Human Rights in Turkey

PENNSYLVANIA STUDIES IN HUMAN RIGHTS
Bert B. Lockwood, Jr., Series Editor

A complete list of books in the series is available from the publisher.

Human Rights in Turkey

EDITED BY
ZEHRA F. KABASAKAL ARAT

FOREWORD BY RICHARD FALK

PENN

University of Pennsylvania Press

Philadelphia

10   9   8   7   6   5   4   3   2   1

Published by
University of Pennsylvania Press
Philadelphia, Pennsylvania 19104-4112

Library of Congress Cataloging-in-Publication Data

Human rights in Turkey / edited by Zehra F. Kabasakal Arat ; foreword by Richard Falk.
    p.   cm. — (Pennsylvania studies in human rights)
  ISBN-13: 978-08122-4000-9 (alk. paper)
  ISBN-10: 0-8122-4000-6 (alk. paper)
  Includes bibliographical references and index.
  1. Human rights—Turkey. I. Kabasakal Arat, Zehra F. II. Series.
JC599.T87 H83   2007
323.09561—dc22   2006051471

To Mehmet Kabasakal for leading by example and being the best big brother

Contents

Foreword   xi
Richard Falk

1. Collisions and Crossroads: Introducing Human Rights
   in Turkey   1
   Zehra F. Kabasakal Arat

PART I: FREEDOMS AND ANTIDISCRIMINATION

2. Freedom of Press and Broadcasting   19
   Dilruba Çatalbaş

3. The Minority Concept and Rights in Turkey: The Lausanne
   Peace Treaty and Current Issues   35
   Baskın Oran

4. The Human Rights Condition of the Rum Orthodox   57
   Prodromos Yannas

5. Linguistic Human Rights and the Rights of Kurds   72
   Mary Lou O'Neil

6. Freedom of Religion: Secularist Policies and Islamic
   Challenges   87
   Özlem Denli

PART II: SOCIAL AND ECONOMIC RIGHTS

7. So Near, Yet So Far: Freedom of Association and Workers'
   Rights   105
   Edward Weisband and *Sera Öner*

8. The Right to Education   123
   Fatma Gök and *Deniz Ilgaz*

9. Environmental Protection and Rights   137
   N. Burcu Taşatar Parlak

PART III: THE RIGHTS OF THE DISPLACED

10. Conflict-Induced Internal Displacement   159
    Alpaslan Özerdem and *Tim Jacoby*

11. Turkish Asylum Policy and Human Rights   170
    Kemal Kirişçi

PART IV: WOMEN'S RIGHTS

12. Women's Rights, Women's Organizations, and the State   187
    Yıldız Ecevit

13. The Effect of CEDAW on Women's Rights   202
    Yasemin Çelik Levin

PART V: CIVIC AND EDUCATIONAL EFFORTS

14. Human Rights Discourse and Domestic Human Rights
    NGOs   217
    Başak Çalı

15. Tensions and Dilemmas in Human Rights Education   233
    Kenan Çayır

PART VI: INTERNATIONAL AFFAIRS AND INTERACTIONS

16. Turkey's Participation in Global and Regional Human Rights
    Regimes   249
    Füsun Türkmen

17. Leveraging Norms: The ECHR and Turkey's Human Rights
    Reforms   262
    Thomas W. Smith

18. Conclusion: Turkey's Prospects and Broader Implications   275
    Zehra F. Kabasakal Arat

Notes   289

References   303

List of Contributors   331

Index   335

Foreword

RICHARD FALK

Few would doubt that there has been great progress in recent years with respect to the protection of human rights in Turkey. Even fewer would question the contention that serious problems pertaining to human rights remain part of the Turkish political landscape. Both observations lend a particular importance to a book that seeks to survey this landscape to take note of progress and of obstacles to further progress.

Beyond this, the future of Turkey, its relationship to constitutional democracy overall, is bound up with two complex external relationships: with the European Union (EU) and the road to possible membership for Turkey in a decade or so; and with the United States as Turkey's longtime principal strategic partner with a variety of implications for the future of the Middle East as a region caught between the contradictory currents of Islamic militancy and American imperial geopolitics. The way these relationships unfold in the coming years is likely to affect decisively the extent to which the impressive human rights momentum of recent years in Turkey is sustained, accelerated, halted, and conceivably even reversed.

In the lead-up to the Iraq War early in 2003, it came as a great surprise to the U.S. government when the Turkish legislature refused to authorize the deployment of American troops on Turkish soil for the purpose of invading Iraq from the north. It was an unexpected and unprecedented Turkish show of governmental independence in the setting of national security policy. Such a Turkish posture had never been a feature of the bilateral relations between these two countries during the course of the entire Cold War. Months later in the same year, Paul Wolfowitz, Deputy Secretary of Defense, while visiting Turkey chided the Turkish military leadership on CNN-Türk for failing to find some way to circumvent this parliamentary decision so adverse to the U.S. policy. The fact that the Turkish decision to refuse the deployment of American troops had the backing of more than 90 percent of the Turkish public seemed to make little difference with respect to American expectations that Turkey would continue to perform its assigned role as a junior strategic partner in the region. After the passage of time, this defection has seemingly been forgotten for the most part on both sides, and the old partnership has been renewed, but probably now with an undercurrent of caution and uncertainty on both sides.

But there are more difficult questions about what the United States wants from Turkey, and for that matter from the region. American leaders sermonize about democracy and human rights, yet pursue familiar geopolitical patterns in relation to their foreign policy goals. Since failing to find weapons of mass destruction in Iraq, the Bush administration has been tireless in the insistence that it came to Iraq to liberate the country from a brutal dictator. It also continually promises to end its occupation of the country as soon as the Iraq people are able to establish an elected democratic government that respects the human rights of its citizens and is able to maintain security. But will Washington be content with an Iraqi government, however democratic, that makes common cause with Iran or that harshly criticizes Israel? I think not. The implications for Turkey are troublesome and clear. These hypothetical possibilities have been brought closer to reality by the Shia victory in a series of Iraqi elections between 2004 and 2006. At the same time, the Shia interest in being protected from the ongoing violence associated with a vicious Sunni-led insurgency complicates the picture still further. The Shia leadership, while strongly opposed to the U.S. occupation, is reluctant to insist upon an American withdrawal so long as the threat posed by Sunni ambitions to restore their control of the country remains a credible danger. Turkey's response to this situation is also likely to be ambivalent, worrying about the implications of a prolonged foreign occupation, even by the United States. The Turkish government is probably even more concerned by the Iraqi Kurdish secessionist aspirations, and the related risk of an outbreak of civil war in Iraq leading to a possible breakup of Iraq as a unified country, and the formation of an independent Kurdish political entity. Under these conditions, the U.S. occupation may be the least bad option among bad options for the main regional political actors. Such a prospect adds dark colors to the human rights picture, particularly with respect to the exercise and meaning of the right to self-determination in the Turkish context, as well as in the regional neighborhood of Turkey. Despite these developments, it would be a mistake to suppose that Turkish behavior with respect to human rights is derivative of U.S. regional priorities and approach. Turkey in recent years has been demonstrating in various ways that it is capable of bold initiatives on its own, and with the revival of the Turkish economy, including the stabilization of its currency and price structure, Turkish self-confidence is likely to grow even stronger.

Approaching the Turkey situation from a different angle, it is striking to note the sweeping legal reforms associated with human rights that have been enacted in the last several years. This is sometimes explained as merely an expression of the natural evolution of a maturing Turkish democracy. It can also be understood, at least until very recently, as following directly from the seeming end of the Kurdish challenge to Turkish unity that followed from the capture of Abdullah Öcalan in early 1999. This event temporarily undermined the will of the Kurdish movement to continue an armed struggle, which in turn reassured the government in Ankara with respect to internal security and secessionist concerns. In the early months of 2006 there was a revival of Kurdish militancy that has been difficult to interpret. Some commentators believe that Kurdish activism was mainly *provoked* by the Turkish armed forces, as part of a wider campaign to undermine the authority of the government, and cast doubts on the capacity of the Justice and Development Party (Adalet ve Kalkınma Partisi, AKP), which remains a controversial and distrusted leadership for much of the Turkish mainstream establishment, to protect the national unity of Turkey. Others believe that the revival of the insurgency was a result of the regrouping of rebels, which took a few years after the capture of Öcalan.

But, perhaps, most important of all, many in Turkey and beyond believe that the political liberalization taking place in Turkey represents a concerted effort by a significant portion of Turkish elites to improve prospects for the country's membership in the EU. At least on the surface, a main stated obstacle to Turkish accession has been its poor human rights record. So conceived, to qualify for EU membership Turkey will have to overcome such sore points as police torture and brutality, violations of minority rights, discrimination against women, abusive prison conditions, and the intrusion of the military into civilian affairs of government, and these are only the most salient issues.

The most daunting issue of all, yet the most fundamental from the perspective of constitutional democracy, relates to the establishment of civilian control over the military. This part of the wider human rights challenge is associated in Turkey with the existence of "the deep state." This invisible yet formidable source of ultimate political authority has in recent decades established red lines that the elected visible government dare not cross if it wishes to remain in political power. These red lines pertain to internal self-determination for the Kurds, the future of Turkish Cyprus, positive strategic relations with the United States and Israel, and most crucially, the containment of political Islam in such a manner as to uphold beyond any doubt the secular principles of the Turkish state as initially established by Kemal Atatürk and embodied in the most recent Turkish constitution (and since his death interpreted by the Turkish military leadership acting as self-appointed guardians of the Atatürk legacy, with the strong backing of the urbanized middle classes and most of the business elite).

These red lines are not inscribed in granite. The outlook of the military leadership has been itself evolving in the direction of moderation and constitutional legitimacy. The dominant elements in the military leadership appear to share the commitment of the elected political leaders to securing eventual Turkish membership in the EU, or at least pursuing this goal as long as it seems like a real possibility. At the same time there is growing apprehension by close observers of the European scene that Turkey will be eventually denied entry to the EU, no matter what it does to improve its image from a human rights perspective. To the extent that it appears that the path toward EU membership is likely to be blocked in any event, it may have the effect of weakening the consensus of recent years that it is beneficial for Turkey to gain international respect by upholding human rights in a more scrupulous manner than in the past. Rejection by the EU, when it comes or even as soon as it is anticipated, could unleash an ultranationalist Turkish backlash that might well be accompanied by backsliding with respect to human rights. The progress of recent years, while enjoying wide backing at present and reinforced by a strengthening economy, is not irreversible by any means, and could prove fragile in times of national crisis. But at the same time this progress should not be underestimated. Turkey has significantly improved its human rights standing since the events of 11 September 2001, an achievement that no other major country can claim, including the most respected and durable constitutional democracies in the world.

The uncertain future interaction between Turkey and the EU is not the only cloud of uncertainty that overhangs the human rights situation. If the Kurdish issue resurfaces as a serious threat to national unity or by way of a move toward an independent Kurdistan in neighboring Iraq, the pressures on Ankara to clamp down on freedoms at home are quite likely to become intense.

This essentially pragmatic and cautiously optimistic interpretation of Turkish reforms can be bolstered by more idealistic and ideological arguments along various lines. It is argued in some circles that to fulfill the Atatürk legacy of building a truly modern Turkish state in the twenty-first century, one that participates successfully in a globalizing world requires the attainment of political legitimacy at home and abroad, and this increasingly depends on a strong human rights record and robust democracy. This political path has been privileged ever since the fall of the Berlin Wall and the collapse of the Soviet Union. In recent years, in the wake of the 11 September attacks, the United States has pursued a diplomacy that proclaims that the future of world peace is dependent upon the democratization of the non-Western world, and nowhere more so than in the Middle East—although such a diplomatic initiative by Washington arouses suspicions and skepticism as to its sincerity and depth, especially in the wake of the Iraq War. Nevertheless, even American rhetorical support for democracy gives new space to political leaders in the region to move in these directions. This support from Washington generally reinforces indigenous democratizing tendencies, although there is some risk that "democracy" can end up with a bad name if it gets too closely linked to U.S. interventionary diplomacy.

If we think along these lines, the European and American external pressures, despite their inconsistencies, are no longer alien to the Turkish reality, but provide some of the impetus to move in a direction that corresponds with a gathering national consensus. This consensus represents a dynamic understanding of what secularism should mean in the Turkish context that has been evolving in generally encouraging directions in the last several years, taking into account changes in social, cultural, and historical circumstances. Perhaps ironically, this national consensus may have been deepened by the rise to prominence in the last few years of the AKP, with its distinctly Islamic flavor that is coupled with a vigorous endorsement and acceptance of the unconditionally secular character of the Turkish state. Such political leadership, although far from oblivious to the potentially intimidating role of the military establishment as the guarantor of the Atatürk legacy, seems genuinely oriented toward a moderate vision of Turkish governance that is respectful of the rights and values of the entirety of the Turkish people, including those who are not practicing Muslims and are members of the small non-Muslim minorities, as well as those influential individuals who remain fearful that any ascent to power by adherents of political Islam could mean the end of a secular Turkey. This latter anxiety helps outsiders understand why the controversy around the wearing of head scarves by Turkish women in public settings, including state universities, has become such an ideological battleground in recent years.

Even with the enactment of legal reforms designed to protect human rights in state/society contexts and as a matter of public policy, there is no assurance that patterns of behavior will adhere to the new more enlightened legal guidelines. Progress in Turkey with respect to human rights has been inhibited to varying degrees by the unwillingness of some personnel in police and security bureaucracies to change their ways. Such bureaucrats have often not entirely abandoned old abusive habits of governance, and at best, will tend to resist a rapid change in dealing with the citizenry, especially if the reforms are widely regarded as inconsistent with prevailing cultural attitudes. India, for instance, has found for decades that a recalcitrant bureaucracy and regressive cultural practices can greatly impede the implementation of positive law when it comes to certain human rights, especially in the countryside at village level where traditional harsh cultural attitudes prevail. In this regard, despite the encouraging official moves of recent years and the corresponding changes in Turkish law, the extent of behavioral adherence will largely depend on the degree of implementation that is achieved locally and in concrete circumstances on a day-to-day basis with respect to the treatment of those individuals and groups that find themselves at odds with the policies and restrictions of the Turkish state. In the end, it is the behavioral realities, not the pious words of politicians, legislative enactments, and executive decrees, or even the genuine sentiments of the public favoring reform, which bring into being and sustain a humane state. A human rights record of a country is generally best tested by the treatment of those who are either at the bottom of the social hierarchy or regarded as opponents of the government. The verdict is not yet in as to whether the encouraging legal reforms and governmental rhetoric in Turkey during the last decade has been effectively and irrevocably translated into consistent patterns of practice. As developments in the United States since 11 September disclose, no country can be entirely confident that its adherence to human rights will stand up well during periods of national crisis.

There is one further factor of relevance to an assessment of the Turkish approach to human rights at the present time. The ascent to power of the AKP in 2002 was accompanied by a positive revival of the Ottoman past in Turkish political consciousness. This is not entirely new, as Turgut Özal had also invoked the glories of the Ottoman past, but it has occurred in a narrower nationalist context of intensifying the modernizing and Westernizing path of Atatürk. There has been recently an upsurge in the celebration of the cultural achievements of the Ottoman era, but more than this, a recognition that Ottoman rule was sensitive to cultural, ethnic, and religious diversity, to what these days is often called multiculturalism. This Ottoman heritage exhibited high degrees of tolerance for non-Muslim religions, and included the conferral of an impressive degree of autonomy upon religious and ethnic minorities, by way of the millet system. It is impossible to overstate the potential significance of this revival of the pre-Atatürk ethos in the contemporary setting, especially in relation to a possible future accommodation of Kurdish aspirations without fragmenting the Turkish state. This way back for Turkey may yet prove to be the best way forward!

It needs to be remembered that Atatürk's extraordinary contributions to modern Turkey was historically associated with avoiding complete disintegration in the face of the collapse of the Ottoman Empire immediately following World War I. It was entirely understandable in such an international setting that the idea of establishing a unified Turkish nation should be given the highest priority. But conditions have changed. Turkey is now a strong and increasingly well-regarded state, and it can improve upon this reality by incorporating and adapting Ottoman ideas that embody a creative tension between unity and diversity. This tension could produce both a softening of nationalism and a welcome onset of receptivity to a greater decentralization of authority and governance within Turkish territorial borders.

What is clear, beyond doubt, is the importance of Turkey and its political development at this stage of history, both for the region and world. Turkey represents, first of all, a country with a large Muslim population that has successfully embraced a Western model of secular democracy. This embrace seems to include a welcome commitment to human rights. This commitment was not upheld in the past, but for the variety of reasons mentioned above, impressive progress toward realizing human rights goals has been made in recent years. At the same time, there remain disturbing indications that much work needs to be done, particularly with respect to the status and treatment of women. As discussed, Turkey is an Islamic country that is seeking to achieve a balance between religious and secular orientations that discourages extremism on either side. Turkey is also seeking to sustain its alliance with the United States and Israel while exercising its own self-interested assessment of policy choices, thereby affirming its identity as a truly sovereign state. And finally, Turkey is moving toward a closer relationship with Europe and with its Arab neighbors, enabling it to have more room for diplomatic maneuver. Of course, none of this will matter much if the Turkish economic development does not begin to benefit the population as a whole, satisfying the basic needs of the poor, including gainful employment for all levels of Turkish society, including those with advanced education. There is a pronounced tendency in the liberal West to overlook the material foundations of a humane structure of governance. I believe this can be explained by a reductive and liberal conception of human rights as involving only that range of issues encompassed by "civil and political rights," ignoring minimal conditions of right livelihood that fall within the domain of "economic, social, and cultural rights." Part of this selective understanding of human rights arises from a fear and loathing of Marxist approaches to political behavior. The rise of neoliberal orthodoxy in this period of globalization accentuates tendencies to overlook the circumstances of those living in poverty, insisting that market forces will over time sort things out, so far as the social effects of poverty are concerned, without imposing any responsibility on government or employers. More than ever, it is crucial to endorse a comprehensive view of human rights, which regards economic and social rights as integral to a serious engagement with human rights and not merely matters for aspirational appreciation. Such a view was fully set forth in the 1948 Universal Declaration of Human Rights, and was carried into positive international law as early as 1966 by the two covenants dealing with both categories of rights.

It is the great strength of *Human Rights in Turkey* that it adopts such a comprehensive view of its theme, developing the subject matter of human rights within a broad spectrum of perspectives. This volume, expertly introduced by its editor, Zehra Arat, also represents the best traditions of social science: respect for evidence, balanced assessment of conflicting viewpoints, reliance on analysis and reasoned argument to clarify controversial issues. From such a detailed examination and mapping of human rights in Turkey there emerges a coherent profile that depicts both progress and concern, thereby reflecting the complex and contradictory realities of the Turkish situation.

One of the most beautiful things to do is to paint darkness, which nevertheless has light in it.

—VINCENT VAN GOGH

Chapter 1

Collisions and Crossroads:
Introducing Human Rights in Turkey

ZEHRA F. KABASAKAL ARAT

In terms of human rights, the twentieth century offered a world of contrasts. It was a period of wars fought with exceedingly destructive machinery, causing unprecedented levels of damage and death. The rise of fascism and other modern forms of authoritarian rule led to the annihilation and devastation of millions of people. Capitalist development paradoxically sustained enormous poverty amid the mounting wealth. Yet, from the middle of this misery emerged a conscientious global effort to respect human dignity and protect the human rights of all people. Starting with its Charter (1945), the United Nations made the promotion of human rights a goal of the member states. Human rights was linked to peace and security, and by adopting the Universal Declaration of Human Rights in 1948, the UN General Assembly paved the way for the establishment of a global human rights regime, which generated international treaties that obliged state parties to respect and protect human rights. Regional organizations also embraced human rights and issued their own declarations and conventions. The emergence of global and regional human rights regimes promised a better world that would not relive the horrible events of the first half of the century.

Yet, warfare and ethnic cleansing continued; torture prevailed; racism, sexism, and other forms of discrimination were not eradicated; mothers kept questioning the whereabouts of their "disappeared" children; the euphoria about liberation from colonialism was eclipsed by economic despair and dependency; and global inequalities and poverty reached record highs.[1] While the propagation of numerous human rights instruments and the incorporation of human rights into international law constituted significant progress in terms of developing normative and legal frameworks, at the dawn of a new century, it is clear that the human rights norms have not been upheld by all, and the principles and provisions of human rights regimes have not been enforced.

The explanations for the overall ineffectiveness of human rights regimes have included overlapping problems: the lack of commitment by states parties, the lack of enforcement mechanisms, cultural relativists' challenge to the notion of universal rights, a partial endorsement of rights with preferences assigned to different kinds, the persistent emphasis on state sovereignty, the prevalence of "realism" in international politics, the global power structure and the inconsistent policies of hegemonic states, the economic or political weakness of the state in developing countries, and the resistance of privileged and powerful groups (Bell, Nathan, and Peleg 2001; Drinan 2001; Falk 2000; Forsythe 1999; Donnelly 1998; Evans 1998; Gillies 1996).

Among all regions, the Middle East has been particularly poor in advancing human rights. The countries in the region lagged behind in both political democratization and participation in the international human rights regimes. But Turkey is usually recognized as an exceptional case for establishing a secular democratic system, which allowed more freedoms and granted several rights to its citizens, and for its willingness to be integrated into the global and regional human rights regimes. When the attacks of 11 September 2001 and subsequent events brought the problems of Muslim-populated states to the public agenda in the United States, Turkey was presented as a model to be followed by other Muslim countries.[2] While the study of human rights in Turkey is important for understanding Turkish politics and the causal links of human rights, the recent proposals about modeling other countries after Turkey adds an urgency and call for an in-depth analysis and appraisal of "the model."

Human Rights as a Political Issue

The term "human rights" entered into the Turkish lexicon and discussions during Ottoman times, mainly in reference to "minority rights," as a result of continuous interventions by the European powers that assumed the role of "protectors" of the non-Muslim population of the Empire (Braude and Lewis 1982; R. Davison 1973; Karpat 1996; Toynbee and Kirkwood 1976). Following the defeat of the Ottoman Empire in the First World War, a group of Turkish nationalists, led by Mustafa Kemal, initiated a movement to liberate the country from the grip of victorious states and the invading Greek army. Seeing the İstanbul government corrupt and disabled, they established an alternative government in Ankara in 1920. The successful military campaigns during this "War of Independence," reinforced the power of the Ankara government and forced its European adversaries to recognize it as the legitimate government to represent the country at the Lausanne Peace Conference, held during the summer of 1923. The nationalists embraced "people's right to self-determination" and a strong anti-imperialist stance.

Declaring its political system a republic on 29 October 1923, the Kemalist regime attempted to "modernize" the country, create a new secular polity, and transform the passive subjects of the Empire into dedicated citizens. Later, as a founding member of the UN and signatory of the Universal Declaration of Human Rights, the Republic also pledged to promote human rights at home and abroad. In 1954, it became a party to the European Convention on Human Rights and Fundamental Freedoms. Despite these commitments, however, the human rights record of Turkey has been a thorny subject, criticized by many human rights organizations and foreign governments (U.S. Department of State 2001; Freedom House 2001; U.S. Congress 1997; Finkel 2000; Human Rights Watch 1999; Yurdatapan 1998; Amnesty International 1996). Nevertheless, these criticisms have been subdued, at least until recently, partially due to the mixed record of Turkey and partially due to the synchronization of its politics with the foreign policy goals of the influential states (Z. F. Arat 2003b).

Some political developments during the last two decades, such as the rise of Kurdish nationalism (Barkey and Fuller 1998; Kirişçi and Winrow 1997; Ciment 1996; Bozarslan 1992; İmset 1992; Gunter 1990) and "Islamist" politics (Öniş 1997; Marulies and Yıldızoğlu 1996; Dumont 1986),[3] reinforced the power of the military and led the country into an armed conflict that was paramount in the Southeast region and not short of the devastating characteristics of a civil war. These conditions created a political environment in which the advocacy of human rights could be perceived or framed as an assault or threat to the territorial integrity and secular identity of the state. The European Union's human rights criteria and Turkey's prolonged candidacy to EU membership have added an international dimension to the controversy (Hicks 2001; Dunér and Deverell 2001; Rumford 2001; Kramer 2000).

Examining human rights policies in Turkey over time, this book intends to move the debate from a highly politicized forum to an arena where human rights issues can be examined at the intersection of domestic and international politics. For this purpose, it includes a review of the history and politics of Turkey that goes beyond the frequently employed center-periphery paradigm that explains the instability of democracy and the uneven modernization of the country by the top-down approach of the Kemalist reforms that alienated the masses (Jung and Piccoli 2001; Özbudun 2000; Mardin 1972; Manstry and Nation 1996). It examines the articulation of human rights by different groups, the state responses to the "rights demands," and the influence of the international human rights regimes on the country's human rights discourse.

Chapters are not guided by a particular theoretical approach, and the book does not attempt to offer a new theory. Yet, as a comprehensive and longitudinal study of the county, it anticipates contributing to the theory-building efforts in the field of human rights. Although the combination of questions encountered by Turkey over time has been historically determined and unique, the issues themselves are prevalent in all of its neighbors and other societies that try to fulfill (at times seemingly contradictory) goals of national security, independence, economic development, and respect for human rights. Specifying the patterns of change in human rights policies in Turkey would shed light on the interaction of factors that help or hinder the legitimization and materialization of specific rights.

Thus, the volume includes research and analyses by Turkish and international scholars who approach the issues from a number of disciplines and fields. Although there is an emphasis on the recent developments, all authors try to employ a historical approach and examine the patterns of change in Turkish governments' policies in a substantial area of human rights. While the thematic division of labor makes the chapters complementary, the overlap among them confirms the interdependency of human rights. (See the concluding chapter to this volume.) Thus, these integrated chapters comprise a volume that is not a typical reader but a threaded narrative of multiple raconteurs.

Historical Eras and Turning Points

The political history of the Republic of Turkey permits a convenient periodization that is followed practically by all students of Turkish politics, with some minor variations. We can chart four periods and highlight the turning points and significant human rights-related events as follows into four periods: (1) nation-state formation, 1920–45; (2) transition to democracy, 1945–60; (3) ideological polarization, 1960–80; and (4) cultural diversity and affirmation (since 1980).

THE PERIOD OF NATION-STATE FORMATION, 1920–45

The first period covers the years of nation and state building. It also corresponds to the hegemonic rule of the Republican People's Party (Cumhuriyet Halk Partisi, CHP), when the attempts to establish alternative parties were quickly repressed. The CHP rule was also personalized, first by Mustafa Kemal, the founder of the state, and later, by İsmet İnönü, his comrade and also a war hero. Mustafa Kemal's notions about the character and values of the new nation were articulated as the six principles of the party, during the Third Party Congress in May 1931. Republicanism, nationalism, populism, étatism, secularism (laicism), and reformism were incorporated into the emblem of the party as six arrows.

The extensive control of the party over the state apparatus during the one-party era resulted in a virtual extension of these into state goals that also defined the character of "the nation." Following Mustafa Kemal's death in 1938, İnönü served as the president of the Republic but dominated both the party and the state as "the national chief," until the 1950 elections that ended the CHP rule.

The one-party era was authoritarian by all means. The Kemalist leadership faced challengers and rivals from the beginning, some of whom organized around ideological and ethnic differences. Several Kurdish uprisings took place in the 1920s and 1930s. Opposition groups and parties were repressed for being communist traitors or religious reactionaries. The desire to forge a national identity led to some assimilationist and discriminatory policies but also to sizeable investments in education and economic infrastructure, which would facilitate the integration of the country and its people.

THE PERIOD OF TRANSITION TO DEMOCRACY, 1945–60

The second period starts with the initiation of the competitive electoral system in 1945 and continues until the first military intervention in 1960. Although the political rules were changed to allow multiparty competitions, the outcome was another authoritarian regime, this time under the Democrat Party (DP) guidance. Ruling between 1950 and 1960, DP governments, led by Adnan Menderes, relaxed some of the "modernization" initiatives imposed by the one-party regime, especially with regard to the religious practices. However, this DP-ruled decade was stamped by economic crisis, increasing social inequalities, social unrest, and political repression, and eventually ended by a military coup launched on 27 May 1960.[4] The government was ousted, and Prime Minister Menderes and some other members of the DP were executed, albeit following a series of accelerated court trials.

THE PERIOD OF IDEOLOGICAL POLARIZATION, 1960–80

The military takeover in May 1960 ushered in a new phase of politics. Although the military rule was by all means repressive, it produced a surprisingly liberal constitution, which was adopted after a plebiscite vote in 1961. The Constitution defined the Republic as a state based on human rights and assigned the state the duty of protecting rights and providing social services. At the same time, however, the military created the National Security Council (Milli Güvenlik Kurulu, MGK); including top generals along with the prime minister and select cabinet members, the MGK helped to institutionalize the political role and influence of the military.

The liberal tenets of the Constitution, combined with the social forces resulting from rapid industrialization and urbanization of the country, turned the 1960s and 1970s into a period characterized by burgeoning organizations, social mobilization, and political polarization. The unprecedented levels of student, labor, and other civic activism, which challenged the state policies as well as the ideological positions of rival groups, involved frequent protests, as well as physical clashes and armed attacks. The Justice Party (Adalet Partisi, AP), which inherited the vision and political constituency of the DP, governed for most of this period either by forming a majority government or as the leading party in a coalition government. Süleyman Demirel and other leaders of this probusiness, conservative party often blamed the Constitution for granting too many liberties, which they regarded as "luxurious" for Turkey. The 1971 military intervention that ousted the elected government and replaced it with a handpicked civilian government took care of some of those "luxuries" by amending the Constitution and placing a good portion of the country under martial law. State repression and terrorism targeted the left, but its chilling effect could be felt beyond these ideological groups.

The polarized political life and its ramifications resurfaced when the country returned to electoral politics and civilian rule in 1973. Political violence became common among ideological rivals, and terrorism vastly increased. The state response was further repression, but also entailed pitting groups against each other. The involvement of the ultranationalist Nationalist Action Party (Milliyetçi Hareket Partisi, MHP) in two coalition governments in the late 1970s was particularly important in reinforcing the ideological divides and stimulating political violence. Its affiliate association, Ülkü Ocakları ([Nationalist] Ideal Hearths), enjoyed the government support and was used against the left-wing groups and individuals.

The Period of Cultural Diversity and Affirmation (Since 1980)

The turmoil of the 1970s ended with the military coup that took place on 12 September 1980, marking a new era. The military government initiated a systematic and largely effective depolitization process. Legitimate political organizations and labor unions were closed, and their leaders, along with those of the illegal ones, were either imprisoned or forced to live in exile. In 1982, a new constitution was devised that spelled out individual freedoms and rights but also provided long lists of conditions under which these rights would be limited. In other words, the 1982 Constitution attempted to curb the "excessive freedoms" of the 1961 Constitution. The military also monitored the transition to the civilian rule and assured the continuation of the military control by installing the coup leader General Kenan Evren as the president of the Republic, albeit through a referendum, and by transforming the function of the MGK from consultation to that of a de facto supra-cabinet.

The first elections after the 1980 military coup d'état brought the Motherland Party (ANAP) of Turgut Özal into power. The trademark of the Özal government became economic liberalization, changing Turkey's industrialization strategy from import-substitution to an export-oriented one. It also rekindled Turkey's aspirations to join the EU by formally applying in April 1987 and making some other overtures to improve Turkey's chances, such as accepting the jurisdiction of the European Court of Human Rights, which became effective in December 1989. The economic and political maneuvers of Turgut Özal, some of which were sustained by the subsequent governments, have had profound impacts on human rights conditions and practices in the country. An inevitable impact of economic liberalization and other structural adjustment policies of the International Monetary Fund, which had been guiding the Turkish economy since the beginning of 1980, was the further distortion of an already skewed income distribution; between 1987 and 1994, the income share fell for all quintiles, except for the highest one (which marked an increase from 49.9 percent to 54.9 percent), and the GINI coefficient for income distribution raised from .44 to .49 (UNDP 1998, 43).

Some institutional adjustments that were favorable to human rights included the creation of administrative agencies to monitor and oversee human rights practices and policies. A parliamentary Commission on Human Rights was set up in 1990,[5] and a year later, a state ministry responsible for human rights issues was established. On 9 April 1997, the Coordinating High Commission of Human Rights (İnsan Hakları Koordinatör Üst Kurulu) was created under the Office of the Prime Ministry to coordinate the human rights efforts by different ministries and agencies.

Also important in this period was the rise of Kurdish nationalism and Islamist politics. When the former was dominated by the armed struggle led by Abdullah Öcalan and his Kurdistan Workers' Party (Partia Karkaren Kürdistan, PKK), the military intervened and the country was dragged into a civil war from the mid-1980s until 1999, when Öcalan was captured in Kenya and brought to Turkey. Beyond its economic and political costs, this conflict is estimated to have taken 30,000–40,000 lives. In addition to the deaths occurring due to the clashes, both the military and the PKK intimidated the population living in the Southeast to reach their own goals and penalized those they deemed collaborators of the other side. Ten provinces in the region were placed under the state of emergency, and the Özal government created village guards as a counterforce against the PKK militia. By the mid-1990s, the number of village guards reached approximately 70,000. The PKK did not hesitate to employ overtly terrorist strategies, at least until the end of 1994; then, it decided to heighten the diplomatic efforts and formally issued a "Declaration of Intent," indicating its decision to abide by the humanitarian law and rules of war as established in the Geneva Conventions and subsequent international protocols ("Kurdistan Workers' Party").

Some Islamist groups were also engaged in armed struggle and maintained organized and trained militia. The Hizbullah Kurdish Revolutionary Party was particularly notorious in the Southeast. However, it was tolerated by the state because of its anti-PKK activity and successful liquidation of numerous intellectuals, activists, politicians, and journalists who were considered to be pro-PKK, between fall 1991 and March 1993. Then it signed a "cooperation protocol" with the PKK (Karmon 1997).

Islamists pursued their power struggle also through party politics and street demonstrations. Women's demand to wear head scarves at universities and government offices—a practice that had been banned by the agencies' bylaws or regulations, as a part of the secularization and westernization project in the 1920s—has become the symbolic issue for those who want to assert their religious identity and freedom, but it was seen as an open assault on secularism and an attack to the republican character of the state by the armed forces and other state officials. The militarism of these two movements allowed the state to capitalize on the separatist or antisecular threats to repress dissident voices and close down pro-Kurdish and Islamist political parties. Moreover, the continuation of terrorist attacks, which included also some left-wing groups such as the Revolutionary People's Liberation Party/Front (DHKP/C) and the Turkish Workers and Peasants Liberation Army (TİKKO), have established an excuse for taking further repressive measures and undermining human rights by the state.

The landslide victory of an Islamist party, the Justice and Development Party (AKP, Adalet ve Kalkınma Partisi), in the November 2002 elections, however, put the Islamists in power in a majority government. As the "reformist" split from the closed-down Virtue Party, AKP leaders distanced themselves from the conservative Islamist "Milli Görüş" (National Vision) philosophy and their former mentor, Necmettin Erbakan, who led a sequence of religious parties from 1960s through the 1990s. Claiming that they have left their radical and militant past in favor of secularism, they emphasize a nonreligious rhetoric and prefer to be branded as "conservative democrats" instead of Islamists. Similarly, many Kurdish nationalists, who have effectively used the human rights discourse to gather the sympathy and support and of government officials and public in European countries, started to capitalize on Turkey's desire to the join the EU and tried to advance their cause through the use of diplomatic and political means.

Human Rights Issues and Policies

FREEDOMS AND ANTIDISCRIMINATION

In discussing the freedom of press and broadcasting in Chapter 2, Dilruba Çatalbaş presents a detailed chronological assessment, showing that the news media in Turkey have been subject to numerous and frequently applied restraints and repression. Yet, she notes that although the relations with the state have always been difficult and complicated, the freedom of press has never been totally absent. Investigating political, social, and economic forces that influence the freedom of print and broadcast media, she argues that while political and legal constraints were the main concerns in news publishing and broadcasting, there have been some promising legal reforms in these areas, including the partial removal of the ban on broadcasting in Kurdish and in some other languages. However, as a growing area of concern, she points to the market pressures that increase the corporate control over the media.

Chapters 3–5, by Baskın Oran, Prodromos Yannas, and Mary Lou O'Neil respectively, examine the link between freedoms and antidiscrimination. The protection of minorities under the Lausanne Peace Treaty of 1923 is the focus of Oran's chapter, in which he contends that state officials in Turkey have followed a very narrow interpretation of the treaty. By construing that all rights mentioned in the treaty are applicable only to non-Muslims, and by defining non-Muslims as the Greek Orthodox, Armenians, and Jews, the state effectively denied various rights (e.g., language rights, religious freedom) to a wide variety of groups (e.g., Kurds) and certain rights that would apply to all citizens. He also notes that even within the narrow interpretation, the rights of the three minority groups continued to be violated, because non-Muslims in Turkey have been constantly treated as "foreigners" and suspected of disloyalty.

In Chapter 4, Prodromos Yannas's study of the situation of the Greek Orthodox in Turkey follows up on Oran's arguments by providing details for this particular group. Pointing to the substantial decline in the Greek minority population over the years, Yannas argues that the decline in the Greek Orthodox population is related to the continuous violation of their human rights, which in turn is shaped by Turkey-Greece relations. The conflicting claims over Cyprus, which is populated by both Turkish and Greek descents, have been especially problematic, since each "Cyprus crisis" between the two countries has led to some restrictions or hardship imposed upon the Greek minority in Turkey.

Kurds constitute a sizable ethnic group in Turkey, but they have not been recognized as such by the state. In fact, the existence of such a distinct ethnic group was denied for a long time. In Chapter 5, Mary Lou O'Neil explores the discord over the Kurdish language, invoking the concept of linguistic human rights and Turkey's responsibilities under international law. Highlighting the importance of language to national identity, she notes that as Kurds demanded language rights to assert their national identity, government and state officials repeatedly restricted the use of Kurdish to repress precisely that identity. Nevertheless, the reformulation of their demands in a human rights discourse has allowed Kurds to gain some ground.

In the early days of the Republic, Kurdish national identity was blended with a religious one, and uprisings such as that led by Sheik Said resulted in the banning of all religious orders and dervish lodges in 1925 (Berkes 1998b, ch. 15–17). The regime perceived the religious establishment as a threat, both a source of political opposition and an antithesis of its modernization project. Thus, it pursued reforming the Islamic institutions and their doctrinaire interpretations. In 1924, the Directorate of Religious Affairs (Diyânet İşleri Başkanlığı) was created, in order to assure the "proper" teaching and practice of Islam. Özlem Denli in Chapter 6 examines the development of Turkish "laicism," which is different from the conventional understanding of secularism as the separation of church and state but involves asserting the state control over religion. She also discusses Islamists' challenge to laicism. Focusing on the articulation of a "pluralist" Islamist view that defines the state control over religion as a human rights violation, she explores the prospect of an alternative Islamic theory of state that would respect the religious freedom of all.

SOCIAL AND ECONOMIC RIGHTS

In addition to the persistent violations of civil and political rights, the respect for and protection of social, economic, and cultural rights have been less than satisfactory. Besides poor quality, the access to health care has been limited, and only about half of the population (51.61 percent) has been insured (State Institute of Statistics, c. 2004). The culmination of problems related to the shortage and poor quality of housing was demonstrated by the devastating Marmara earthquake of 1999, which caused 17,127 deaths and 43,953 injuries (General Directorate of Disaster Affairs), displacement of 300,000 to 600,000 persons, and job losses reaching 31 percent (World Bank 1999, 2–4). While earthquake is a natural disaster, its impact is aggravated by human negligence and government policies.

The chapters on labor and educational rights in this volume point to a pattern of decline in social and economic rights, which is contrary to the expectations set by the International Covenant on Economic, Social and Cultural Rights. The Convention specifies: "Each State Party to the present Covenant undertakes to take steps, individually and through international assistance and cooperation, especially economic and technical, *to the maximum of its available resources*, with a view to *achieving progressively the full realization of the rights* in the present Covenant by all appropriate means, including particularly the adoption of legislative measures" (Article 2/1, emphasis mine).

In Turkey, however, although the wealth and resources of the country have been expanding over the years, the realization of social and economic rights seems to have *progressively declined.*

Edward Weisband and Sera Öner, in Chapter 7, explain the numerous violations of internationally recognized labor rights and the declining access to and power of unions by interrelated factors such as state repression, union structures, and the neoliberal economic policies and their consequences. They see the exploitative effects of these developments particularly striking in the form of gender discrimination, reliance on illegal migrants, and recruitment of child labor. In fact, the State Institute of Statistics reported that in mid-1990s, about 31 percent of households in Turkey lived in poverty, and in 1999, 10.2 percent of children between the ages of six and seventeen worked—a portion approximately 7.5 percent of the total labor force (Libal 2001). There is no doubt that economic hardship, unemployment, and declining unionization inevitably undermine other social and economic rights, such as the right to livable wages, social security, and health care for large segments of the population.

Writing on the right to education, in Chapter 8 Fatma Gök and Deniz Ilgaz contend that the founders of the Republic of Turkey emphasized education as a part of their secularization and modernization project and as a vehicle of forging a nationalist ideology. This created an educational system that did not stress creativity or independent thinking, but the emphasis placed upon public education and schooling allowed many to gain access to education in the early days of the Republic. However, the authors note that the economic changes and government policies followed since the 1980s, in particular, resulted in a variety of discrepancies and discrimination. Reductions in budget allocations, combined with population increase and income gaps, eroded the quality of public education and created a large private education industry that caters to the well-to-do. These concurring patterns effectively diminished access to education and violated the right to education for many, especially for girls, children of low-income families, village kids, and those living in the less developed eastern and southeastern provinces.

N. Burcu Parlak's piece on environmental rights, Chapter 9, argues that in Turkey environmental issues did not become a public concern until the 1970s, and they are still not addressed as human rights issues. She documents the proliferation of legislative and institutional arrangements, as well as the environment-focused NGOs, but finds them ineffective in preventing environmental deterioration and pollution, preserving natural resources, and providing a healthy environment. Nevertheless, she finds a glimpse of hope in the increasing use of litigation and protest activities by the public, as well as in the state's recent interest in providing environmental and human rights education.

THE RIGHTS OF THE DISPLACED

While human rights violations are common, certain groups of people tend to be more vulnerable. People who are forced to leave their home or even their country for various reasons constitute such a category. In Chapter 10, Alpaslan Özerdem and Tim Jacoby indicate that there may be as many as 3 million internally displaced people (IDP) in Turkey, the vast majority being from southeast Anatolia, mainly from the ten predominantly Kurdish-populated provinces, which were subject to the "emergency administration" since the mid-1980s. Examining the historical development of the displacement problem in Turkey, they hold that the legacy of earlier policies continues to contribute to and aggravate the IDP problem, but the increasing public awareness about human rights issues and treaties, as well as Turkey's candidacy to the EU membership, may help Turkish citizens to "discover" their civil identity and to begin to see the importance of nongovernmental initiatives in facilitating further social and economic changes.

Chapter 11, by Kemal Kirişçi's, on the other hand, focuses on the rights of asylum seekers in Turkey. The author notes that contrary to the common belief, Turkey has had a long tradition of receiving and accommodating asylum seekers, and was both a drafter and a signatory of the 1951 Geneva Convention Relating to the Status of Refugees. However, it is one of the few countries that continue to maintain a "geographical limitation" to the applicability of the Convention, which puts many asylum seekers in a vulnerable position. Thus, Turkey has been pressured to lift the limitation by the EU and international advocacy groups, and some important steps have been taken, such as the opening of administrative decision on asylum to judicial review and the closer cooperation between Turkey and the UN High Commissioner of Refugees.

WOMEN'S RIGHTS AND CIVIL SOCIETY-STATE RELATIONS

Among all human rights issues in Turkey, perhaps the most mystifying one is that of women's rights, because the Kemalist regime targeted improvements in women's status, both as a means of economic development and modernization and a symbol of the country's secularization and westernization, but it fell short of seeking gender equality. In assessing the progress made in advancing women's rights, Yıldız Ecevit in Chapter 12 challenges the common notion that women in Turkey were granted rights without a struggle. Focusing on the relationships between the state and women's organizations since the establishment of the Republic, she argues that there were always organized efforts by women, but by resorting to the alternative strategies of cooptation and repression, the state managed to suppress autonomous women's organizations. However, the diversity and concerted efforts of women's organizations that emerged after 1980 have allowed women to maintain their autonomy and participate in the policy process with effective voices.

In Chapter 13, Yasemin Çelik examines the progress in women's status and lives, with an emphasis on the impact of the UN Convention on the Elimination of All Forms of Discrimination against Women (CEDAW), to which Turkey became a party in 1985. The author highlights the pro-women legislation that was adopted after the ratification of the CEDAW, as well as the state agencies created to promote women's rights and monitor the implementation of the CEDAW. Although she finds these legislative and institutional treatments significant and consequential, her chapter suggests that various issues such as women's reproductive rights, "honor killings," and discrimination in various areas necessitate change not only in law but also in culture.

Both Ecevit and Çelik emphasize the role of women's organizations and the recent women's movement in bringing about changes favorable to women. NGOs have been critical to the advancement of international human rights since the beginnings of the UN, if not earlier, and are gaining prominence globally (Korey 1998; Z. F. Arat 2006, ch. 1). They have been particularly effective in reframing many issues as human rights issues, as in the case of the campaign to ban land mines (Ottawa Convention), and strengthening the mechanisms of international accountability, as in the case of creation of the International Criminal Court (Rome Statute) (Davenport 2002–3). The role of the domestic human rights NGOs is the subject of Chapter 14 by Başak Çalı. Focusing on four main human rights NGOs in Turkey, Çalı finds them instrumental in transforming the human rights discourse in Turkey since the 1980s. However, she notes that they have been less effective in influencing state policies, mainly due to the state officials' skeptical attitude toward human rights NGOs. Çalı's crediting human rights NGOs with the transformation of the human rights discourse in the country, a position backed by other authors who point out the increasing use of human rights language and treaties by otherwise ideologically diverse groups, counter some prevailing arguments about the limited acceptance of human rights in Turkey, such as the one by Ümit Cizre (2001), who claims that there is a "wide spectrum of aversion to human rights as a cause":

Human rights values have not aroused Turkey's centrist-liberal passions fully. Nor have they been translated into popular discourse. . . . For Turkey's millions in the urban middle classes, the human rights landscape is still unsafe, not worth the time and energy to extend sympathy, support and commitment in terms of the future returns it offers. Only some professional segments that perceive integration with global entities and dynamics in their own objective interests, intellectual dissidents, and those who suffered materially and psychologically under human rights abuses have engaged with the cause of human rights with some zeal and devotion. (55)

While these observations may be valid, one can question if they are unique to human rights, since political activism and participation in civic organizations have always attracted a limited number of people in Turkey. The causes of this hesitancy, if not apathy, must be rooted in the political culture and social values that equate organized activity, especially one with political undertones, with youthful restlessness or sinister and self-promoting challenges to the state authority.

Nevertheless, it is clear that changes in favor of human rights cannot be achieved without a change in individuals' values and attitude. Thus, there is a growing international consensus on the importance of human rights education, and the UN declared the years between 1995 and 2004 to be the UN Decade for Human Rights Education. In sync with the UN, a National Plan of Action was formulated in Turkey in 1999, and several programs on human rights education were launched in schools and incorporated into professional training. Kenan Çayır's chapter (Chapter 15) provides an overview of these programs, as well as a critical assessment of the textbooks prepared for the seventh and eighth grade human rights courses. Çayır argues that by privileging collective security and national duties over individual liberty and rights, the textbooks fall short of cultivating a human rights culture. Moreover, the content and methodology of all educational programs are far from meeting their stated goals.

INTERNATIONAL HUMAN RIGHTS REGIMES AND TURKEY

Turkey has been a participant in the global and European human rights regimes, and it became a party to numerous treaties that promote human rights. The impact of Turkey's integration into the international regimes in terms of human rights outcomes, however, has not been clear, and the authors in this volume present different views on this subject. For example, Çelik finds the CEDAW as instrumental in prompting legislative and institutional arrangements for women's rights, and Oran sees the European Convention on Human Rights as becoming a higher law and the European Court of Human Rights as effectively acting like a supreme court. Similar positive assessments are implicit in the Kirişci chapter, as well as that by Özerdem and Jacoby. Most of the other authors, however, especially those who write on social and economic rights, point to the gap between the norms and the actual practices, and at least imply that the commitment expressed by the ratification of treaties has not been matched in their execution.

In the last two chapters, the authors take on these controversies and try to assess the impact and meaning of Turkey's participation in international human rights regimes. Füsun Türkmen (Chapter 16) compares Turkey's integration into and level of participation in the European human rights regime and the UN-led global human rights regime. Arguing that Turkey's human rights policy has been shaped by concerns of realpolitik, she contends that with the goal of membership to the EU and accepting the jurisdiction of the European Court of Human Rights, Turkey has been more responsive to the monitoring and demands of the European regime. On the other hand, she contends that Turkey has generated less controversy within the global human rights regime, largely due to the nature of the UN's human rights machinery.

In Chapter 17, Thomas W. Smith focuses on the impact of the European Court of Human Rights (ECHR). Arguing that the ECHR is mostly about creating legal norms, he notes that "the Court has taken a key role in reforming Turkey's legal system," especially by prompting reforms in pretrial detention, trial procedures, freedom of expression, and freedom of assembly and association. He attributes the positive influence of the court partially to the fact that the compliance with the ECHR rulings has been a material condition for Turkey's EU membership, and partially (and implicitly) to the widely accepted argument that Europe has the world's strongest human rights regime.

Taken together, chapters in this volume depict a country that has been exposed to human rights language and claims for at least a century, but whose population has experienced repression more often than the enjoyment of human rights. However, emphasizing a host of recent developments that favor human rights, the authors expect a brighter future. These predictions and their assessments are discussed in the Conclusion, along with the international and theoretical implications of Turkey's experience.

Part I
Freedoms and Antidiscrimination

Chapter 2
Freedom of Press and Broadcasting

Dİlruba Çatalbaş

Freedom of expression is a fundamental human right and as such is protected in international human rights instruments, including the Universal
Declaration of Human Rights (Article 19), the International Covenant
on Civil and Political Rights (Articles 19 and 20), and the European Convention for the Protection of Human Rights and Fundamental Freedoms
(Article 10). Freedom of expression cannot be fully realized without the
freedom of press. Freedom of press also allows news media to play a crucial role in liberal democracies, by providing citizens with wide-ranging
news, information, and ideas, and by creating opportunities for different
views and interests to be publicly expressed. However, no legal system
grants unqualified support to the freedom of press. For example, the
European Convention permits restrictions "in the interests of national
security, territorial integrity or public safety, for the prevention of dis-
order and crime, for the protection of health and morals, for the protection of reputation and rights of others, for preventing the disclosure
of information received in confidence or for maintaining the authority
and impartiality of the judiciary" (Article 10/2). However, the European
Court of Human Rights has ruled that any infringement on freedom of
expression "must be prescribed by law," must be "necessary in a democratic country" (i.e., must be justified by a "pressing social need"), and
must be "reasonably proportionate to the aim of responding to that need"
(Robertson and Nicol 1984).

In Turkey, there have been frequent government restraints and restrictions placed on freedom of expression, as well as on freedom of press.
The Turkish news media have usually operated within very limiting legal
frameworks, particularly during periods of political instability. Although
Turkey ratified the European Convention in 1954, the laws on press and
other legislation contained restrictive provisions in relation to freedom
of expression. A survey, conducted by the Turkish Press Council in 1995,
identified 152 laws that restricted press freedom in Turkey (*Milliyet*, 3
April 1995). Moreover, in an effort to adapt its conduct to the exigencies

of the circumstances and reap their possible political and economic rewards, Turkish press, since its inception, developed a rather complex web of relations with the state, the military, politicians, and powerful economic interest groups. Particularly after the 1980s, these relations, usually guided by media proprietors and elite executive journalists, created overt and covert pressures over editorial decision making and reinforced self-censorship. This, in turn, caused a serious decline in independent and objective reporting and, thus, severely undermined the credibility and respectability of journalism (Tunç 2004). Other equally important factors that have long undermined the freedom of press in Turkey are embedded in the political economy of the media sector; ideological and sociocultural background of journalists; the issues of democratic governance, representation, and deunionization within news organizations; ineffectiveness of journalists' associations; organizational and internalized self-censorship mechanisms; limited local news outlets; and the excessively commercial media culture, which treats news as a part of the show business.

However, it should be noted that while the media-government relations in Turkey have been always difficult and complicated and the structural factors shaping journalism have been less than favorable, freedom of press has never been totally absent. On the contrary, there have been several periods in which freedom of press thrived and the voices of dissent and resistance continued even under the military and martial law rules. These contradictory elements are described by Human Rights Watch (1999):

> The press in Turkey—in the vernacular of psychiatry—suffers from multiple personality disorder. When reporting on the vast majority of issues, such as domestic party politics or the economy, the media today is lively and unrestricted—indeed often sensational. . . . Alongside the arena of free discussion there is a danger zone where many who criticize accepted state policy face possible state persecution. Risky areas include the role of Islam in politics and society, Turkey's ethnic Kurdish minority and the conflict in southeastern Turkey, the nature of the state, and the proper role of the military.

The constraints on the reporting and discussion of certain "taboo" subjects continue to be the source of contention between Turkey and the European Union. Trying to meet the political conditions for EU membership, set in the Copenhagen criteria, several reform packages were adopted since the beginning of 2000, but they are received with caution.

This chapter provides a brief summary of the historical development of the freedom of press in Turkey by focusing on the legal and political hindrances that journalists and broadcasters had to encounter. Identifying the constraints stemming from political, legal, and market pressures, it contends that while the authoritarian politics and legal restrictions have been the main obstacles to the freedom of press, economic issues, namely the concentration of ownership, increasing corporate control, and the invasion of the newsrooms by a commercial ethos constitute growing areas of concern. "Turkey has a lively press and there is no overt censorship, but it remains a difficult environment for independent journalism" (Karaelmas 2001).

Struggle for Freedom of the Press: A Historical Perspective

The history of journalism in Turkey reflects the troubles and the fundamental transformations that Turkish society has undergone since the reforms carried out by the Ottoman Empire in the nineteenth century. Its decisive moments, therefore, have coincided with the major turning points in the political system, including the declaration of the Tanzimat (reforms), the Constitutional Monarchy, the armistice, and the establishment of the Republic of Turkey (Mazıcı 1996).

The first newspapers in Turkish were published in the mid-nineteenth century and were almost entirely financed by either the Palace or the foreign embassies (Bozdağ 1992, 141). They were published and mostly read by an influential minority of intellectuals, who usually occupied public offices (Gürkan Pazarcı 2004). As newspapers and journalist started to voice opposition, they became targets of repressive measures. The 1864 Press Law, by requiring all newspapers to obtain a prior permission, imposed the first legal restrictions on the freedom of press (Mazıcı 1996, 18). Three years later, a government decree (Ali Kararname) gave the state authorities the right to close down newspapers that posed a threat to the regime.

Although the 1876 Constitution stated that "the press was free as prescribed by law," this freedom did not last long, and all publications became subject to strict censorship during the long reign of Sultan Abdülhamit (1878–1908). The proclamation of the second Constitutional Monarchy, in 1908, brought an atmosphere of freedom, as the 1909 Press Law did not require a prior permission but demanded a notification to be made to the authorities. However, the persecution of the press continued under the rule of the Committee of Union and Progress, when the first politically motivated killings of journalists took place (Özgen 2000). After the First World War, the parliament was dissolved and censorship was reimposed in December 1918. Following the occupation of İstanbul in March 1920, the occupation forces played a prominent role on the censorship board.

THE ONE-PARTY RULE (1920–50)

The national resistance movement, organized under the leadership of Mustafa Kemal, divided the Turkish press into two hostile camps: the

İstanbul papers, which were loyal to the sultan, and the Anatolian papers, which worked as a propaganda arm of the struggle for independence (H. Çakır 2002). The National Assembly convened in Ankara, on 23 April 1920, in defiance of the sultan, and passed a law that rendered any criticism on the legality of the Assembly as treason. On 17 June 1920, the Anatolian News Agency, which had been formed to spread news about the independence war, was brought under the authority of the Press and Intelligence Directorate, and all communications with İstanbul began to be censored.

The 1921 Constitution adopted by the National Assembly did not have any provisions on the press, and there was no specific press law. The country was still at war, and all that was expected from the press was to support the government (Alemdar 2004). The victory in the independence war allowed Mustafa Kemal to create the Republican People's Party (Cumhuriyet Halk Partisi, CHP), which would run the country until 1950. On 8 December 1923, soon after the proclamation of the Republic of Turkey on 29 October 1923, an Independence Tribunal was sent to İstanbul to try those journalists who opposed the Ankara government.

The 1924 Constitution stipulated that newspapers would not be subject to any prior inspection or control. However, all CHP governments were as suspicious of press as their predecessors in the Ottoman times, and they took harsh measures to discourage all critical reports and opposition. Following the suppression of a rebellion in the southeast, launched by a local Kurdish leader, Sheik Said, the government declared martial law on 13 February 1925, and on 4 March 1925, it passed the Law on the Maintenance of the Order (Takrir-i Sükun). The law, which gave the government the power to ban newspapers and other publications, allowed the trial of some leading journalists by the Independence Tribunals with the charges of inciting the rebellion. On 3 June 1925, the government closed down the Progressive Republican Party (Terakkiperver Cumhuriyet Fırkası), which had been formed on 17 November 1924 by a split group from the ruling party, for its alleged role in the unrest. During the four years that Takrir-i Sükun law remained in force, the opponents of the regime were silenced, mainly through summary trials by the Independence Tribunals (Kabacalı 1990).

Nevertheless, the 1920s also witnessed two media-related developments that ran counter to the bureaucratic/conservative/controlling attitude of the government (Alemdar 2004). First, in 1925, the Anatolian News Agency (AA) was transformed from a state agency to a limited company. Second, the Turkish Wireless and Telephone Company (TTTAŞ), a private monopoly, was granted a license to carry out radio broadcasting between 1927 and 1936. In addition to trying to create a westernized nation-state through a set of top-down reforms in various areas, ranging from the alphabet to people's attire, the founders of the Republic were also interested in stimulating the development of a national bourgeoisie (Kejanlıoğlu 2003). However, the autonomous structure of the AA could not be maintained, and in 1933, as a result of growing dissatisfaction with the operations of the TTTAŞ, and a shift to étatist economic policies, Turkish government decided to nationalize the radio broadcasting company.

The establishment of the Free Republican Party in 1930, as another attempt to break the one-party rule, divided the press, and the ensuing fierce dispute forced the founder of the party to dissolve it. In 1931, several journalist parliamentarians from the ruling party called the government to put an end to what they called "poisonous reports" by the opposition press (Mazıcı 1996). Until 1946, a large portion of the Turkish press wholeheartedly supported the ruling ideology, Kemalism, and perceived itself responsible for the preservation of it. Kemalist principles were used to define the nature of the state and represented the idealist formulations of central elites, including the journalist intelligentsia, on *how* to transform Turkey into a modern, Western-style state. Thus, when it meant to deter challenges to the ruling ideology, many journalists did not hesitate to support censorship and even condemn and inform about fellow journalists (Oktay 1987, 45). As a result, the new Press Law, adopted in 1931, gave the Council of Ministers the power to ban publications and close publishing houses that were deemed to contradict the "prevalent politics/policies of the country" (Özgen 2000, 22). It also allowed the government to ban the circulation of newspapers and magazines published in foreign countries. The aim of the law was to create "a responsible press" that would support and help the regime. The concept of "responsible press" was reiterated by the government at the first Press Congress, which was convened in Ankara on 25 May 1935. The Congress reached the agreement that the state would support the press and, in return, the press would help the state to generate public support for the Kemalist reforms (Bozdağ 1992, 175).

The 1931 Press Law was later subjected to five amendments, the most extensive ones taking place on 27 June 1938, which required a prior permission and a security payment in order to publish a newspaper, and demanded publishers not to have a "bad reputation," an ambiguous word the interpretation of which was left to the bureaucrats (Topuz 1996, 95). Also in 1938, all practicing journalists were required to join the Press Association. The executive board of the association was composed of journalists who were members or deputies of the ruling party. Other measures of government control included regulating the imports of newsprint and printing equipment and rewarding the prominent supportive journalists by having them elected to the parliament. It is noted that during the 1920–38 period, more than forty of the deputies had their professional background in journalism (Kabacalı 1990, 141).

During the Second World War, the state control over the AA was reinforced by the Press and Broadcasting Directorate. Trying to stay out of the war, the government attempted to prevent newspapers from influencing the public opinion in support of either of the warring sides, but could not stop some papers from adopting an openly pro-German stance (Arabacı 2004, 116). However, the martial law, declared in November 1940 and lasting until 1947, tightened the government's grip on the press. Leftist newspapers and journalists, accused of making communist propaganda, became the main target. On 4 December 1945, the premises of *Tan,* a daily paper known to be the staunchest critic of the CHP, the ruling party, was attacked and destroyed by a mob of students, who were allegedly provoked by the CHP İstanbul office (Topuz 1996, 98). Some prominent journalists also took part in the provocation.

After the Second World War, Turkey was pressured by its Western allies to become a pluralist and liberal political system. In 1945, the American Freedom of Press Commission visited Turkey to promote the concept and advocate the exercise of self-control instead of censorship (Özgen 2000, 26). Employing a similar liberal language, the Democratic Party (DP), formed on 7 January 1946, gained widespread support from the press. To regain the backing of the press, the CHP government amended the 1931 Press Law, on 1 June 1946, to make the closing of newspapers permissible only by court order. However, the martial law commanders were able to prohibit any news that would cast doubts on the results of elections. After the annulment of the Press Association Law by the government, on 10 June 1946, journalists established the Journalists' Association. The censorship and repressive measures against the press, which were particularly harsh on the opposition papers, began to invoke criticisms in the international arena. In 1948, the CHP government announced its intention to change the antidemocratic features of the Press Law. But before the draft amendment was discussed in the parliament, the elections of 14 May 1950 brought the DP to power.

THE MULTIPARTY SYSTEM (1950–80)

The press, like most of the electorate, largely welcomed the DP government, since it had promised greater freedoms in economic, social, and cultural spheres. The DP policies, which attempted to end the hegemony of the elitist intellectual, bureaucratic, and military consensus in politics, allowed a more pluralist press to emerge, which even included left-wing papers. The 1950 Press Law, enacted on 15 May, permitted the publication of newspapers without acquiring prior approval from the state authorities. Under this law, charges against the press would be taken to special press courts, and newspaper proprietors would not hold any criminal liabilities. Despite the protests by the newspaper owners, in 1952 the DP government also adopted the first law that recognized and protected the labor rights of professional journalists.

However, the honeymoon period did not last long, as the DP government quickly became intolerant of criticisms and claims that its policies were undermining the Kemalist principles. The Cold War and the Soviet threat, which had rendered Turkey a part of the Truman doctrine, were used to suppress the press and socialists. The closure of the Turkish Communist Party in 1950 and the trial of its 173 members echoed the communist witch hunt pursued in the United States (Bozdağ 1992, 183). Prior to the 1954 elections, the DP government, frustrated by increasingly tense relations with the opposition, passed a law on "the crimes committed through the press and radio," which led to the trials of many journalists, particularly those who supported the CHP. As a result of the riots of 6–7 September 1955, in İstanbul, during which many mainly Greek businesses were assaulted and looted, the government put the martial law into effect (see Chapter 4, by Prodromos Yannas, in this volume). During the nine months of the martial law rule, the martial law administrators issued several bans on the press. By 1956, Prime Minister Adnan Menderes was convinced that extending freedom of press in 1950 had been a mistake (Kabacalı 1990, 172). As a result, fourteen articles of the Press Law were amended to tighten the control over the press.

During the 1950s, the press was manipulated also through the allocation of newsprint and the allotment of public announcements and advertisements. Papers that were offered generous financial resources from public funds were called the "foster-child press" (*besleme basın*) by critics. The DP government also put pressure on judges and public prosecutors to obtain banning orders. Between 1954 and 1958, 1,161 journalists were interrogated, and 238 of them were prosecuted (Oktay 1987, 51). The International Press Institute protested the DP government for putting editors on trial for publishing a critical piece on the DP administration in 1959 (Topuz 1996, 117). Yet on 18 April 1960, the DP government formed a parliamentary commission to investigate the CHP and the press, and authorized it to ban publications. These policies, as well as the partisan use of the radio, intensified the opposition to the DP rule, particularly among university students and intellectuals. Following the street protests that began on 28 April, the martial law was declared again. One of the first actions taken by the martial law commanders included imposing a ban on reporting the protests.

The ten-year rule of the DP ended by a military coup d'état on 27 May 1960. The Committee of National Unity (Milli Birlik Komitesi, MBK), composed of the leaders of the coup, abolished the law "on the crimes committed through the press and radio" but did not tolerate the news reports that were critical of the charges and lawsuits brought up against the DP leaders, as well as the harsh penalties imposed by the courts. The MBK, however, also took some measures in favor of freedom of press. On 2 January 1961, it passed a law that established the Press Advertising Corporation (Basın İlan Kurumu), in order to prevent the discriminatory allocation of public advertisements. This was followed by Law No. 212, which involved protective clauses on the rights of professional journalists. In protest of the latter act, the owners of nine major newspapers decided not to go to print for three days. Demonstrating an unprecedented example of solidarity, journalists published their own paper, by using the facilities at the office of the Journalists' Association and with the support of the MBK (Özsever 2004, 84). This event speaks to the popularity of the 1960 coup among journalists.

The new Constitution, adopted by a public referendum on 9 July 1961, produced a more liberal regime and affirmed that the press was free, not subject to censorship (Article 22). The restrictions could be defined only by law, and there could be no prohibitions unless ordered by a court judge. However, before the elections on 9 July 1961, the MBK passed a law outlawing statements that portrayed the military takeover, or those that defended the DP government, as illegal or unjust (Kabacalı 1990, 189).

The liberal character of the post-1960 regime allowed the left to re-enter the political arena. The Turkish Workers' Party was established in 1961, and several socialist publications were launched. However, it was mainly through the writings of some influential left-wing journalists, who wrote for the mainstream papers, that the leftist ideas began to permeate into the society (Oktay 1987, 58). The proliferation of the left-wing ideological groups, fueled by the rapid urbanization and industrialization processes, annoyed the subsequent governments established by the right-wing Justice Party (Adalet Partisi, AP). As the main heir of the DP, the AP exerted pressures mainly on the leftist press.

During the 1960s, there were a few important developments in favor of freedom of press and broadcasting. First, the Press Honor Council (Basın Şeref Divanı) was founded as a self-regulating authority, which continued its operations, though ineffectively, until 1967. Then, a law (no. 359) issued on 1 May 1964 established the Turkish Radio and Television Broadcasting Corporation (TRT), as an "autonomous public juridical person" (and as a reaction to DP's partisan conducts). However, throughout the 1960s, the TRT management continuously faced restrictive political and economic pressures from AP governments, which considered the TRT a leftist outlet (Şahin 1981).

At the beginning of the 1970s the growing polarization between the right- and left-wing ideological groups and the escalating violence on university campuses and on the streets led to another military intervention.

A memorandum of armed forces, issued on 12 March 1971, forced the prime minister to step down, and on 26 April the martial law became effective in 11 cities, where the martial law commanders had the authority to control and censor publications and close down printing houses. The interim government, picked by the military, argued that the 1961 Constitution was idealistic, too liberal, and a "luxury" for a developing country such as Turkey (Pevsner 1984). An amendment to the 1961 Constitution, passed on 22 September 1971, gave the government and the public prosecutors the right to confiscate newspapers. The martial law commanders took several journalists into custody. The autonomy of the TRT was annulled, and a three-star general was appointed as its director general. The repressive regime was criticized by the 1972 Congress of the International Federation of Journalists, which was held in İstanbul.

Although the martial law regime ended with the parliamentary elections held in 1973, political instability and social unrest continued throughout the 1970s. Newspapers, like other segments of the society, were deeply divided and ideologically polarized. While some journalists were in favor of the annulment of the Articles 141 and 142 of the Penal Code, which punished left-wing activities, others strongly opposed it (Özgen 2000, 52). Moreover, in the 1970s, decreasing circulations forced newspapers to resort to some commercial strategies such as lotteries and paved the way for the later moves into tabloidization. A significant assault to the freedom press was the trial of eleven newspapers and two news agencies that were charged with disclosing the state secrets on the Cyprus issue in 1974 (Kabacalı 1990, 207).

SINCE 1980

The 1980 coup ended a period of political crisis and civil violence. A year after the dissolution of the Parliament, all political parties, including Atatürk's CHP, were closed down. The mass media could not escape restriction. The martial law administration issued new bans almost on daily basis. Newspapers were closed "until a further notice," and the editors of the mainly leftist newspapers were sentenced to prison terms for hundreds of years.

The preamble of the 1982 Constitution stated that "no protection shall be afforded to thoughts or opinions contrary to Turkish national interests." Although Article 28 stated that "the press is free and shall not be censored," a number of provisions made it an offense to write or print any news or articles that threaten the security or "the indivisible integrity of the State with its nation and territory." In the same manner, although Article 31 forbade restrictions on the rights to information, to access ideas and opinions, and to engender public opinion through the use of mass media and press, Article 13 allowed extensive exceptions and permitted restrictions on the grounds of protecting national security, public order, public peace, public interest, public morals, and public health. Moreover, Articles 26 and 28 contained a clause that banned the use of languages "prohibited by law." As Feroz Ahmad puts it, the "1961 Constitution had permitted Turkish society to be politicized; the 1982 version attempted to reverse the process" (Ahmad 1985).

In October 1983, the National Security Council imposed additional restrictions on the freedom of press. The Emergency Rule Law, adopted on 25 October 1983, also enforced censorship. The new broadcasting Law No. 2954, dated 11 November 1983, ended "autonomy" by allowing the government to control the appointment of the TRT directors, which made the TRT a mouthpiece of the government. The law granted to the prime minister, or a minister designated by him, the authority to prohibit the transmission of news items on the grounds of protecting national security.

Contrary to its liberal economic policies, the government established by the Motherland Party (ANAP), which won the November 1983 elections and ran the country until 1991, pursued a conservative policy in cultural and political matters. In March 1986, the ANAP government revived an old law with the aim of protecting minors from obscene publications. An amendment of Article 24 of the Civil Law, adopted on 4 May 1988, gave individuals the right to demand the prevention of publications that were deemed to insult their personality. Several cases of alleged insults were brought to the courts and the leader of the ANAP, Turgut Özal, had the highest number of lawsuits demanding pay for damages (Kabacalı 1990, 235).

The liberal economic policies pursued by the ANAP throughout the 1980s not only opened up the Turkish economy to the world markets but also produced "new mental images, desires, aspirations and motivations" (Abadan-Unat 1991, 180). Turkish society started to embrace a consumerist culture. The press, which refrained from addressing controversial political issues, focused more and more on entertainment and popular culture. The emergence of cheap and sensational tabloid papers like *Tan*, which quickly captured large numbers of readers, contributed to the depoliticization of the society and a decline in quality journalism. Another significant change during the 1980s was the entry of the non-media capital into the publishing industry. One of the first acts of the new media bosses, such as Aydın Doğan, was the removal of unions from their papers, thus depriving the journalists of their right to association.

In 1991, Articles 141, 142, and 163 of the penal code—typically used to punish communists, separatists, and the Islamists—were repealed. In the previous decade socialist papers had been confiscated frequently with the charges of communism and separatism. However, the Antiterrorism Law, passed in April 1991 as a measure against the terrorist organization PKK (Partia Karkaren Kürdistan, or Kurdistan Workers' Party), introduced further limitations on the freedoms of expression and press. Article 7, meanwhile, prohibited assisting the members of illegal organizations, and Article 8 outlawed separatist propaganda. Initially the scope of Article 8 was very wide, as it took no account of the intent or method employed. These restrictive provisions of the laws were used particularly against the Kurdish nationalist and Islamist presses, which were seen as threats to the unitary structure of the state, its territorial integrity, and its secularist foundations.[1]

The economic liberalism of the ANAP government and the increasing public pressure to end the state monopoly in broadcasting led to the mushrooming of private satellite channels in the 1990s. The liberalization of broadcasting allowed some very controversial topics (e.g., the Kurdish insurgency, Islamic fundamentalism, and secularism) to be discussed on television and radio. However, the producers of some programs that were critical of state institutions, especially the military, faced prosecution.

Although private satellite stations started in 1990, the private electronic media had no legal basis until 8 August 1993, when the official abolition of the state monopoly was ended with an amendment of Article 133 of the 1982 Constitution. The amendment defined the TRT as an "autonomous" corporation, but this was not translated into Law No. 2954. A new broadcasting Law No. 3984, which was passed on 13 April 1994, established a Radio and Television Supreme Board (Radyo ve Televizyon Üst Kurulu), with extensive powers, to assert a tight control over the broadcasting media. Law No. 3984 immediately received criticisms and calls for rectification of its imperfections from different quarters, and some of its provisions were amended on 7 June 2001. Although the large media conglomerates welcomed the changes, the president of the Republic vetoed them on the grounds of excessive commercialization and monopolization. However, almost a year later, on 15 May 2002, the parliament overruled the veto and upheld the amendments. A more recent law (no. 4756) also allowed the Radio and Television Supreme Board to monitor Web sites and impose heavy fines for defamation and dissemination of "false news." President Sezer forwarded the law to the Constitutional Court and asked for the annulment of the articles that he deemed harmful to freedom of press and to the diversity of public sphere. In the end, on 12 June 2002, the Constitutional Court ruled for the annulment of five provisions and some paragraphs of Law No. 4756.

Persistent Constraints

Until the present century, the news media in Turkey faced extensive restrictions. Covering controversial issues, such as Kurdish identity and nationalism, several journalists, including a few foreign correspondents, faced prosecution. The laws most frequently invoked in restricting the freedom expression and press included Articles 155, 158, 159, and 312 of the Penal Code, Articles 7 and 8 of the Antiterrorism Law, and the law concerning crimes committed against Atatürk. In addition to prosecutions, there were also overt or covert political pressures, emanating from some state institutions like the military and the National Security Council. Journalists have been also subject to pressures from underground organizations that used intimidation and violence, and some journalists became victims of assassinations. Most of the assassinated journalists had worked for radical, far-left papers or Kurdish-nationalist publications that appeared sympathetic to the PKK. The security forces were also heavy-handed in their treatment of journalists. As a result, Turkey attracted serious criticisms from the EU, various journalists' associations, and human rights NGOs. In fact, the European Court of Human Rights frequently decided against Turkey on matters related to freedom of expression (see Chapter 17 in this volume).

Legal Changes

On 17 October 2001, a number of constitutional amendments were adopted to improve the freedom of expression and press and to bolster the country's prospect to join the EU. The new preamble of the Constitution did not mention "thoughts or opinions," but affirms that "activity" that is "contrary to the Turkish national interests, the principle of the indivisibility of the existence of Turkey with its state and territory," is not protected. The amended Articles 13 and 14 state that fundamental rights and freedoms might be restricted only by law without infringing upon their essence, and restrictions should not be in conflict with the requirements of the democratic order of the society and the secular Republic and the principle of proportionality. Moreover, the prohibition on the use of "language prohibited by law" was removed from Articles 26 and 28.

These changes were followed by several more legislative reforms. A "minidemocracy package," passed in February 2002, revised Articles 159 and 312 of the Penal Code and brought penalty changes to Article 7 and 8 of the Antiterrorism Law. The second reform package, which came into effect on 8 April 2002, included modifications to the Press Law. The third package, which was approved in August 2002, altered Article 159 of the Penal Code in such a way that the written, oral, or visual expressions of opinion that did not carry any intention to insult institutions would not be penalized. It also introduced an article to Law No. 3984 that permitted broadcasting in "different languages and dialects used traditionally by Turkish citizens in their daily lives," which thus allows broadcasting in Kurdish and other languages. In addition, six different articles of the Press Law were amended to replace prison sentences with fines.

Pledging to speed up Turkey's efforts to join the EU, the AKP government passed the fourth package of harmonization on 2 January 2003. The package included an amendment of Article 15 of the Press Law to state that editors and journalists could not be forced to disclose their sources. Following the fifth package, which entered into force on 4 February 2003, another set of changes was passed on 19 July 2003. With these private radio and television stations are obliged during the election periods to abide by the regulations in the TRT Law. The National Security Council Secretariat was excluded from the Video, Music, and Works of Arts Supervisory Board. Moreover, Law No. 3984 was amended to permit "broadcasts by state and private radio and television stations in different languages and dialects, which are traditionally used by Turkish citizens in their daily lives." However, the most significant change was the abolition of Article 8 of the Antiterrorism Law. The seventh reform package, which was approved by the President Sezer on 6 August 2003, amended the second paragraph of Article 7 of the Antiterrorism Law, as well as the last paragraph of Article 159, and Articles 169, 426, and 427 of the Penal Code. The amendments excluded the works of arts and science from the scope of "immoral publications" proscribed in Article 426. These constitutional and legal changes expanded the freedom of expression and press in Turkey a great deal. However, many observers agreed that how these changes would be put into practice was more important than their existence on the paper, and would prove to be the test case for their success and effectiveness in the long run.

On 17 July 2003, the AKP government announced its plans to replace Press Law No. 5680, which stated that distribution of a newspaper or other published material may be suspended by the decision of a judge, or in the event delay was deemed prejudicial, by the written order of the public prosecutor. According to this law, periodicals and other published work could be temporarily suspended from one day to fifteen days if they were found guilty of publishing material that contravened "the indivisible integrity of the state with its nation and territory," national security, and public morals. Any publication that would be the continuation of a previously suspended periodical was also prohibited and would be seized upon the decision by a competent judge. Press Law No. 5680 also demanded that the provisions in relation to damages caused by false news and defamation would be applied to electronic newspapers and the Internet.

The draft press law, which abolished restrictive provisions of Law No. 5680, received an enthusiastic welcome from several prominent journalists. Another development, which added to the optimistic mood, was the approval on 9 October 2003 of Law No. 4982 on the Right to Obtain Information, which allowed citizens to demand information from state institutions (Ekşi 2003). However, the new Press Law No. 5187, which was enacted on 26 June 2004, felt short of meeting the expectations. Although it contained certain improvements such as extending the right not to disclose news sources to documents as well, the law had its drawbacks. The Turkish Association of Journalists criticized the Press Law for retreating from the principle of converting prison sentences for editors to fines, and claimed that exorbitant fines would economically destabilize the local media. The association also argued that the regulation on the coverage of court cases was too restrictive and not suitable for a transparent society. Moreover, by prohibiting the sale and distribution of illegal materials published in foreign countries, the Law No. 5187 reintroduced the Article 31 of its predecessor (TGC). The Union of Journalists was further disturbed by the fact that that the law did not provide any protective measures against the abuse of media proprietors. The Union of Journalists has long argued that "the trend for monopolization, emerging through the collection of ownership of media companies in the hands of a few employers and the cartels established by those employers, eradicate the freedom of press, free distribution of publications, free employment right of journalists and the editorial independence" (International Federation of Journalists).

Finally, the enactment of the new Penal Code on 26 September 2004 constituted a major improvement on the previous one by several measures, but it is not advanced on promoting freedom of press. The Global Coordinating Committee of the Press Freedom Organizations called Turkey to remove the provisions on defamation and insult as they would have "a paralyzing effect on the media profession as a whole," and would "encourage censorship by making journalists fearful of writing investigative stories that criticize the state" (*Alert*). On 28 November 2004, thirty-seven journalists' associations in Turkey demanded the amendment of some provisions that impose prison sentences on journalists. Claiming that these provisions would undermine the liberating effect of the recent legal reforms, journalists contended that the new Penal Code would make Turkey the world's biggest journalists' prison. As a result of the growing public protests by journalists' associations and objections and concerns voiced by some legal experts over the imperfections in the law, the AKP government decided on 31 March 2005 to postpone the implementation of the new Penal Code until 1 June 2005.

Economic Changes and Market Pressures

Private ownership of press in Turkey is as old as the history of journalism. What started as opinion papers, owned and published by members of political and cultural elite in the first half of the nineteenth century, evolved into partisan papers in the early years of the Republic. The establishment of *Hürriyet* in 1948 signaled the beginning of dailies with mass circulation. The arrival of television in 1968 forced newspapers to embrace new technologies and adopt more aggressive commercial strategies. This forced the major papers to form closer relations with business circles in search of more advertising revenues. Leftist publications could not survive, as they were not able to meet the marketing requirements of advertisers.

Until the end of the 1970s newspapers were mostly owned by families that were in journalism for generations, or by cultural and political organizations. In the 1980s, some entrepreneurs, who made their fortunes in other industries, began to acquire well-known and high-volume papers such as *Milliyet* and *Hürriyet*. The transfer of the newspaper ownership from journalist families to corporate entrepreneurs started to change the dynamics and structure of the news media in Turkey. Becoming a part of larger corporate entities increased newspapers' dependence on capital with significant stakes in several nonmedia sectors.

When the Turkish electronic media was started to be privatized in 1990, the press barons, such as Aydın Doğan and Dinç Bilgin, took it as an opportunity to diversify their media operations (Sönmez 1996). Other nonmedia corporations also scrambled to grab a share in the media business, which was not only a flourishing market but would also allow the use of the media power as a "weapon" to bargain with politicians and scare their competitors (Sönmez 2003a). As the corporate takeover gained a momentum, newspapers moved from their traditional premises in the city center to new suburban corporate campuses with rising media towers, which usually combined broadcasting and printing facilities. A factor that facilitated the corporate takeover of the broadcasting sector in the 1990s was the generous public subsidies granted to assure the favorable coverage of the government (Söylemez 1998). The increasing trends of cross-ownership and concentration of ownership provided the media companies with considerable power to further their economic interests and to negotiate with the politicians for further privileges.

In the 1990s, two media conglomerates, the Doğan and the Medi groups, controlled around 70 percent of newspaper sales and a large proportion of television advertising (Nebiler 1995). Their growth was largely due to the advertising provided by the also flourishing and competitive banking and finance sectors. Consequently, the bankruptcies of many banks and subsequent contraction of the banking sector during the financial crises of November 2000 and February 2001 had profound effects on the media companies. Especially the 2001 economic crisis forced downsizing and restructuring, which resulted in massive layoffs, including those of a large number of journalists.

Since the 1990s, the ownership of some media companies has kept changing due to the financial instabilities or transactions among different groups, reinforcing the concentration of ownership. Recent studies on the Turkish media, conducted by Turkish or international researchers or organizations, identify the concentration of ownership as a major impediment to the freedom of press and broadcasting, and one of the primary causes of the degeneration of journalistic integrity and ethics in Turkey (*Journalism and the Human Rights Challenge* 2002).

Conclusion

The freedom of press and media are crucial to the development of democratic life and politics. However, the governments and other state officials in Turkey have tended to view the press and media as culprits of instability and have tried therefore, in different ways and with various degrees of success, to manipulate and control their operations. Thus, the state control of the press and broadcasting has been the major obstacle to the freedom of press in Turkey, but the recent changes in the legal framework promise some significant improvements. Since the 1980s, the emergence of large media conglomerates raised new concerns, and economic and commercial considerations gained ascendancy. The phenomenal transformation in the 1990s of television broadcasting into a multichannel competitive system was another important change that deeply influenced Turkish journalism. The increased sensitivity to the market pressures started to define what is worth covering and broadcasting, especially during the prime time. As the concentration of ownership and the media connection to the corporate world continues, there is a real danger that "the tyranny of the market may replace or supplement governmental pressures" (Randall 1993). These recent developments in Turkey demonstrate that freedom of press and broadcasting cannot be seen as threatened only by the political pressures but must be defended against powerful economic interest groups as well.

Chapter 3

The Minority Concept and Rights in Turkey: The Lausanne Peace Treaty and Current Issues

BASKIN ORAN

The definition of the concepts of minority and minority rights in Turkey has been based on a peace treaty that was signed in Lausanne on 24 July 1923, between the British Empire, France, Italy, Japan, Greece, Romania, and the Kingdom of Serbs, Croats, and Slovenes on oneside, and Turkey on the other. Following the Turkish nationalists' victory in the War of Independence against Greece, backed by England (which had occupied the country after the First World War), this treaty replaced the Treaty of Sèvres of 10 August 1920, which had been imposed upon the Ottoman Empire after the war, and it recognized the Ankara government as the representative of Turkey.

When the League of Nations was formed after the First World War, a tripartite criterion was employed to define minorities in racial, linguistic and religious terms. Minorities fitting into any of these three categories were granted not only equal rights with the majority but also internationally guaranteed rights that did not apply to the majority (e.g., building their own schools and using their own languages).

However, the Turkish delegation in Lausanne did not accept the full criterion as applicable to Turkey; it recognized only "non-Muslims" as constituting a minority, a position that was accepted at the conference. Since then, Turkey has insisted on using this definition, always invoking the Lausanne Treaty in its international treaty agreements by appending an "interpretative statement" (a term employed by the Turkish Ministry of Foreign Affairs) that reads: "The Republic of Turkey reserves the right to implement Article [number of article] of this agreement in accordance with the relevant articles of the Turkish Constitution and in accordance with the relevant articles and procedures of the 24 July 1923 Lausanne Peace Treaty and its annexes."

This chapter analyzes the content of the Lausanne Peace Treaty, examines its interpretation and application by Turkey, and discusses the validity and consequences of such interpretations. It makes the following arguments. (1) Turkey has employed a very narrow definition of "minority" and used it to limit the applicability of the rights articulated in the Lausanne Treaty as well as the subsequent human rights treaties. (2) Even the rights of non-Muslim minorities that were recognized by the state have been continuously violated. (3) The official position on minority definition and rights, framed by the political conditions of the 1920s and 1930s, is outdated and out of sync with the rest of the world. (4) The official position and state policies have been counterproductive, but with the recent legal reform packages, an irreversible course in favor of human rights has been set in Turkey. (5) These reforms carry a special weight for being enacted at a time when the country's political climate was charged by the "Sèvres syndrome," which summoned an aura of McCarthyism against the advocates of minority and human rights.

The Official Position on the Definition of Minority

The official position of Turkey on minority rights can be viewed by dividing it into two aspects: (1) in the Lausanne Treaty, the term "non-Muslims" is used to replace the minority criteria prevalent at the time; and (2) the international rights recognized by international organizations are granted only to non-Muslims.

Limiting the Definition to Non-Muslims

A distinctive characteristic of all the minority protection agreements signed immediately after the First World War was the recognition of race, language, and religion in defining minorities. This became the standard practice and was imposed by the victors, the Principal Allied and Associated Powers (PAAP, i.e., United States, Great Britain, France, Italy, Japan) on some of vanquished states (Austria, Bulgaria, Hungary, and the Ottoman Empire), on some victorious countries that expanded their territories (Greece and Romania), and on countries established after the war (Poland, Serbian-Croatian-Slovenian State, and Czechoslovakia). In fact, the Polish Minorities Treaty, which was the first of such instruments, served as a template for the subsequent treaties.[1] However, the "racial, linguistic and religious minorities" reference is replaced in the text of the Lausanne Treaty with the term "non-Muslims." This may be explained by the relatively higher negotiation power of the Turkish delegate, which emerged victorious from the Turkish War of Independence (1919–22).

Moreover, the definition of minorities in the Lausanne Treaty was not based on an inclusive parameter of "religion." Even the "religion" criterion was reduced to a "non-Muslim" reference. Had the parameter of religion been accepted, as noted by Dr. Rıza Nur (1967, 1044), the deputy head of the Ankara delegation at the Lausanne negotiations, the Alavis, whose religious practices are very different from Sunni Muslims, would have been also recognized as a minority and therefore covered by international guarantees.

INTERNATIONAL RIGHTS

The second fundamental differentiating characteristic of all the minority protection agreements following World War I is that the rights granted to racial, linguistic, and religious minorities are "provisions of an international character." This provision, spelled out in Article 12/1 of the Polish Agreement, and carried into the Lausanne Treaty as Article 44/1, reads: "Turkey agrees that, in so far as the preceding Articles of this Section affect non-Muslim minorities of Turkey, these provisions constitute obligations of international concern and shall be placed under the guarantee of the League of Nations. They shall not be modified without the assent of the majority of the Council of the League of Nations."

Although the system of the League of Nations does not exist today, the treaty and the issue of rights is a matter of international political responsibility for Turkey, and a part of its national law (Law No. 340). Moreover, according to Article 90/5 of the 1982 Constitution, "International agreements duly put into effect carry the force of law. No appeal to the Constitutional Court can be made regarding these agreements, on the ground that they are unconstitutional." Therefore, the Lausanne Treaty has at least the same force as the Constitution.

Thus, according to the provisions of the Lausanne Treaty, *it is legally correct for Turkey to consider only non-Muslims as minorities.* This legal inference also corresponds to the general conviction in Turkey that only non-Muslims should be considered as minorities—a conviction that is determined by historical, political and ideological factors. Historically, the millet system, maintained by the Ottoman Empire since 1454, treated only non-Muslims as minorities because within this system, all Muslims, whatever their ethnicity or sect, were considered as one "Islam Nation" (Ümmet) and first-class members of the majority (*millet-i hakime*). Only non-Muslims formed separate millets of second-class citizens, and each millet was defined with respect to its religion and confession (e.g., Greek Orthodox, Armenian, Protestant, Catholic, Jewish). Politically, the protective attitude of the European countries over the Christian minorities in Turkey gained speed and strength in direct proportion to the weakening of the empire, and it was used as a pretext for interfering in the internal affairs of the empire. Consequently, the Muslim majority has always considered these minorities as "the other." Ideologically, the founders of the Republic were determined to avoid further disintegration of the country, and thus they did not grant international minority rights to the Muslim flank of the population, which formed the bulk of the mosaic inherited from the Ottoman Empire. This impulse became stronger especially after the Kurdish insurgence of 1925, which erupted only sixteen months after the proclamation of the Republic.

Denial or Violation of Rights Recognized by the Lausanne Treaty

Although Turkey may be following the proper definition of minority, as stated by the Lausanne Treaty, it has been failing to implement the Treaty's provisions fully. Turkey has not only been violating the rights granted to its non-Muslim population, but it has been also denying some rights granted by the Lausanne Treaty to various non-Muslims groups, under Section 3.

THE RIGHTS GRANTED TO NON-MUSLIM CITIZENS HAVE NOT BEEN FULLY IMPLEMENTED

The violation of the non-Muslim population's rights takes two forms: (1) Not all of the non-Muslims are allowed to enjoy the rights granted to minority groups. These applied only to the three largest minority groups: Greeks (Rum), Armenians, and Jews. Although the treaty consistently employs the term "non-Muslim," nowhere in its 143 articles are these three groups singled out. Yet, smaller Christian groups, such as Syriacs, Caldeans, Assyrians, and Nestorians, have been left out of the treaty's protection, deprived of the right to "establish, manage and control . . . any . . . schools with the right to use their own language . . . freely therein" (Article 40), and of the right to establish foundations, and so forth. The reason for excluding these groups from the protected minority is not clear. One possible explanation may be the lack of a kin-state that would serve as an advocate of these groups. (2) Some rights spelled out in the treaty are denied even to the three major non-Muslim minority groups. The financial assistance enumerated in Article 41/2 was not actualized not until after the 1950s; the special commissions established in Article 42/2 were not implemented. The rights related to religious foundations that are clearly expressed in Article 42/3 were not put into use from the 1970s through 2002.

The notorious "1936 declaration," related to non-Muslim foundations (referred to as "Community Foundations" in Turkish law), is a striking example of discrimination against non-Muslims. In 1936, the Law on Foundations (*vakıf*) ordered all the foundations to submit a property declaration listing immovables and other properties possessed by the foundation. The underlying reason for this law was to dry out the financial resources of the "Islamic" foundations, which were seen as threats to the new secular regime. After Mustafa Kemal Atatürk's death in 1938, those property lists were forgotten, but the escalation of the Cyprus conflict to a military confrontation between Turkey and Greece in the 1970s changed the situation. The General Directorate of Foundations required non-Muslim foundations to resubmit their regulations, called "Vakıfname." However, none of them had a Vakıfname because these foundations had been established under the Ottoman rule by individual decrees of the sultan of the day. The General Directorate of Foundations responded to this problem by ruling that the declarations of 1936 would be considered their Vakıfname. In case these declarations did not carry a special provision entitling the foundation to acquire immovable property, the General Directorate would expropriate all of the immovable property acquired after 1936.

The non-Muslim foundations challenged the ruling, arguing that the declarations submitted in 1936 were merely a list of immovable properties possessed by each foundation at that date, but they argued to no avail. No matter how these properties were acquired (purchases, donation, lottery, inheritance, etc.) expropriations went ahead, despite the fact that they were in violation of the Lausanne Treaty. The expropriated properties were returned to their previous owners or to their beneficiaries at no cost, and if there were no inheritors, they were acquired by the treasury at no cost.

When the case was brought to the Supreme Court of Appeals (Yargıtay), the Second Legislative Branch of the court upheld the policy in its unanimous ruling of 6 July 1971, which included the following statement in its justification: "It is evident that the acquisition of immovable property by non-Turkish legal persons is forbidden" However, the legal person that the court referred to and banned from acquiring property, the Balıklı Greek Orthodox Hospital Endowment (Balıklı Rum Hastanesi Vakfı), was not a "foreign" endowment. When the issue was brought before the General Board of Legislation of the court on 8 May 1974, the same ruling and justification were maintained. The following year, the court's First Legal Department reached a similar verdict:

Except under the conditions specified by either Law No. 1328 or in Article 44 of the Law No. 2762, foreign nationals are forbidden from acquiring real estate in Turkey. Because these decrees concern the public order, there is nothing against the law for the plaintiff institution to challenge the unlawful behavior of the defendant institution, or in taking legal action for the annulment of the unlawful disposal. Therefore, based on the reasons explained above and on the other reasoning indicated in the court verdict, it is unanimously decided that the improper appeals be rejected and the court decision be approved.[2]

The attorneys of the Balıklı Greek Orthodox Hospital Endowment appealed for the reevaluation of the verdict. This time the same branch supposedly admitted the mistake in considering some Turkish citizens as foreigners because they were non-Muslim, but insisted on its discriminatory position in the new ruling of 11 December 1975: ". . . the reference to 'the laws that forbid foreigners to own real estate' in the decision of approval is due to an error. . . . [The court decides] to delete that phrase by amendment [and] otherwise . . . denies the request for correction of judgment."[3]

THE RIGHTS GRANTED TO GROUPS OTHER THAN NON-MUSLIMS ARE NOT HONORED

It is true that according to the Lausanne Treaty, the definition of minority covers only non-Muslims, but Section III of the text also provides rights to some other people. They can be categorized into four groups (Oran 2001):

A. *Non-Muslim citizens of the Republic of Turkey.* Members of this group should enjoy full freedom of movement and of migration (Article 38/3), as well as the same civil and political rights enjoyed by Muslims (Article 39/1). They have equal rights to establish, manage, and control, at their own expense, any charitable, religious, and social institutions, and any schools and other establishments of training instruction and education, with the right to use their own language and to practice their own religion freely (Article 40). In towns and districts where there is a considerable proportion of Turkish nationals belonging to non-Muslim minorities these minorities are assured an equitable share in the enjoyment and application of the sums that may be provided out of public funds under the national, municipal, or other governmental budgets for education in their mother tongue (Article 41/1 and 2). The state should respect non-Muslim minorities' traditions and customs in regard to their family or personal status (Article 42/1). These minorities cannot be compelled to perform any act that would constitute a violation of their faith or religious observances, and they cannot be forced to perform official business on their weekly day of rest (Article 43). It goes without saying that the rights extended to other three groups would also apply to this group.

B. *Citizens who speak languages other than Turkish.* Members of this group would be given adequate facilities for the oral use of their own language before the courts (Article 39/5). The rights of this group would also include the rights recognized for groups in categories C and D.

C. All citizens. Article 39/3 of the Lausanne Treaty clearly stipulates that "differences of religion, creed or confession shall not cause any discrimination, and Article 39/4 articulates the right to use any language in matters relating to citizens' private or commercial relations. The rights of this group also include the rights of Group D.

D. All inhabitants. All inhabitants would enjoy "full and complete protection of life and liberty without distinction of birth, nationality, language, race and religion" (Article 38/1), and would be entitled to free exercise of religion or belief (Article 38/2), and without distinction of religion, they would be equal before the law (Article 39/2).

To each of these four groups of people, the Lausanne Treaty grants different rights that cannot be annihilated (Article 37). However, the non-Muslims are privileged in two ways. First, they have more numerous rights compared to the other groups. Second, as indicated in Article 44/1, their rights and privileges are placed under international guarantee. Nevertheless, by articulating the rights for "all Turkish citizens," and even for "everyone living in Turkey," Section III makes the Lausanne Treaty a document of human rights (twenty-one years before this term made its formal entrance to international law), not simply one of minority rights.

However, the comprehensive nature of the document has been neglected and even actively rejected by many. Those who treat the Lausanne Treaty as limited to addressing the rights of non-Muslim minorities tend to advance two arguments: (1) since the heading of Section III is "Protection of Minorities," there can only be minority rights under it; (2) rights were granted only to non-Muslim minorities.

1. *There can only be minority rights under Section III.* However, a careful study of the historical context of the document would reveal the otherwise. First, although the PAAP primarily started out to solve the minority problems in Central and Eastern Europe—problems that were one of the two catalysts for World War I—they also granted rights to everybody living in those countries. They were compelled to do so to protect their own citizens who were engaged in trade in these countries. In fact during the Lausanne Conference, Sir Horace Rumbold, a British man who was head of the Subcommission of Minorities, eventually consented to the Turkish delegation's demand on limiting minority rights to non-Muslims, on the condition of using a broader reference for some other categories. Minute number 9 of the session held on 23 December 1923 reads: "Sir Horace Rumbold stated that if the Turkish Delegation agrees that the term 'all inhabitants of Turkey' is used instead of the term 'minorities' in the paragraph 1 of the new Article 2 [the article was later finalized as Article 38/1 and 2], he would agree with the usage of the term 'non-Muslim minorities'" (*Lozan Barış Konferansı* 1970, 206).

Second, and more important, even though the term "human rights" was introduced as early as 1789, its use was limited to the national context only. This term first appeared in the international field after World War II, with Article 1/3 of the United Nations Treaty. Since the term "human rights" was not in circulation before then, regardless of the drafters' intentions, it could not be possibly used in the heading of Section III of the treaty in question.

Third, the term "minority" is not a specific term but a generic one. According to the 1969 Vienna Convention on the Law of Treaties, nongeneric terms used in a treaty should be taken with their regular meanings at the time of the signing of the treaty. But the meaning of generic terms has to be determined in line with the subsequent developments in international law over the years. As a matter of fact, while interpreting the statement "disputes regarding the territorial status of Greece," the International Court of Justice, in its decision of 1978 on the case Greece versus Turkey concerning the Aegean Continental Shelf, stated that this term should be interpreted according to its meaning in 1978 rather than (as the Greek part argued) its meaning in 1928 or 1931 (par. 77–80).[4]

2. *Rights were granted only to non-Muslim minorities.* This position can have some support in the report presented by Jules Cesar Montagna, chairman of the Minorities Subcommission, to Lord Curzon, chairman of the First Commission, on 7 January 1923, and by Lord Curzon's response, as recorded in minute number 19 of the session on 9 January 1923: "The Sub-Commission considered that, based on an article of general context (see Article 2 of Draft Bill), the application of these provisions could be limited to non-Muslim minorities. The Sub-Commission considered it impossible to insist that the Muslim minorities be included in the said protection" (*Lozan Barış Konferansı* 1970, 309–10). This "Draft Bill, Article 2," was later to be finalized as Article 38 of the Lausanne Treaty.

However, when these references are placed in a larger context, the view that the rights were granted to non-Muslims only cannot hold for two reasons. First, according to the general principles of law and also to Article 32 of the Vienna Convention on the Law of Treaties, preparatory studies and minutes are taken into consideration only if the text of a treaty is not clear. Articles 37 and 39 of the Lausanne Treaty, on the other hand, are unambiguously clear. Second, what Montagna and Curzon meant was minority rights "under international guarantee," because that was the only meaning attributed to the term "minority rights." The issue here is not whose rights are mentioned but whose rights are guaranteed by the League of Nations. The international guarantee, granted in Article 44/1 of Section III, covers only non-Muslims; such a guarantee is not applicable to the rights granted to people belonging to the other three groups noted above.

THE SCOPE AND INTERPRETATION OF ARTICLE 39

The language provisions of Article 39 are particularly relevant today to the rights of Kurdish citizens of Turkey, and deserve a special attention. The full text of Paragraph 5 of the article reads: "Notwithstanding the existence of the official language, adequate facilities shall be given to Turkish nationals of non-Turkish speech for the oral use of their own language before the Courts." "Turkish nationals of non-Turkish speech" does not mean those who cannot speak, nor can it mean those who know languages other than Turkish. What is meant is "those whose best language (mother tongue) is other than Turkish." This provision allows an exception to the rule of exclusive use of Turkish as the official language at state offices, and it is undoubtedly based on a concern over the proper defense of one's rights in court.

The full text of Article 39/4 is as follows: "No restrictions shall be imposed on the free use by any Turkish national of any language in private intercourse, in commerce, religion, in the press, or in publications of any kind or at public meetings." We can highlight three points in interpreting this clause. First, it grants all Turkish citizens the right to use any language of their choice in all private and public spaces, except in conducting official business and in state offices. Second, since in the early 1920s radio broadcasting was available only in the United States and television did not exist, the expression "in the press, or in publications of any kind" should now be read to include radio and television broadcasting as well. Finally, although this clause concerns all Turkish citizens, it mainly benefits Turkish citizens whose mother tongue is not Turkish.

However, it is frequently argued that the purpose of the signatories was not granting the language rights to Kurds or other Muslims who speak a different mother tongue. They should be reminded that Muslims had been using different languages, both in public and private affairs, prior to the establishment of the Republic (e.g., it was a regular practice to submit a written petition in Arabic in Baghdad). Inheriting a linguistically diverse population and needing to accommodate them, the Turkish delegation at the Lausanne Conference did not object to these clauses of language rights, even though the official language of the new state would be Turkish. In fact, these provisions did not stir any debates during the drafting stage. The text of Articles 39/4 and 39/5 were directly copied from the Poland Minorities Treaty (Articles 7/3 and 7/4) by the Turkish delegate, which incorporated them as Articles 3/4 and 3/5 into its draft proposal presented on 18 December 1922.[5] In other words, Article 39 was in fact proposed by the Turkish delegation as well.

Yet, it should be noted that apart from these two clauses of Article 39, the Kurds (and other Muslim Turkish citizens whose mother tongue is not

Turkish) do not have any positive rights, and the rights recognized by the treaty do not fall under international guarantee. However, as mentioned before, all these rights are protected under the Turkish national jurisdiction.

We can summarize the human rights implications of the Lausanne Treaty for today as follows:

1) The definition of a minority and the rights brought by the Lausanne Treaty should not be contracted. It defines as minority the non-Muslims only but it articulates certain rights for some other groups as well, albeit without providing international guarantee. Therefore,

2) The argument that Article 39 recognizes certain rights of Muslim groups, such as the Kurds, is correct. Protected by Article 37, this article clearly rules out the notion that no language other than Turkish can be used for radio and TV broadcasting in Turkey.

3) The above-mentioned interpretation would not contradict the official position on minorities issue, because the rights and liberties articulated in Article 39/4 concern not the minorities but "all Turkish citizens." In fact, the rights recognized in Article 39/5 have been implemented since the beginning of the Republic, albeit with some interruptions in exceptional periods such as the aftermath of the military coup that took place on 12 September 1980.

Whether the Kurds constitute a minority is a complex issue, because in addition to the official rhetoric and practice that refuse to recognize Kurds as a minority, the Kurds themselves, especially the nationalist ones, object to being treated as such. The official line is well known: "The Lausanne Treaty only recognizes the non-Muslims as minorities." The nationalist Kurds' objection to the minority reference stem from different concerns: (1) Minority classification would be a degradation, because in Turkey the concept of minority has been conditioned by the Ottoman millet system, which considered the Muslims as the "sovereign nation" and the minorities (non-Muslims) as second-class citizens. (2) Kurds are one of the two founding peoples of the Republic of Turkey; the War of Independence was fought together with Turks, but later the Kurdish input was dismissed. And most importantly, (3) Kurdish nationalists consider themselves to be a "people," rather than a minority—this approach, in international legal theory, would place them in a category much closer to external "self-determination" (independence).

The Minority Issue in Legislation and the Courts

The Turkish state officials' defensive position and reluctance to recognize the diversity of the populations in Turkey find their expression in their understanding of two constitutional principles: Article 3/1 states, "The Turkish State, with its territory and nation, is an indivisible entity. Its language is Turkish." And Article 4 adds that this paragraph "shall not be amended, nor shall its amendment be proposed."

THE PRINCIPLE OF THE "INDIVISIBLE UNITY OF THE NATION"

"Territorial integrity" of a state is a principle advocated by all and protected in international law. Thus, all international instruments on minority rights take two standard measures to prevent division: (1) they use the term "the rights of individuals belonging to minority groups" to emphasize that the rights are not given to groups (collectivity) but to individuals; and (2) they include a clause such as: "These rights shall only be exercised with the condition that the territorial integrity of the country is respected" (Çavuşoğlu 2002, 127–28)

However, the Turkish Constitution also refers to the "integrity of the nation," which is contrary to the very essence of democracy. As aptly put by Oktay Uygun, "the concept of the indivisibility of the nation is unfamiliar to the Europeans" (quoted in Kaboğlu 2002b, 380), because claiming that a nation cannot be divided would assume that it is monolithic in nature, suggesting policies of assimilation, which would be inevitably shaped by the values of the dominant ethnic and religious groups and take oppressive forms. In Turkey, a monolithic concept of nation was employed in the early days of the Republic, and that authoritarian and oppressive attitude was rectified by subsequent military interventions, especially by the military coup of 12 September 1980. The approach not only denies the existence of minorities or minority rights, other than *what were deemed to be articulated in the Lausanne Treaty*, but also punishes those who make contrary claims and suggestions. This punitive approach has had numerous expressions in Turkish legislation and court decisions:

The Antiterrorism Law of 1991 (Law No. 3173) describes terrorism as "any kind of act carried out by one or more persons belonging to an organization with the aim of changing the characteristics of the Republic . . . , damaging the indivisible unity of the State with its territory and nation" (Article 1). Before it was abolished in June 2003, Article 8/1 of the same law was amended on 6 February 2002, to read: "Written, oral or visual propaganda and assemblies, meetings and demonstrations aimed at damaging the indivisible unity of the Turkish Republic with its territory and nation will be punished. . . . If this act is committed in a form that encourages the use of terrorist methods, the sentence will be increased by a third and in case of repeated commitment of this act, the penalty of imprisonment will not be converted to monetary penalty."

"The indivisible unity of the state with its territory and nation" is mentioned also in other laws:[6] Article 8 and Annexed Article 7 of the 1934 Law on the Duties and Authority of the Police (no. 2559); Article 5/A of the Law on Turkish Radio and Television (no. 2954); Article 4 of the Law on the Establishment and Broadcasting of Radio Stations and Television Channels (no. 3984); Articles 44 and 55 of the Law on Associations (no. 2908); and Articles 78 and 101 of the Law on Political Parties (no. 2820).

These restrictive legislative expressions are based on the assumption that all claims about the existence of minority groups based on ethnic and linguistic differences would threaten national unity and territorial integrity. Consequently, those who make such claims can be punished for "separatism" or "destructiveness." Until its amendment on 2 January 2003, Article 5 of the Law on Associations imposed the following restrictions: "It is forbidden to found an association with the aim of claiming that there are minority groups in the Republic of Turkey based on racial, religious, sectarian, cultural or linguistic differences or of creating a minority group by protecting, developing or spreading any language and culture other than Turkish." The 2003 amendment mitigated the language: "No association can be founded with the aim of creating differences of race, religion, sect or region or creating minorities based on these differences and with the aim of changing the unitary state structure of the Republic of Turkey . . . in violation of . . . the national security and the public order."

Article 81 of the Law on Political Parties included more restrictive clauses: "Political parties shall not a) claim that there are minority groups in the Republic of Turkey based on the differences of . . . ; b) aim at and work for damaging the unity of the nation by creating minority groups in the Republic of Turkey by protecting, developing and spreading languages and cultures other than Turkish."

The restrictions in the Law on Political Parties were derived from Articles 68 and 69 of the Constitution. Article 68 states that "the statutes and programs, as well as the activities of political parties shall not be in conflict with the independence of the State, its indivisible integrity with its territory and nation." And Article 69 affirms that a political party will be dissolved "if the Constitutional Court determines that the party in question has become a center for the execution of such activities." Consequently, the Constitutional Court has frequently banned political parties for violating the principle of "the indivisible unity of the State with its territory and nation" and for violating the prohibition against "creating minority groups."

The Principle That "the Language of Turkey Is Turkish"

All states declare one or more official languages and conduct their business and provide education in those languages. In Turkey, the 1982

Constitution and other laws not only define an "official language" by defining Turkish as "the language of the State," but they also restrict the use of other languages within the private domain. Law No. 2932, enacted in 1983 by the military rule (repealed in 1991), prohibits "the declaration, circulation and publication of ideas in a language which is not the first official language of a State recognized by Turkey" (Article 2). This article targets Kurdish (which was the second official language of Iraq at the time), practically banning its use in all public spaces, without using the word "Kurdish." Article 3 of the law asserts that the "Mother tongue of the Turkish citizens is Turkish language." This law and others that restrict the use of languages and non-Turkish cultural expressions (e.g., the Law on Census (no. 1587) prohibits parents to give their children names "that are not appropriate to our national culture") have been found all in violation of the Lausanne Treaty. Several constitutional and legal amendments, undertaken since 1991, relaxed these restrictions but are still short of allowing full freedom (see Mary Lou O'Neil in this volume, Chapter 5).

THE CONSTITUTIONAL COURT'S INTERPRETATIONS

The Constitutional Court has the authority to close down political parties, and indeed has banned numerous political parties, frequently by invoking the principle of the "indivisible unity of the nation." This has happened especially in their dealings with left-wing parties, including the following instances:[7]

- The Court closed down the Turkish Workers' Party (Türkiye İşçi Partisi,TİP) in July 1971, by referring to Article 57 of the 1961 Constitution, which protected "The indivisible unity of the State with its territory and nation," as well as Article 81 of the Law on Political Parties.
- The verdict that closed down the Labor Party of Turkey (Türkiye Emekçi Partisi,TEP) in May 1980 finds the Party guilty of "attempting to create a sense of minority in the minds of a certain group of citizens [that] is contrary to the concept of the unity of the State with its territory and nation." Referring to Article 83 of the Constitution, it notes: "In addition to official correspondence, education and national culture should be based on Turkish. In other words, the only national culture in the country is Turkish culture." It also specifies that the Constitution does not allow behavior that would lead to the disintegration of the nation based on elements such as [differences of] religion, language or race in a manner contrary to the principles of Turkish nationalism. On July 1991, the Court closed down

the Turkish United Communist Party (Türkiye Birleşik Komünist Partisi, TBKP) with a similar verdict.

- The Socialist Party (Sosyalist Parti, SP) was closed down in July 1992 by invoking the constitutional clauses and the Law on Political Parties (no. 2820), by noting, "People of every origin live in every part of the country. From a scientific point of view, there are no sufficient [ethnic] characteristics or elements to be considered as minorities."
- The Freedom and Democracy Party (Özgürlük ve Demokrasi Partisi, ÖZDEP) was banned in November 1993, on the grounds that it "intends to divide the unity of the Turkish nation . . . into two as Turks and Kurds. . . . [The] clauses in the program aim at destroying the unity of the country and the nation."
- The Socialist Turkey Party (Sosyalist Türkiye Partisi, STP) was banned on November 1993 on the grounds that various sections of its program violated Articles 78/a and 78/b of the Law on Political Parties, which articulated restrictions on divisive activities aimed at the indivisible unity of the State with its territory and nation.
- When the Democracy Party (Demokrasi Partisi, DEP) was closed down in June 1994, the court verdict specified that "granting minority status based on racial and linguistic differences is not compatible with the integrity of the territory and nation." It also noted that "there is one State, one whole territory, a single nation," and the Lausanne Treaty recognizes only non-Muslims as minorities.
- In February 1997, when the Labor Party (Emek Partisi, EP) was banned, the court verdict noted that "by claiming the existence on Turkish territory of minorities of national or religious culture or of confession, race, or language, the goal of violating the national unity is being pursued by creating minorities through means of protecting, developing, and spreading languages and cultures other than Turkish language and culture."

In most of these cases, the following lines are repeated verbatim to describe the offense: "To create, among citizens who are in such an unprivileged position, the feeling and thought of belonging to a minority, and to demand that they be subjected to a policy of restricted rights, and to expect them to become a minority when they are the very nation itself, can only be interpreted as a violation of the unity of the nation" (Çetin 2002, 80).

The court's verdicts on two cases are particularly illuminating. First, in the TEP case the ruling does make a distinction between "acknowledging differences" and "creating minorities":

to mention in an objective way that the language or religion of a certain group of citizens within a nation is different from that of other groups does not entail, in and of itself, the claim that "there exists a minority." In addition to this, it must be claimed that the community in question must be granted a special legal security for it to maintain its existence and characteristics that distinguish it from other groups, that is to say there must be an open or covert claim that these people have a right to take advantage of the "minority legislation." This . . . is the situation defined and forbidden as "claiming the existence of minorities." (Çavuşoğlu 2002, 135–36)

Thus, the court appears to accept the existence of different identities as harmless, as long as the claims do not go too far to suggest that these identities have a right to benefit from the minority law. However, the court verdict takes a different turn in the subsequent paragraphs: "[But] in view of the fact that the term 'creating minorities' is closely related to 'the claim that minorities exist,' the former must be interpreted in the same direction as the latter. The conclusion to be reached with such interpretation is that the term 'creating a minority' can only mean 'the creation of the idea, within the community of citizens, that it is necessary for them to benefit from the law of minorities'" (Çavuşoğlu 2002, 136).

The verdict on case of the DEP is more explicit on a monolithic idea of nation and fear of disintegration. It notes that Article 66 of the Constitution, which specifies that "anyone who is attached to the Turkish state by way of citizenship is Turkish," would not mean "the denial of the ethnic roots of the citizens." Thus, "the purpose of legal regulations" on this matter is not "the prohibition of diversity and of their languages and cultures," or "what is banned is not the expression of cultural differences and cultural wealth; it is the employment of these with the aim of destroying the unity of the nation and in connection with this, the construction of a new state order based on divisions by means of creating minorities on the land of the Turkish Republic." It concludes that "the demands for the recognition of cultural identities—which initially seem acceptable demands [but] which aim at separatism—will in time incline toward a break from the whole" (Çavuşoğlu 2002, 127, 141, nn. 23–25).

Fearing that the recognition of diverse identities will lead to the disintegration of the state, the Turkish Constitutional Court considers minority rights not as universal human rights but as a subject of national legislation and within a limited understanding of the Lausanne Treaty. In other words, it finds the universal human rights incompatible with "the indivisible unity of the country and the unitary state."

Changes in International Notions of Minority and Turkey's Resistance

Since the 1920s, especially after the establishment of the UN in 1945, both the concept of "minority" and international protection of rights evolved.

Space here does not allow a review of these changes, but it is important to note that especially in the 1990s, the concern over minorities moved from "prevention of discrimination" to "protection of minorities." This change expands the obligations of the state. In addition to avoiding discriminatory conduct, which may be defined as a passive/negative duty, the state is assigned an active duty and required to take positive action toward protecting minority rights and creating the conditions for such protection. In various documents, both the Organization of Security and Cooperation of Europe (e.g., 1990 Paris Charter) and the UN (e.g., the 1992 UN Declaration on the Rights of Persons Belonging to National or Ethnic, Religious, and Linguistic Minorities) make it clear that the question of whether any minorities exist in a particular country is not left to the judgment of that country. International human rights organizations and other NGOs reinforce this new understanding and pressure the states to undertake proper protective measures. As evident in the practice of the Council of Europe's European Commission against Racism and Intolerance (ECRI), the violation of minority rights is increasingly considered to be on a par with racism.

In terms of treaty ratification, Turkey has been active in several human rights systems. In practice, however, it has been reluctant to change. The resistance stems from two interrelated factors that affect the collective political psyche of the country, the intertwined relationship between the supra-identity and sub-identity, and the "Sèvres syndrome."

The Relationship Between Supra-Identity and Sub-Identity in the Republic of Turkey

The Ottoman Empire included many sub-identities: Turkish, Kurdish, Georgian, Abkhazian, Armenian, Albanian, Greek, Jewish, and so on. All were recognized by the state, but none of them coincided with the "Ottoman" supra-identity. The same sub-identities continued to exist in the Republic of Turkey, but the supra-identity was changed to being "Turkish." Since this identity coincided with the "Turkish" sub-identity, it created an imbalance in favor of Turks.

The term "Turk" can mean different things. In forging a national identity, the republican regime originally subscribed to a definition of "Turk" based on culture, not race. Even in the 1930s, when the nationalist ideology of the state was pursued in its most rigid form, the main criterion for incoming refugees was "to be attached to the Turkish culture," not being an ethnic Turk. Mustafa Kemal underscored his preference for the "subjective" identity (the one chosen by the individual) against the "objective" identity (the one assigned at the birth) in a dictum pronounced in his famous "Tenth Year Speech" by saying, "How happy is the one who calls himself a Turk" (instead of "How happy is the one who is born/who is a Turk"). Earlier, during the War of Independence, he preferred employing the territorial reference, "Türkiye," to the ethnic reference, "Türk." For example, he favored using "Türkiye Halkı" (People of Turkey), instead of "Türk Halkı (Turkish People).[8] In fact, Mustafa Kemal was arguably the first person to ever us the term "Türkiyeli" (one from Turkey). Moreover, he had the term incorporated into four separate articles of the bill proposed to amend the first (1921) Constitution of Turkey (*Türkiye Cumhuriyeti İlk Anayasa Taslağı* 1998).

However, influenced both by the European racist theories that swept the world in the 1920s and 1930s, and threatened by the Kurdish uprisings of the very same period, the regime employed a racial definition of "Turk," from time to time. The desire to eliminate the sense of inferiority created by the term "Sick Man of Europe" also stimulated efforts to forge a strong Turkish identity. These culminated in some extreme policies in the 1930s. Skull measurements were taken to prove that the Turks belonged to the highest echelon of humankind. The 1934 Law on Settlements (no. 2510) used the term "Turkish race." Until the 1950s, an admission requirement for the military schools was "belonging to the genuine Turkish race" (*öz Türk ırkından olmak*), which was later replaced with "being a Turkish citizen."

Moreover, the "Turkish" supra-identity involves religion as much as ethnicity. As a residue of the Ottoman's millet system, only those who are Muslims, better yet Sunni Muslims, are considered to be "Turk." Non-Muslims are referred to by their ethno-religious identity as Greek, Armenian, or Jewish, and so on. This attitude has been codified into the state's policies. Until the 1940s, non-Muslim citizens were registered in the "Ecanip Defterleri" (Foreigner Registry). A government decree called Protection from Sabotages, published on 28 December 1988, listed non-Muslims as "domestic foreigners (Turkish citizens) and those from other races in the country" as the most likely population that would yield saboteurs. At time of this writing, Article 24/1 of the Law on Private Institutions of Education (no. 625), which stipulates that a Turkish assistant director "of Turkish origin and a Turkish citizen" is to be assigned to "schools opened by foreigners," is applied also to the minority schools (Çetin 2002, 70, 75, 78). In February 2003, a lawsuit to annul the land registry of a non-Muslim minority school building was filed on behalf of the treasury against the Surp Haç Armenian Lycée Foundation: "By a decision taken by the Subcommittee for Minorities of the Interior Ministry that monitors the activities of minorities in regard to national security, the foundation under the name Surp Haç is not legitimate, . . . for this reason the annulment of the title deed of the foundation's immovable property and its registry on behalf of the Treasury is thereby requested."[9]

These examples show that the Republic of Turkey continues to view its non-Muslim citizens as foreign nationals and to suspect their loyalty. Moreover, the supra-identity of "Türklük" (Turkishness), used instead of "Türkiyelilik" (being from Turkey), alienates both the non-Muslims and Kurds, the second largest group after the Turks.

While some citizens and advocates of human rights try to reform the culture and politics of Turkey, there is a significant number of people and institutions that resist any transformation of this supra-identity due to a fear of disintegration. Referred to as "chosen trauma" by professor of psychiatry Vamık Volkan (Volkan and Itzkowitz 1994, 7), this collective psychology in Turkey might be called "Sèvres syndrome."

HISTORICAL AND POLITICAL FOUNDATIONS: THE SÈVRES SYNDROME

The Ottoman Empire had to sign the Peace Treaty of Sèvres after its defeat in the First World War. The Sèvres Treaty partitioned the Ottoman land to create several new states, including a Kurdistan and a greater Armenia (see Mary Lou O'Neil's chapter in this volume). Although the Lausanne Treaty replaced the Sèvres Treaty with more favorable conditions for Turkey, the fear that the country would be subject to partitioning again as a result of the collaboration between its minorities and their foreign allies has prevailed. This fear has been intensified by the terrorist attacks and activities of the ASALA (the underground Armenian Army for the Liberation of Armenia) and the PKK (Partia Karkaren Kürdistan, or Kurdistan Workers' Party), which were intense from the 1970s through the 1990s and gave the impression that the Armenians and Kurds would complete a dismemberment left unfinished by the unapplied Sèvres Treaty. The burgeoning Iraqi Kurdish organizations in the "safe haven" created in northern Iraq after the 1991 Gulf War added to the threat. Most important, the fact that the ASALA and PKK were received with sympathy in Western countries led to the perception that Turkey's allies were participating in this dismemberment. The syndrome turned into paranoia.

The ASALA terror ended in the mid-1980s. The ensuing Armenian Genocide resolutions have receded in the last few years. The PKK terror stopped after the capture of the PKK leader Abdullah Öcalan in 1999. But the Sèvres paranoia has been inflamed at every minor incident, leading to numerous urban legends, some of which were hyped up by the sensationalist press (e.g., the Fener Greek Orthodox Patriarchate is buying up property in İstanbul "in order to create a second Vatican"). For some people, the fragile situation faced by the founding fathers in the early days of the Republic still prevails, and the country should take measures to maintain its territorial and national integrity. Others, however, are eager to make Turkey a "European country," fulfilling the Kemalist quest of reaching the "contemporary civilization" (*muasır medeniyet*) by joining the European Union.

The EU and Reform Packages

With the advent of accession to the EU, however, reforming human and minority rights practices became a focus of the legislative agenda. Since the end of 2001, the parliament adopted eleven "EU Harmonization Packages," which included new laws or amendments. We can highlight the progress toward the recognition and protection of minority rights within these legislative reforms.

The Second Harmonization Package (26 March 2002). Ban on publishing in a language prohibited by law was repealed from the Press Law.

The Third Harmonization Package (3 August 2002). The Law on Learning and Teaching of Foreign Languages was changed to lift restrictions on the right to learn "languages and dialects traditionally used by Turkish citizens." The Law on the Establishment and Broadcasts of Radio and Television Channels (LEBRTC) was amended to allow broadcasting in different languages and dialects traditionally used by Turkish citizens. Article 159 of the Turkish Penal Code (TPC) was modified to make freedom of expression in line with the norms of the European Convention on Human Rights. The Law on Foundations was amended to enable non-Muslim foundations to acquire immovable property with the authorization of the Council of Ministers. The Code of Criminal Procedure (CCP) was amended to allow for retrials both in civil and penal law cases after the decision of the European Court of Human Rights (ECHR).

The Fourth Harmonization Package ("Copenhagen Package," 2 January 2003). The Law on Foundations was amended again to replace the Council of Ministers' authorization with that of the General Directorate of Foundations, but the unequal treatment of the Muslim and non-Muslim foundations was not totally eliminated; the law (no. 4771/4) requires the General Directorate of Foundations to "solicit the recommendations of the related Ministries and Public Agencies" prior to approving non-Muslim foundations' request to buy or dispose real estate—a procedure not required for the applications of other foundations. Since the state agencies alluded to here are the Ministry of Foreign Affairs and the security and intelligence agencies, it can be deduced that the reformed law still treats the non-Muslim citizens as "foreign" and suspect. The discriminatory impact of this law has been already observed. According to a news report by the daily *Radikal*, dated 5 May 2003, out of 1,813 applications made by non-Muslim foundations for registration of real estate, 574 were refused, 579 were found "incomplete," and 226 applications were returned as "invalid."

The Fifth Harmonization Package (23 January 2003). The CCP and the Code of Legal Procedure have been amended to allow for retrials for cases finalized at the time the package entered into force, as well as for the applications submitted afterward.

The Sixth Harmonization Package (19 June 2003). With an amendment to the Antiterrorism Law, the use of force or violence is incorporated into the definition of the crime of terror. Moreover, Article 8 of the same law was repealed to expand freedom of thought and expression. According to the amendments to the LEBRTC, both private and public radio and TV stations can broadcast in languages and dialects used traditionally by Turkish citizens in their daily lives. The application submission period allowed for non-Muslim foundations to acquire real estate is prolonged. Several articles of the Law on Construction are rephrased to address the need for places of worship for people of different religions and faiths. The amendment made to the Law on Census removed the restrictions imposed on parents in choosing names for their children. Finally, new provisions that make retrials for the administrative law cases were adopted in the light of the ECHR rulings.

The Seventh Harmonization Package (30 June 2003). With an amendment to Article 159 of the TPC, the minimum penalty for those who "openly insult and deride Turkishness, etc." is reduced and the freedom of expression is supported by decriminalizing thoughts that involve criticisms with no intention of insult. The scope of Article 169 of TPC, concerning the crime of assisting and abetting a terrorist organization, is limited further. A new article, added to the CCP, requires that the cases related to torture and maltreatment be handled without delay. The language restrictions are relaxed further (see O'Neill in this volume).

The Second Constitutional Amendment Package (May 2004). The most important change for minority rights was the paragraph added to Article 90/5 of the Constitution: "Should the international treaties on the fundamental rights and freedoms that are duly put into effect and national laws contain contradictory stipulations on the same subject, the provisions of international law would prevail."

In October 2004, a new Penal Code was adopted. People had expected the new law to shift the focus and replace the concerns over "state security" with an emphasis on the protection of individual rights and freedoms. The expectations were very high, but so has been the disillusionment. Soon after it entered into force in June 2005, lawsuits challenging the freedom of expression of intellectuals, journalists, writers started to pour in. They have tended to invoke Articles 216 and 301, which respectively correspond to Articles 312 and 159 in the old Penal Code, as well as a new article that allows one to charge anyone who comments on a court case with the offense of "tying to influence the judiciary" (Article 288). Moreover, some "nationalists" started to take upon themselves to alert the prosecutor about speeches and newspapers that "denigrated Turkishness," and called for the prosecution of the perpetrators. Prosecutors have been acting on these "call for prosecution" (*suç duyurusu*), as if they were obliged to do so. When the same nationalists approach the courts, claiming that "Turkishness is denigrated. We are Turks. Therefore, we want to be accepted as *partie civile*,"[10] judges comply, again as if they were obliged to do so.

The rise of ethnic Turkish nationalism has been buttressed by two factors: (1) the backlash to the process of integration and globalization, which is perceived by the ordinary citizen as a top-down modernization imposed by foreigners (e.g., the EU harmonization packages); and (2) the militant Kurdish nationalism and PKK terrorism. These can be summed up under the heading "Sèvres paranoia."

Conclusion

In the 1920s, the Kemalist "revolution from above" had transformed a feudalistic Ottoman Empire into a monistic nation-state. It was a unique development, resulting from the westernized national elites introducing Western culture without involving any direct imperialistic Western intervention. Turkey is now experiencing another "revolution from above" that tries to modify the assimilationist "nation-state" into a pluralistic structure. I think this, too, is a unique transformation, closely linked to the previous experience.

The first modernization project was introduced by the Kemalists, and it created a religious reaction of resistance from below. The second one is now being led by the governing Justice and Development Party (AKP), which embodies the spiritual grandchildren of the 1920s reactionaries. Now, the reaction from below comes from the promoters of the Sèvres paranoia, who happen to be the grandchildren of the Kemalists of the 1920s. This ironic turn of events makes Turkey valuable as a social laboratory, not only for showing how external dynamics can create successful internal dynamics but also for pointing out that even progressive ideologies can impede change and development if not reinterpreted in the light of changing conditions.

As already stated, the legislative reforms required a great deal of effort that was largely fueled by the EU. Their implementation is likely to be stagnated, if not impeded, by the Sèvres paranoia. Moreover, the differences in the ways the terms of minority and minority rights are used by the EU and how they are understood by the majority of people in Turkey complicate the process. However, in this dynamic country, where the ECHR is slowly becoming a sort of supreme court above the Turkish Court of Appeals, and where the national court decisions violating the European Convention on Human Rights are subject to retrial, the reversal of the progress and a diversion from the reform path seem most unlikely.

Chapter 4

The Human Rights Condition of the Rum Orthodox

PRODROMOS YANNAS

In the Ottoman Empire the Greeks comprised the Rum millet. As a community, they were quite prosperous, residing in the major cities of İstanbul (Constantinople) and İzmir (Smyrna). With the succession of the Ottoman Empire by the Modern Turkish state the condition of the once thriving Rum Orthodox minority deteriorated drastically, and its numbers began to dwindle.[1] From close to 111,000 residents in 1923, the minority has been reduced to barely 2,000–3,000 members at present. The fact that the rights of the minority have been spelled out and safeguarded by an international treaty, the Treaty of Lausanne, makes the steady deterioration of the Rum Orthodox condition in Turkey harder to explain.

This chapter traces the condition of the Rum Orthodox population from 1923 to the present and discusses the international and domestic factors that have shaped the policies of the Turkish Republic toward this minority and to the center of Eastern Christianity, the Fener Patriarchate (the Ecumenical Patriarchate) in İstanbul. I argue that during the 1923–45 period the nation-building policies of the state undermined minority rights and discriminated against all non-Muslim minorities, including the Rum Orthodox.[2] In the post-World War II period, international factors became more important. In the case of the Rum Orthodox minority the pivotal role was played by the Cyprus conflict, especially at critical junctures of 1955, 1964, and 1974, in worsening the human rights conditions. I maintain that whenever diplomatic developments on the Cyprus front were perceived as not favorable to Turkish interests or as threatening to the Turkish Cypriot community, the Rum Orthodox community became a target for reprisals.

The Road to the Lausanne Treaty of 1923

The Turkish War of Independence (1919–22) ended with the defeat of the Greek forces by the Turkish army, led by Mustafa Kemal (Atatürk). On

30 January 1923, in conjunction to the peace treaty signed in Lausanne, Greece and Turkey agreed to a compulsory exchange of populations whereby approximately 1.2 million Greek Orthodox and 400,000 Muslims were forced to abandon their homes and relocate to Greece and Turkey respectively.[3] Two groups were exempted from the compulsory exchange: the Rum Orthodox community in İstanbul and in the islands of Gökçeada and Bozcaada, as well as the Muslim minority of Western Thrace.[4]

The Treaty of Lausanne concerned the rights of the "non-exchange-able" or "established" minorities in respective countries. In 1934, a League of Nations mixed commission for the exchange of populations estimated the number of the "established" Rum Orthodox residing in Turkey as 111,200. A breakdown of the total figure revealed that 73,000 were Rum Orthodox with Turkish nationality, 30,000 were residents of İstanbul with Greek nationality, 7,000 were inhabitants of the island of Gökçeada (Imbros) and 1,200 were in Bozcaada (Tenedos) (Alexandris 1983, 143; 1988, 39). The Treaty of Lausanne defines minorities in religious terms and articulates the rights of the non-Muslim minorities of Turkey in Articles 37–45 in Section III. Aside from the enjoyment of civil and political rights, which apply to all Turkish nationals, the Treaty of Lausanne grants non-Muslim minorities, among others, the freedom of religious practice and the rights to use and be taught in their own language, to establish and administer educational, religious, and charitable institutions (Articles 38–41). It obliges the Turkish government to respect the customs of religious minorities in family and personal matters and to protect churches and other religious establishments (Article 42). It deals with the rights of the Rum Orthodox as Turkish citizens but makes no explicit references to the status of the Ecumenical Patriarchate. However, it is noted that the Turkish delegation verbally acquiesced at the negotiations to the Greek demand that the Patriarchate remain in İstanbul on the condition that its authority would be solely confined to spiritual matters (Alexandris 1983, 103).

The Period 1923–45

The national modernization project encompassing the sweeping Kemalist reforms aimed at the secularization of Turkish society and the creation of a homogeneous society that bears no resemblance to the multinational Ottoman Empire. The new leaderships' concerns about developing a new national identity and the nationalist aspirations of the Rum Orthodox in previous years did not work in favor of the Republic's Rum Orthodox minority.

At the turn of the century, a period that can be characterized by the clash of nationalisms in the Balkans and the eastern Mediterranean, the

Greeks, motivated by the urge to fulfill their irredentist claims (Megali Idea) and backed by the Allied powers, landed troops in İzmir in 1919 and occupied parts of western Anatolia (M. Smith 1998). The occupation (liberation in the Greek frame of mind) increased the determination of the Turkish nationalist forces. As put by Bernard Lewis (1968, 241), "the thrust of a neighboring and former subject people into the heart of Turkish Anatolia was a danger—and a humiliation—beyond endurance." Turkish nationalist forces repelled the aggressor and entered İzmir on 9 September 1922. For the Turks, the military victory led to the establishment of the modern republic. For the Greeks, this defeat came to be known as the "Asia Minor Catastrophe," resulting in the expulsion of many merchants and Ottoman elites, which counted among the 1.2 million of Orthodox Christians who were forced to abandon their homes (Hirschon 2003; Courbage and Fargues 1998, 112).

The place of the economically dominant Greek Ottoman subjects was taken over by the creation of a nationally minded Turkish middle class that owed its existence and claim to prosperity to the policies of the Turkish state. Non-Muslim property owners and professionals were hit the hardest. Property confiscated or left behind that belonged to Rum Orthodox was given to Turkish business interests, and barriers to practice were erected for professionals who belonged to minority groups (Alexandris, 1983, 106–12; Keyder 1997, 40). Foreign and state companies and financial institutions were asked to adopt a Muslim employment policy only, and many Rum Orthodox businesses were urged to engage in partnership with their Turkish counterparts in order to continue with their operations (Alexandris 1983, 106–12). While considerable numbers of Rum Orthodox preferred to flee to Greece or elsewhere, many who wanted to remain in Turkey were unable to do so. Approximately 40,000 Rum Orthodox, who had fled Turkey at the time of the War of Independence, were considered "undesirables" by the Republic and not allowed to return to Turkey. The outstanding property issues, including compensation for property seizure of those who could not return to Turkey, were not settled until the Greek-Turkish Convention was signed in Ankara in June 1930, by Turkish foreign minister Tevfik Rüştü Aras and Greece's ambassador in Ankara, Spyridon Polychroniades (Alexandris 1988, 72). A few months later, on the occasion of the signing of a series of bilateral Greek-Turkish agreements in October 1930 in Ankara, the two governments redefined "established" to mean all Rum Orthodox who were present in İstanbul by the time of the signing of the Convention (Alexandris 1983, 178). As a result, 73,000 Rum Orthodox acquired Turkish citizenship and received "non-exchangeable" certificates (*nüfuz*). Similar certificates were issued to the 8,200 "established" of Gökçeada and Bozcaada, whereas resident permits were given to 30,000 holders of Greek passports

(Alexandris 1988, 91). However, some subsequent policies of the Turkish government forced several of these residents to leave Turkey.

In July 1932, the Turkish National Assembly passed a law (no. 2007) that prohibited thousands of foreigners from practicing their professions. It is estimated that 10,000 "established" holders of Greek passports left İstanbul in the period of 1934–35 (Alexandris 1983, 189; 1988, 99). Similarly, an estimated 8,000–10,000 Thracian Jews were forcibly removed from their homes in the areas of Edirne and the Straits zone and found refuge either in İstanbul or fled the country, because Law No. 2510 stipulated that some areas including Eastern Thrace were to be restricted only to Turks (Brown 1987, ix–x). In line with the principle of nationalism, a campaign aimed at increasing the usage of the Turkish language in public places (*vatandaş Türkçe konuş*) was initiated in mid-1930s. When all citizens were required to adopt last names by Law No. 2525 in 1934, minority members were advised to adopt Turkish endings (e.g., -*oğlu*).

Some other policies, which did not intend to single out and harm minorities, had adverse effects and run counter to the provisions of the Lausanne Treaty. For example, Law No. 2596, dated 1934, which forbade the clergy from wearing their clerical garb outside houses of prayer, was a part of the general policy of secularization and was indiscriminate in its application to the priesthood of all faiths. Nevertheless, it constituted a violation of Article 43 of the Treaty of Lausanne (Alexandris 1983, 198–200). Similarly, Law No. 2762, dated 1935, which made provisions for the appointment of a single trustee accountable to the Department of Religious Foundations (Vakıflar) went counter to the minority' s right to be responsible for the management of religious, charitable, and social institutions as specified in Article 40 of the Treaty of Lausanne (Alexandris 1983, 202; 1988, 97).

During World War II, Greek, Jewish, and Armenian males between the ages of eighteen and forty-five were singled out and sent to special labor camps in the interior of Anatolia, where many of them perished because they were unable to withstand the harsh living conditions (Brown 1987, x).

By far the most damaging measure directed against non-Muslim minorities was the 1942 Law of Capital Levy (Varlık Vergisi, no. 4305), passed by the Grand National Assembly on 12 November (Ökte 1987, 23). The avowed purpose of the measure was to tax war profiteers who were taking advantage of wartime commodity shortages to raise prices, benefiting from black markets. The tax applied to both Muslim and non-Muslim merchants, but at different rates. According to Faik Ökte (1987, 19), a governmental official responsible for the assessment and execution of the tax, taxpayers were classified into categories of Muslims, non-Muslims, Dönme Turks (converts), and foreign nationals. The application of the law, which lasted from November 1942 until mid-March 1944, had a devastating impact on non-Muslim minorities, who not only provided an easy scapegoat to blame for the misfortunes of the war but also shouldered a disproportionate burden of the tax. For instance, of the 315 million Turkish liras that the Turkish government had amassed by February 1944, a month before the law's cancellation, 280 million liras had been collected from the "wealthy minorities" (Weisband 1973, 235–36). Non-Muslims, and in many cases foreign nationals, paid ten times as much the rate of Muslims, and Dönme Turks paid twice the Muslim rate (Lewis 1968, 298).

For the Muslim middle class, the imposition of the tax was received as a mixed blessing. The payment of the tax, albeit at reduced rates compared to the non-Muslims, turned the Muslim merchant class against the state bureaucracy, the very institution which had helped them through the étatist policies that had stimulated the accumulation of wealth since the founding of the Republic (Keyder 1988, 204–5). On the other hand, the tax offered Muslim merchants the opportunity to buy out, at favorable prices, the businesses and property of non-Muslim merchants who had no choice but to sell in order to meet their tax requirements (Keyder 1987, 113).

Discrimination was also evident in the case of tax defaulters. Their property was seized, some were imprisoned, while others were deported to the labor camp at Aşkale, near Erzurum. Of the 300 people who were garthered at Aşkale in March 1943, only 3 were Muslims (Weisband 1973, 233).

The abolition of the tax in 1944 brought some relief, but the biggest losers were law-abiding minority members who had paid their debts or had given up their property and could not benefit from the cancellation provisions of Law No. 4530. The Capital Tax, inspired by nationalism and racist doctrines, did hurt the international reputation of modern Turkey as a tolerant country. Faik Ökte assessed its economic impact as follows: "The major Greek, Armenian and Jewish merchant figures were shaken and dislocated. The middle class was feeble and powerless. . . . the Muslim Turks also felt, at least indirectly, the impact of the Capital Tax. . . . Many of the ruined non-Muslim taxpayers never managed to recover financially" (1987, 91).

The Period 1945–82

During this period of interrupted multiparty democracy, which ends with the development of a new constitution, the Cyprus issue became the source of the problems for the Rum Orthodox minority. Things took a turn for the worse, beginning with the London tripartite conference in 1955, and major clashes occurred in 1963–64 and 1974.

From 1571 to 1878, Cyprus was part of the Ottoman Empire. In 1878, the island was transferred to Britain and remained a British colony from 1914 until the year it gained its independence in 1960. Independence, though, was not high on the priority list of Greek Cypriots, Turkish Cypriots or their "mother countries," Greece and Turkey. The mother countries were harboring designs to make Cyprus part of their own territory. Greek Cypriots wanted Enosis (Union) with Greece and thought of an anticolonial struggle as a precursor to self-determination. In 1955, they launched under the banner of EOKA (Ethniki Organosis Kyprion Agoniston, National Organization of Cypriot Fighters) a military anticolonial struggle that was opposed by both the British and the Turkish Cypriots. The Turkish Cypriots, conceiving EOKA as their archenemy, sided with the British and before too long the struggle against British colonial rule turned into an intercommunal ethnic conflict (Ioannides 1991, 57). To resolve matters, in August 1955 British prime minister Anthony Eden hosted a Tripartite Conference on Cyprus, in London, with Britain, Greece, and Turkey as participants.

Soon after the conference, on 6 and 7 September, riots targeting primarily Rum Orthodox neighborhoods broke out in İstanbul, and to a lesser extent, in the Marmara islands and İzmir. The crowds looted and destroyed property, including houses, stores, factories, churches, schools, and organizations belonging to the Rum Orthodox minority, and severely injured members of this minority. Although the perpetrators of the events were under orders not to spill blood, the human toll included three dead and hundreds injured (Linardatos 1978, 331). The majority of the perpetrators were not even residents of İstanbul; they carried destructive tools, which were loaded off trucks, and were provided with lists of non-Muslim houses and shops (Christides 2000, 347–48 and 351–52). The İstanbul prefecture estimated that more than 1,000 houses, more than 4,000 shops and businesses, 73 churches, and 26 schools were damaged (Christides 2000, 359). The Turkish government paid compensation to the victims but the amounts received covered a portion of the claims, submitted by minority members.

The September events caused a social hysteria that could not be contained by the government, pitting the have-nots against the relatively well-off. The government rushed to put the blame for the events on communist extremists. However, some identified the Menderes-led government as the real culprit that had incited the rugged underprivileged masses to engage in looting (Nesin 1999, 73–74).[5] In fact, a court trial in September 1961, at Yassıada island, after Menderes government was ousted by the 1960 military coup, revealed the government's hand behind the atrocities and held former Prime Minister Adnan Menderes and former Foreign Minister Fatin Rüştü Zorlu accountable.

The pretext for the launching of the orchestrated attacks against the minority was the news that a bomb had exploded outside Atatürk's birthplace house in Thessaloniki. The news was circulated instantly by the media and by leaflets distributed by the Kıbrıs Türktür (Cyprus Is Turkish) Association (Christides 2000, 346). The activities of the Cyprus Is Turkish Association and the late August 1955 London conference point to a direct link between the Cyprus issue and the events against the Rum Orthodox minority. Opposing the Greek Cypriots for their Enosis designs, the Cyprus Is Turkish Association and its leader Hikmet Bil were inflaming Turkish nationalism and circulating stories that the Greek Cypriots were about to commit atrocities against the Turkish Cypriots in mid-August. The association also called for a mass rally on 9 September. Hikmet Bil had Menderes convinced that İstanbul prefect's ban on mass meetings should be lifted (Christides 2000, 353).

A number of statements by high-level Turkish officials before the 1955 Tripartite London Conference on Cyprus highlight the interface between the international and the domestic levels, the links between the Cyprus issue and the September events. For instance, at a press briefing on 24 August, a few days before the departure of the Turkish delegation to London, Prime Minister Menderes voiced his concerns about atrocities that would be committed against Turkish Cypriots. Although this scenario did not materialize, a few bombs that went off in Cyprus near police stations and military installations on 31 August and 3 September respectively did not calm the situation (Linardatos 1978, 324–25). By the end of 1955, the Rum Orthodox minority declined from an estimated 88,680 in 1945 to 65,000 (Akar 2003, 244–45).

Another blow against the Rum Orthodox community occurred in 1964. Again, the Cyprus issue was the main culprit, and a mass exodus of thousands of Rum Orthodox from Turkey followed the events. As a result of disagreements over constitutional amendments by the Greek and Turkish Cypriot leaderships, intercommunal violence broke out in the island on 21 December 1963. The hostilities, which continued until August 1964, resulted in killings and atrocities on both sides and brought Greece and Turkey to the brink of war. In reaction to atrocities committed against Turkish Cypriots, the Ankara government not only threatened to intervene militarily in order to protect Turkish Cypriots, who had fled their homes and moved into enclaves, but also took retaliatory measures against the Rum Orthodox community in Turkey.[6]

An initial measure that was revoked within a few days was forbidding Patriarch Athenagoras from visiting Jerusalem for a scheduled meeting with Pope Paul VI. The meeting finally took place on 4 January 1964 (Linardatos 1986, 371). Other measures targeted against the Ecumenical Patriarchate in İstanbul included the expulsions of archbishops Aimilianos of Selefkia and Jacob of Philadelphia for engaging in "subversive" activities; the closing down of the patriarchal printing house in April 1964; and prohibitions against all foreign nationals, including minority members holding Greek passports, from studying at the Theological Seminary of Chalki (Alexandris 1983, 299). More important, on 16 March 1964, Prime Minister İsmet İnönü decided not to renew the 1930 Greek-Turkish friendship agreement, that had been signed on 28 October 1930 (Demir and Akar 1999, 39–62). The effect of the decision was the expulsion of approximately 12,500 members of the Rum Orthodox community holding Greek passports (N. and H. Pope 1997, 116; Oran 1996, 137; Demir and Akar 1999, 91 and 114). Turkish officials regarded the Greek passport holders as suspects, "agents" of Greece who were financially aiding the Greek cause on Cyprus. The expulsion policy assumed a massive character within a short period. The cases of deportation were increasing monthly, reaching a climax in September 1964, when the 1930 Greek-Turkish Convention expired. The deportees increased from 16 in February 1964, to 36 in May, to 333 in June, to 613 in July (Bitsios 1975, 177). In August 1,073 were deported, but by September 1965 their number had surpassed 6,000 (Alexandris 1983, 283). The property of the affected minority members was either confiscated by the government or was abandoned in the hope that it could be reclaimed at some future date. The expulsion policy dealt a fatal blow to the Rum Orthodox minority of Turkey. Between 1960 and 1965, marking two population censuses, the Rum community of İstanbul registered a net loss of 21,000 persons and the Rum Orthodox share of the total Christian population decreased from 46 percent in 1960 to 35 percent in 1965 (Dündar 2003, 56). After 1964, the Rum Orthodox minority in Turkey numbered an estimated 30,000–40,000 (Akar 2003, 246).

The 1963–64 Cyprus crisis also led to measures taken against the property rights and the educational and cultural institutions of the Rum Orthodox community. On 2 November 1964, Turkey's Ministerial Council approved Decree No. 6/3801, which forbade Rum Orthodox of Greek nationality from carrying out juridical acts regarding the purchase, sale, transfer, exchange, or donation of their property.

For a long time, minority members felt helpless, seeing their estates confiscated, without being able to challenge the decree in courts by the mere fact that the decree remained "secret," not being published in the government's gazette. The situation took a turn for the better only in 1988, when Prime Minister Turgut Özal of Turkey, responding to the Greek government's pressure exerted on European Union Council of Ministers in the context of Turkey's membership application to the EU, announced the withdrawal of the decree during the summit meeting with Greece's prime minister Andreas Papandreou in Davos.

The farm property owned by the Rum Orthodox in the islands of Gökçeada and Bozcaada was also taken away from their owners under the 1964 Law on Land Expropriation (No. 6830). Moreover, in direct violation of Articles 14, 37, 38, and 40 of the Lausanne Treaty, Turkey transferred convicts from the mainland to the open farm prisons created on the nationalized land in Gökçeada. This act, which altered the demographic composition of the island, along with several other measures that affected the education of children (e.g., the expropriation of schools' property in Gökçeada and Bozcaada, the closing down of the only school for minority children in Bozcaada, and the ban on the teaching of the Greek language, Law No. 502, in 1964) compelled many islanders to emigrate. Whereas in 1964 there were 8,000 Rum Orthodox and 250 Turks in Gökçeada, and 1,220 Rum Orthodox and 600 Turks in Bozcaada, the balance has shifted overwhelmingly in favor of Turks. In the 1990s, 7,900 Turks and 260 Rum Orthodox were residing in Gökçeada, and 2,000 Turks and 37 Rum Orthodox were living in Bozcaada (Christophoridis 1996, 76).

Restrictions were also imposed on the activities of minority educational and charitable organizations in İstanbul. Law No. 222, in 1961, took away the "communal" character from minority schools, which was implied in the minority clauses of the Lausanne Treaty, and turned them into private schools, by putting them under the Department of Private Schools in the Turkish Ministry of Education. Other new regulations that went into force in 1964 stipulated that: (a) Turkish assistant headmasters would be appointed to all schools; (b) morning prayer and Greek textbooks would be banned; (c) Orthodox clergymen would be prohibited from entering the schools (Alexandris 1983, 286–87); (d) repair work at school buildings or permits for new schools would not be granted; and (e) elected minority school boards would not be recognized (Helsinki Watch Report 1992, 15).

The third set of Cyprus-related events that had devastating effects on the Rum Orthodox broke up in 1974 with the military intervention of the Greek junta and continued with the Turkish intervention that was carried out as a response. By the time of the 1974 Cyprus crisis, only a few thousand Rum Orthodox remained in İstanbul. The July-August crisis in Cyprus expedited the exodus of 7,800 Rum Orthodox who were ambivalent about leaving Turkey until then (Akar 2003, 246). The heightened nationalist fervor forced the inhabitants of the village of Kastro in Gökçeada to abandon their homes, and the village cemetery was desecrated (Pan-Imvrian Committee of Athens 1996).

Since 1982

As a result of the restrictive and repressive policies followed by subsequent Turkish governments over the years, the once vigorous, dynamic, and prosperous Rum Orthodox community has dwindled. Today in İstanbul, for example, it is consisted of approximately 4,000–3,000 and mostly elderly residents. The people who have chosen to remain in Turkey and not emigrate are trying very hard to safeguard their identity, their religion, and their language, and to rescue whatever property belongs to the community or to its members. In religious affairs, the sole institution that holds the community together and reminds it of its historical heritage is the Ecumenical Patriarchate, the seat of the Orthodox Patriarch and spiritual leader of all Orthodox faithful around the world. Thus, the human rights concerns of the community during the last decade have concentrated on religious freedom and autonomy.

The legal status of the Fener Patriarchate (Fener Rum Patrikhanesi) has been an issue of contention since 1923. The Ecumenical Throne in İstanbul is considered "first among equals" of all Orthodox churches. The reach of the Patriarchate is global and extends beyond its small diocese in İstanbul to Europe, North and South America, Asia and Australia. The center of Orthodoxy has been located in İstanbul for more than sixteen centuries. It is true that the negotiations in Lausanne in 1923 confined the role of the Patriarchate to purely religious matters. However, the Lausanne Treaty also obliges Turkey to protect the religious establishments of the minorities (Article 42).

Turkey recognizes the Patriarchate as a Turkish institution limited to serving the Rum Orthodox minority in İstanbul. As the global reach and recognition of the Patriarchate increases, the official position has become more pronounced. A recent expression of official displeasure is a communication from the office of Prime Minister Tayyip Erdoğan to government officials in July 2004 urging them not to attend a reception hosted by U.S. Ambassador Eric Edelman because the latter had sent invitations referring to Vartholomeos as "ecumenical patriarch" (Helicke 2004). The official position also has had some resonance in public. For example, bombing attacks were launched on the Patriarchate grounds in 1994, 1996, 2004, and 2005 by fringe elements representing extreme nationalist or Islamic fundamentalist groups.

However, a number of positive steps were initiated as well. For instance, Turkish authorities did not interfere with the list of candidates for the patriarchal election in 1990, as they had done in 1972. Moreover, Turkish authorities granted permission for rebuilding the church and facilities of the Patriarchate in 1987. Since 1999, they have eased the bureaucratic procedures related to the repairs of religious and charitable facilities. Archimandrite Dositheos (2000; 2002) has recorded more than sixty churches that have been renovated and restored in recent years.

A major problem that confronts the Ecumenical Patriarchate is the lack of a theological seminary where it could train its future clergy and theologians. The Theological Seminary at Heybeliada (Chalki), founded in 1844, was demoted from university status to a training school in 1964 and was closed in 1971, under a Constitutional Court decree that nationalized all non-Turkish private universities. In November 1998, Turkish authorities charged the seminary's lay board of trustees with mismanagement and anti-Turkish propaganda and dismissed them (Law Library of Congress 2000, 142).

Both former Ecumenical Patriarch Demetrios and current Ecumenical Patriarch Vartholomeos have made repeated requests to the Turkish government to reopen the seminary. Patriarch Vartholomeos considers the reopening of the seminary vital to the renewal of the clergy at the patriarchal throne and has launched a concerted effort to generate international interest that could put pressure on the Turkish government. He believes that the training of Orthodox clergy is an essential function of the church and the reopening of the seminary would demonstrate that there exists freedom of religion in Turkey and that all religions enjoy equal opportunities to train and educate their clerics. During the August 1994 celebrations, which marked the 150th anniversary of the founding of the seminary, Patriarch Vartholomeos appealed to the Turkish government to permit its reopening.[7] He reiterated his appeal in a meeting with Turkish Prime Minister Tayyip Erdoğan on 28 August 2003.

However, progress on the issue has been slow. Turkish authorities are reluctant to pass a law that would grant, in their view, preferential treatment to Rum Orthodox, which may then open the door for the operation of Islamist schools (Law Library of Congress 2000, 143). Instead, some government officials are willing to consider a proposal that would allow the Heybeliada Theological Seminary to function as part of a Faculty of Theology at İstanbul University. The Patriarchate authorities find two problems with this solution. First, since İstanbul University is a public institution, there is apprehension over the state's control and the seminary's ability to recruit students and teachers from abroad who would eventually be able to join the ranks of the church and acquire Turkish citizenship. The second problem relates more to the type of education and training that would be offered. In a university setting courses are theoretical and students would not be able to deliver sermons, perform liturgical practices, and experience the liturgy first hand. Commenting on this point, Patriarch Vartholomeos succinctly stated that "this combination of theory and praxis does not exist at a university faculty of theology. . . . Liturgical life in Orthodoxy plays a central and essential role. The entire theology of our church is concentrated, lived, and expressed in the divine worship" (Gilson 2002).

Recently, the issue concerning the reopening of the theological seminary at Heybeliada has gone through several ups and downs. There seems to be a split within the Turkish state between supporters of the reopening and opponents who consider a potential reopening as a threat to the internal security of Turkey. The Turkish Foreign Ministry, sensing the beneficial effects of the reopening on Turkey's candidacy to the EU, has put forth a proposal in favor of reopening. The proposal calls for the establishment of a postsecondary two-year theological school that would be under the supervision of the Ministry of Education (Mavridis 2004, 8). This positive view is countered by circles close to the military that have influence within the National Security Council. According to press reports that came to light in November 2004 (Ergin 2004; Berkan 2004), the theological seminary at Heybeliada is designated as a threat to the internal security of the country in the new National Security Political Document (Milli Güvenlik Siyaset Belgesi). This new development came as blow to minority circles and the issue of reopening has been suspended.

Other pending human rights issues concern property and education rights. Article 40 of the Lausanne Treaty grants non-Muslim minorities the right to establish and manage religious, charitable, and social foundations. These foundations, which amount to approximately 70 sites for the Rum Orthodox community, are supervised by a government agency, the General Directorate of Foundations (Vakıflar Genel Müdürlüğü) (U.S. Department of State 2001). Contrary to Article 40, the Turkish government has, since 1935 and up until recently, enacted legislation that placed obstacles to the purchase, sale, and use of properties owned by charitable foundations. In 1935, the government passed Law No. 2007, which forbade the donation of property to churches and charitable foundations (Helsinki Watch Report 1992, 23). The following year, a law was passed specifying that only properties declared under Law No. 2762, of 1936, would be recognized, otherwise they could be confiscated by the Turkish state (Commission of European Communities 2002, 38). In the aftermath of the Cyprus crisis in 1974, the Turkish Supreme Court of Appeals ruled that minority religious foundations could not buy or sell property acquired since 1936 (Law Library of Congress 2000, 141). The above-mentioned laws, partly originating from a nationalist conception that viewed the activities of minority institutions with suspicion, violate the antidiscrimination rules since the foundation laws have applied to Muslim and non-Muslim communities differently (see Baskın Oran in this volume, Chapter 3). The situation regarding the foundation properties improved considerably starting in August 2002 and continuing with the subsequent reform packages that would harmonize Turkish legislation with the Copenhagen criteria for the EU membership. However, a reversal in connection with property rights occurred on 21 October 2004, when Turkey's Supreme Court did not recognize the Rum Orthodox community as the rightful owner of the Rum Orthodox orphanage at Büyükada (Prinkipos).

The legal amendments in line with Turkey's bid for membership in the EU are still short of establishing freedom of religion and equal treatment of the followers of different faiths (see Chapter 3, by Baskin Oran, in this volume). In this regard, it is noteworthy that the Christian communities of Turkey (Rum Orthodox, Armenian, Assyrian, and Roman Catholic) forwarded in October 2003 to the Human Rights Committee of the National Assembly a document outlining a set of common demands. The document called for the following: (a) the lifting of legal restrictions that would grant legal personality to Christian patriarchates and churches; (b) the granting of Turkish citizenship or work permit to clergy originating from abroad; (c) the operation of theological schools for training of the clergy; (d) the right of churches and minority foundations to own and administer their property; (e) the return of property that had been confiscated; and (f) an end to practices that cast doubt on the loyalty of non-Muslim citizens ("Aitimata ton Christianon tis Tourkias" 2003, 6).

In the field of education, the Treaty of Lausanne provides that the Rum Orthodox minority in Turkey has the right to Greek-language education in reciprocal terms with the provision of Turkish-language education to the Muslim minority in Western Thrace in Greece. The Treaty of Lausanne is supplemented by two educational protocols signed by Greece and Turkey, in 1951 and 1968 respectively.[8] Under the 1951 Education Protocol, each party reserves the right to establish schools in the territory of the other. Aiming to foster educational exchanges, the protocol allows for the mutual recognition of diplomas received in each other's countries and grants each state the right to establish schools in the territory of the other. The 1968 Educational Protocol of the Greek-Turkish Cultural Commission addresses the issue of reciprocal exchange of teachers to provide instruction in minority schools, and discusses at length the production and use of textbooks in minority schools, granting each country the right to publish textbooks for its respective minority in the other country (Human Rights Watch Greece 1999, 10–12).

Undoubtedly, the mass exodus of Rum Orthodox after the crises of 1955, 1964, and 1974 resulted in substantial decline in enrollments in Rum Orthodox schools. Whereas there were approximately 15,000 students in the Rum Orthodox school system in 1923, the total number declined to 6,589 students in the 1955–56 school year, to approximately 5,000 in the 1964–65 school year, and to barely 294 students in the 1998–99 school year (Helsinki Watch Report 1992; Anastasiadou-Dumont 2000; Soltarides 2000). For the 2004–5 school year, the total number of students stood at 221. This resulted in closing of many schools, leaving in operation one kindergarten, ten primary schools, and four secondary schools. Some students opted to continue their education in Greece, perhaps without considering a return (U.S. Department of State 2002). Yet, it can be argued that there are no major problems recently in the school system of the Rum Orthodox minority. This qualitative improvement is due to the new approach that Greece took in the early 1990s toward its own Muslim minority in Western Thrace and to the recent rapprochement in Greek-Turkish relations, which began in late 1990s, with the acceptance of Turkey as a candidate for membership country at the December 1999 European Summit Council meeting in Helsinki and due to the signing of a number of protocols between Greece and Turkey on "low-politics" issues in 2000.

Conclusion

In this chapter, I have traced the history of the Rum Orthodox minority from the founding of modern Turkey until the present. The rights of this minority were articulated in the Lausanne Treaty. The national modernization project of the Turkish elites and the arousal of Turkish nationalism at critical junctures in the historical trajectory were the cause of much misfortune and of violations of human rights that were experienced by all non-Muslim minorities including the Rum Orthodox. For the latter, the violations have been aggravated by the Cyprus problem, especially after 1955. Although I agree with Tözün Bahçeli (1990) that the initiation of restrictive measures was not part of a grand design to rid Turkey of the minority, I do not share his assertion that these measures would have been pursued even in the absence of hostilities created by the Cyprus problem. This is not to deny that the Turkish government often took measures against the minority in retaliation for adversarial acts of the Greek government against Muslims in Western Thrace. The same can be said of restrictive Greek measures toward the Muslim minority in the period 1967–74, which Sevasti Troumbeta interprets as belated reprisals for the mass exodus of the Rum Orthodox the previous years (2001). However, without major events, like the Turkish War of Independence and the Cyprus crises, it would have been difficult to "invent" events that would have resulted in sufferings and emigrations of such large scale, which would then be retaliated.

Identifying the Cyprus problem as a significant cause of the gradual worsening condition of the Rum Orthodox minority of Turkey in recent history calls for a solution to this problem. Both the UN and the EU have pushed the interested parties to reach a settlement. In November 2002, the secretary-general of the UN submitted to the two communities in Cyprus the so-called Annan Plan. After a number of talks and revisions, the two communities were asked to vote in simultaneous and separate referenda for or against the finalized version of the Annan Plan. On

24 April 2004, Greek Cypriots rejected the plan with a majority of 75.83 percent and Turkish Cypriots voted in favor of the plan with a majority of 64.9 percent. The negative vote of the Greek Cypriot community was a clear setback both for the settlement of the Cyprus problem and, indirectly, for improving the condition of the Rum Orthodox in Turkey. A resolution of the Cyprus problem would have positive repercussions in Ankara, paving the way for the reopening of the theological seminary at Heybeliada and clearing the way for the resolution of other outstanding issues. With the Cyprus problem still unresolved, the Rum Orthodox in Turkey cannot expect major breakthroughs on issues that concern them. However, they stand to benefit from negotiations for the accession of Turkey to the EU and the strengthening of Turkey's democracy.

Chapter 5
Linguistic Human Rights and the Rights of Kurds

Mary Lou O'Neil

Since its establishment, the Republic of Turkey has had a problematic relationship with its Kurdish population, an ethnic and linguistic group primarily living in eastern Anatolia. The conflict between Turks and Kurds over the control of the region predates the Republic, stretching back to the Ottoman Empire. At times, especially during the 1980s and 1990s, the strife between the Turkish state and the Kurds has proved particularly violent and costly for the parties and the entire country. The capture of Abdullah Öcalan, the leader of the Kurdistan Workers' Party (Partia Karkaren Kürdistan, PKK), in February 1999, stopped violent encounters for a while, but the "Kurdish question" has not been solved.

For much of the history of the Republic of Turkey, a major contention between the state and its Kurdish population has been the use of the Kurdish language, the cornerstone of Kurdish culture. On various occasions, the Republic has banned its use in private and public, and some state officials and Turkish citizens have gone so far as to deny the very existence of Kurds and the Kurdish language.

Since the early twentieth century, language rights have grown in importance, and have become a part of numerous international human rights agreements. The international legal protection of language rights stems both from general human rights provisions, such as freedom from discrimination, and freedom of expression, as well as specific instruments for the protection of language, although no single international treaty expressly dedicated to the protection of language is in force today. The level of protection ranges from simply ensuring freedom from government interference to more positive action, such as requiring states to provide services and education in minority languages. The protection of language rights under international law also stems from a number of different organizations, such as the United Nations, the European Union, and the Council of Europe.

This chapter examines the restrictions placed on the use of Kurdish as an issue of human rights and a violation of international law that protects language rights. The first section provides a summary description of Kurds in general, as well as the Kurds in Turkey, and reviews the Turkish state's policies toward this ethnic group, particularly on the use of language as a means of subduing the Kurds. The second section examines linguistic human rights in various international and regional human rights conventions and discusses Turkey's treaty obligations. The last section discusses the reasons for resistance to granting language rights to the Kurds in Turkey as well the future for any language rights the Kurds might claim. The struggle over Kurdish demonstrates the fundamental role language plays in the struggle between Turkey and its Kurdish population, and that language is of vital importance to the national identities of both Kurds and Turks. Subsequent Turkish governments have proved particularly sensitive to the use of the Kurdish language, and thus have used varying prohibitions on Kurdish as a means to try to subdue the Kurds. Finally, I contend that Turkey as a party to numerous international human rights treaties has an obligation to safeguard the linguistic rights of all of its citizens, including the Kurds.

The Kurds and Their Status in Turkey

Despite a lack of agreement about the origin of the Kurds, Kurdish people have existed as an identifiable group in the Middle East for approximately two thousand years (McDowell 2000, 2). People who identify as Kurds have lived primarily in the area that today falls in the border of Turkey, Syria, Iraq, and Iran. Although defining who the Kurds are proves difficult, due to the fact that the term applies to a wide group of people, some broad characterizations are still possible. Historically, the Kurds constituted a nomadic tribal people. After years of voluntary and involuntary migration to cities, the tribal organization of Kurds collapsed, at least in Turkey, yet some tribal ties remain intact, albeit not in the same ways that existed in the past (P. White 2000).

In terms of religion, the vast majority of Kurds (75 percent) subscribes to Sunni Islam, and the rest are scattered among various sects of Islam, although not all Kurds practice Islam (McDowell 2000, 10). In Iran, the majority of Kurds practice the same brand of Shia Islam subscribed to by the majority of Iranians. In Turkey, alongside Sunni Kurds, who constitute the majority, there exists a strong community of Alevi Kurds, who follow a form of Shia Islam (McDowell 2000, 41). Until recently, many Yazidi Kurds also lived in Turkey, but a number of Yazidis, whose faith represents a blend of Zoroastrianism, Judaism, Christianity, and Islam, have fled to Germany in recent years to escape the repressive political conditions in Turkey (McDowell 2000, 17).

Kurds appear to be linguistically diverse as well. Although they speak Kurdish—an Indo-European language that is closely associated with the Iranian group of languages—a number of Kurdish dialects exist. Two major dialects are in use today. Kurmanji is the dialect spoken primarily in the north, and most common in Turkey; Surani is most prevalent in the south and among the Iraqi Kurds. Other dialects include Kirmanshahi, Gurani, and Leki, which are primarily used in Iran. In Turkey, there is also a Kurdish community that speaks Zaza, though there is some controversy over whether Zaza is actually a Kurdish dialect, because there are substantial differences between Zaza and the other Kurdish dialects (P. White 2000, 16).

While it is clear that a Kurdish community exists and is substantial in size, determining the exact numbers of Kurds proves elusive due to the reluctance of various governments in keeping and providing accurate population statistics. Estimates vary widely, but the most reasonable estimates place the overall population of Kurds at around 20–25 million (McDowell 2000, 3; Garr and Harff 1994, 30). Approximately 12 million, or nearly half all Kurds, are said to live in Turkey (McDowell 2000, 3; Garr and Harff 1994, 37). By this estimate, Kurds may constitute as much as 20 percent of the current population in Turkey.

The Struggle of Kurds in Turkey

Historically, Kurds have experienced peaceful coexistence with Turks under the Turkish rule, yet they faced state repression and struggled to assert their identity. This struggle dates back to the Ottoman Empire, which included several upheavals. During the First World War, the Ottoman government authorized and partially implemented a plan that forced Kurds to move out of the east, and resettled them in western Anatolia while trying to assure that in these resettled areas, the population of Kurds did not exceed 5 percent (McDowell 2000, 105). While the plan was only partially implemented by the Ottoman government, it was reintroduced several times by the republican governments as a way of dealing with the ever troublesome Kurds. The Republic also waged a concerted campaign to subdue the Kurds and forcibly assimilate them into the "Turkish" society. In order to achieve a unified Turkish state, successive governments have employed strategies such as forced migration and resettlements, bans on Kurdish publications, and prohibitions on using the Kurdish language in private or public. In line with the state policy, many Turks started to deny the existence of the Kurds, claiming that Kurds are actually "mountain Turks," and therefore not a distinct group, and that Kurdish is a dialect of Turkish.

On 20 October 1920, the Ottoman government reluctantly signed the

Treaty of Sèvres, bringing to a close its involvement in World War I. The terms meted out by the victorious Allies were particularly harsh, especially regarding Anatolia. While an Ottoman government was to remain in existence, its territory was to be severely curtailed. The straits between the Mediterranean Sea and the Black Sea were to be placed under international control and Anatolia was partitioned between the victors. France, Italy, and Great Britain were to be allowed to form "spheres of influence" in Anatolia, while the Greeks were awarded Thrace and the Anatolian port city of İzmir (Cleveland 1994, 154). All of the former Arab provinces of the Ottoman Empire were to be divided between France and Great Britain. Finally, the Allies also dictated that in eastern Anatolia an independent Armenian state would be founded and the Kurds would be provided with an autonomous region of their own (Cleveland 1994, 154–55). This treaty, however, was never ratified by the Ottoman government in İstanbul and proved wholly unacceptable to the nationalists led by Mustafa Kemal (Atatürk), who waged a war from 1919 to 1923 to overturn the treaty terms and free Turkey from the invading forces.

With the victory of the Turkish nationalists and the signing of the Treaty of Lausanne in July 1923, the Treaty of Sèvres was nullified. This also brought an end to the hopes for an autonomous Kurdish area at that time, as the Treaty of Lausanne provided for Turkish sovereignty over Anatolia. Although most Kurdish tribes fought alongside the nationalists in Turkey's War of Independence (Aydın 2000, 158), and helped securing the victory for the new Republic, the Treaty of Lausanne had little to offer to the Kurds, while granting explicit protections in the areas of religion, language, and schools to non-Muslim minorities.

As early as 1922, language became a central issue between Kurds and Turks.[1] The Turkish Grand National Assembly proposed the formation of a Kurdish National Assembly but insisted that the language of the assembly be Turkish (McDowell 2000, 188). Also under this plan, the governor general of the Kurdish areas would be allowed to encourage the use of Kurdish, provided this did not lead Kurdish to be the official language (McDowell 2000, 189). The plan was never implemented, but it marks the importance of language in forming a national identity and the Turkish nationalists' sensitivity about this issue.

By 1924, the battles over language reached the zenith. The Turkish government began to replace the Kurdish names for places with Turkish ones, and the Constitution, adopted in October 1924, defined Turkish as the official language (McDowell 2000, 191). Turkish also became the exclusive language of education, except for some non-Muslim groups. Denied access to education in Kurdish, Kurds were deprived of the equal opportunity for education. Between 1923 and 1938, Turkey witnessed a number of armed uprisings by Kurds, and the response of the Turkish government ranged from attempts at assimilation to outright repression. The Settlement Law of 1934 (Law No. 2510) divided the country in three parts: the first area was intended for inhabitation by people already considered "Turks"; the second area included regions where those not in possession of Turkish culture and language could be placed and assimilated into Turkish culture; and the third area covered those parts which were to be fully evacuated (Kirişçi and Winrow 1997, 99; Gunter 1997, 6). Villages or urban centers where Turkish was not the mother tongue were to be dissolved, and inhabitants were to be removed to mainly Turkish-speaking areas. Gatherings at which the majority of persons did not speak Turkish were also prohibited. It was also proposed that Kurdish children be placed in boarding schools where they would be compelled to learn and speak Turkish (Gunter 1997, 6). Although it is not clear if the boarding school project was fully implemented, in 1961 such a proposal became law, when the Turkish parliament allowed for the establishment of boarding schools (McDowell 2000, 404). The effect, if not the intent, of such a policy was assimilation of Kurdish children into the "Turkish" society.

As a response to their treatment by the Turkish government, in 1937 the tribal chiefs from the Kurdish populated area of Dersim (Tunceli) sent a letter to the secretary-general of the League of Nations. This letter, which catalogued what the Kurdish leaders described as the "tyrannies of the Turkish government against human rights and the Kurdish nation" (P. White 2000, 81), is significant for its use of the use of the term "human rights." It appears to be the first time that Kurdish leaders characterized their struggle against the Turkish government as one concerning human rights. The chiefs' appeal to the League of Nations for assistance brought no relief, and the Kurds were left to fend for themselves, which resulted in major upheavals in the Dersim area.

The last of the uprisings in and around Dersim in 1938 ended with such a suppression of the Kurds that little or no further organized movements appeared until the 1960s. In the 1960s, the liberal Constitution of 1960 allowed a number of Kurdish publications in both Turkish and Kurdish, but they were frequently banned, and the writers and publishers were often charged with separatism, especially if they attempted to discuss Kurdish issues. In 1967, the parliament passed a law forbidding the importation and distribution of Kurdish language materials from abroad (McDowell 2000, 404; Gunter 1997, 6–7). Earlier in the decade, the government had once again begun to change Kurdish names of places to Turkish, since Kurdish names were perceived as "names which hurt public opinion and are not suitable for our national culture, moral values, traditions and customs" (McDowell 2000, 410).

In the midst of the turmoil, the Marxist Revolutionary Eastern Hearth Organization was founded in 1969, but members were subsequently arrested in October 1970. During their trial, those arrested presented a lengthy document defending their Kurdish identity and rights to their history, language, and society (Gunter 1997, 10). The Workers' Party of Turkey (Türkiye İşçi Partisi, TİP) also raised the issue of Kurds in Turkey, but after the 1971 military coup, the Constitutional Court ordered the party's closure for advocating separatism.

Another group that took up the plight of Kurds in Turkey was the PKK, a Marxist, separatist organization led by Abdullah Öcalan. The PKK, in its attempts to win an independent Kurdish state, pursued guerrilla war against the Turkish state, attacking military installations and troops in the southeast of Turkey, where the population of Kurds is concentrated. The Turkish government responded in kind, and through much of the 1980s and 1990s Turkey found itself embroiled in a civil war.

In the aftermath of the 1980 military coup, as the war against the PKK escalated, the government again used language as a weapon to try to subdue the Kurds. In 1983, reinforcing provisions of the new constitution, Law No. 2932 was passed, stating that it was "forbidden to express, diffuse or publish opinions in any language other than the main official language of states recognized by the Turkish state" (Gunter 1997, 10). Needless to say, Kurdish was not a recognized language. The same law also declared Turkish as the mother tongue of all Turkish citizens, and forbade the use of any language other than Turkish as a mother tongue (McDowell 2000, 425). The state once again prohibited the use of Kurdish, and parents were forbidden to give their children Kurdish names (Houston 2001, 99). Also, more place names were changed from Kurdish to Turkish. Later in the 1980s, most of the Kurdish-dominated southeast of Turkey was placed under emergency rule, and its governor general was granted ever increasing powers. He could close publishing houses if they were deemed to have "misrepresented" the situation in the southeast. In a return to the earlier policies, the governor could also forcibly remove persons from their villages. There were also extensive numbers of detentions and arrests, and torture was widely used (Kirişçci and Winrow 1997, 129; McDowell 2000, 427).

In 1991, however, Turgut Özal, president of the Republic at the time, was able to persuade the Turkish parliament to legalize the private use of Kurdish (McDowell 2000, 429), but the military maintained its hardline stance against such moves. The same parliament, however, also passed the Antiterrorism Law, which forbade any kind of protest that sought to change the character of the state—of course defined as Turkish (429). The armed confrontations between the PKK and the military continued, resulting in thousands of casualties. This armed struggle persisted until 1999, when Abdullah Öcalan, the leader of the PKK, was captured in Nairobi, Kenya. After his capture, Öcalan was returned to Turkey, where he was found guilty of treason and is currently serving a life sentence. Following the capture of Öcalan, and the ending of Syrian support for the PKK, the war in the southeast has virtually ended, and the state of emergency has been lifted in many of the southeastern provinces. Moreover, as Turkey has tried to strengthen its candidacy for the EU, the parliament has passed important legislation with the intention of improving human rights, including easing restrictions on the use and teaching of the Kurdish language.

Recent years witnessed a pitched battle over the language issue, culminating in changes in the government's policies concerning the Kurdish language. A substantial number of students submitted petitions and requested that optional Kurdish courses be made available in Turkish universities. This was met with stiff resistance by the government and the Higher Education Council (Yükseköğretim Kurulu,YÖK). In this primarily student led protest, many were detained by police and some were even arrested ("Police Detain 29 People" 2002). Many of those students who signed petitions were expelled from their universities ("Kürtçe İsteyen 40 Öğrenciye Ceza" 2002). Expelled students later initiated a campaign to file suit against the university rectors who dismissed them ("Students Signing Petitions" 2002).

In September 2002, the parliament, in hopes of winning the EU approval, legalized Kurdish as a language, lifted some of the restrictions on broadcasting and publishing in Kurdish, and thus paved the way for the provision of privately offered Kurdish language classes. One of the largest changes made by the Turkish government involved Article 26 of the Turkish Constitution, removing the restriction that "no language prohibited by law shall be used in the expression and dissemination of thought." This provision had banned the use of Kurdish, as Kurdish was a language prohibited by law. The removal of this restriction also allowed for changes in legislation regarding broadcasting in Kurdish. Changes in the law governing the Radio and Television Supreme Board (Radyo ve Televizyon Üst Kurulu, RTÜK) in 2002 and 2003 allowed for "broadcasts in the different languages and dialects used traditionally by Turkish citizens in their daily lives" (Commission of European Communities 2002, 34). These changes provide for broadcasting in Kurdish (as well as a few other minority languages) on both public and private radio and television stations, yet broadcasts are limited to 45 minutes per day, 4 hours per week on radio and 30 minutes per day, 2 hours per week on television. Moreover, radio programs in languages other than Turkish must be followed by the same programs in Turkish, and non-Turkish television programs must have Turkish subtitles (Global IDP Project, "Despite Legislative Reforms"). Of course, the restriction on broadcasts that "contradict the fundamental principles of the Turkish Republic and the indivisible integrity of the State" remains in place (Commission of European Communities 2002, 34).

The last of the major changes made in August 2002 concerned the Law on Foreign Language Education and Teaching. Mirroring the language in the revised RTÜK law, the new foreign language education law allows for the learning of the different languages and dialects used by the people of Turkey. However, the learning must take place in private language courses, and these courses must in no way contradict "the indivisible integrity of the state" (Commission of European Communities 2002, 41). In June 2003, amendments to the Law on the Census removed the prohibition on parents giving their children Kurdish names. Although the official prohibition on Kurdish names has been lifted, names may not include the letters *q*, *w*, and *x*, which are common in Kurdish but do not exist in Turkish. This is despite the fact that these letters are commonly seen in the names of companies and television and radio stations (Minority Rights Group International 2004). Moreover, Article 42 of the Turkish Constitution, stating that "no language other than Turkish shall be taught as the mother tongue to Turkish citizens at any institutions of training or education," remains unchanged (Commission of European Communities 2002, 41).

The move toward tolerance has not been smooth, either. As recent as the year 2002, individuals were still being prosecuted for listening to Kurdish songs, television and radio stations were still subject to periodic closure if they broadcasted in Kurdish, and at least one book written in Kurdish has been removed from circulation (Commission of European Communities 2002, 42). Starting in 2004, broadcasting in Kurdish and some other languages were allowed, but only on the state-owned media. Reflecting the back-and-forth nature of the Turkish government's moves toward tolerance, December 2005 saw RTÜK approve regulations allowing for Kurdish language broadcasts on private radio and television stations ("Turkish Radio-TV Board Approves").

Linguistic Rights and Turkey's Obligations Under International Law

The Republic of Turkey, as a member of the UN, the Council of Europe, and the Organization for Security and Cooperation in Europe, and as a party to a number of international agreements maintains a certain level of obligation to protect the language rights of all its citizens. The linguistic rights of individuals stem from a number of general human rights guarantees, as well as specific international instruments that focus on the rights of minorities. The level of protection provided by various international and regional instruments also varies from noninterference to taking positive action by the participating state. At present, international law requires little more than noninterference from Turkey regarding the language rights of its Kurdish citizens.

Turkey's first international obligation to respect minority rights begins with the Treaty of Lausanne, which is still in force. It guarantees some minorities in Turkey certain rights such as the right to speak and publish in their languages, as well as the right to establish their own schools and teach their language alongside Turkish in those schools. However, to date the treaty has been interpreted by the Republic of Turkey as only applicable to non-Muslim minorities, leaving Turkey's Kurdish citizens unprotected. (See Baskın Oran in this volume, Chapter 3, for an argument that the language provisions provided in the treaty are also applicable to the Kurds.)

As a member of the UN, the Republic of Turkey maintains some obligations, albeit not necessarily legal, to create conditions in line with the Universal Declaration on Human Rights. Two of the most basic guarantees contained in that document focus on nondiscrimination and freedom of expression for all individuals. Specifically, under Article 2, discrimination on the basis of language is prohibited, even though the proscription against discrimination is not absolute. States are not required to provide services or conduct state business in every language that is used within their borders, as this would prove far too burdensome. Freedom from discrimination in terms of language represents a balancing act between states' legitimate interests, that is, maintaining an official language, and the rights of nonmajority language speakers to live free from discrimination. Moreover, the Declaration is not a binding document, although some scholars argue that the norms embodied in the Declaration now comprise international custom and therefore constitute a basis for international law. Nevertheless, Turkey has consistently denied these basic rights to its Kurdish citizens, and those who challenged these denials or even tried to discuss the Kurdish issue have been jailed and silenced.

The European Convention for the Protection of Human Rights and Fundamental Freedoms embodies many of the same provisions found in the Universal Declaration of Human Rights. Unlike the UN Declaration, the European Convention represents a fully binding multilateral international treaty. As a party to the Convention, Turkey has an obligation to uphold its provisions and to ensure that all of its citizens and residents are guaranteed the rights outlined in it. Like the UN Declaration, the European Convention provides for freedom from discrimination based on language (Article 14) and freedom of expression (Article 9). These provisions allow for private newspapers and radio and television broadcasters to use any language without undue interference from authorities. Certainly, a state can require a broadcasting license and insist that the private media conform to all existing laws, but it may not make distinctions based on language in their provision, as this would violate the principle of nondiscrimination. The situation for state-owned media is less clear, however; states parties to the European Convention are bound by the principle of nondiscrimination, and this would appear to require state-owned media to provide some broadcasting in nonmajority languages. The European Convention also provides that in criminal proceedings individuals are informed about the reasons of their arrest and the charges against them in a language that they can understand. It also requires that individuals who are charged with a criminal offense be provided with an interpreter, if they cannot understand or speak the language used in the proceedings (Article 6e).

Preventing discrimination based on language, the Convention obliges Turkey to refrain from discriminating against Kurds. Therefore, in terms of freedom of expression, the Kurds must be afforded the right to communicate in Kurdish if they choose to do so. The right to freedom of expression also extends to media and provides the right to "receive and impart information and ideas without interference by public authority and regardless of frontiers" (Article 10). Under this provision, private media should be allowed to broadcast in Kurdish, and freedom from discrimination may also require time for broadcasting in Kurdish on the state-owned media. Private media also extends to newspapers and magazines, which have a right to publish in Kurdish, and individuals are guaranteed the right to import Kurdish materials if they choose.

The single most important binding international treaty, which directly impacts language rights, is the International Covenant on Civil and Political Rights (ICCPR). Turkey ratified the treaty in December 2003 and thus assumed the obligation of upholding its provisions. The ICCPR contains important guarantees of freedom of expression and freedom from discrimination, including freedom from discrimination based on language (Articles 2, 19, and 26). The covenant also provides for specific language rights to be safeguarded in criminal proceedings. Most significantly, Article 27 specifically addresses the issue of linguistic minorities: "In those states in which ethnic, religious or linguistic minorities exist, persons belonging to such minorities shall not be denied the right, in community with the other members of their group, to enjoy their own culture, to profess and practice their own religion, *or to use their own language*" (emphasis mine). This represents a relatively straightforward noninterference clause limiting the extent to which governments can curb the cultural, religious, and language practices of minority groups (Varennes 1996, 136).[2]

As a binding international treaty, the ICCPR places on Turkey obligations similar to those included in the European Convention, including equal treatment of individuals regardless of their language, freedom of expression, and informing the person in criminal proceedings in a language he or she can understand. But Turkey placed a reservation on Article 27, which specifies that minorities should have the right to "use their own language."

Turkey has also ratified the UN Convention on the Rights of the Child (1989) but placed a reservation on three separate articles that relate to language rights (Articles 17, 29, and 30). The provisions at issue concern mass media and broadcasting that is sensitive to the linguistics needs of minority children, education that develops respect for the child's cultural identity language and values, and finally a clause that mirrors Article 27 of the ICCPR in calling for children belong to minority groups to be allowed to practice their religion, enjoy their culture, and use their language. Turkey has reserved the right to interpret and apply certain provisions of this treaty in accordance with the "letter and the spirit of the Constitution of the Republic of Turkey and those of the Treaty of Lausanne of 24 July 1923" (Declarations and Reservations to the Convention on the Rights of the Child, n.d.). This, of course, effectively removes any protections this convention could have offered Kurdish children, as Turkey interprets the minority protection provided by Treaty of Lausanne as applicable only to non-Muslim minorities.

Most recently, Turkey has signed and ratified the UN Convention on the Elimination of All Forms of Racial Discrimination. Although this is a general human rights treaty, it has some impact on language rights. In addition to requiring the elimination of racially discriminatory practices, the Convention also insists that parties to the treaty ensure that all citizens have the right to freedom of expression and a right to education and training (Article 5(d)(viii) and Article 5(e)(v)). As a state party, Turkey is legally bound to ensure that all of its citizens, including the Kurds, enjoy these rights without discrimination.

Alongside the UN, regional organizations have also attempted to advance linguistic rights. European agreements involving human rights tend to go farther than those of the UN. Whereas the UN treaties that relate to language rights focus on noninterference, many of the European treaties require positive action by states parties.[3] Aside from bilateral agreements, which are too numerous to cover here, there are four main documents that outline significant language rights for individuals in Europe: Central European Initiative Instrument for the Protection of Minorities (1994); European Charter for Regional and Minority Languages (1992) (European Charter); Framework Convention for the Protection of National Minorities (1995) (Framework Convention); Document of the Copenhagen Meeting of the Conference on the Human Dimension of the Conference on Security and Cooperation in Europe (1990) (Copenhagen

Document 1990). These documents follow the same basic principles and require states parties to create conditions that would promote equality and guarantee that minorities can "preserve and develop their ethnic, cultural, linguistic identity" (Central European Instrument for the Protection of Minority Rights, Article 4; Document of the Copenhagen Meeting of the CSCE, 1990, Article 31). In addition to freedom of expression and freedom from discrimination, all four documents include the right to education in one's mother tongue and minorities' right to establish their own institutions, including schools. They require positive action by states parties in three areas: the promotion of equality, the provision of education, and governmental administrative services. The European Charter and the Framework Convention further emphasize positive action in the areas of creating equality, providing education and administrative services in less commonly used languages. The Republic of Turkey, however, has declined to sign both the European Charter for Regional and Minority Languages and the Framework Convention for the Protection of National Minorities, nor is it a party to the CEI Instrument. While Turkey is a member of the Organization for Security and Cooperation in Europe, the Copenhagen Document is not binding and therefore Turkey is not obligated to ensure the rights provided in that document. With the acceptance of Turkey as an official candidate for the EU, however, these instruments may take on added significance and increase the pressure on Turkey.

Turkey has also refused to sign the UN Convention against Discrimination in Education (1960) which allows, among other things, "the establishment or maintenance, for religious or linguistic reasons, of separate educational systems or institutions offering an education which is in keeping with the wishes of the pupil's parents or legal guardians" (Article 2b). Aside from the non-Muslim minorities protected by the Treaty of Lausanne, the Republic of Turkey has made it very clear that it will not allow for the establishment of a separate school system, private or otherwise, for its Kurdish citizens.

Given the nature of the treaties Turkey has ratified and the reservations it has placed on them, Turkey's legal responsibility regarding the language rights of its Kurdish citizens is one of noninterference. Turkey currently has no positive duty to provide education in Kurdish or to extend government services in Kurdish. However, the lack of state-sponsored education may give rise to a claim of discrimination, especially given the number of Kurds currently living in Turkey. The only principles the Republic of Turkey is bound to uphold under international law are those of nondiscrimination and freedom of expression. This means that Turkey cannot prohibit the use of Kurdish; nor can it ban publications or broadcasts in Kurdish. All of these fall under the protection of freedom of expression and nondiscrimination. Certainly, the state can regulate and require permits and licenses to publish and broadcast, but it cannot formulate licensing policies on the basis of language requirements. Though legally Turkey is only bound to a position of noninterference, and this may seem to offer minimal protections, they are not, in fact, insignificant. Even guaranteeing these basic rights would be a major break with past policies of the Republic.

Conclusion

Despite Turkey's obligations under international law to respect the language rights of its Kurdish citizens and the many reforms undertaken by the government in recent years, resistance to the Kurdish movement and the Kurdish language remains strong. At the same time, the prospects for the language rights of Kurds living in the Republic of Turkey are brighter than they have been in recent memory. The changes the Turkish government made in 2002 and 2003 indicate a softening of the once strict opposition to using Kurdish in any context or medium. Unfortunately, many of the reforms that have been made were passed as a direct result of pressure applied by the EU. The EU made it clear that in order for Turkey to proceed to the candidate status, it would have to change its approach to the Kurds, including legalizing all aspects of the Kurdish language. While there is little doubt that the changes that have been made are substantial in and of themselves, they do not represent any kind of real change in attitude, on the part of the state or the people, toward the Kurds.

The main source of the resistance to the Kurdish movement seems to stem from two intertwined concepts: the indivisibility of Turkey as both a state and a nation, and the Turkish national identity as one that supersedes all others. Article 3 of the Turkish Constitution proclaims, "The Turkish state, with its territory and nation, is an indivisible entity. Its language is Turkish." Underscoring the seriousness of the state's commitment to this ideal, the Constitution also states that this section cannot be amended nor can amendments be proposed (Article 4). While provisions to protect the territorial integrity of a nation-state are common and recognized within international law, the idea of an indivisible nation is more problematic, in part because, as Barkey and Fuller point out, this position creates the impression that Turkey is a "unitary state with a uniform national identity" (1998, 133). Although Turkey is a country populated by many different peoples representing a multitude of nationalities, the Turkish national identity essentially subsumes all others. As Yeğen argues, "the Constitution and exclusion of Kurdish identity were intrinsically related to the project of transforming an a-national, de-central, and disintegrated political, administrative and economic space into a national, central and integrated one" (1996, 226). This belief still holds that recognition of any other identity proves a direct challenge to not only to the unity of the state but to the nation's identity as solely Turkish. Baskın Oran, in Chapter 3 of this volume, describes this collective fear of disintegration as the "Sèvres syndrome." Largely as a result of this fear, the state has, at times, forcibly defined that national identity as solely Turkish.

One of the most important tools that have been used to reinforce these ideas is language, and that the primary language of Turkish citizens is Turkish. Article 42 of the Constitution still states that, "No language other than Turkish shall be taught as a mother tongue to Turkish citizens at any institutions of training or education." Once again any recognition of languages other than Turkish as the mother tongue of Turks is taken a direct challenge both to the idea of state unity and the nation's identity as Turkish. Although Kurdish may now be used in broadcasting and taught in private courses, neither must be seen as presenting a challenge to the unity of the state and nation.

In many ways, full recognition of the Kurds and the Kurdish language requires a reformulation of the understanding of what it means to be Turkish as well as rethinking the idea of the Turkish nation-state. These involve deep-rooted ideas that extend into each and every apparatus of the Turkish state and nation and will not change easily or quickly. At this point, the Turkish government has shown no desire to even begin to discuss, let alone dismantle, this ideology. What may, however, prove interesting is the recent (re)emergence of the idea of "being" European. Now that Turkey has been accepted as a candidate for the EU, the idea of belonging to Europe and what that may mean for Turkish identity represents a potentially interesting turn in the discussion. Can one be Turkish and European at the same time, or Turkish, Kurdish, and European? Will there come a time when the dominant identity is neither Kurdish nor Turkish but European? Or will we once again see the fear of disintegration take hold and the Turkish state demand the exclusive allegiance of all its citizens?

Turkey is at the beginning of a long process that may lead either to the extension of further language rights or to a return to the repressive policies of the past. Perhaps if the changes made can be implemented with few problems, the Turkish government and the military will realize that language rights for the Kurds do not have to constitute a threat but instead represent an integral part of a democratic, multicultural society. If the current situation holds, this may allow for the removal of reservations placed on Article 27 of the ICCPR but Turkey also needs to remove the reservations on the Convention on the Rights of the Child. This would go a long way toward ensuring full freedom of expression for Kurds.

After the basic language rights of the Kurds are protected and some measure of good will and trust have been established between the state officials and Kurdish citizens, further rights of education in Kurdish can be addressed. In the near future, Turkey should also accord the same educational rights to the Kurds that are currently enjoyed by non-Muslim minorities. Even more importantly, if and only if the basic human rights, including language rights, of the Kurds are respected, will Turkey witness the full integration, rather than the assimilation, of Kurds into the Turkish society. It is only on a basis of respect for the human rights of all its citizens that Turkey can hope to move forward in peace and security.

Chapter 6

Freedom of Religion: Secularist Policies and Islamic Challenges

ÖZLEM DENLİ

The Justice and Development Party (Adalet ve Kalkınma Partisi, AKP), led by a splinter fraction of the Islamic-oriented Welfare Party (Refah Partisi, RP), emerged with a sweeping victory from the parliamentary elections held on 3 November 2002. The AKP government committed formidably to the goal of full membership in the European Union, and displayed political will to enact constitutional and legal reforms in order to harmonize the Turkish legal system with the Copenhagen criteria, stipulating a well-established human rights regime.

This development is just one striking example of the drastic changes the Turkish political scene has been going through since the 1990s. An important variation has been the entry of the language of human rights and individual freedoms into the political language. Various Islamic movements and organizations are no exception to this trend.

Basic institutions and decision-making procedures in a constitutional democracy must be acceptable on premises internal to different kinds of political, moral, and religious views existing in that society. The political and cultural leverage that Islam has acquired in Turkish society since 1980s adds to the importance of deriving normative support for human rights from within an Islamic frame.

This chapter discusses various consequences that the official policy of secularism has generated, regarding the freedom of religion and belief, and examines the Islamic "rights language" that has emerged in relation and contrast to the official position and application. More specifically, I attempt to fulfill a twofold purpose: (1) to examine the major turning points in the development of the existing human rights regime and explore the legal framework and basic policies of secularism; (2) to provide a brief review of an individual Islamic approach that disputes the official stance, and exemplifies an internal transformation toward principled accommodation of religious liberty through a reinterpretation of Islamic concepts and values.

Here, I have to note that what I refer to as Islamic discourse and Islamism in the framework of this study is an exclusively Sunni phenomenon.

Alevis largely left behind organizational strategies based on religion after the establishment of the Turkish Republic (Aktay 2000, 67). Even though Alevis are also diverse in terms of religious beliefs and interpretations, they have largely adopted a secular public-political discourse and formulated their rights demands therein.

Religious Liberty as a Human Right

The freedom of religion and belief is regarded as among the pillars of modern pluralism, protected as a fundamental principle by international human rights instruments. Article 18 of the Universal Declaration of Human Rights (UDHR) establishes the principle of the freedom of religion or belief and lists the specific aspects intrinsic to the enjoyment of the liberty in question. Article 18 reads: "Everyone has the right to freedom of thought, conscience and religion, this right includes freedom to change his religion or belief, and freedom, either alone or in community with others and in public or in private, to manifest his religion or belief in teaching, practice, worship and observance."[1]

Putting human rights issues into practice often involves conflicts of varying degrees, and the principle of nondiscrimination demands that these divergent claims are dealt with equitably in specific instances.[2] Since the demands of various religions differ substantially, the nondiscrimination principle requires sensitivity to these differences (Krishnaswami 1998, 17). The institutional setting should assure the equal enjoyment of the freedom of religion or belief, and no group of individuals, who can be defined in terms of criteria salient to religion or belief, should be put into a position of systematic disadvantage.

The internationally negotiated and accepted norms are designated to accommodate diverse cultural and religious contexts. Thus, the key human rights documents do not prescribe any particular juridical relationship between the state and religious institutions; they allow the state parties to implement the norms by using different institutional arrangements.

In Turkey, the broad principle of secularism has framed the scope of rights in relation to the freedom of religion or belief. The following section provides a broad delineation of the secularization process in the Ottoman-Turkish society and official policies of the Republic of Turkey on religion.

A Brief History of Secularization in Turkey

THE OTTOMAN LEGACY

Although it was a major Islamic empire, the Ottoman Empire was not a theocracy. The political and moral legitimacy of the Ottoman state was based on its ability to assure the autonomy and difference of each millet (religious community). Confronted with the challenge of holding together a multiethnic and multireligious empire, the Ottoman rulers were compelled to develop a body of public law that was not derived from the Islamic law (Turan 1991, 33). Public law was enforced as the law of the land and consisted of the decrees by the dynastic ruler, whereas the Islamic law applied to mainly personal status law and transactions within the Muslim community. The Ottoman government established effective control over the ulema by turning them into state functionaries (Mardin 1995, 118).[3] The jurists who coded and interpreted the Islamic law loosely organized themselves into schools of jurisprudence, but they developed no hierarchies comparable to, for instance, that of the Catholic Church. Partially due to the fact that the Muslim community was not a political unit, the political institutions had the capacity to control the religious one (Berkes 1997, 17).

The state furnished the setting for the application of the Islamic law and privileged Sunni Islam vis-à-vis other religions and different sects of Islam within the Ottoman territories. Consequently, the polity conferred as much legitimacy upon religion as religion did upon the polity. Sunni Islam relied on its position as state religion to secure prevalence over the heterodox cults, sects, mystical orders, and the Shia Islam (Turan 1991, 41). Ottoman bureaucrats, who were trained in the palace system, rather than in the religious schools, had a definite view of the interrelation of politics and religion. Şerif Mardin describes it as the primacy of *raison d'état*: "The Ottoman bureaucrat saw the viability of the state as essential for the preservation of religion: since the state was necessary to keep religion flourishing, it had priority over religion" (1989, 139).

The Ottoman administrative practice was strongly marked by this bias. Because of the primacy assigned to the state, Ottoman bureaucrats reacted fiercely against any religious influence that could pose a challenge to the central authority. Religious heterodoxy was tolerated as long as it posed no threat to the political establishment. Every organization and institution was constrained by the duty to protect the state, which, in turn, acted in the name of the sacred (Berkes 1997, 18).

MODERNIZATION, WESTERNIZATION, AND SECULARIZATION

The process of secularization in the Ottoman Empire was initiated by the ruling elite in the 1800s. However, since the ruling elite tried to achieve transformation within the confines of the existing sources and language of legitimization, the reforms in the nineteenth century created a duality at the heart of the judicial and educational institutions, where the old existed side by side with the new (Mardin 1994, 45).

The most important turning point in the process of secularization of the Ottoman-Turkish society was, no doubt, the establishment of the Turkish Republic. The founding of a new nation-state, led by a splinter fraction of the old ruling class, required a rapid break with the old basis of legitimacy. Kemalist reformism concentrated its efforts on defining a political system that would be free of religious and dynastic legitimization and, therefore, constituted the Republic on a secularist-nationalist basis (Keyder 1987, 86). Immediately after the establishment of the Republic, the Kemalist cadres commenced a program to eliminate the institutional structures of religion in the society. The caliphate and Islamic courts were abolished, tombs and shrines were closed, and mystical orders were banned. The traditional institutions of religious education were closed down, and all education was brought under the supervision of the Ministry of National Education.

Niyazi Berkes argues that religious institutions, represented in Turkey by the term "Şeriat," were gradually but steadily abolished and the term was finally limited to the innermost core, namely the legal relations clustering around family. Accordingly, the decisive moment was the secularization of the civil law, which represented the fall of the legal dimension of a structure, the traditional and temporal basis of which was already abolished (Berkes 1998a, 467). In 1926, the new Civil Code adopted from the Swiss Civil Code, was legislated by the National Assembly (470). Berkes writes: "the aim of the makers of the code was not to establish and regulate the civil relations of the people according to the existing customs and mores, or religious provisions. On the contrary, it was to shape these relations according to what the makers of the code believed they should be" (471). The cultural transformation and modernization were pursued through a series of reforms. Imams, *hocas*, and preachers were permitted to wear clerical garb only while performing their duties. In 1925, the so-called Hat Law outlawed the traditional head garments for men in favor of the Western hat, though no comparable policies were implemented for women. The Latin script was adopted in 1928, and the use of the Arabic script in all public affairs was prohibited. Again in 1928, the teaching of Arabic and Persian was removed from the school curricula. Instructions on religion were dropped from the urban and village school curricula in 1930 and 1933 respectively. A law passed in 1934 prohibited the use of religious titles such as *hacı*, *hafız*, and *molla* as official titles (466–77).

In 1928, Islam was disestablished as the state religion, and in 1937 the principle of laicism became an integral part of the Turkish Constitution. The Kemalist laicism did not "separate" the religion and state. The Turkish Republic followed the Ottoman tradition of incorporating the religious establishment into the administrative apparatus. Two state institutions were created to control the religious domain: the Directorate of Religious

Affairs (Diyânet İşleri Başkanlığı); and the Directorate of Pious Foundations (Evkaf). The Directorate of Religious Affairs was established to oversee all religious practices; the Evkaf administered religious endowments and maintenance of mosques. After 1931, it assumed the administration of cleric remuneration (A. Davison 1998, 139).

The head of the Directorate of Religious Affairs was appointed by the president, on the recommendation of the prime minister. Attached to the office of the prime minister, this directorate's functions included:

the dispatch of all cases concerning the Exalted Islamic Faith which relate to beliefs [itikad] and rituals [ibadet]. These included the administration of all mosques . . . and of dervish houses . . . and the appointment and dismissal of all imams, hatibs [orators], vaizs [preachers], şeyhs [leaders of dervish houses], müezzins [callers to prayers], kayyıms [sextons] and all other employees of a religious character . . . entailed responsibility for distributing "model" sermons [hutbe] and translating, editing, and publishing authentic religious works for the public. (A. Davison 1998, 39)

Laicism, as understood by the republican elite, meant not only state dominance and control of religious institutions, but also implied regulating the lived Islamic tradition and expressions of popular religiosity (Sarıbay 1995, 59–61). The directorate has attempted to fulfill its mission by subscribing to and promoting a particular school of Sunni Islam, the Hanafi Medhab.

Despite the imposed restrictions, religion was never meant to be completely eliminated in the official discourse of national identity. The majority of the republican cadres viewed religion as something to be modernized and reformed, not as a mere anachronism. Considering the Protestant movement and the Reformation as milestones central to the modernization of Europe, they implemented Lutheran-inspired reforms. Translation of the Qur'an into Turkish, changing the language of the call for prayers from Arabic to Turkish, researching the possibility of an Islamic work ethic, can be listed among the state effort to create a national religion, which in turn could serve as the basis of public morality (Mardin 1995).

These rigid and restrictive policies of the state encountered resistance among the population. The Sheik Said revolt in the eastern Turkey, lead by a prominent Nakşibendi leader, was not only the most noteworthy of the sporadic reactions that took place at that time, but, with its dual nature, expressed a multidimensional opposition to the nationalist project. While the leadership of the revolt was motivated by the desire for an autonomous or even independent Kurdistan, the rank and file acted from religious motives, demanding the restoration of the holy law and the caliphate (Zürcher 1993, 178). The government took strong measures, which included the closing of Nakşibendi and all other sufi orders (tarikat), as well as forbidding all sufi activities.

The regime's repressive attitude toward religion during the 1930s and 1940s was relaxed in the cultural, if not the political, realm of policies; after the introduction of multiparty politics, both major parties started to court the Muslim vote. The ruling Republican People's Party (Cumhuriyet Halk Partisi, CHP) itself changed its course after the party congress in 1947, reintroducing elective courses on religious education in schools, establishing the Faculty of Divinity, and allowing rituals at tombs and shrines, starting in 1949. At the same time, the CHP tried to guard against any religious reaction in politics, by enacting Article 163 of the Penal Code, which strictly prohibited propaganda against the secular character of the state (Zürcher 1993, 244).

The Democrat Party (Demokrat Parti, DP), which came to power in 1950, continued with the policies of moderation. The prayer call in Arabic was made legal again, religious education was expanded, and the number of preacher schools was increased. Consequently, there was a marked increase in the building of mosques, and the sale of religious literature was allowed again. Although the DP's understanding of the secularist character of the state was not radically different from that of the CHP, a significant divergence was the fact that the DP accepted the existence of autonomous religious organizations, such as the brotherhoods, and even legitimized them by accepting the support of the Nurcu movement in the 1954 and 1957 elections (Zürcher 1993, 244).

The DP government was criticized heavily, by the Committee of National Unity (Milli Birlik Komitesi, MBK) leadership, for using religion for the purposes of a political agenda. The party was ousted with the military coup in 1960, yet there was no return to the strict policies of the early years of the Republic. Geyikdağı (1984) argues that most members of the MBK wanted to make Islam a national instrument of the state, in order to prevent its manipulation by conservative interest groups and political parties. Efforts were made to cut the ground from under the feet of Islamist currents by increased attention to the building of mosques and the restoration of shrines and to religious education in schools. They tried to propagate a modern, rationalist version of Islam. The curriculum of the colleges for preachers was changed to include sociology, economy, and law. The Directorate for Religious Affairs started publication of "enlightened" sermons, and the Qur'an was published in Turkish translation. At the same time, the military, similar to İnönü's government after the war, guarded itself against the emergence of religious rivals; it maintained the prohibition of the political use of religion, which had been incorporated into the High Treason Law in 1925 and into the Penal Code in 1949, now as an article in the new Constitution introduced in 1961 (Geyikdağı 1984, 89).

The Kemalist notion of secularism prevailed throughout 1960s and

1970s. In 1970, Necmettin Erbakan left the center-right Justice Party (Adalet Partisi, AP) and formed the National Order Party (Milli Nizam Partisi, MNP), which had an Islamic orientation. The MNP was banned and resolved after the military coup of 1971 but reemerged in 1972 as the National Salvation Party (Milli Selamet Partisi, MSP). In the elections of 1973, the MSP got 48 seats in the National Assembly. Geyikdağı states, "This was the first time in the history of the Republic that a pro-Islamic party, campaigning with pro-Islamic slogans and, along with a socioeconomic and welfare program, came to occupy a relatively important position in the parliament" (1984, 105). Nonetheless, far from being perceived as an extremist party that can pose a threat to the secular foundations of the state, the MSP formed a coalition government with the secularist CHP.

During the late 1970s, the MSP also took part in two right-wing coalition governments; the first and second Nationalist Front (Milliyetçi Cephe, MC) governments, established in 1974 and 1977, respectively. Milliyetçi Cephe governments allowed the graduates of the imam-hatip schools (secondary schools to train imams) to pursue university education. At the same time, the elective courses on religion, offered at academic schools, were allowed to be taught only by the graduates of the Higher Islamic Institutes (Yüksek İslam Enstitüsü) (Geyikdağı 1984, 109).

THE MILITARY COUP OF 1980 AND ONWARD

Religious groups and parties were present and active throughout the 1960s and 1970s, despite some restrictions. However, Islamist groups emerged as a major challenge to the state monopoly and the laic foundation of the state only after the 1980 coup, which was paradoxically carried out by the historically secularist armed forces.

Alarmed by heightened political polarization and the prevailing radical left-wing discourse of the 1970s, the military leaders commenced a policy of depoliticization, which relied on the supposedly stabilizing function of a "religious culture" (Ahmad 1994a, 219). As argued by Faruk Birtek and Binnaz Toprak, "The idea of the Islamic *ummah*, a community of believers who are united by the same faith, seems to have set the model for a new sense of community which can consolidate social unity and solidarity and thereby eliminate the conflicts of opposing ideologies" (1993, 195).

The state's investment in promoting and controlling religion increased substantially. The number of the imam-hatip schools increased sharply from 258 to 350 during the three-year military rule. The number of students attending those schools rose dramatically to 270,000. There was also an increase in the number of the lower-grade Quranic schools; before 1980, there were 2,610 such schools, but their number reached 4,715 by

1989 (Ahmad, 1994a, 219–21). In 1982, the military government made religious instruction a part of the required curriculum in all primary and secondary schools—except for the schools of non-Muslim minorities.[4] Obligatory religious instruction took a confessional attitude and became synonymous with teaching Sunni Islam.

The aim of the military, certainly, was not to provoke Islamization of the political and legal institutions. The Constitution of 1982 reiterated the provisions safeguarding the secular character of the state. Furthermore, it accorded special protection to the eight "Principal Reform Laws" (Özbudun 1996, 31) enacted under Atatürk's leadership and embodied the principles of Kemalist laicism: establishing secular education; instituting civil marriage; adopting the Turkish alphabet; using the international numerals; introducing the Western hat; closing the dervish convents; abolishing religious titles; and prohibiting the wearing of certain garments. The central measure protecting the secular character of the state, namely the constitutional provision banning the use of religion for political purposes,[5] was copied directly from the Constitution of 1961.[6]

The same period was also marked by the controversy over wearing head covers by university students and by primary and secondary school teachers, and the universities became the crux of the conflict. In 1982, a directive issued by the Council of Higher Education prohibited students from wearing head covers while attending classes. The decision and its implementation, which meant interruption of the education of the "pious Muslim" students, caused widespread protest actions and political mobilization. Moreover, Islamist parties and their followers have become subject to intimidation and prosecution. The Welfare Party and its subsequent reincarnations under different names were closed down by the order of the Constitutional Court.

The seemingly contradictory policies of the state, promoting Islamic education while restricting its public manifestations, actually illustrate the state's continuous manipulation of the religion. The main intention underlying the official policy was to elicit the Islamic loyalties of the population for political stability under an authoritarian institutionalization. According to this "religiously based moral authoritarianism," the nation came to be understood as a homogenous unit based on a synthesis of the family, the mosque, and the barracks (Birtek and Toprak 1993, 193).

IMPLICATIONS IN TERMS OF THE FAIR ENJOYMENT OF RELIGIOUS LIBERTY

Accommodation of cultural diversity and the equal enjoyment of the freedom of religion or belief in modern societies typically involve a separation of religion and the state. Indeed, constitutional democracies are expected to refrain from establishing or promoting any particular religion; they are expected to allow persons to be free in their private lives to espouse or reject religion. Referring to this democratic norm, Robert Audi proposes three guiding principles (Audi and Wolterstorff 1997):

1. The libertarian principle saying that the state must permit the practice of any religion, though within certain limits.[7]
2. The egalitarian principle dictating that states may not give preference to one religion over another. This principle not only rules out an established church—the existence of which might be arguably consistent with the libertarian principle—but also precludes such things as legally requiring a certain religious affiliation as a condition for public office.
3. The neutrality principle stating that the state should not favor or disfavor religion as such. That is, the state cannot give positive or negative preference to institutions or persons just because they are religious.

The third item on the list is, admittedly, the more controversial and less acknowledged of Audi's principles. Its rational is based on the idea that religious liberty, broadly conceived, includes the freedom to reject religious views. If the state shows preference for religious institutions, or for the practice of religion in general, there may be pressure to adopt a religion, or even discrimination against those who do not. Governmental preference for the religious as such is intrinsically unequal treatment of the religious and the nonreligious.

An alternative view is presented by Richard Kraut (1999), who claims that the position of neutrality provides too weak a foundation for the kind of free and diverse society we would all like to live in. Kraut's alternative conception allows the state to take special measures to insure that those religious institutions or practices not be threatened or weakened. In this case the state recognizes that religious institutions play a central role in the way the good is conceived by many citizens. In protecting and helping these institutions, the state is partisan to a widely held conception of the good. These broad political and economic regulations can, nonetheless, be compatible with the principle of equal treatment and concern. In these instances public authorities do not support one religion/sect over another but acknowledge that religion may be significant for most members of the society and play an organizing role for many citizens in their efforts to lead meaningful lives. The state places all religions in a special category and takes special measures to insure availability of general means that enable meaningful enjoyment of the freedom of religion or belief (Kraut 1999, 315–32).

Putting this relatively controversial stance on the *neutrality principle* in parentheses, we can try to evaluate the Turkish policies in terms of the other two principles: the *libertarian principle* and the *equalitarian principle*.

1. The *libertarian principle*. Official policies on religion nominally permit the practice of any religion within the limits of protecting basic human rights. Yet, not just non-Muslim minorities and non-Sunni sects of Islam, but the Sunni creed as well suffer from limitations on the right to manifest one's religion or belief. Non-Muslims encounter numerous official difficulties in maintaining their temples, educating religious functionaries and providing religious literature (see Oran and Yannas, Chapters 3 and 4, in this volume). Alevis face similar difficulties regarding building *cemevi*. On some occasion Alevis have even been coerced to build mosques in their villages (Tanör 1994, 47). Also the widely contested ban on the use of head covers at universities can be listed among examples of the violation of this principle.

2. The *equalitarian principle*. The Republic of Turkey followed the Ottoman tradition of "the political domination of the spiritual" by coopting the Islamic religious establishment into the state and asserting state control over religious activities. As had been the case in the Ottoman Empire, Islam meant solely Sunni Islam. İlter Turan writes: "What was built was a political community of Turks who were also Muslims. Islam did not legitimize the regime, nor was it necessarily the appropriate ideology on which to base political action, yet one's claim to membership in the political community, in behavioral terms, was validated by the possession of Islamic credentials" (1991, 40).

The Lausanne Peace Treaty of 1923 guaranteed the freedom of religion and equal protection by law for the non-Muslim citizens of Turkey. Similarly, Article 88 of the 1924 Constitution stipulated, "The People of Turkey, regardless of religion and race, are Turks in regards to citizenship." In practice, however, certain citizenship rights have not been available for non-Muslim citizens of Turkey, in spite of the principle of secularism that has been part of the Constitution for more than sixty years.[8]

While state funding and support conferred legitimacy upon the Sunni creed, this was achieved not only at the expense of other religions and other Islamic sects but also by the delegitimization of the alternative interpretation of Sunni Islam by autonomous actors. Public resources are used to promote Sunni teaching by sponsoring the imam-hatip schools, Qur'an courses, emissions on state radio and TV, and ultimately by initiating compulsory religious education in the 1980s. The substantial number of Alevis and followers of other Shia sects, are denied access to similar resources (Tanör 1994, 47).

Thus, far from honoring the egalitarian principle, official secularist policies in Turkey are inherently biased, exclusionist, and discriminatory.

THE EU MEMBERSHIP PROCESS

Turkey's candidacy for membership to the European Community was confirmed in the Helsinki Summit of 1999. In the Copenhagen Summit of 2002 Turkey was given date of December 2004, and signed a protocol with the EU that specified the steps it needed to fulfill the Copenhagen criteria. Political standards stipulated by the Copenhagen criteria require that the candidate country have a consolidated democracy, rule of law, and a well-established human rights regime.

Since 1999 Turkey adopted constitutional reforms and altogether eight comprehensive reform packages instituting improvements regarding the protection of fundamental rights and liberties, primarily in the areas of freedom of religion and conscience, freedom of expression, and freedom of association. Özbudun notes that all in all, more than one-third of the original text of the Constitution was amended in the process (Özbudun and Yazıcı).

Turkey also acceded to a significant number of international human rights instruments, both within the UN framework and within the framework of the Council of Europe. Moreover, a constitutional amendment has established the supremacy of international agreements in the area of fundamental freedoms over internal legislation (*2004 Regular Report on Turkey's Progress*, 29). Prior to these developments, Turkey had already recognized the right to individual application to the European Commission of Human Rights in 1987, and accepted the binding judicial competence of the European Court of Human Rights in 1989 (Özbudun and Yazıcı, 25).

The first reform package passed in 2002 amended Article 312 of the Penal Code, declaring incitement to hatred on the basis of the differences of social class, race, religion, sect, and region. With the amendment, only the expressions that may create danger for public order would constitute a criminal offense (Özbudun and Yazıcı, 19). No amendments were made to Article 24 governing the freedom of religion and conscience. But the third reform laws package, which went into force on 9 August 2002, recognized the right of community foundations (meaning non-Muslim foundations) to own immovable properties and to dispose of them freely.[9] The sixth reform package, which went into force on 19 July 2003, recognized the right of non-Muslim communities to build places of worship subject to the approval of the competent administrative authorities (Özbudun and Yazıcı, 9).

On the other hand, the European Commission's 2004 accession report on Turkey observes, "As far as the situation of non-Sunni Muslim minorities is concerned, there has been no change in their status. Alevis are not officially recognized as a religious community, they often experience difficulties in opening places of worship and compulsory religious instruction in schools fails to acknowledge non-Sunni identities. The parents of an Alevi child have a case regarding compulsory religious education pending before the ECHR" (*2004 Regular Report on Turkey's Progress*, 44).

Nevertheless, Alevis present diverse views in regard to the state's rate. While some criticize the exclusion of Alevis from the institutional structure of the Diractorate of Religious Affairs (Diyânet İşleri Başkanlığı), many other Alevis "claim that as a secular state Turkey should treat all religions equally and should not directly support one particular religion (the Sunnis) as it currently does through the *Diyânet*" (*2004 Regular Report on Turkey's Progress*, 45).

As to the religious freedom of Sunnis, the single most important issue seems to be removing the ban on head covers at universities and for state employees. Yet, some Sunni groups and intellectuals also hold that an institution like Diyânet İşleri is in violation of the freedom of religion and belief.

All in all, legal reforms enacted to this day introduce significant yet inadequate improvements in the area of religious liberty, and Islamic criticisms as well as demands are formulated largely with reference to concepts such as pluralism, cultural heterogeneity, civil society, and human rights. Turkey's participation in international human rights regimes, including the individual's right to take a case to the European Court of Human Rights, facilitated the employment of human rights terminology as an intrinsic part of the political vocabulary and public debate. The incorporation of rights language into Islamic discourses constitutes an ideological rupture.

Levent Köker (1995, 227) argues that the nation-building secularist intellectuals in Turkey have enhanced the hold of the state over social dynamics and produced an authoritarian concept of national culture that emphasized unity and solidarity. The definition of "nation" reflected a desire for cultural homogeneity and was construed within the grid of a community unified in the singularity of its moral tradition. The Kemalist conception of national sovereignty claimed to represent the genuine feelings and desires of the nation but had little tolerance for cultural, religious, or linguistic plurality and divergence. The "general interest" was deemed to be grasped by the elite fathoming the "real" consciousness of the people (Heper 1985, 50).

In the 1980s, with their newly acquired political and cultural leverage, it was the Islamist movements that claimed to represent "the deeper and cherished" values of people. This was done by criticizing the direction of state intervention, but without problematizing the act of intervention itself. They challenged the official view of "national unity" by creating a binary conflict between an essentially Muslim community and a secular state. Yet, they too failed to acknowledge the diversity within the Turkish society.

Therefore, the transformation of Islamism and, in a broader sense, Islamic views and expressions in the 1990s and in the new millennium pose a fundamental question: are these human rights-based arguments grounded in actors' fundamental values, or do they derive their urgency from short-term political interests?

Similar questions are raised for the AKP government and its orientation towards the EU. Kalaycıoğlu (n.d.) states that in the past not all AKP deputies were in favor of the EU and the party is led by a leader and elites who shared immaculate Sunni Islamist credentials and notes that "some critics argue that the main goal of AKP will be to push through legislation that cohere with the previous careers of the party elite in the National Vision (Milli Görüş) movement. Hence, the reform packages will be motioned and legitimated on the grounds of rendering the Turkish democracy more liberal, yet their main and "hidden" objective will be to liberate the forces of the Islamist movement in Turkish politics and society" (Kalaycıoğlu, 12).

Still, the fact remains that Islamists have entered the political forum with human rights demands and employed the human rights terminology to justify and clarify their positions.[10] In the next section I will briefly delineate a line of reasoning that shows the internal transformation of Islamic positions toward internalizing human rights values through novel interpretations of Islamic concepts sources. My aim here is not to argue that this is a generalizable line of thought, but to demonstrate that genuine normative justification of fundamental human rights principles within Islamic discourses is indeed possible.

State, Society, and the Individual: Islam as a Religion of Community

According to the opinion widely held among Islamists, the Turkish state constructs and propagates an "official Islam" in line with its political imperatives, and restructures Islam's internal premises to fit a secularist-republican agenda (Canatan 1997, 18). Islam, which has a comprehensive meaning in Muslims' lives,[11] is fragmented and its precepts on social order and religious practice are placed under the jurisdiction of the state and the Directorate of Religious Affairs, respectively (Canatan 1997, 20–21).

This particular vein of Islamic critique not only questions the state control on the religious establishment but also rejects the notion of having a dominating official doctrine, secular or religious. This approach is significant for affirming Islam's internal plurality, seeing diversity as endemic in its lived tradition, and accepting that fundamental sources of Islam can be interpreted differently. The pluralistic vision of the social realm underlying the position briefly delineated here is based on a gap posited between the divine will and the acquired knowledge of it.[12] The argument is as follows. The divine will reveals itself in the world of phenomena in a plurality of ways and there is a disparity between the divine essence of the revelation and the human acquisition of it. The divine will is always the co-presence of all its elements. Therefore, the essence behind complex appearance cannot be inferred from the knowledge of its worldly expressions, which is bound to be relative and partial. Consequently, what is divine cannot be reduced to the products of human effort (Bulaç 1993a, 41–42; 1993b, 50). The immediate conclusion drawn is that there cannot be a single methodology that would legitimately bring out a single interpretation. Human acquisitions of the divine will cannot be monopolized by elite or placed at the disposal of a political authority. The quest for a single "true" reading can easily be a hostage to the political authority that aims at promoting a particular Islamic interpretation for its own purposes.

In this approach, Islam is treated as the religion of a community, not as the religion promoted and controlled by the state, since the divine will resides in the *ummah*, and the political authority must be organized in a way that would avoid official orthodoxy but allow the plurality, which stems from the lived traditions of the community (Canatan 1994).

An important aspect of this pluralist vision is abandoning the political aim of forming an Islamic state and disengaging the individual salvation from the issue of statehood. This position is supported by the claim that Islam does not authorize the duty of establishing an Islamic state, and the fundamental sources of Islam do not furnish political models that can be implemented universally. Political authority is not a sacred instance but a mode of organizing the coexistence of Muslims, as well as that of Muslims and non-Muslims, in a way congenial to Islamic principles. In summary, Islam provides no legal and institutional closure, and its basic tenets can be implemented in a variety of institutional settings.[13] The legitimating basis for government is declared as not theological or metaphysical but functional and political. In this respect, Islamists in question find it more appropriate to talk about "the state of a Muslim society" instead of an "Islamic state."

Limiting the intervention capacity of the modern state into the life of communities and the individual seems to be a supporting aim. Köktaş notes that "if there is such thing as an Islamic form of government, it is the minimum government" (1995, 48). Thus, the pluralist view presents an immanent critique of the overarching political institutions in Turkey and calls for a system that enables dynamic and community-shaped religious life for every religion or belief.

A critical question here is the extent to which the modern principles of freedom and equality are accommodated in this pluralistic vision. As formulated in Article 1 of the UDHR, the very idea of human rights is founded on the "freedom and equal dignity" of all human beings, which is, in turn, translated into the idea of equal rights.

Some Islamist thinkers seem to be taking the idea of equal worth and moral capability of every human being for affirming or rejecting faith and related ways of life, as the starting point for appreciating the moral significance of equality in a more general sense.[14] This may prove to be a successful route toward accepting the individual as the primary rights holder, which, in turn, is essential for counteracting the communitarian tendencies so widespread among Islamists, for religious communities can be rather repressive entities.

For the time being, it is important to note that there is a growing tendency toward articulating liberal positions in Islam, which do not contradict fundamental modern values and can actually contribute to their endorsement.[15] I agree with A. E. Mayer in her assessment of the power the normative resources of Islam can have for accommodating religious pluralism, and for deriving support for human rights (1992, 133). This position does not imply that the Muslim mind responds solely to Islamic stimuli. Instead, it underscores the significance of transforming mentalities and enhancing the legitimacy of human rights in ways that are acceptable from Islamic points of view.

Conclusion

In this chapter, I have provided a brief outline of the historical relation between the state, society, and religion in Turkey, with an emphasis on official policies regarding religion since the founding of the Republic. Then I introduced few arguments exemplifying a pluralist Islamic approach to human rights, which employs the language of human rights in order to justify and support demands for religious freedom.

It seems that, informed by human rights questions, the rereading of Islamic texts and the normative sources of Islam to ponder concepts of diversity, pluralism, and social contract cannot only stand for the internal secularization of the discourse itself but can also contribute to the endorsement of a political morality that can be shared across religious, political, and other ideological divide.

Part II
Social and Economic Rights

Chapter 7
So Near, Yet So Far: Freedom of Association and Workers' Rights

EDWARD WEISBAND AND SERA ÖNER

Freedom of association and workers' rights in Turkey, like all other freedoms and rights, have been affected by the country's volatile politics, as well as its structural economic constraints. Tensions and contradictions have been paramount: between the need to promote social and economic rights, workers rights and freedom of association, on the one hand, and the desire to pursue rapid economic growth, on the other.

This chapter examines the development of workers' associational rights with an emphasis on the current legal and economic environment. Although workers in Turkey gained substantial legal rights after 1960, these rights have been subject to legal restrictions and workers have frequently encountered various forms of political repression. We contend that ineffective and unaccountable governments chastened by labor demonstrations and generally frightened by organized labor, in combination with the chronic weakness of Turkish labor unions in defending freedom of association rights, have contributed to the basic problem. In addition, neoliberal policies stressing strategies of privatization, pursued since the 1980s, have aggravated the structural obstacles to unionization and left some segments of the labor force, especially female workers, in vulnerable situations. The chapter acknowledges the considerable progress made in recent years with respect to workers' and trade unions' rights in Turkey, but it also reveals how much further the country must go toward full realization of workers' and freedom of association rights. Thus, it is a matter of "so near and yet so far."

Industrial Relations in Turkey: A Brief Overview

Starting in the late Ottoman era (Ahmad 1994b, 143), workers in Turkey have asserted their rights by engaging in organized collective actions whenever political conditions permitted. A rising sense of working-class

consciousness and attendant grievances prompted dock, postal, and rail-
way service workers to undertake spontaneous strike actions during much
of the late nineteenth century (Baydar 1998, 5). The Constitution of 1908
and the Young Turk government created new opportunities. In 1909, for
the first time, workers were allowed to celebrate May Day and to petition
employers. However, the Young Turk government remained restrictive
(Ahmad 1994b, 135). A new law, Tatil-i Eşgal Kanunu (the law on work
stoppage), adopted in 1909, did not ban unions but it prohibited requiring workers to strike and it prevented the establishment of unions in
workplaces that provided public services. Nevertheless, between 1919
and 1922, workers once again began to agitate on behalf of improved
working conditions (Baydar 1998, 5). This continued during the War of
Independence, when many workers sided with nationalist armies led by
Mustafa Kemal against the regime in İstanbul and the invading Greek
army (Ahmad 1994b, 134). Mustafa Kemal recognized the contribution
of organized workers in the national struggle by permitting them to participate in the 1923 İzmir Economic Congress (136).

The history of industrial relations in the Republic of Turkey can be
divided into four periods. During the first period (1923–45), no specific
legislation on industrial relations existed. The Law on the Maintenance
of Order (Takrir-i Sükun), which was passed on 4 March 1925, as a direct
response to Kurdish uprisings, however, represented a major blow to all
associational rights by restricting workers' ability to organize and carry
out collective action, including strikes. Employer-worker relations were
regulated within the scope of the Turkish Civil Code. This changed in
1936, in connection with industrialization (Koray 1992, 6), and as a result
of the promulgation of the first Turkish labor law that defined minimally
acceptable labor standards and working conditions and established the
basic industrial relations structure. The law did not ban trade unions but
prohibited strikes (Baydar 1998, 5). The first attempts to regulate Turkish industrial relations were modeled along the lines of European cor-
poratism. Corporatist patterns of industrial relations were created that
were suggestive of dirigisme, or intensive forms of state control over industrial, labor, and competitive policies. These encouraged paternalistic
forms of state intervention within the private sectors of the economy.
The Law on Associations, also adopted in 1936, prohibited the establishment of "class-based" organizations. This effectively limited the use
of rights granted by the labor law provisions.

The second period, started at the end of World War II, was characterized by the introduction of labor laws and practices reflective of slightly
greater political freedom. Until then, workers in Turkey had worked without trade unions to defend or promote their interests. In 1947, the ruling
Republican People's Party (Cumhuriyet Halk Partisi, CHP) passed the

Trade Union Act, which legally sanctioned the formation of trade or labor unions. However, the law also maintained restrictions on collective bargaining and the right to strike. This dual approach would also serve to color all future efforts to build democratic forms of industrial relations in Turkey: Unionization would be allowed to proceed, but only under strict state control (Koray 1992, 7). The opposition party, the Democrat Party (Demokrat Parti, DP), promised to legalize the right to strike. But once it attained power in 1950, it failed to implement promised concessions, in part, presumably, on account of Cold War fears and ideological concerns over the spread of communism. On the other hand, the DP somewhat encouraged the establishment of what came to be known as the Confederation of Turkish Labor Unions (Türkiye İşçi Sendikaları Konfederasyonu· TÜRK-İŞ). However, association rights continued to decline in the 1950s, and workers became increasingly restive. Ultimately, the military coup of 1960 and its martial law regime dominated all functioning trade unions and suppressed all expressions of freedom of association rights (Ahmad 1994b, 142).

The 1961 Constitution recognized workers' right to strike but lacked provisions on collective bargaining (Ahmad 1994b, 146–47). In 1963, however, the Labor Unions Act (no. 274) and the Collective Bargaining, Strikes, and Lockout Act (no. 275) came into force. These initiated the third period (1963–80), which allowed greatest labor freedoms to date and a proliferation of unions (Koray 1992, 7). In 1967, the Confederation of Revolutionary Workers' Trade Unions of Turkey (Devrimci İşçi Sendikaları Konfederasyonu, DİSK) was established by unions discontent with TÜRK-İŞ. Emphasizing the need to combine political with economic struggle, DİSK introduced an approach that defined employer-worker relations in class terms and challenged the state to advance both democratic political rights and workers rights. During this time, unions became more prestigious and appeared stronger (Çetik and Akkaya 1999, 56). Economic and political problems during the late 1970s forced many workers to protest government policies and to threaten strikes; unions started to pursue increasingly militant and aggressive actions (Koray 1992, 7). Meanwhile, political conflicts and divisions between right and left political parties and factions created deep dissension throughout Turkey. Mounting tensions leading to the prospect of armed clashes and the specters of civil insurrection provoked fears that the country was drifting into chaos. These dynamics culminated in 1980 with the military coup d'état that summarily ended strident collective action.

The fourth period began in 1982, with the promulgation of a new constitution, which was in effect, a reaction against the democratic Constitution of 1961. It recognized the rights to unionize and strike but included quite detailed provisions aimed at suppressing the fundamental freedoms accorded by virtue of freedom of association rights. It redesigned industrial relations in Turkey. First, it distinguished between illegal and legal procedures in collective bargaining, thereby expanding the purview of the former; second, it restricted the choices open to trade unions as a result of an enlarged role for executively appointed labor mediation committees. Such committees, although nominally tripartite and corporatist in nature, favored not only the influence of employers relative to workers and trade unions, but would permit intensified forms of state or government intervention in the collective bargaining process (Çetik and Akkaya 1992, 91).

The undemocratic social policy provisions of the Constitution were further reinforced by means of the Law on Labor Unions (no. 2821, Sendikalar Yasası), the Labor Law (no. 1475, İş Yasası), and the Law on Collective Agreement, Strike, and Lockout (no. 2822, Toplu İş Sözleşmesi, Grev ve Lokavt Yasası), in 1983. Later, the economic liberalization policies initiated by the Özal government, which was formed following the 1983 elections, fostered changes in the public sector through establishment of the Coordination Council for Collective Bargaining in the State Economic Enterprises. The Özal government embarked on a series of measures that today are identified as reflective of neoliberalism of the "Washington consensus," including opening up the economy to foreign markets; increasing foreign capital entry; reducing state intervention in corporate and industrial policy decisions; permitting the fluctuation of the Turkish lira; and liberalizing export-import policies. But liberalization stopped at the border's edge of labor markets. The Özal government sought to regulate trade union activities and to restrict the levels of wage increases granted through collective bargaining (Kazgan 1988, 353). Specifically, its foreign economic policies pursued two standard neomercantilist objectives: greater labor force productivity, and suppression of wages and salaries (Çetik and Akkaya 1999, 91). Lower industrial wages were to allow Turkish exporters to compete successfully in foreign markets. Moreover, new managerial regimes were gradually introduced into Turkish industrial production and marked a shift from Fordist industrial economy to the managerial practices of neo-Fordism (or post-Fordism), which included "flexibilization," privatization, part-time work, and quality circles (Çetik and Akkaya 1999, 58). Thus, industrial wages were kept officially low for a decade. As a reaction to mounting worker grievances, many employers resorted to large-scale dismissal of unionized workers. The situation was aggravated by the seeming indifference of government authorities, who refused to carry out reforms beneficial to workers or their unions.

The policies designed to lower real wages and salaries, presumably to promote macroeconomic growth and to reduce inflation, led to a series of strikes actions. According to the Turkish Ministry of Labor and Social Security, the workers who engaged in strike activities steadily increased from 561 in 1984 to 166,306 in 1990 and 199,867 in 1995. The number of strikes also increased from 4 in 1984 to 458 in 1990, but declined to 120 in 1995 (Çalışma ve Sosyal Güvenlik Bakanlığı 2002c). Many employers responded to these strikes with lockouts and dismissals. In 1991, for example, number of locked-out workers reached nearly 61,000 workers. During the early 1990s, thousands of union members and workers were sued, and many were sentenced to imprisonment, especially public sector workers and civil servants (Koç 1999, 63).

The 1990s thus appears to have been the most problematic period for industrial relations in Turkey. Labor union leaders experienced pressures from their membership to press for increases in real wages and salaries; employers resisted such demands on account of their presumed undesirable macroeconomic and inflationary implications (Çetik and Akkaya 1999, 228). Employers began to call for new legislation designed to support greater flexibility in employment, that is, the adoption of a workplace regime that would sanction part-time work, work based on contract, temporary work, flexible hour plans, and so on. (Çetik and Akkaya 1999, 59 and 101). They reached this objective with legislation of a new labor law (no. 4857), on 9 June 2003. Article 7, which covers details of flexible working plans and work based on contract, benefits the employer and hinders unionization.

Unions started to lose members because of economic privatization and their inability to provide meaningful or substantive assistance to Turkish workers. The lack of democratic governance within the unions also contributed to decline in trade union credibility and unionization rates. According the Turkish Ministry of Labor, unionization rates of workers (not including civil servants) dropped from nearly 68 percent (2,695,627 unionized out of 3,973,306 workers) in 1996 to 58 percent (2,854,059 workers unionized out of 4,916,421 workers) in July 2004 (Çalışma ve Sosyal Güvenlik Bakanlığı 2003).

The Vectors of the Informal Economy: Unemployment, Privatization, Gender Discrimination, and Clandestine Workers

Unemployment is high in Turkey and results from a set of macroeconomic conditions that include rapid population growth, insufficient development of human and social capital, and technology-induced labor market surpluses. These forces, combined with the dynamics of privatization and gender discrimination, have operated as vectors to produce a large informal economy in Turkey.

Since the 1960s, large-scale migrations from rural to urban areas have swelled the ranks of the informal economy, with increasing number of female and child laborers. However, the aggravated unemployment currently faced by Turkey is largely the result of privatization policies and the shift toward service sector employment. Through the 1980s, Turkey was a country that allocated more than half of its fixed capital investments to the industrial sector. Later, this proportion decreased rapidly, and investments in industrial sector were replaced by investments in the service sector and real estate (Tan, Ecevit, and Üşür 2001, 33). As of 2006, the service sector was creating greater employment opportunities relative to its share in gross domestic product (GDP) than the industrial sector, which was employing a mere 18 percent of the total workforce. The process of deindustrialization, along with the privatization of the SEEs, the State Economic Enterprises (Kamu İktisadi Teşekkülleri), was rapidly eroding traditional industrial relations structures, reinforcing the dynamics of informality, and setting the stage for the forces of deunionization.

Privatization of the SEEs has been main culprit since 1985. Supported by international financial institutions that promote economic liberalization, the objectives of privatization policies in Turkey include the reduction of chronic national deficits plus increasing state revenues through the sale of publicly owned assets; lessening the inflationary impacts brought on by nonproductive forms of employment; and eliminating excessive employment resulting from clientelism, nepotism, and other kinds of informal networking. However, privatization, which justifies the dismissal of thousands of workers and suppression of wages in the name of efficiency, also results in exponential rise in numbers seeking to gain livelihoods in the informal sector. In addition to these, deunionization is fostered by the direct threats of dismissal posed by the management of newly privatized SEEs.

The threats are often realized (Petrol-İş 1996, 245–300).[1] The Ministry of Labor reports the number of workers dismissed on account of privatization between 1992 and 1997 as 2.5 million (Petrol-İş 1999, 106). In addition to the banking sector, large-scale dismissals occurred in the privatized SEEs in many industrial and service establishments, which include: Meat and Fish Products Organizations (Et Balık Kurumu, EBK); Milk and Milk Products Institute (Süt ve Süt Ürünleri Enstitüsü, SEK); Çukurova Electric Utility (Çukurova Elektrik Anonim Şirketi, ÇEAŞ); Cement Industry (Çimento Sanayi, ÇİTOSAN); Airport Ground Transportation Services (HAVAŞ). The negative causal link between privatization and unionization rates is perhaps best illustrated in the energy sector. After the privatization of the SEEs, such as ÇEAS, Aktaş Electric, and Kayseri Electric, the unionization rate dropped from 100 percent to 36 percent (PETROL-İŞ 1996). Some of the dismissed workers were replaced by new workers employed by subcontractors (named *taşeron*). These workers, however, are not unionized and cannot claim benefits obtained through collective bargaining.

Moreover, there is virtually no legislation protecting against arbitrary dismissals of workers at privatized SEEs, while the legal procedures governing worker reinstatement take years.[2] Besides reinstatement and job security issues, the problem with privatization as an economic policy is the inadequacy of unemployment insurance schemes or any other form of safety-net available as a form of compensation to dismissed workers (Petrol-İş 1996, 263).

Although it may be difficult to define the informal economy in a way that applies to all economies, its essential features are unrecorded and unregulated work (Lordoğlu 2001b). Informal sector workers do not enjoy health benefits, social protections, permanent job status or guarantees of safe and clean working conditions. More than half of the Turkish labor force currently works under conditions of labor informality (Lordoğlu 2001b, 114–15). It is estimated that no less than 10.9 million persons out of the 21 million of the total labor force work in the informal economy. Moreover, 34.1 percent of workers in urban areas do not come under social security coverage, while 84.6 percent of agricultural sector workers are nonregistered, the majority of them women (Uras 2002).

The forces leading to an expansion of the informal market serve as indicators of the precarious state of female employment in Turkey, driven by widespread gender discrimination. Given their role, especially in agricultural, handicraft, and throughout the service sectors, Turkish women produce major proportions of the annual GDP. Female labor tends to be concentrated in the agricultural sector, constituting unpaid family work, as well as in the manufacturing sector (Tan, Ecevit, and Üşür 2001, 22–23). Yet women continue to suffer from discrimination, lower wages, substandard and often demeaning working conditions, sexual harassment, the lack of adequate social protections, and the absence of freedom of association and worker rights—conditions that are much more common in the informal sector.

Despite Turkey's ratification of international human and labor rights treaties, women remain largely unprotected in terms of job security and equal pay for equal work, notwithstanding their revised domestic legal status (Tan, Ecevit, and Üşür 2001, 23). They still lag behind in education, employment, and in terms of equal pay for equal work. Moreover, girls' limited access to education (see Fatma Gök and Deniz Ilgaz in this volume, Chapter 8) reduces female workers' ability to participate in the formal labor markets and drives them into the informal sector.

The State Planning Organization recognizes that Turkey is in need of new mechanisms and policies to eliminate gender discrimination in employment and at work, and to bring the informal economy under regulatory control in ways that ameliorate the working conditions that women face (Yedinci Beş Yıllık Kalkınma Planı 1996, 151–52). The European

Commission's 2002 and 2004 reports called on Turkey to eliminate discrimination and gender-based restrictions to certain jobs and positions. Fortunately, the Turkish Job Security Act (İş Güvencesi Yasası), adopted in August 2002, includes a provision that is designed to insure that work contracts and their termination will no longer be based on reasons related to sex, race, marital status, family obligations, pregnancy, religion, political views, ethnicity, or social roots (Council of Europe 2002, 91–92).

Clandestine immigrants, whose numbers have increased during the last decade, also facilitate the growth of unemployment, informal sector, and deunionization. Arriving from Iran, Iraq, Afghanistan, Moldova, Ukraine, Russia, Romania, Georgia, Bulgaria, Syria, Algeria, Morocco, Egypt, and Turkic Republics, among other places, they join the ranks of Turkish informal sector workers, leading to large volumes of untaxed commerce.

The Turkish labor market structure is especially suitable for clandestine work because of the latent or side effects of official fiscal policies. Employers confront government-mandated levels of high worker insurance, for example, while registered workers face deep deductions in gross wages and salaries (Karadeniz 1999, 425). This sets the stage for the informal economy to flourish under the tables of Turkish business enterprise. Owners of small and medium-size enterprises that generate an estimated 45 percent of employment in Turkey (Aydemir 1995), for example, are especially prone to hire illegal aliens (Karadeniz 1999, 416–25). Illegal aliens entering Turkish labor markets have limited recourse to any means of obtaining job security, since Turkey has not as yet implemented a system similar to those of many European countries that permit aliens to pursue legal job status in temporary and flexible ways. Turkish labor law specifies primarily the sanctions and fines that are to be imposed in cases of violations (Lordoğlu 2001b, 126).[3]

The dynamics of interrelated factors, including privatization, unemployment, deindustrialization and growth of the service sector, and illegal workers, all contribute to the growth of the proportion of the informal sector of the economy and deunionization. Consequently, only 13 percent of the total civilian labor force over the age of fifteen are today unionized or affiliated with a workers' association (Uras 2002).

Freedom of Association Rights in Turkish Law and Practice: 1982 to the Present

Workers, as well as trade or labor unions, in Turkey do not function in an environment in full compliance with the international labor standards. Freedom of association rights press claims that link democratic values with the standards of social and economic justice. They assert workers' right to organize to seek their interests and undertake collective action, particularly within systems of collective bargaining or industrial relations. Thus, freedom of association rights are not only an integral part of the fundamental freedoms that comprise the architecture of democratic rights, but they hold a special allure for workers who find in the assertion of such rights a means to counter the ravages of poverty, marginalization, injustice, and/or exploitation.

The bases for workers' freedom of association rights in international law are the International Labour Organization (ILO) Conventions 87 and 98, which were ratified by Turkey in 1998 and 1951, respectively. Convention 87, the Freedom of Association and Protection of the Right to Organize (1948), recognizes the legal capacities of workers and employers to exercise freely and fully their associational rights absent all forms of discrimination, and thus "to form and to join organizations of their own choosing" in order "to further and defend their interests." Subsequent provisions permit worker associations "to draw up their own constitutions and rules" and "to organize their administration and activities and to formulate their programs." In particular, trade unions or representative organizations enjoy the capacity to acquire "legal personality" in unrestricted ways. ILO Convention 98, the Right to Organize and Collective Bargaining (1949), upholds the rights of workers to participate in collective bargaining and establishes the validity of complaints and claims arising from antiunion discrimination or prejudicial acts against individuals as a result of their trade union affiliation. In a noteworthy gesture toward continuing expansion of freedom of association rights, promoted by the process of negotiating Turkish accession into the European Union, Article 90 of the Turkish Constitution was amended to strengthen the status of international conventions ratified by Turkey; international treaties and conventions automatically prevail in instances when domestic laws and/or practices conflict with international obligations. Thus, ILO Conventions 87 and 98 represent inviolable undertakings within the statutory frameworks of Turkish national law.[4]

Among the restrictions imposed by the 1982 Constitution was the denial of the right of public sector workers to unionize and thus to engage in collective bargaining. However, persistent pressures exerted by and on behalf of primary and secondary school teachers in the early 1990s, led to an alteration of Article 53 of the 1982 Constitution, in 1995, to recognize public sector workers' freedom of association rights by granting them the right to organize. The amendment also allows their participation in collective bargaining talks, but without having the right to sign off on a collective bargaining contract. This is, of course, discriminatory against the public sector workers.

Nevertheless, the amendment resulted in the formation of additional unions in the public sector, including the Confederation of Public Labor

Unions (Kamu Sendikaları Konfederasyonu, KAMU-SEN); the Confederation of Civil Servants' Unions (Memur Sendikaları Konfederasyonu, MEMUR-SEN); the Confederation of National Health Laborers (Ulusal Sağlık Emekçileri Konfederasyonu, USEK); and the Confederation of Public Laborers' Unions (Kamu Emekçileri Sendikaları Konfederasyonu, KESK). In 2001, the parliament extended the coverage of such rights to include a full complement of public sector workers, except police and military personnel. Finally, in July 2002, the Ministry of Labor decreed that public sector trade unions would be allowed to participate in full-fledged collective bargaining negotiations across a range of sectors and services: banking and insurance services; education, health, and social services; local government services; press, broadcasting, and communication; artisan and cultural services; construction and rural services; transportation; agriculture and forestry; energy, industry, and mining; religious affairs and foundation services. Consequently, approximately half of the 1.4 million public employees became eligible for unionization (Çalışma ve Sosyal Güvenlik Bakanlığı 2002b).

Collective bargaining in Turkey in recent years has covered such issues as wage/salary negotiation as well as training, productivity, job performance evaluation, protection against accidents, job security, and health issues (N. Tan 1999, 6). Today, all established trade or labor unions in Turkey freely represent the views and interests of their organizations and their memberships. But they do so under a panoply of legal and statutory restrictions aimed at insuring government micromanagement of freedom of association rights. Most notably, trade or labor unions must obtain prior governmental authorization for gatherings and demonstrations, and they must officially invite police authorities to attend and to report on the proceedings of major meetings, particularly the union conventions. The right to strike is not granted to a range of workers in such sectors as mining and petroleum, education, sanitation, in addition to the police and the military. Labor disputes in these sectors must ultimately be determined by binding arbitration.

Workers employed within the nine Turkish free export zones have not been permitted to strike during the first ten years of their company's legal incorporation. In 2002, however, Turkey repealed the ten-year ban on strikes, lockouts, and mediation in free trade zones within the framework of industrial relations reforms. On the other hand, strikes organized by workers who are not registered to any union remain illegal, despite the fact that ILO Convention 87 states that "workers and unions" have the right to strike.

Various statutory restrictions regulate collective bargaining in ways that have consistently called into question the legitimacy of Turkish procedures.

What is legally sanctioned, for example, before, during, and after strike actions are called, require trade or labor unions to meet exacting criteria that easily invites government intrusion or the threats of employer lockouts. Article 54 of the 1982 Constitution authorized employer prerogatives with respect to lockouts. These were amplified and given added statutory legitimacy by the Law on Collective Agreement, Strike, and Lockout (no. 2822). According to Article 25 of this act, a strike is defined "as stoppage of labor activities in a workplace or going-slow on duties or work based within an agreement by workers or by calls for a strike by labor union(s)." Article 25 delineates the procedures that must be followed for enjoyment of the right to strike.

Formal modes of collective bargaining must precede all strike actions, and a tripartite committee consisting of government, employers association, and trade or labor union representatives must first be convened in order to initiate the process of collective bargaining. If the parties to a labor dispute cannot reach an agreement during the formal phases of collective bargaining, they are obliged to accept the mediation of a board prescribed by legislation (Articles 22–23/2821). Collective bargaining is the sole avenue through which trade or labor unions must pass before a strike may be legally called. Strikes are deemed legal only if disagreements emerge in the course of collective bargaining. Then, and only then, are strikes considered officially sanctioned. Trade or labor unions may not call strikes before or during collective bargaining talks, nor after talks have successfully concluded with a bargaining agreement. For a strike to be considered legal, therefore, collective bargaining must have reached an impasse. This means that trade or labor unions must first submit to and reject the outcome of nonbinding mediation. Such procedures are often time-consuming and costly. But if such measures are not carefully followed, employers are legally enjoined to threaten and eventually to undertake lockout action supported by government authority. Other examples of statutory restriction in Turkish laws and practices with respect to the exercise of freedom of association rights include the following:

- the right of government authorities to reject initiation of strike action on the basis of official claims alleging that legal paperwork procedures remain incomplete;
- restrictions on strike leaders and their activities, including a ban on union shelters where strike leaders may stay or assemble during strikes;
- requirements that oblige workers to leave their workplaces in cases of strikes;
- ban on salaries or wages that might be given to workers as compensation for their days on strike;

- limitations on printed materials such as handouts and leaflets distributed for purposes of the strike;
- obligation to begin strikes within sixty days after legal permission is granted;
- legal permission to organize a strike can be suspended for sixty days with the decision of the Cabinet or for national security reasons;
- once labor unions become legally entitled to organize a strike, they must notify the employers at least six days in advance of their intentions (Article 37/2821);
- in the event that workers seek to assemble within urban city centers, local or regional public authorities must designate the location and specify the duration.[5]

Under Turkish law, however, employers are not permitted to transfer administrative staff to perform tasks normally undertaken by striking workers, nor to hire "scabs," that is, replacement workers hired for the purpose of breaking a strike. Employers are enjoined not to terminate unionized workers who have engaged in a strike or who have encouraged other workers to do so. Antiunion discrimination laws and the Turkish Constitution also make it a violation for employers to discriminate against those workers who provide trade union leadership or to discriminate against those who seek to become trade union members. In practice, employers do discriminate against workers involved in strikes. Thus, workers often face the dilemma of either accepting unsatisfactory working conditions or risking their livelihood by going on strike.

Governments in Turkey may also suspend strikes for a sixty-day period on the grounds of national security or safety and health. Trade unions may petition the Council of State to rescind such decrees. Failure to be granted such an injunction may lead to compulsory arbitration to resolve the dispute in question. The broad and nonspecific nature of the definitions of national security, safety, and health provided in Turkish labor law have led several international monitoring agencies, including those of the ILO, to question whether Turkish practices function in ways that satisfy freedom of association standards.

Multilateral Monitoring of Turkish Labor Laws and Practices: The ILO and the EU

As a result of this somewhat ambiguous situation regarding freedom of association rights, Turkey has come under the surveillance and criticism of the monitoring agencies of the ILO. Among other issues raised by the ILO, are the following:

- violations of the right to assembly and demonstration;
- violations of freedom of opinion and expression;
- restrictions of the right of workers to set up and join organizations;
- restrictions of the right of trade unions to draw up their constitutions and rules, elect their representatives in full freedom, and to organize and administrator their activities;
- limitations on the right to strike;
- suspension of organizations by administrative decision; and
- restricted rights of organizations to form federations and affiliate with international organizations.

Since 1982, the ILO Committee on Freedom of Association (CFA) has considered numerous complaints that have included allegations of the following: interference in the right to strike and to become unionized; denial of the right to strike with respect to public workers; officially authorized but arbitrary termination of labor union activities; unlawful detention, arrest, and trials of labor union leaders; bans on May Day demonstrations; antiunionization state policies particularly with respect to recruitment and deposit of union funds.[6] Further restrictions that apply with respect to collective bargaining and the right to strike include the following: committees established for the purposes of collective bargaining often consist of a majority of employers or are dominated by employers (N. Tan 1999, 17–18); the procedures that apply in cases of alleged unfair dismissals are grossly inadequate; part-time workers and workers within small and medium enterprises do not enjoy full application of the legal rights to collective bargaining; small and medium-size enterprises deter their workers from becoming unionized (N. Tan 1999, 64). A new Turkish labor law passed in 2003 better specifies worker safety but at the cost of granting greater flexibility to employers to sanction part-time work in ways that hinder trade unionization and prevent extension of freedom of association rights.[7]

Perhaps the most provocative challenge to the full enjoyment of freedom of association rights, however, centers on the "10 percent threshold." Turkish labor laws require that a trade or labor union, before it can be officially registered as a collective bargaining agent, must inscribe at least 51 percent of all employees salaried or waged at a given work site and, in addition, at least 10 percent of all workers employed within the respective sector or industry as defined by their occupation. Moreover, according to the Law on Collective Agreement, Strike, and Lockout (no. 2822), in order to acquire the legal authority to participate in a process of collective bargaining, a trade or labor union has to register 10 percent of the workers in a specific labor field and, in addition, must sign up an absolute majority of the workers in a specific workplace (Article 12). These high thresholds create a "barrier to entry" for new unions and favor established unions, such as TÜRK-İŞ, the labor confederation that represents nearly three-quarters of organized labor in Turkey. They imply a government effort to maintain the status and control of a few established labor unions by creating disincentives against the creation of smaller and perhaps more radical ones. Consequently, while no less than 912 labor unions functioned in Turkey in 1978, as of 2001 the entire Turkish organized labor movement was consolidated into approximately ten major confederations or unions (Çalışma ve Sosyal Güvenlik Bakanlığı 2002c) (see Table 7.1). Among these, only three, TÜRK-İŞ, DİSK, and the Confederation of Real Trade Unions (Hakiki İşçi Sendikaları Konfederasyonu, HAK-İŞ) enjoy relatively large memberships.

Membership levels thus represent a vital concern for Turkish trade or labor unions. Statutory restrictions declare that workers who are not registered to a labor union are not allowed automatically to benefit from the advantages gleaned from collective bargaining or to enjoy the same

TABLE 7.1. MAJOR LABOR UNIONS AND CONFEDERATIONS

TÜRK-İŞ	Türkiye İşçi Sendikaları Konfederasyonu (Confederation of Turkish Labor Unions)
DİSK	Devrimci İşçi Sendikaları Konfederasyonu (Confederation of Revolutionary Workers' Trade Unions)
HAK-İŞ	Hakiki İşçi Sendikaları Konfederasyonu (Confederation of Real Trade Unions)
MİSK	Milli Sendikalar Konfederasyonu (National Labor Unions Confederation)
PETROL-İŞ	Türkiye Petrol Kimya Lastik İşcileri Sendikası (Petroleum Chemical Rubber Workers Union of Turkey)
EĞİTİM-SEN	Eğitim Bilim ve Kültür Emekçileri Sendikası (Union of Education, Science, and Culture Workers)
KAMU-SEN	Kamu Sendikaları Konfederasyonu (Confederation of Public Labor Unions)
MEMUR-SEN	Memur Sendikaları Konfederasyonu (Confederation of Civil Servants' Unions)
USEK	Ulusal Sağlık Emekçileri Konfederasyonu (Confederation of National Health Laborers)
KESK	Kamu Emekçileri Sendikaları Konfederasyonu (Confederation of Public Laborers' Unions)
METAL-İŞ	Metal İş İşcileri Sendikası (Metal Workers' Trade Union)

rights to collective bargaining as their unionized colleagues. But, a "side-system" called *teşmil* is used to accommodate nonunionized workers. The *teşmil* system exists in law and allows the benefits of collective bargaining given to union workers to be extended to nonunionized workers, but it entails substantial paperwork and complex procedures that impede efficient implementation. It can only be administered to nonunionized workers in a specific workplace if and when the Cabinet and the Ministry of Labor approve. Thus, while the promise of benefits regardless of union membership discourages unionization, the unfulfilled promise disappoints many workers.

The thresholds force the unions into playing a numbers game.[8] The Ministry of Labor requires that labor unions regularly list the numbers of their members, but the mere process of doing so creates incentives for misrepresenting the lists. Trade unions fall into a kind of competition for larger lists of members relative to other trade unions. Falsified membership registration is considered unlawful, but the 10 percent threshold tends to reward organizations that occasionally inflate their listings. It has also been alleged that it is common practice for some labor unions to provide fake names and false addresses in order to obtain the legal rights to representation. The practice of transferring nominal memberships from one union to another also occurs.[9] In addition, trade or labor unions have been criticized on several grounds: for not actively working on recruitment of members; for failing to implement democratic procedures; and for failing to provide opportunities for members, especially women, to advance into positions of leadership.

Turkey ratified the European Social Charter in 1989 with major reservations (Gülmez 1990), with respect to the following articles: Article 2 on the right to just conditions of work; Article 4 on the right to fair remuneration; Article 3 on the right to safe and healthy working conditions; Article 5 on the right to organize; Article 6 on the right to bargain collectively; Article 7 on the right of children and young persons to protection; Article 8 on the right of employed women to protection; and Article 15 on the right of physically or mentally disabled persons to vocational training, rehabilitation, and social resettlement (Gülmez 1990, 124; Çetik and Akkaya 1999, 98). During the XIII and XIV Inspection Periods (1990–98), the Committee of Independent Experts of the Council of Europe evaluated Turkey's compliance with the European Social Charter using a statistical methodology based on benchmarks. Within this eight-year period, Turkey was alleged to have noncomplied with 2 articles and 17 clauses (Gülmez 1999). The substantive nature of the supposed infractions concentrated on the availability of various forms of social protection to certain subsets of the working population in Turkey, including foreign workers, self-employed refugees, stateless persons, and migrant workers.

As of 2002, Turkey was in noncompliance with the following articles of the European Social Charter:

- Article 12 /4 on equal treatment for the nationals of other contracting parties with respect to social security
- Article 13/1 on the right to social and medical assistance
- Article 16 on the right of the family to social, legal, and economic protection
- Article 19/4 on treating migrant workers not less favorably than nationals with respect to employment, trade union rights, and accommodation
- Article 19/10 on the extension of protection and assistance to self-employed workers
- Article 19/10 on the extension of protection and assistance to self-employed migrants
- Article 19/8 on security against expulsion, and Article 19/10 on the extension of the protection and assistance to self-employed migrants.

Some steps have been taken concerning the social protection of unemployed people. In April 2002, payments of unemployment benefits were made for the first time. The Regular Report on Turkey's Progress Towards Accession, released by the Commission of the European Communities in 2002, noted some progress as well, including a claim by the Turkish government that a program has been established so that employees subject to layoffs due to privatization would henceforth receive unemployment benefits for six to eight months (Council of Europe 2002). Nevertheless, the report also noted that Turkey still lagged behind in adopting the EU norms in terms of social and economic rights (Lordoğlu 2001b, 49–51). The commission boldly summarized its findings: "In the area of labor law, no concrete progress was made." But it noted that a "scientific" committee had been set up to prepare a revision of the Turkish Labor Code (Council of Europe 2002, 91), specifically to address the perceived substandard practices, and spell out the areas of labor law where improvements should be benchmarked to European and ILO international labor standards: collective redundancies; insolvency; working time, fixed-term, and part-time work; young people at work and posting of workers; health and safety in fixed-term and temporary employment; European Works Councils employer-worker consultative structures.

   Inadequate protection of worker and freedom of association rights continues to loom as a major obstacle in the way of Turkey's admission to the EU. This may propel Turkish society and government toward fuller realization of fundamental freedoms and labor rights. The EU has specified necessary improvements in certain areas: job security, particularly in the aftermath of privatization; social protection relative to contract work; social security for nonregistered workers; guaranteed health care for all workers; amelioration of the worst forms of child labor; greater regulation of the informal sector; elimination of discrimination based on gender, particularly unequal payment for equal work that discriminates against women throughout Turkey; development of social protections for workers with disabilities.

The 2002 Commission Report, in particular, called on Turkey "as a matter of priority" to expand the bipartite mechanisms and tripartite structures intrinsic to the promotion and efficacy of "social dialogue" among employers, workers, and government representatives. Among its litany of complaints leveled against current Turkish labor laws and practices, the commission specified that "Turkey should make rapid progress towards establishing full trade union rights that includes elimination of restrictive thresholds for forming a trade union branch and requirement of 10 percent threshold for a trade union to be eligible for collective bargaining at company level" (Council of Europe 2002, 94). The report also stressed the need to deliver full freedom of association rights to workers in the public sector, noting that there remain "restrictive provisions relating to the exclusion of the right to strike and to collective bargaining" (94). It called on Turkey to extend freedom of association rights and social protections to a broader range of its population beyond the 15 percent currently covered by collective agreements and to strengthen the administration of labor law across the board. Subsequent reports continuously stressed the need for Turkey to promote social dialogue in ways that strengthen freedom of association rights, specifically within the private sector, and stated that restrictive thresholds on trade unions with respect to their eligibility to become agents for collective bargaining and all other similar limitations placed on representational rights, including the right to strike, must be abolished, especially with respect to public service workers (Council of Europe 2004, 109–11).

Conclusion: Glimmers of Hope

The EU also called for the deepening of constitutionalism and the expansion of civil society as a condition for Turkey's accession. This bears directly on issues pertaining to social dialogue and freedom of association rights. Within this context, Turkey in 2004 established a Tripartite Advisory Board to issue advisory opinions on matters relevant to working life, to foster cooperation and dialogue among the social partners, and to monitor legislative developments in the field of labor law. This advisory panel met for the first time in May 2004. Glimmers of hope may also emanate from the Turkish Economic and Social Council (ESC) that was created in the early 1990s. But this depends on how and to what extent the ESC develops structural depth and programmatic effectiveness. The draft of law on the ESC was prepared in 1992, but without adequate provisions specifying its structure, functions, and duties. As a consequence, confusion has surrounded the role, status, and operations of ESC ever since. The ESC was actually established in 1995 by means of a decree approved by the Prime Ministry. ESC meetings concluded at the time of its establishment did not produce a set of bylaws that defined in formal ways either its mission or its objectives.

The enunciated objective of the ESC was to create a consultative platform to foster social dialogue and to provide a forum aimed at the strengthening of administrative capacities in the field of domestic labor laws. ESC members were predominantly government representatives. Ostensibly, the ESC will function to enhance social dialogue with respect to a range of compelling issues affecting labor and workers, including: the promotion of sustainable growth; the strengthening of Turkey's competitiveness in international markets; the pursuit of expanded exports and foreign direct investments; methods for decreasing chronic inflation; unemployment and the expansion of job opportunities; adaptation of new technologies to enable Turkey to become a "knowledge" society; improvement in education and training levels of the national labor force (Evren 1999). Among the issues amenable to the ESC review is the state of domestic labor laws and practices.

In 2004, the EU, in the name of bringing Turkey closer to the accession *acquis*, called for a major improvement in the performance of the ESC and an end to the predominance of government representatives so as to promote greater social dialogue. Future ESC meetings and of similar agencies thus will provide a meter or litmus test to measure the extent of Turkey's commitments to the reasonable aspiration, so near and yet so far, that someday soon all Turkish citizens and all residents in Turkey will enjoy fundamental freedoms and access to unimpaired human rights and that this will include promotion of workers' rights and the unhindered practice of freedom of association rights.

Chapter 8
The Right to Education

FATMA GÖK AND DENİZ ILGAZ

*Dedicated to the memory of the teacher and 84 students of State Regional
Boarding Primary School in Çeltiksuyu town of Bingöl, who lost their lives
under the ruins of their school building that was poorly constructed and
collapsed during a 2003 earthquake.*

This chapter explores the major issues concerning the right to education
in Turkey. The right to education is articulated in the 1948 Universal
Declaration of Human Rights as an individual right of every person regardless of sex, race, ethnicity, nationality, or any other status. Increasingly
considered as a precondition for the exercise of other human rights, the
statement about right to education takes place in Article 27 of the International Covenant on Civil and Political Rights (ICCPR), and in Articles
13 and 14 of the International Covenant on Economic, Social, and Cultural Rights (ICESCR). Under Article 13, states parties agree that education will be directed at the full development of the human personality and
strengthen respect for human rights and fundamental freedoms.

The right to education is specified also in Article 3 of and by a protocol
to the 1952 European Convention for the Protection of Human Rights
and Fundamental Freedoms, and addressed in several other international
human right instruments, including: of the UNESCO Convention against
Discrimination in Education (1960, Article 5(1)(c)); the Convention on
the Elimination of All Forms of Discrimination against Women (1979,
Article 10); the Convention on the Rights of the Child (1989, Articles 28
and 29); the Declaration of Minimum Humanitarian Standards (1994);
the Council of Europe Framework Convention for the Protection of
National Minorities (1995); Article 13 of the San Salvador Protocol to
the 1969 American Convention on Human Rights; African Charter on
Human and Peoples' Rights; and the 1990 Copenhagen Document of the
Conference on Human Dimension of the Organisation on Security and
Cooperation in Europe.

As articulated in these documents, the right to education requires the state to provide educational opportunities accessible to all and free of charge. All forms of education are to be provided without discrimination of any kind as to social class, race, color, sex, language, religion, political or other opinion, national or social origin, property, birth or other status. The equal rights of men and women in the enjoyment of the right to education must be ensured. Although it is a party to most of these treaties, Turkey is far from fulfilling the requirements of the international norms. In this chapter, we contend that the secular and westernized education, which in the early days of the Republic aimed at social and economic development and infliction of patriotic connection to the state, received considerable public support and created opportunities for many, but never fulfilled the goal of equality in access. We argue that the class system and the unequal distribution of wealth in the society, gender discrimination in family and society, inadequate financial resources allocated to education, failings in birth registrations, lack of respect for cultural differences, and inadequate adult education are the main obstacles to the realization of the right to education in Turkey.

The Education System and the Right to Education in Turkey

Education was first recognized among the duties of the state during the late Ottoman period, after the Royal Tanzimat Decree of 1839. The General Education Regulation of 1869 (Maarif-i Umumiye Nizamnamesi) declared that primary education was compulsory and free for all citizens (Akyüz 1994, 142), but the Ottoman state failed to fulfill this responsibility. After the establishment of the Turkish Republic in 1923, the Constitution of 1924 recognized primary education as a right of citizens and a responsibility of the state by declaring it compulsory and free for both sexes. Strict centralization was the most striking characteristic of the educational system of the republican period. A significant step was taken in 1924, with the enactment of the Law on the Unification of Education, which consolidated all scientific and educational institutions under the Ministry of National Education, abolished all religious educational and training institutions, and brought foreign schools, as well as those of minorities, under state control. A national secular education system, modeled after the Western European school system, was established.

The education policies of the one-party era (1923–46) emphasized education for modernization and development purposes and used schools and adult education programs for political and cultural socialization. The Ministry of National Education issued a circular on 19 December 1923, declaring: "schools are obliged to indoctrinate loyalty to the principles of the Republic" (Akyüz 1994, 286). Curriculum and course books were designed to instill a modern, urban, Western lifestyle. The party-run

People's Houses in cities and People's Rooms in rural areas were established for adult education.

Moreover, education was seen as vital for an economically poor country,
with limited physical, human, and financial resources, which also needed
to increase agricultural and industrial production. "Traveling village
women's classes" and "village men's vocational classes" were introduced
in 1938 and 1939 by the Ministry of National Education. In order to meet
the educational needs and to support social and economic development
of the 40,000 villages in Anatolia, 21 teacher training schools, called the
"Village Institutes," were established in different regions of the country
(Ilgaz 1999). In the beginning of the republican era, education was mainly
offered by public schools and financed by the government, and there were
only a few private schools.[1]

The right to education was fully recognized in the liberal Constitution
of 1961, under the section on the individual rights and duties, as well as
on the social and economic rights and duties. The state was assigned the
obligation of supporting the physical and moral development of the individual; religious education would be on a voluntary basis; the freedom
in the arts and sciences would be recognized; private education would
be possible at all levels but subjected to some limitations; the academic
and administrative autonomy of the universities was recognized.

The emphasis placed upon education in the earlier years of the Republic can be observed in the annual allocations to national education from
the national budget. Table 8.1 shows that the percentage of allocations
from the annual national budget for education starts with 3.2 percent in
the early 1920s and shows a steady increase up to 16.6 percent in the
mid-1960s; then a period of decline starts and a low figure of 6.9 percent
is reached in 2003. The budgetary decline takes place despite the increase
in the number of students and schools, meaning that the state spends less
on each school and student in later years. Noticing this declining trend,
the UN pecial rapporteur Katarina Tomasevski, reporting on the right
to education in Turkey in 2002, agreed with the UNESCO recommendation for doubling the national spending on education from the current 2.7 percent of GNP to 6.0 percent.[2]

The Issue of Access and Obstacles to the Right to Education

Education in Turkey is a big sector that includes more than 17 million
students, 600,000 teachers, and 50,000 schools, including nonformal education (Ministry of National Education 2004, 15). However, its share in
the national budget has been declining. According to *Eurostat Yearbook
2004*, the allocation of funds per student has been far below those of EU
member states and candidate countries, and at the primary level, the
figure for Italy is nearly ten times that of Turkey; 80 percent of the funds

allocated to education are spent on salaries of teachers and other personnel. Due to the lack of public funds, many school administrators ask students to bring money for heating, cleaning and repair of the building, and purchasing of equipment, which creates tension and conflict between schools and families (Gök et al. 2002).

In addition to the inadequate funding, there is the issue of inequality. The Turkish Ministry of Education claims that no discrimination in education exists in Turkey. Yet, the special rapporteur of the UN expresses her concern about the lack of quantitative and qualitative data and indicates that the process of exposing and eliminating discrimination has not even started in Turkey. She notes that "the official enrollment statistics record the number of children who are enrolled but are silent on those who should be in school but are not" (Tomasevski 2002, par. 43).

The issues related to the right to education can be analyzed on two dimensions. The first dimension involves the participation in schooling

TABLE 8.1. BUDGET, STUDENT, SCHOOL, AND TEACHER STATISTICS, 1923–2005

Year	Percent of consolidated budget spent on education	Number of students	Number of schools	Number of teachers
1923	3.20	361,514	5,133	12,266
1930	3.60	528,274	6,797	18,838
1935	4.60	763,339	6,596	19,136
1940	6.60	1,096,415	11,019	27,330
1945	8.40	1,503,111	14,589	36,891
1950	11.80	1,760,271	18,248	46,841
1955	12.60	2,222,972	19,835	56,324
1960	13.40	3,341,620	33,670	87,158
1965	16.60	4,634,668	43,150	121,287
1970	11.60	6,275,052	55,608	187,269
1975	13.30	7,276,223	66,745	247,124
1980	11.50	7,897,309	85,116	326,675
1985	8.40	9,554,205	98,156	350,399
1990	13.12	10,803,033	65,499	396,479
1995	10.17	11,970,053	63,888	448,048
2000	7.13	12,646,693	51,010	492,081
2001	8.37	12,879,507	51,612	528,816
2002	7.61	13,686,616	52,616	557,759
2003	6.91	13,852,429	56,321	563,200
2004	8.22	14,039,609	58,458	589,004
2005	9.57	14,482,337	61,144	596,096

This table was prepared by Nimet Yılmaz, using Kaya 1989; Ministry of National Education publications dated 2000 and 2001 (see References for full citations); Milli Eğitim İstatistikleri, State Institute of Statistics, Ankara, 2001; and the online sources of Ministry of National Education (www.meb.gov.tr) and State Institute of Statistics (www.die.gov.tr). Schools include preschools, primary schools, secondary schools, high schools, and vocational schools that are equivalent to high schools.

and can be assessed in quantitative terms. The second dimension involves more complex, controversial, hidden matters such as the method of teaching, content, teacher's attitude, school climate, in other words, the issues related to the essence of educational process and everyday experiences of school life.

Participation Rates

At the quantitative level, the rapidly growing educational system and the increasing number of students are shown in Table 8.1. But an important problem is the fact that there are many children who are not enrolled. The rate of literacy has increased from a low 11 percent in 1927 to 85.7 percent in 1999, and it is lower for some segments of the population, especially for women (see Table 8.2).

Less than half the population hold a primary school diploma, largely due to the inadequate facilities in rural areas, urban poverty, patriarchal gender roles, and the poor enforcement of the mandatory education rule in primary education. While registration of all newborn children constitutes a prerequisite for monitoring the implementation of compulsory education, as noted in the Convention on the Rights of the Child Committee report, some children do not have an identity card and are not registered on the civil registries (Committee on the Rights of the Child

Table 8.2. Literacy Rates for Population Ages Six Years and Over

| Year | Percent literate | | |
	Total	Male	Female
1927	11.0	17.4	4.0
1935	19.2	29.3	9.8
1940[a]	24.5	36.2	12.9
1945[b]	30.2	43.7	16.8
1950[c]	32.5	45.5	19.4
1955	41.0	55.9	25.6
1960	39.5	53.6	24.8
1965	48.8	64.1	32.8
1970	56.2	70.3	41.8
1975	63.7	76.2	50.5
1980	67.5	80.0	54.7
1985	77.4	86.5	68.2
1990	80.5	88.8	72.0
2000	87.3	93.9	80.6

Source: State Institute of Statistics, http://www.die.gov.tr/tkba/t098.xls (accessed 6 June 2005); data for 1927 are from Gök 1987.

[a]1940 data estimated by using data for 1935 and 1945; [b]population seven years and over; [c]population five years and over.

2000, par. 199). The lack of reliable information on the annual number of births is noted to be a problem by other UN agencies as well (United Nations Country Team-Common Country Assessment 2000, 68).

Table 8.3 reports enrollment ratios by educational level between 1990 and 2002, and its breakdown by sex. The declining rate of enrollment in higher levels points to the low "survival rate." The differences in male and female survival rates also point to the gender discrimination.

The highest rate of attrition takes place during the transition from primary to secondary education. According to a longitudinal study, in 1945–46, only 12 percent of those graduating from a primary school started secondary school education. Access to secondary level of education for the age group was 4.4 percent for the same year. In the 1972–173 school year, the rate of transition from primary education to secondary education was still pretty low, at 42.7 percent, and increased to 56.4 percent in 1984–85. The transition ratio increased to 67.3 percent and 66.6 percent during the years 1992–93 and 1996–97 respectively (Gök 2002, 95).

A closer examination of the rate of survival can also point to the areas of discrimination. A panel study that examined the survival rate for 1,586,004 students who started their mandatory primary schooling in 1987–88 and followed them until the 1997–98 school-year, which would be the year of graduation from high school for that group, reports its findings for both sexes. Table 8.4 shows that while there was no notable gender gap in the earlier years (84.85 percent of boys and 85.26 percent of girls completed their compulsory education), the difference becomes striking in upper grades. Only 62.40 percent of the boys and 42.06 percent of the girls (an average of 53 percent) continued with their education in middle school. Another major drop out rate is observed for those students who graduated from middle school, since only 24.77 percent of boys and 21.12 percent of girls (an average of 23 percent) who started their education in 1987–88 made to high school. A mere 5 percent survived to pursue higher education.

The country does not offer many educational opportunities for its citizens beyond the school age, either. There are only 922 adult education centers, which provide literacy courses, vocational training, and social and cultural activities. 579,000 persons attended literacy courses in 1997–2001, 294,629 persons in 2002–3, and 150,133 persons attended in 2003–4 (Ministry of National Education 2004, 206).

QUALITY OF EDUCATION

The quality of education is a problem at all levels. The public school system is often criticized for being dogmatic, emphasizing rote learning

TABLE 8.3. NET ENROLLMENT RATIOS BY EDUCATIONAL LEVEL.

Academic year	Primary school			Junior high school and equivalent			High school and equivalent			University/higher education		
	Total	Female	Male	Total	Female	Male	Total	Female	Male	Total	Female	Male
1990–1991	91.96	88.70	95.06	45.65	34.63	56.18	26.35	20.59	31.82	7.08	5.53	8.57
1991–1992	92.63	89.41	95.69	46.53	32.82	56.76	28.21	22.31	33.85	7.24	5.77	8.64
1992–1993	90.82	87.83	93.66	49.60	38.96	59.76	31.13	24.56	37.41	7.62	6.24	8.93
1993–1994	90.09	87.92	92.13	52.33	43.24	61.00	34.57	28.86	40.00	9.61	7.58	10.48
1994–1995	89.34	87.28	91.29	53.43	44.57	61.89	36.74	30.89	42.35	8.61	7.35	9.82
1995–1996	88.93	86.79	90.94	53.09	44.30	61.51	38.74	33.21	44.05	9.35	8.07	10.57
1996–1997	89.40	86.92	91.80	52.82	44.62	60.63	38.54	33.78	43.10	9.21	8.35	10.58

	Primary school*			High school and equivalent			University/higher education		
	Total	Female	Male	Total	Female	Male	Total	Female	Male
1997–1998	81.08	75.61	86.28	37.56	33.78	41.19	10.61	9.45	11.73
1998–1999	83.59	75.78	91.00	38.16	34.47	41.69	10.98	9.82	12.10
1999–2000	90.45	85.53	95.15	39.12	35.27	42.81	11.62	10.52	12.68
2000–2001	90.80	87.78	93.62	40.09	36.06	43.87	11.49	10.61	12.26
2001–2002	89.79	87.04	92.37	43.16	38.77	47.92	11.84	11.07	12.58

Source: State Institute of Statistics, http://www.die.gov.tr/tkba/t103.xls (accessed 3 June 2005).

*Starting in 1997, mandatory primary school education was increased from five years to eight years.

TABLE 8.4. NUMBER OF STUDENTS AND SURVIVAL RATES

Grade level	Academic year	Male students	Compared to 1987	Compared to previous year	Female students	Compared to 1987	Compared to previous year	Total students	Compared to 1987	Compared to previous year
Primary 1	1987–1988	839,324	100.00	100.00	746,680	100.00	100.00	1,586,004	100.0	100.0
Primary 2	1988–1989	768,503	91.56	91.56	690,511	92.48	92.48	1,459,014	92.0	92.0
Primary 3	1989–1990	765,757	91.23	99.64	686,444	91.93	99.41	1,452,201	91.6	99.5
Primary 4	1990–1991	731,951	87.21	95.59	657,035	87.99	95.72	1,388,986	87.6	95.6
Primary 5	1991–1992	712,156	84.85	97.30	636,636	85.26	96.90	1,348,792	85.0	97.1
Middle 1	1992–1993	523,700	62.40	73.54	314,040	42.06	49.33	837,740	52.8	62.1
Middle 1	1993–1994	480,211	57.21	91.70	300,224	40.21	95.60	780,435	49.2	93.2
Middle 3	1994–1995	415,824	49.54	86.59	275,063	36.84	91.62	690,887	43.6	88.5
Secondary 1	1995–1996	207,912	24.77	50.00	157,689	21.12	57.33	365,601	23.1	52.9
Secondary 2	1996–1997	140,139	16.70	67.40	126,993	17.01	80.53	267,132	16.8	73.1
Secondary 3	1997–1998	152,906	18.22	109.11	134,875	18.06	106.21	287,781	18.1	107.7
University	1998–1999							80,048	5.0	27.8

Source: Compiled from statistics provided by the State Statistical Institute by Abuzer Yakarylmaz, Dilek Çankaya, and Onur Seçkin, students at the Department of Educational Sciences of Boğaziçi University, in 2003.
Numbers for middle and secondary schools include all types of schools (e.g., academic and vocational).

and stifling creative thinking. Students are subjected to an ideologically restrictive and didactic interpretation of the principles and reforms of the founder of the Turkish Republic, Mustafa Kemal Atatürk, and are not encouraged to acquire the methods of critical and analytical thinking. Curricula are uniform in content, as well as in application, and the teachers are usually poorly educated and lack in-service training (Gök 2004).

Economic gaps and limited access to education contribute to the problem of child labor. According to a study by Tuncer Bulutay, 12 of every 100 children in the six- to twelve-year-old age group were working in 1995, and out of 11,889,000 children of the six- to fourteen-year-old age group, nearly 3,848,000 (32.2 percent) were working children; and the rate was higher for girls and rural kids, reaching up to 30–40 percent (Bulutay 1999, 9–26).

The method of discipline at schools is another area of concern. According to a survey study, corporal punishment is common; one in four teachers routinely beats pupils (Eğitim ve Bilim Emekçileri Sendikası).

Inequality and Discrimination

In addition to persistent gender discrimination, income, social class, ethnic background, age and disabilities are important factors in determining one's access to schooling, as well as the quality of education that one receives. Moreover, rural communities and the eastern and southeastern provinces receive fewer services and lag behind both in terms of enrollment and quality of education.

REGIONAL GAPS

While the enrollment ratio for the primary education for the entire country is 97.6 percent, for the Blacksea region is 84.3 percent, and for the eastern region is 85.6. The rate for high school for Marmara region is 82.3 percent and for southeastern region is 42.7 percent. For women, the situation is likely to be more severe. Table 8.5 exhibits how schooling ratios differ significantly from one region to another.

The regional discrepancies in the quality of education can be observed in national test scores. Higher scores on selection and placement tests for both secondary schools and universities tend to be obtained by students from the Western and wealthier provinces. The lowest scores and lowest placement rates are the predicament of students from the three least developed cities located in Southeastern Region: Şırnak, Bitlis, and Hakkari.[3]

NEOLIBERAL POLICIES, PRIVATIZATION, AND INCOME GAPS

Class differences and income gaps have been always important in determining one's access to education and the quality of education received. The neoliberal economic policies initiated by the military rulers in 1980 and followed by the subsequent civilian governments resulted in wider income gaps and lower social services. The issues related to educational inequalities are strongly embedded in problems of income distribution, class system, and other types of social stratification. The impact of highly skewed income distribution on education has been the creation of a dual system, in which the private schools cater to the rich and provide high-quality education, and the overcrowded public schools with depleting resources serve the lower- and middle-income groups.[4]

The post-1980 era displayed a major shift in the state's approach to education. The structural adjustment policies of the International Monetary Fund, adopted by the Turkish government on 24 January 1980, focused on reducing the state spending and encouraged privatization of state enterprises and services. As the neoliberal philosophy of the international financial agencies was internalized by the state officials in Turkey, the welfare state stated to be viewed as passé, and the Kemalist notion, which treated education as a tool of development, modernization, and secularization that should be supported and controlled by the state, has been progressively undermined. For example, General Kenan Evren, the leader of the 1980 military coup d'état, questioned the merit of free education. In 1986, he asked: "Is it social justice if a man with twelve children can send all twelve of his children to state schools for free?" (Gök 2002, 97).

As a result of the adoption of neoliberal social and economic policies, financial resources allocated to education from state funds diminished steadily (see Table 8.1). Expenditures for salaries make up most of the national education budget in Turkey. Yet salaries of teachers, as it is the

TABLE 8.5. SCHOOLING RATIO BY REGIONS, 2003–4

Regions	Primary school	High school
Marmara	111.5	82.3
Aegean	97.1	72.6
Mediterranean	94.6	66.5
Central Anatolia	89.0	71.8
Blacksea	84.3	32.1
Eastern Anatolia	85.6	45.1
Southeastern Anatolia	93.2	42.7
Total	95.2	66.5

Source: Küçüker 2005.

case for all public employees, have remained extremely low, far from providing a decent living. Low salaries at public schools lead well-trained and successful teachers to switch to private schools, which pay salaries three to five times higher.

More important, the reduction in the public spending on education has taken place along with a rapid increase in population. With half of the population being under twenty-five, the result is overcrowded public schools leads conscientious and well-to-do parents to seek alternatives; the increasing demand for private education then leads to the further deterioration of public school education. Currently, the average class size in private schools is 20–25, whereas in public schools it is 60–70. In crowded shantytown neighborhoods, a class may have 100 students. Annual tuitions of the private schools range from $3,000 to $13,000, depending on the reputation of the school ("Özel Okul Fiyatları Oxford Gibi" 2003).

Private schools, furthermore, receive subsidies in a variety of ways, which include credits, exemption from income and corporate taxes, and direct provision of public funds. Privatization of education flourished rapidly after 1980. While there were only 57 primary schools and 36 high schools in 1932, their number increased to 164 and 76 respectively in 1965, but jumped to 676 and 650 by 2004. In terms of the number of students, while there were 25,727 primary school students and 12,867 high school students in 1965, by 2004 the figures reached 172,348 and 71,253, respectively (Gök 2002, 98; Ministry of National Education 2005).

One significant indicator of crisis in the education system in Turkey is the establishment of quasi-private schools by the state itself. These "super high schools" and "Anatolian high schools," which are free and have English as the medium of instruction, have created a two-tier system within the public education. There is extreme competition to get into these schools, as in the case of private schools. In this hierarchal system, private schools rank at the top, with Anatolian high schools and the super high schools following, and at the bottom are the regular public high schools.

In addition to the primary and secondary schools, the private sector has penetrated into university system, creating an entire "college preparation industry." Since the establishment of the Republic, universities and other higher educational institutions have been a part of the public educational system. In the mid-1960s a number of higher educational institutions were founded privately, but the Constitutional Court later banned them. In the post-1980 era of neoliberalism, the private university notion was reintroduced as nonprofit "foundation universities." Ironically, the first private university (Bilkent University) was established by the same person who was in charge of the Higher Educational Council (*Yükseköğretim Kurulu*, YÖK), which has been a target of criticisms for its centralized and authoritarian structure and negative impact on academic freedom. Since 1986, the number of foundation universities has increased steadily, from 3 in 1995, to 17 in 1997, and to 24 in 2004. The number of universities is still far from meeting the demand. In 2004, out of the 1,786,963 students who took the university entrance examination, only 57.6 percent were able to get the required score of 185 that made them eligible to be considered for admission (National Student Selection and Placement Center).

Another discriminatory process is related to the preparatory classes for the highly competitive entrance examinations for the selective high schools and all universities. Middle-class and well-to-do families spend fortunes to send their children to such private classes or to private tutors. Public high schools are reduced to institutions that do not provide much education but that enroll students who then can be recruited by a private preparatory program. Operating for profit, these private programs mark the commercialization of education (Gök 2002, 98).

THE GENDER GAP

The unequal distribution of education between males and females is one of the most striking characteristics of the educational system in Turkey. The illiteracy rate for women is 30.4 percent, whereas it is 10.1 percent for men. The rate of female illiteracy in urban areas is 18.7 percent, while the rate is 4.5 percent for males (KA-DER 2003, 6).

The lower rate of participation in educational system by women is only part of the gender discrimination. The gendered curriculum and socialization process at schools tend to reproduce the traditional gender roles and stereotypes (Gök 1990; M. Tan, 2000). Schoolbooks tend to present more prestigious social roles and occupations as appropriate for men and depict women in domestic and caring roles. It is often emphasized that "a woman's greatest obligation is motherhood" (Bilgen et al. 2002, 26, 61, 63).

In *Citizenship and Human Rights Education* textbooks, used in seventh and eighth grade, women are studied separately, under two headings: "The Place of Turkish Women in Society" and "The Place of Turkish Women in Business Life." The texts are written to make Turkish women feel grateful to the Republican regime and Atatürk for the granting them some rights. A survey of nine textbooks revealed 19 pictures depicted women in a position of authority, as opposed to 90 such pictures for men (Gök 2004).

The Issues of Freedom and Choice

The 1982 Constitution stipulates that "no one would be deprived of the right to education." The right to education is defined as a social right, and education is to be provided to serve the aims of Atatürk's principles and reforms. The national education policy of the state has always been quite restrictive in terms of teaching methods and curriculum contents. The constitutional provision, which makes it obligatory to provide Religion, Culture, and Morality courses in primary and secondary schools face the challenges of the Alevi community, since they teach mainly the Sunni Islam. Another religion-related debate has been about the state ban on head scarves at schools, which imposes a restriction on the educational rights of female students. The Turkish Constitutional Court found the wearing of the head scarves incompatible with the principles of secularism (Constitutional Court 1989). Two student cases were taken to the European Court of Human Rights, but the Commission of the Court found them inadmissible.

Kurdish is the mother tongue of many citizens, but the law imposed a ban on the use of Kurdish in public places. Such a ban made education in Kurdish or the study of Kurdish as a second language impossible. Those who demanded the language rights have been subjected to prosecution and repression (see Mary Lou O'Neil in this volume, Chapter 5).

The Freedom and Democracy Party (Özgürlük ve Demokrasi Partisi, ÖZDEP), which proposed to create a system whereby "Everyone will have the right to basic education in his mother tongue," was dissolved by the Constitutional Court decision, for attempting to create minorities. When the decision was appealed at the European Court of Human Rights, the European Court found the closing of the party in violation of the charter. Eğitim-Sen, a progressive teachers' union with 170,000 members, is under the threat of being closed, because its bylaws includes a clause that promotes the right to receive education in one's mother tongue. Nevertheless, recently the laws were changed to allow teaching of mother tongues in private courses and broadcasting of news in various languages.

However, the change is slow and reluctant, and Turkey has been subject to international criticisms. For example, in its concluding observations of 8 June 2001, the Committee on the Rights of the Child expressed a concern over "the reservations made by the State Party [Turkey] under Articles 17, 29, and 30 of the Convention in some cases, in particular in the field of education, freedom of expression, and the right to enjoy own culture and use one's own language." The committee added that this "may have a negative impact on children belonging to ethnic groups which are not recognized as minorities under the Treaty of Lausanne, in particular children of Kurdish origin" (Committee on the Rights of the Child 2000).

Conclusion

Recognition of education as a right has a long history in Turkey. Provision of education has historically been accepted as the responsibility of the state, but the state has failed to provide adequate and equal access. Discrimination based on class, region, sex, and ethnicity prevented many from enjoying the benefits of even primary education.

As neoliberal policies became the norm and the state's commitment to public education declined after the 1980s, the resources allocated to public education from the national budget diminished steadily. The impact of declining funds was further aggravated by the high population growth rate. In a country like Turkey, where the distribution of income is unequal and there exists an elitist and competitive system of schooling, leaving the education of the young generation to market forces creates an alarming situation that violates the right to education of many, especially that of the poor. We are yet to see if the reforms in connection to Turkey's candidacy to the EU and the EU projects and programs related to education and training will lead to some improvements.

In its 2004 "Recommendation on Turkey's Progress Towards Accession," the Commission of the EU communicated to the Council and the Parliament that in education and training, Turkey's participation to the EC programs was quite satisfactory and that Turkey was showing an effort to enroll girls in less-favored regions. Turkey had amended some and made a number of new laws concerning education since 2001, in order to ensure the implementation of the EU *acquis*, and had completed the legal process for Turkey's participation in community programs, such as Socrates, Leonardo da Vinci, and Youth Community Action Programme. The Turkish National Agency operates as a department within the State Planning Organization in Ankara. The Ministry of National Education and the Ministry of Labor and Social Security participate in studies within the context of the European Training Foundation established by Council Regulation (EEC) 1360/90.

Chapter 9

Environmental Protection and Rights

N. Burcu Taşatar Parlak

Despite its rapid industrialization during the last fifty years, Turkey has been mainly an agricultural society. Thus, concerns over environmental pollution and conservation were addressed not until the 1970s, when the negative environmental impact of industrialization, urbanization, and overcrowding in some cities became striking.

This chapter reviews the development of public awareness about environmental issues and discusses the legal and administrative measures taken by the state to prevent environmental deterioration. The main argument holds that although the state and public awareness of environmental problems have been increasing, framing of these problems as a human rights issue is very new and far from becoming the dominant approach in the near future.

Constitutional, Administrative, and Legal Approaches

Constitutional Framework

In line with the late development of environmental consciousness, constitutions of the Republic of Turkey have not been attentive to environment either. Neither the 1924 Constitution nor the 1961 Constitution included any references to environmental issues and rights. Even though the 1961 Constitution defined the Republic of Turkey as a state based on human rights, its conceptualization of rights did not include environmental rights. The closest reference to environmental rights would be Article 49, which addressed the right to health and indirectly implied the right to a clean and healthy environment: "It is the duty of the state to ensure that everyone leads their lives in conditions of physical and mental health and to provide medical care" (Article 49).

The 1982 Constitution provided the first constitutional recognition of environmental rights and assigned the responsibility of the environmental protection to both the state and citizens. Article 56 reads: "Everyone has the right to live in a healthy, balanced environment. It is the duty of the State and citizens to improve the natural environment, and to prevent environmental pollution." The 1982 Constitution also includes provisions for environmental protection, which include: Article 43 on the protection of coastal areas; Article 44 on protections against soil erosion and other hazardous activities; Article 45 on the protection of agricultural lands, forests, minerals and other natural resources; Article 57 on the right to habitat and protection of urban environment; Article 63 on the protection of historical, cultural, and natural heritage; and Articles 168 and 169 on the protection of forests. Moreover, the Constitution protects the environmental rights indirectly, by setting boundaries on other individual rights it protects. For example, Article 35 protects property rights but also places a limit to the use of property rights to protect "public interest."

Planning Approach

A systemic approach to environmental issues in Turkey was first attempted in the Third Five-Year Development Plan (1973–77). The plan acknowledged that although some measures had been taken by different agencies, especially by local governments, environmental policies lacked national coordination. It emphasized the need to have a national effort to address environmental problems through special constitutional, legal, institutional, and technical measures and arrangements. It also included initiatives that would help public agencies, private organizations, and individual citizens in incorporating the goal of environmental protection into their actions. These concerns were reiterated in the subsequent development plans, which identified the problem areas, prioritization, and some policy approaches.

The Fifth Five-Year Development Plan (1985–89) related the environmental problems to the prevention of natural disasters and erosion, as well as the management of social changes such as urbanization, rapid industrialization, and the modernization of agriculture (Keleş 1997, 50). The Sixth Five-Year Development Plan (1991–95) incorporated the issue of environment for the first time into all of its economic sector-based development approaches and strategies (*Johannesburg Summit 2002*). Yet, it was the Seventh Five-Year Development Plan (1996–2000) that included environment concerns among its "Objectives, Principles, and Policies," under the heading "Protection and Improvement of the Environment." Its proposals and prioritization can be summarized as follows:

emphasizing pollution prevention rather than clean-up; using an appropriate combination of economic and regulatory instruments; developing regional and eco-basin strategies; strengthening the system of environmental management; ensuring that policies and solutions are in accordance with the EU norms and international standards; revising and enhancing the financing system for environmental protection, management and improvement; promoting environmental awareness through formal and non-formal channels; harmonizing legislation to ensure compatibility between economic development and environmental protection. (NEAP 1999, chap. 2)

The Eighth Five-Year Development Plan (2001–5) also stipulated: "It is essential to protect human health, ecological equilibrium and cultural, historical and aesthetic assets in economic and social development and emphasizes the sustainable development approach" (*Johannesburg Summit 2002*).

ADMINISTRATIVE AND INSTITUTIONAL ARRANGEMENTS

As environmental concerns started to be addressed in planning and led to legislative measures, it became necessary to create specialized institutions that would implement the policies and enforce the environmental law. The first such institution was the Permanent Board of Consultants for Environmental Problems; established in 1974, it prepared the Turkey Report for United Nations Environment Programme (UNEP). Then, in 1978, the Environment Organization was created under the prime minister's office, as was a General Directorate of Environment in 1984, which was transformed into the Undersecretariat of Environment in 1989.

The Ministry of Environment (ME) was established in 1991, by government Decree No. 443, in order to conduct and coordinate activities to protect and improve the environment. These activities were defined as ensuring appropriate land use, protection of natural resources, flora and fauna, and preventing pollution. Its duties included drafting laws, preparing rules and internal regulations, creating institutions (such as national laboratory for environmental analysis, village environment associations, and commissions to manage waste), supervising and planning environmental designs, taking interventionist initiatives and actions as appropriate, managing watershed water quality and regional waste, creating environmental policies and strategies, coordinating environmental activities at international and national levels, conducting research, applying measurements, monitoring compliance, collecting data, managing finances, and carrying out education and training. The ME formed special consultative organs at three levels to ensure the participation of people in line with the requirements of environmental protection and development activities: the Environment Council (ENC), the Higher Council for the Environment (HCE), and Local Environment Committees (LECs).[1] At the provincial level, "Provincial Directorates of Environment" were organized in 33 provinces, in 1995 (NEAP 1999, chap. 2). However, the ME lacked the structure and technology necessary to perform its duties. Since its structure allowed activity only through political power, the ME could not be very effective. Similarly, the Councils for Preservation of Natural and Cultural Entities were also hampered by several problems (chap. 2). Critics also noted that local authorities had limited personnel to meet the responsibilities, and political patronage often biased "the selection, appointment and promotion of municipal staff" (chap. 2).

In May 2003, the Ministry of Environment was merged with the Ministry of Forestry to create the Ministry of Environment and Forestry (MEF) by government Decree No. 4856. The new ministry was assigned the following responsibilities: to protect and rehabilitate the environment; to assure the use of land and natural resources effectively and properly in rural and urban areas; to protect and develop natural habitat, flora, fauna, natural resources, forests; to prevent environmental pollution; to protect, develop, and expand forests; to protect the living conditions of the population living in forests or near forests; to develop an industry of forestry. The extent to which the merge will address the structural and technical shortcomings of the ME is not clear.

LEGISLATIVE APPROACH

The first legislation on environment, Environmental Law No. 2872 (1983), defined environment as a common property of all citizens and included measures to protect and improve environment by pursuing the following objectives: "to protect and improve the environment which is the common property of all citizens; to protect and make optimal use of land and natural resources in rural and urban areas; to prevent water, soil, and air pollution; and to improve and assure the protection of health, culture, and lives of the present and future generations by preserving the nation's plant and animal life and its natural and historical wealth" (Turkish Environmental Law and Some Other Related Legal Provisions 1988, 9).

This law also embodied the "polluter pays principle" adopted by other countries, and set forth the concept of "absolute liability" to operationalize it. It also banned certain polluting operations and required environmental impact assessments (EIAs) for various activities taken by private and public industrial production and construction projects. The law specified the regulation procedures to be followed, plans to be prepared, standards to be met, and activities to be prohibited. It also authorized different agencies, particularly government agencies and municipalities, to enforce the law, through monitoring and imposing fines and other penalties as specified by law. In addition to fines, enforcement involved imprisonment, factory closings, or prohibitions on the right to build or operate facilities. Violators were allowed to appeal penalties in courts (NEAP 1999, chap. 2).

Since Turkey was late to pursue environmental regulations for at least ten years, in this law, regulatory mechanisms were designated to be the primary tools for managing the environment. Thus, it was weak on direct preventive actions and mainly included remedial provision. Development was given priority over preserving the environment (Akıncı 1996, 220–23).[2]

As national and international environmental NGOs and other international organizations pointed to the limitations of the Environmental Law No. 2872, several regulations were devised to protect the environment: the Environmental Pollution Prevention Fund Regulation (1985); the Air Quality Regulation (1986); the Noise Control Regulation (1986); Regulation of National Parks (1986); the Regulation Concerning the Establishment of Guilt in Fines to be Levied on Ships and Other Marine Vessels (1987); the Water Pollution Control Regulation (1988); the Water Pollution Control Regulation Revision (2004); Regulation of Coastal Law Applications (1990); Radiation Safety Regulation (1991); Solid Waste Regulation (1991); Regulation on Control of Medical Wastes (1993); Environmental Impact Assessment Regulation (EIA) (1993); Environmental Impact Assessment Regulation Revision I (1997); Environmental Impact Assessment Regulation Revision II (2002); Environmental Impact Assessment Regulation Revision III (2003); Environmental Impact Assessment Regulation Revision IV (2004); Regulation on the Control of Dangerous Substances and Preparations (1993); Regulation on the Control of Dangerous Substances and Preparations (1993), changed to Regulation on Dangerous Chemical Substances in (2001); Regulation on the Control of Hazardous Wastes (1995); Pastures Regulation (1998); Regulation of Reducing Substances that Deplete the Ozone Layer (1999); Regulation of Licensing of Pesticides and Similar Substances Used for Agricultural Purposes (1999); Regulation of Preparation Principles of Environmental Systematic Plans (2000); Regulation of Insulating of Heat in Buildings (2000); Regulation of Air Pollution from Insulting of Heat in Buildings (2005); Regulation of Radioactive Wastes That Do Not Require Special Process (2000); Regulation of National Application in Case of a Nuclear Accident or Radiological Emergency (2000); Regulation of Application for International Trade in Endangered Species of Wild Fauna and Flora Convention (2001); Soil Pollution Control Regulation (2001); Regulation of Protection of Wetlands (2002); Environmental Inspection Regulation (2002); Regulation of Organic Agriculture Principles and Applications (2002); Disposal of Waste Oils Control Regulation (2004); Protection of Waters against Pollution Caused by Nitrates from Agricultural Sources (2004); Quality of Petrol and Diesel Fuels Regulation (2004); Packaging and Packaging Waste Control Regulation (2004); Waste Batteries and

Accumulators Control Regulation (2004); Radiation Security Regulation Revision (2004); Control of Combating of Air Pollution from Industrial Plants Regulation (2004); and Industrial Zones Regulation (2004).

In addition to these regulations, as of 2006, there are some 40 laws that are also related to environmental problems and issues, some going back to the 1950s. They include the Straits Law No. 2960 (1983), Coastal Law No. 3621 (1990), and Forest Law No. 6831 (1956). The new Penal Code (2004) also addresses the pollution of the environment and assigns significant penalties, but its provisions on environmental pollution will enter into force later than the other components of the law, with a considerable delay on 1 April 2007. Also questionable is the level of enforcement that the law will enjoy.

The inadequacies of the Law No. 2872 were evident immediately, and a new Environmental Law was drafted in 1995. After numerous revisions, on 26 April 2006, the parliament adopted the new bill (no. 5491). This new legislation increased the penalties and centralizes the regulatory power at the ministry. An important aspect of the bill is its brief reference to environmental rights for the first time (Article 3(e)). The bill also extends the function of the HCE to include the responsibility of determining legislative and administrative measures that would incorporate environmental concerns into economic decisions to ensure the fulfillment of the sustainable development principle.

While the recent legal reforms are promising, it should be noted that the earlier legislative and administrative measures have been ineffective due to limited means, structural problems, the lack of enforcement, political manipulations, and the lack of education and communication. For example, a survey of public officials found that 75 percent lacked adequate information on EIAs; only 5 percent could translate legal arrangements on environmental protection into practice; 35 percent had no notion of whether the laws were sufficient; 21 percent felt the laws did not clearly identify implementing agencies; 73 percent indicated that their colleagues had no idea about the Environment Act; and 94 percent had not accessed the act's regulations (NEAP 1999, chap. 2).

International Treaties and Turkey's Participation

The right to the environment is considered in a new category of human rights, referred to as the "third generation rights," which also include the rights to development, peace, ownership of common heritage, and communication.[3] The Universal Declaration of Human Rights (1948) is not explicit on environmental rights. However, it recognizes that "Everyone is entitled to a social and international order in which the rights and freedoms set forth in this Declaration can be fully realized" (Article 28), and it is generally accepted that the "order" to which the Declaration refers also covers the environmental concerns. Turkey was among the original signatories of the Declaration.

The International Covenant on Economic, Social and Cultural Rights (1966) makes implicit references to environmental rights in several articles: Article 1 on the "right of peoples to self-determination and to freely dispose of their natural wealth and resources"; Article 11 on the "right to an adequate standard of living, and to be free from hunger," which obliges state parties with providing "programmes to improve methods of production, conservation and distribution of food; disseminating knowledge of principles of nutrition; measures to achieve the most efficient development and utilization of natural resources; equitable distribution of world food supplies"; Article 12 on the "right to health; steps to be taken for the healthy development of the child, improvement of all aspects of environmental and industrial hygiene"; and Article 15 on the "right to enjoy the benefits of scientific progress and its applications". However, enforcement mechanisms of the covenant have been weak, and Turkey ratified it only at the beginning of 2003.

The Stockholm Declaration on the Human Environment, issued as the final document of the 1972 UN Conference on Environment, is the first important international document that establishes a link between the human rights concept and environmental protection. Principle 1 states, "Man has the fundamental right to freedom, equality and adequate conditions of life, in an environment of a quality that permits a life of dignity and well-being, and he bears a solemn responsibility to protect and improve the environment for present and future generations" (International Association of Universities).

The UN Convention on the Rights of the Child (1989) explicitly refers to the need for the education of the child to be directed, inter alia, to "the development of respect for the natural environment" (Article 29). Moreover, as with most other instruments, many of its provisions intended to be implemented from an ecological standpoint, bearing in mind the relationship between the environment, development, and human rights (Ksentini).

On 6 March 1990 the UN Commission on Human Rights adopted Resolution No. 1990, 41, entitled "Human Rights and the Environment," in which the link between the preservation of the environment and the promotion of human rights is underscored. On 16 May 1994, an international group of experts on human rights and environmental protection convened at the UN in Geneva and drafted the first-ever declaration of principles on human rights and the environment. The Draft Declaration of Principles on Human Rights and the Environment declared the following principles:

1. Human rights, an ecologically sound environment, sustainable development and peace are interdependent and indivisible.
2. All persons have the right to a secure, healthy, and ecologically sound environment. This right and other human rights, including civil, cultural, economic, political, and social rights, are universal, interdependent, and indivisible.
3. All persons shall be free from any form of discrimination in regard to actions and decisions that affect the environment.
4. All persons have the right to an environment adequate to meet equitably the needs of present generations and that does not impair the rights of future generations to meet equitably their needs.

In addition to the normative advancement of environmental rights within the international human rights regime, international conferences on environment yielded a significant body of treaties. The UN Conference on Environment and Development, held in Rio de Janeiro in 1992, has been particularly important. The Rio Declaration on Environment and Development (1992) linked environmental rights to the right to development and identified the principles for a global effort. Principle 1 states, "Human beings are at the center of concerns for sustainable development. They are entitled to a healthy and productive life in harmony with nature" (Ksentini). Moreover, the Rio conference has been noteworthy for issuing 27 agendas to be followed in pursuing development and environmental protection. Although Turkey has not been a signatory or party to several of these instruments, it signed the declaration, which involves no mandatory obligations, and ratified Agenda 21, which set forth important changes environmental protection policies and management systems.

Another significant international development has been the Convention on Access to Information, Public Participation in Decision-Making, and Access to Justice in Environmental Matters, prepared by UN European Economic Council and opened for a signature on 23–25 June 1998 in Aarhus, Denmark (Turgut 1998; Silicon Valley Toxic Coalition). The Aarhus Convention was negotiated by the UN Economic Commission for Europe as part of its pan-European environmental legal framework. It intended to lift environmental secrecy and strengthen citizens' environmental rights. It has been called "a remarkable achievement not only in terms of protection of the environment, but also in terms of the promotion and protection of human rights" (Robinson). It is important also for providing procedural rights irrespective of citizenship and place of residence ("Environmental Accountability in Africa (EAA)").

Neither the European Human Rights Convention nor its Social Charter has direct references to environmental rights. However, over the years several instruments were devised to improve environmental rights and protection. It is noted that Turkey has been more involved in the European human rights regime (see Füsun Türkmen and Thomas W. Smith in this volume, Chapters 16 and 17). Table 9.1, which summarizes Turkey's status on major environmental agreements, supports this argument.

TABLE 9.1. TURKEY'S STATUS ON MAJOR EUROPEAN CONVENTIONS ON HUMAN RIGHTS AND ENVIRONMENTAL PROTECTION

Neither signed nor ratified

Protocol No. 13 to the Convention for the Protection of Human Rights and Fundamental Freedoms, Concerning the Abolition of the Death Penalty in All Circumstances

Additional Protocol to the Convention on Human Rights and Biomedicine concerning Transplantation of Organs and Tissues of Human Origin

Convention on the Protection of Environment through Criminal Law

Protocol of Amendment to the European Convention for the Protection of Vertebrate Animals Used for Experimental and Other Scientific Purposes

Convention on Civil Liability for Damage Resulting from Activities Dangerous to the Environment

Protocol No. 10 to the Convention for the Protection of Human Rights and Fundamental Freedoms

Protocol of Amendment to the European Convention for the Protection of Animals Kept for Farming Purposes

European Convention on the Recognition of the Legal Personality of International Nongovernmental Organizations

European Agreement Relating to Persons Participating in Proceedings of the European Commission and Court of Human Rights

Signed but not ratified

Protocol No. 12 to the Convention for the Protection of Human Rights and Fundamental Freedoms

Additional Protocol to the Convention for the Protection of Human Rights and Dignity of the Human Being, with regard to the Application of Biology and Medicine, on the Prohibition of Cloning Human Beings

Convention for the Protection of Human Rights and Dignity of the Human Being with regard to the Application of Biology and Medicine

Convention on Human Rights and Biomedicine, European Agreement relating to persons participating in proceedings of the European Court of Human Rights

Protocol No. 9 to the Convention for the Protection of Human Rights and Fundamental Freedoms

European Convention for the Protection of Pet Animals

European Convention for the Protection of Vertebrate Animals Used for Experimental and Other Scientific Purposes

Protocol No. 7 to the Convention for the Protection of Human Rights and Fundamental Freedoms

Protocol No. 6 to the Convention for the Protection of Human Rights and Fundamental Freedoms Concerning the Abolition of the Death Penalty

Table 9.1. (*Continued*)

Ratified

European Landscape Convention

Protocol No. 11 to the Convention for the Protection of Human Rights and Fundamental Freedoms, Restructuring the Control Machinery Established thereby

European Convention on the Protection of the Archaeological Heritage (revised)

Convention for the Protection of the Architectural Heritage of Europe

Protocol No. 8 to the Convention for the Protection of Human Rights and Fundamental Freedoms

Additional Protocol to the European Convention for the Protection of Animals during International Transport

Convention on the Conservation of European Wildlife and Natural Habitats

Protocol No. 5 to the Convention for the Protection of Human Rights and Fundamental Freedoms, amending Articles 22 and 40 of the Convention

---

By 2003, Turkey has become party to 90 international treaty instruments that address environmental rights. It has been a signatory to several others. Moreover, the National Assembly is considering the ratification of the Antidesertification Convention. The country also participates in several regional initiatives such as the Mediterranean Environmental Technical Assistance Program (METAP), the Mediterranean Action Plan, Black Sea Environmental Program, and Regional Agenda 21.

At the international level, Turkey strives to play a dynamic role in diverse environmental activities, particularly in the Mediterranean, the Black Sea, the Caucasus, and Central Asia, by contributing to the formulation of regional agendas in line with the principles adopted in Rio in 1992, hosting the Program Coordination Unit for the protection of the Black Sea, and taking an active part within the Mediterranean Action Plan process. Turkey is also taking concrete steps toward the establishment of a Regional Environmental Center in Turkey, to assist the Central Asian and the Caucasian countries, in increasing public awareness on environmental issues, and in facilitating investments in this field. Furthermore, Turkey launched an ambitious initiative to host a regional center in line with the principles of the İstanbul Habitat Conference, organized in 1996, which generated new momentum on urban policies and shelter issues within the context of "sustainable human settlements" ("Environmental Accountability in Africa (EAA)").

Since 1981, Turkey has been a member of the International Energy Agency (IEA), but it has been frequently criticized by the IEA for its limited efforts to reduce air pollution. In its annual report on member countries (2003), the IEA states that Turkey needs to maintain and possibly increase investments in public transport, especially in urban areas, as well as improve the implementation of existing regulations on air quality. "Although Turkey is beginning to take steps to improve air quality (including a switch toward unleaded gasoline by 2005), the increased number of automobiles on Turkish streets is hampering this effort" (Energy Information Administration). Additionally, the IEA has recommended that Turkey "consider the promulgation of appropriate energy conservation laws," "[strive] to limit the growth of greenhouse gas emissions," "tighten efficiency standards on industrial boilers and electric motors," "consider establishing fiscal and economic incentives for conservation . . . in all sectors," and "further promote fuel switching from high-sulfur lignite to natural gas" (Energy Information Administration).

Turkey's carbon emissions have risen in line with the country's energy consumption. Turkey's energy-related carbon emissions have jumped from 18 million metric tons in 1980 to 55 million metric tons in 2000. Although this is low in absolute terms compared to other IEA countries, the rate of increase is rapid.

Turkey is not a party to the Kyoto Protocol, meaning the country has no binding requirements to cut carbon emissions by the 2008–12 period, as most other IEA countries have. However, Turkey has established a National Climate Coordination Group (NCCG) to carry out the national studies in line with those conducted by all countries of the UN Framework Convention on Climate Change (UNFCC), which Turkey signed on 24 May 2004. The ministry is preparing a "National Climate Report" upon which the decision to sign the Kyoto Protocol will be taken. Turkey's "greenhouse inventory" will be determined by the report, which aims to clarify the global warming scenarios, and action will be taken according to the outcome.

Harmonization of the Legislation with the European Union

For membership in the European Union, candidate countries must align their national laws, rules, and procedures, including those relevant to the environmental sector, with those of the EU contained in the *acquis communautaire*. The Accession Partnership sets out the principles, priorities, immediate objectives and conditions decided by the European Council. The Turkish government announced its own national program for the adoption of the EU *acquis* on 19 March 2001 and submitted it to the EU Commission. The national program is composed of 29 chapters, including a chapter on the "environment" (*Johannesburg Summit 2002*).

Earlier, the National Environmental Action Plan (NEAP) had been developed in 1999, to contribute to the Eighth Five-Year Development Plan (prepared in 1998), as well as to act as a key building block for the National Agenda 21, prepared with UN Development Programme support.

The NEAP acknowledged the positive developments such as the creation of legislation and institutional structures, the preparation of environment strategy and action plan, and increased public sensitivity toward a clean environment. These are followed by a series of adversities and shortcomings that can be summarized as follows:

- environmental management systems have not reached the desired level of effectiveness;
- pressures on natural resources caused by rapid urbanization have increased, leading to greater amount of wastes and other environmental problems, especially on coastal areas and seas;
- improvements regarding education, processes of participation in decision-making, and decentralization remain inadequate;
- environment policies have not been incorporated into economic and social policies;
- "an efficient and coordinated environmental monitoring system" has not been established, as the authority and responsibilities of the ME, other related ministries, and the local administrations governments have not been redefined as needed;
- progress regarding the creation of data and information access systems, environmental monitoring and measuring infrastructure, environment inventories, and statistics and standards concerning the environment and development has not been sufficient;
- the implementation process of the regulation of EIA is not as satisfactory as desired. (*Johannesburg Summit 2002*).

The plan calls for certain legal and institutional arrangements, including the enactment of the Biosafety Law and the establishment of the National Biosafety Board by making the necessary amendments in the related laws (*Johannesburg Summit 2002*). Turkey's revised the version of the National Programme for Adoption of the *Acquis* and the "Decision on the Implementation and Coordination and Monitoring of the NPAA," indicating the short- and long-term priorities in the field of environment as well as the other issues, was put into force in July 2003. According to the program, short-term priorities are to increase the effectiveness of environmental impact assessment and enhance the accession of environmental information, midterm priorities, on the other hand are the alignment of waste control regulations to those of the EU. MEF is prepared new waste control regulations to consider alignment. It is estimated that the cost of harmonization in environmental sector is around $U.S.20–30 billion ("Relations with the European Union in the Field of Environment").

The same year, a new regulation on environmental impact assessments (EIA) was devised and environmental inspections have subsequently been improved and strengthened. Air and water quality will be improved through more effective regulation and enforcement, resulting in cleaner environment for the citizens. A national database on environmental information is in the process of being established, which will substantially increase public awareness and public participation. The Ministry of Environment has been coordinating activities with other relevant ministries and institutions in Turkey, in order to ensure that environmental policies are more effectively integrated with other policies (*Johannesburg Summit 2002*).

The Turkish system for protecting and managing environment is criticized an a few accounts, including: "(a) over-reliance on regulatory mechanisms; (b) little integration of environmental factors in planning; (c) limited public participation; (d) inadequate enforcement capability to implement environmental laws; (e) little use of environmental information; (f) over-centralization of budgets, authority and information; (g) low levels of awareness about environmental rules; and (h) inadequate environmental content in the educational system" (NEAP 1999, chap. 2).

According to the progress report released on 6 October 2004 by the European Commission of the EU General Secretariat, even if Turkey makes the necessary investments into the environment, the desired outcome will not be achieved until the 2030s. In an assessment of the problems that Turkey will face during the negotiation process, the EU General Secretariat has listed the requirements that Turkey will have to meet, in order of difficulty. Turkey will not be able to finish the necessary investments until the 2030s and the total cost of the investments is between 30 and 50 billion euros. Despite some progress, Turkish legislation is at a low-level adaptation level for EU environmental legislation. In order to make progress toward the EU legislation, more effort needs to be made in the areas of air quality, waste control, water quality, environmental protection, industrial pollution, and risk management (Representation of the European Commission to Turkey).

Turkey joined European Environmental Agency with government Decree No. 4794 in 2002. Two years later, the Ministry of Environment and Forestry started a project to establish an autonomous environment agency.

Civil Society Organizations and Environmental Conservation

The last two decades witnessed a significant increase in the number of nongovernmental organizations (NGOs) in Turkey. However, a survey study based on a sample of 1,793 voluntary organizations, associations, and foundations, revealed that in the late 1990s only 7 percent of a total of 60,000 NGOs worked on environmental issues (NEAP 1999, 16). Table 9.2

TABLE 9.2. MAJOR NONGOVERNMENTAL ORGANIZATIONS IN TURKEY THAT WORK ON ENVIRONMENTAL POLLUTION, ENVIRONMENTAL EDUCATION, FORESTRY PROTECTION, AND RECYCLING

Name and founding date of establishment	Air	Soil and land	Water quality	Sea	Pesticides	Solid waste	Education	Forestry	Recycling
Environment Foundation of Turkey, 1978*	X	X	X	X	X	X	X	X	X
Turkish Foundation for the Protection of Monumental-Environmental-Tourism Assets, 1976	X								
WWF-Turkey World Wild Life Protection Foundation, 2001**			X	X			X	X	
Environmental Protection and Greenification Council of Turkey, 1972			X						
Association of Turkish Municipalities (and regional unions of municipalities)			X			X			
Aegean Mediterranean Service Foundation, 1991			X						
TEMA, Turkish Foundation for Reforestation, Erosion Combat and Protection of Natural Assets, 1992		X							
SSST, Soil Science Society of Turkey, 1964		X							
Forestry Society of Turkey, 1924								X	
Green Turkey Forestry Society, 1950								X	
Society of Forest Technicians, 1958								X	
Chamber of Forest Engineers, 1954								X	

TABLE 9.2. (Continued)

Name and founding date of establishment	Air	Soil and land	Water quality	Sea	Pesticides	Solid waste	Education	Forestry	Recycling
Foundation for the Protection of Forestry and Nature, 1986									
Environmental Protection/Beautification of Ayvalık Society, 1981								X	
Biologists' Association, 1975					X	X			
Society for Technical Beekeeping, 1985					X				
CEVKO, Environmental Protection and Packaging Waste Recovery and Recycling Trust, 1991									X
CEKUL, Natural and Cultural Environment Protection Foundation, 1990							X		
TURCEV, Turkish Environmental Education Foundation, 1993							X		
TURMEPA. Turkish Marine Environment Protection Association, 1994				X					
Greenpeace Mediterranean, 1994	X	X	X	X		X		X	
Chamber of Agriculture Engineers, 1954		X							
Association of Peace with Nature, 1993				X		X	X		
Chambers of Environmental Engineers, 1992	X	X	X	X	X	X			X

*EFT, United Nations Environmental Programme National Committee for Turkey since 1992 (UNEP c. 2004). *Turkish representative of World Wild Life Fund 2001, formerly Society for Protection of Nature (WWF-Turkey c. 2003).

lists major environmental NGOs and their activity areas. Most of these are located in four major industrial cities and are relatively new, with 62 percent established after 1991. Typically their revenues are limited to membership fees.

Environmental NGOs have been particularly successful in raising and addressing issues about air, water, and sea pollution, coastal zone management, protection of endangered species, soil erosion and forestry (tree plantation activities), environmental education, protection on animals, mining, and nuclear energy. However, their overall effect on improving the environment has been limited, due to several obstacles: limited or unproductive relations with the MEF and government agencies; the lack of interorganizational solidarity; limited membership and the lack of mobilization; ineffective management structures and procedures; reliance on remedial approaches and solutions; limited access to the media, limited finances, technical equipment, and self-assurance (NEAP 1999, chap. 2).

Most important for our purposes, environmental problems still are not fully addressed within a human rights framework. However, some recent developments may change the pattern to make environmental conservationism and protection a human rights issue: (1) references to environmental rights in litigation; (2) increasing public awareness and protests; and (3) introducing environmental education to the younger generations.

LITIGATION

The Turkish Foundation for Reforestation, Erosion Combat, and Protection of Natural Habitats (Türkiye Erozyonla Mücadele, Ağaçlandırma ve Doğal Varlıkları Koruma Türkiye Erozyonla Mücadele, Ağaçlandırma ve Doğal Varlıkları Koruma Vakfı, TEMA) is an NGO established in 1992. TEMA's legal department has focused on the contentious issue of land use in Turkey. It has taken legal action and sought the repeal of several government decrees that opened up ecosystems to tourism, allowed legal loopholes that would result in deforestation, or permitted the use of agricultural land (including Turkey's most productive croplands) for non-agricultural purposes. Recently, "it won rulings overturning decrees instigated by the Prime Ministry and Tourism Ministry in 9 separate cases to turn areas of natural wealth for tourism development," which are mostly "situated in fragile coastal zone ecosystems" where "development would have devastating effects on flora and fauna habitats" (Turkish Foundation for Reforestation).

Another important case of litigation involved the community of Bergama, which won a legal ban on cyanide in Turkey. In May 1997, the highest Turkish administrative court overturned approval given by the Department of Environment for a proposed gold mining project. The

Bergama villagers sued the international mining consortium Eurogold for using cyanide. After a rally by 10,000 local people, with 1,000 tractors that occupied the mine site, the Council of State ruled that the company must halt its gold mining operation using the cyanide-leaching process. Referring to the Constitution and its guarantee of a healthy environment, the court judged that a cyanide-based mining technology was at odds with these constitutional rights (Project Underground). The office of İzmir's governor subsequently ordered Eurogold to cease its activities, and the company was forced to ship its equipment abroad ("Bergama Villagers Worry" 1999).

In addition to actions taken by citizens and NGOs, environmental rights found support in the Constitutional Court. In 1986, the Constitutional Court annulled some articles of the Building Law No. 3194 for being in violation of Article 56 of the Constitution.[4]

PUBLIC PROTESTS

Parallel to proliferation of laws, state agencies and NGOs on environment, public awareness about environmental issues increased, albeit slowly. While protest activities used to focus on other human rights issues, recently there have been cases of organized protest that focus on environmental issues and rights. For example, in May 2001, Greenpeace activists climbed the chimney of a waste incinerator in the northwestern city of İzmit to protest pollution from the plant. Due to its potential health hazards the plant had been closed in 1998, by the Turkish Energy Ministry, but reopened in 1999 (Energy Information Administration).

The country's first nuclear power plant, planned for Akkuyu on Turkey's Mediterranean coast, also raised the ire of environmentalists, who had been arguing that what was needed is not more power generation but more efficient relay and distribution systems. They also point to the fact that the proposed site is less than 15 miles from an active geological fault line, which stirs safety fears in light of the earthquakes of 1999. As a response to the protest activities that started in 1996, in March 2000, the Turkish government once again delayed an announcement of the winning bid for Akkuyu (Energy Information Administration).

ENVIRONMENTAL EDUCATION

Environmental education has been provided in formal preschools, and in primary, middle, and high schools since 1992. In 1995, the Global Learning and Observations to Benefit the Environment (GLOBE) Protocol was signed between the governments of Turkey and the United States. In line with this protocol some of the private schools in İzmir initiated environmental education programs. The South Eastern Mediterranean Environment Project (SEMEP) was organized by UNESCO. The Middle East Technical University Development Foundation College started environmental education under the name ecoschool project in SEMEP scope (NEAP 1999, chap. 2). Further, programs related to the environment are offered in at least 21 Turkish universities and courses such as ecology, environmental law, and policies are offered at the undergraduate and postgraduate levels. In addition, university groups and clubs focus on the environment and nature. Nonformal education programs, which attract about a million people a year, also include some form of environmental education and training. They involve subjects such as nutrition, health, child care, environmental care and cleanliness, and the impact of the environment on the spread of diseases (chap. 2).

Moreover, when the years between 1995 and 2004 were designated by the General Assembly of the United Nations as the UN Decade for Human Rights Education, Turkey joined the effort in 1998 and adopted a national program that called for the incorporation of human rights courses into the curricula of junior and senior high schools. Although the content and effectives of these courses are subject to criticisms (see Kenan Çayır in this volume, Chapter 15), their proper revision and inclusion of environmental rights would make the next generation more aware of environmental issues and rights. In fact, the new bill on environment (no. 5491) requires kindergartens and primary schools, related to the Ministry of National Education, to include environment-related subjects in the curricula (Article 6(1)). Moreover, the state-owned television stations have to broadcast programs about environment at least two hours in a month and private radio stations have to broadcast at least half an hour in a month. At least 20 percent of these programs have to be broadcasted during the highest rating/listening time of the stations. The Radio and Television Supreme Council will be in charge of monitoring these programs.

Conclusion

The progress toward acknowledging environmental problems and taking measures to protect the environment has been late and slow. However, the last few years witnessed a significant leap, as evident in the proliferation of legislation, state agencies, NGOs, as well as Turkey's increasing participation in international environmental protection and human rights regimes. In addition to the state effort, the public awareness about the environmental issues and willingness to take action, either at courts on streets, have been on the rise.

However, all these developments and efforts show that even though environmental issues are identified, they are seldom addressed as human rights issues. That will probably be the contribution of the next generation, which is being exposed to environmental and human rights education at school and through media reports on environmental issues and public protests.

Part III
The Rights of the Displaced

Chapter 10
Conflict-Induced Internal Displacement

ALPASLAN ÖZERDEM AND TIM JACOBY

The term "internally displaced persons" has gained wide usage since it was first coined in the early 1970s, and is currently defined as follows: "Persons or groups of persons who have been forced or obliged to flee or to leave their homes or places of habitual residence, in particular as a result of or in order to avoid the effects of armed conflict, situations of generalized violence, violations of human rights or natural or human-made disasters, and who have not crossed an internationally recognized State border" (Global IDP Survey 1998).

Internally displaced persons (IDPs) are the largest "at-risk" population in the world (Cohen and Deng 1998). Although the causes of flight for IDPs from their homes and livelihoods may be similar to those of refugees, the fact that they remain inside the boundaries of their own state means that they are not entitled to international "protection." In legal terms, they are not guaranteed asylum and admission or the restoration of national protection upon return/resettlement. As such, the United Nations High Commission for Refugees (UNHCR), the specifically designated agency for the provision of international protection and assistance to refugees, cannot offer the same level of assistance to IDPs as those who have crossed an internationally recognized border.

Forced internal displacement can be divided into two groups according to its main trigger: Conflict-Induced Displacement (CID) and Development-Induced Displacement (DID). Displacement caused by "natural" disasters can be considered to be an aspect of DID because of the interwoven relationship between development and the exacerbation of societal vulnerabilities. There are strong parallels and overlaps between these two groups of displacement, as both are triggered by acute change and fears over "human security," and both are frequently understood through a rights-based analytical discourse. Despite the fact that the former receives considerably more attention that the latter, their commonalities mean that they should both be considered within a human rights context (Muggah 2000; Pettersson 2001).

The number of conflict-related IDPs in 2003 was estimated to be between 20 and 25 million (Global IDP Project c. 2005). If development-induced and natural and human-made disasters related displacements are considered, however, the number of IDPs is generally quoted at around 50 million. Considering that there is little access to countries such as Myanmar and China, the figure might be as high as 100 million. While the numbers of refugees (those who have crossed an international border) have remained relatively stable over the last few years, the continued rise in intrastate conflicts and civilian causalities has produced year-on-year increases in conflict-related displacement (Sandole 1999). This chapter will thus focus on the phenomenon of CID. It will look at three levels of analysis—the international, the national, and the community (Korn 1999). First, it will consider issues relating to multilateral intervention, then present a review of the displacement crisis in Turkey from the early 1990s onward. In particular, it will argue that there is currently a window of opportunity for reconsidering conflict-induced displacement issues within a human rights context as a result of recent sociopolitical developments. The chapter will then analyze various opportunities and challenges for improvements in the national protection of conflict-induced displaced persons in Turkey.

Sovereignty, National Protection, and Displacement in South Eastern Turkey

In most cases, the international response to the plight of IDPs is based on "assistance" that, theoretically at least, is apolitical. For many host countries, both the international interest in their IDPs and the accompanying discourse of human rights are, however, heavily politicized and not fully separable from the social dynamics that displaced their citizens in the first place. It is clear, though, that assistance and protection cannot be isolated from each other as altogether different responses. The World Food Programme (WFP), for example, advocates the provision of assistance that promotes future protection, while the UNHCR holds the view that assistance without protection is unlikely to improve the situation of displaced populations in any sustainable way.

In response to the fact that IDPs cannot claim political asylum, have no recourse if their human rights are abused, and are unable to seek the international protection and assistance of the UNHCR, the UN appointed Dr. Francis Deng as the Secretary-General's Representative for Displaced People (RSG) in 1992. His brief was to recommend an effective system of protection and assistance with the overall objective of providing IDPs with an adequate standard of living including sufficient shelter, food, water, sanitation, and essential health and education facilities. The resultant

Guiding Principles on Internal Displacement (Reliefweb 1998) drew on human rights and analogous refugee law to outline a coherent set of rights for IDPs, as well as the obligations of governments and other actors toward them. The thirty principles cover issues of protection against displacement, the management of IDPs during displacement and postconflict return and strategies for their successful reintegration. However, these are not legally binding, so signatory states can only be encouraged and cajoled into acknowledging their responsibilities. Since each has the sovereign power to exercise its own authority over its territory and citizens built into the UN Charter, little more can be done.[1]

It is clear that this principle of nonintervention does pose a challenge not only to the protection of IDPs but also to human rights in general. At essence, it is a question of whether human rights should be considered within a state's domestic domain or as part of an international moral code. It is argued, by proponents of the latter position, that the state does not only have territorial jurisdiction, but also the responsibility of meeting its citizens' basic economic and social needs. For some, a state is unable to claim the right of sovereign authority over its people without satisfying these conditions. In other words, if a state does not respect its responsibilities to IDPs and other vulnerable groups within its borders, then it fails the test of minimum international legitimacy (Hathaway 1991). The issue then becomes focused on the international community's right, or obligation, to violate a state's sovereignty and protect the civil liberties of its citizens. NATO's military intervention in Kosovo in 1999 was, for instance, justified on the grounds that the Yugoslav state was unable to ensure the human rights of a section of its population. However, as Chomsky (2000) points out, the universal ideals of humanitarianism seem to be used to facilitate incursions into small and strategically unimportant territories and not stronger, yet equally reprehensible, regimes. Of these, Turkey's treatment of its Kurdish minority appears to be a case in point. Apart from Ankara's policy decisions and the conducts of its security forces (both of which will be discussed in more detail below), a key area of international concern has been the Turkish state's inability to deal with the large numbers of IDPs emanating from the 13 predominantly Kurdish-speaking provinces of southeast Anatolia.

These areas of Turkey have long been a source of peripheral disquiet and, since Ottoman times, the state has struggled to extend its political infrastructure into what remains an area of well-institutionalized cultural traditions and of topologically difficult terrain (Jacoby forthcoming). Rebellions against central administration have occurred in each stage of Turkey's development. The most notable of these were led by Badr Khan in 1836 against Sultan Mahmud, by Ubaidullah in 1880 against Sultan Abdülhamit, and by Sheik Said in 1925 against Mustafa Kemal. Following the transition to multiparty politics in the 1940s, the representation of this region became increasingly important as a source of electoral support. During the 1960s, Kurdish-speaking delegates, enjoying considerable support from migrant groups within the slums of Ankara and İstanbul, developed ties with broadly leftist organizations, which, in the 1970s, gave rise to a number of direct-action groups. Foremost among these was the Kurdistan Workers' Party (Partia Karkaren Kürdistan, PKK). Following a period of significant activity in 1978 and 1979, the PKK were driven into Syria by the military intervention of 1980. In 1984 they returned with a renewed program of terrorist activities predominantly aimed at feudatories and state functionaries based in the southeast (İmset 1992).

The state's response has largely been to delegate administrative responsibility to the military (Jacoby 2004). Under emergency legislation, provincial governors were given unprecedented powers to restrict civil liberties and to implement highly aggressive policy measures. Kemal Kirişçi identifies three main factors for the causes of internal displacement in the region (1998). First, the military imposed a program of village evacuation as it was claimed that local populations, willingly or unwillingly, provided logistical support for the PKK. In disregard of the UN Resolution on Human Rights No. 77 (1993), Turkish troops, supported by irregular and largely unaccountable paramilitaries, cleared thousands of villages and, as in the case of Lice in 1994, a number of reasonably substantial towns (P. White 1998; Medico International and Kurdish Human Rights Project 1996). It is estimated that around 350,000 people have been "evacuated" from about 3,500 villages (Global IDP Project c. 2002). In addition, the region's print media have been heavily circumscribed with only one Kurdish weekly, *Walate Me*, appearing on a regular basis. The broadcast media have also been prevented from scheduling Kurdish language programs and even the lyrics of popular or traditional Kurdish songs have been seen as potential vehicles of information for the PKK and frequently banned under the Article 8 of the 1991 Antiterrorism Law (Kurdish Human Rights Project 1996). Such programs of repression and forced migration are, in fact, a long-established method of dealing with peripheral dissent for the Turkish state. The infamous displacement of Armenians during the First World War and the wholesale destruction of Dersim in 1937 are cases in point (Hallı 1972). Indeed, Süleyman Demirel, the former president of the Republic, acknowledged that the Turkish state's attitude has changed little when he stated that the PKK was "being dealt with like the previous 28 revolts" (Kurdish Human Rights Project 1996, 4).

Such conflict-induced displacement has been aggravated by the Southeastern Anatolian Development Project, or "GAP," which represents one of the world's most ambitious hydroelectric power and irrigation schemes and has, according to the Global IDP Project, displaced over 200,000 people.[2] For example, the İlisu Dam—one of nineteen planned power plants and part of an irrigation scheme covering over 1.7 million hectares costing over US$32 billion—will alone necessitate the compulsory resettlement of more than 16,000 people (GAP). GAP is also considered to be the state's main response to the region's underdevelopment and, by extension, to the root causes of the armed conflict that has plagued Turkey since 1984. In this sense, the unequal distribution of wealth, poor infrastructure, and poverty of southeastern Turkey are not only linked with the conflict cycle, but they can themselves be the causes of "voluntary" displacement or economic migration. As such, it is, in the Turkish case, extremely difficult to differentiate between the conflict dynamics and broader socioeconomic changes as the main cause of displacement.

A second cause of internal displacement in Turkey has been the pressure imposed by the PKK on those villages that did not support their "liberation struggle." Within the education sector, for instance, the PKK had, by 1995, murdered 150 teachers and burned down 192 schools, forcing the abandonment of teaching provisions in many areas and the closure of 5,210 schools. The government responded by establishing a village guard system, under which Kurdish villagers were rewarded/coerced into organizing anti-PKK militia. By 1994 this had grown to a militia of 60,000 men, which, coupled with the organization of apparently state-sponsored counterterrorist groups, significantly added to the militarization of the region and further intensified the conflict, as village guards and their families became a primary target of PKK operations (McDowall 1992). It has also "created a cycle of action and reaction between Turkish security forces and their allies in the village guard and the PKK that has forced hundreds of thousands, perhaps millions, of persons from their homes in south-eastern Turkey," thereby helping to create a third, more diffused, cause of internal displacement which has chronically eroded social morale in the area (U.S. Committee for Refugees 1997).

In parallel to the intensive military clashes in the first half of the 1990s, conflict-induced displacement reached its peak in 1996—the magnitude of which is still open to widespread speculation. The total number of displaced in 2002 is thought to be around 1 million people, but due to the difficulties in separating the different causes of displacement, this figure may also include those who migrated as a consequence of economic pressures (Global IDP Project c. 2002). Whatever the true figure may be, it is certainly the case that very large numbers of people arrived in urban centers such as Batman, Hakkari, Şanlıurfa, and Van. The population of Diyarbakır, for example, swelled from 400,000 in 1990 to about 1.5 million by 1997 (Kirişçi 1998). Some of those IDPs took shelter with extended family members, but most constructed informal dwellings on the outskirts of these conurbations. Some of the displaced also moved to cities outside the thirteen provinces governed by emergency law at the time (Adana, Gaziantep, and Kahramanmaraş, for example) as well as western cities like Ankara, İstanbul, and İzmir (Kirişçi 1998). However, since the southeastern region has a GDP-per-capita which is much lower than the country's average of around U.S.$6,120 (2002 purchasing power parity), the socioeconomic consequences for that region have been particularly acute (UNDP 2001). IDPs have generally had to live in makeshift housing outside major towns without proper access to clean water, sanitation systems, health care, and educational facilities (Human Rights Watch 2002). Moreover, the resultant population increases have exacerbated the already dire labor markets in the majority of the cities affected. Part of the reason for this was that the state's response has largely focused on action at the community level. Unsurprisingly then, the Turkish government's policy toward its IDPs during the early 1990s was mostly limited "to the provision of food and materials for very basic housing" (Kirişçi 1998).

In 1994, for instance, the Village Centers Project was initiated, which intended to settle people from mountain areas into large, centralized sites on publicly owned lands near major cities. The state planned to provide housing and arable land based on loans to be paid back within a fifteen- to twenty-year period. However, this project was geared neither specifically to the displaced nor to the people of southeastern Turkey. It was particularly criticized, as it did not provide mechanisms for bottom-up participation. A year later, this scheme was replaced by the Return to the Village Project, which, more ambitiously, offered villagers rehousing at (often heavily subsidized) construction costs in their area of origin. Supported by funding of US$22 million, it also intended to facilitate their reintegration by encouraging cattle raising, bee –keeping, and weaving. As of mid-2000, however, nearly two-thirds of the return applications were ruled "inappropriate" due to security concerns (Global IDP Project c. 2002). Occupancy has clearly become "part of the reward system tied to the village guard structure" demonstrating the lack of coherence and concern regarding the welfare of IDPs at the national level (Global IDP Project c. 2002). Indeed, Human Rights Watch has recently found that many displaced people continue to "believe that once they return, the cycle of detention and harassment by government security forces may start again" (Human Rights Watch 2002, 4). This perception of displaced communities cannot easily be overcome without trust-building initiatives and a wider involvement of civil society in return programs.

To do this, the Turkish state must impose stronger administrative structures onto its resettlement agencies. In particular, it must redress the chronic lack of information and reliable statistics on both the implementation and assessment stages of its policies. To date, this has not been the case. In June 2001, for instance, "no officials could show Human Rights Watch anything on paper to describe the aims or methods of the return project" (Human Rights Watch 2002). The Turkish government was also criticized for avoiding the involvement of expert international organizations in the Return to the Village Project despite the fact that such a program "would stand a good chance of receiving international funding and expertise" (Human Rights Watch 2002). Indeed, the government has showed a great deal of reluctance in cooperating with the international community over its displacement crisis in general. Turkey has, for instance, successfully managed to bar international involvement in the southeastern provinces, where "even ICRC [International Committee of the Red Cross] has been unable to operate," and, up until 2002, refused to respond to the RSG's requests to visit the country (Cohen 1999). Consequently, it is generally concluded that the Turkish government is falling "far short of the international standards on the treatment of internally displaced persons embodied in the United Nations Guiding Principles on Internal Displacement" (Human Rights Watch 2002, 5).

Opportunities and Challenges

More recently, though, the establishment's attitude appears to be beginning to change. According to the Interior Ministry, 35,513 people have now returned to 6,000 new homes in 470 settlements at the cost to the state of over US$3 million (Global IDP Project c. 2002). Indeed, perhaps the best indicator of this new approach is the invitation of the government of Turkey to the RSG and Dr. Deng's subsequent visit to the country in May 2002. During his discussions with the authorities, Deng explained that his mandate "is based on recognizing the problem as internal and therefore falling under state sovereignty, but seeing sovereignty not as a barricade against international cooperation, but as a positive concept of state responsibility to protect and assist its citizens, if necessary, with the support of the international community" (UNHCR n.d.). In this way, the RSG emphasized the importance of adopting a *national* strategy to protect and assist IDPs.[3] Deng also noted an "openness and transparency on the part of the authorities to discuss the various aspects of the displacement problem," prompting him to conclude that "an opportunity now exists for the international community to assist the Government of Turkey in the challenging task of facilitating the voluntary return, resettlement and reintegration of the displaced population."

In seeking to understand the changes which have, at least ostensibly, occurred in the state's approach to the protection of human rights since 1999, three factors are important, all of which are particularly relevant to IDPs from southeast Anatolia. The first involves a decline in conflict intensities between Ankara and the PKK. The Syrian government's decision to withdraw support for the PKK in October 1998 set in motion a process of collapse which led to the arrest of the organization's leader, Abdullah Öcalan, in 1999. Following an initial outburst of violence in both Turkey and some European cities, a period rapprochement began. Öcalan issued a statement praising the Turkish military and offering to end PKK activism permanently in return for a democratic solution that "will bring wealth, unity and peace" (cited in Gunter 2000b, 849–70). President Sezer responded by criticizing constitutional restraints upon the expression of non-Turkish identities. Amid a 90 percent decline in fighting in the Kurdish provinces, the then chief-of-staff Hüseyin Kıvrıkoğlu subsequently refused to endorse the court's decision to sentence Öcalan to death.[4]

The second element was the catastrophic earthquake of August 1999. It devastated the wealthiest and most densely populated region of Turkey. It killed more than 17,000 people, hospitalizing a further 44,000 and causing estimated material damage of between U.S.$9 and $13 billion (Özerdem and Jacoby 2005). Responsibility was placed firmly on the state's inability both to ensure that building regulations were adhered and to respond adequately during the disaster's aftermath. The fact that over 90 percent of Turkey's cities are within an active earthquake zone, and that there have been 55 major tremors during the twentieth century (three in 1996–2006) at the cost of over 70,000 lives, led many to question the state's capacity to represent the interests of civil society as a whole (Özerdem and Barakat 2000). In place of the state's traditional image of a protective "father" (*devlet baba*), a new instrumentalism has emerged within civil organizations (Özerdem 2003). While in Rita Jalali's view it may be "doubtful if pressures emanating from organized sectors of society and the victims can do much to change the Turkish state" as a whole, demands for a political system with higher organizational capacities, less corruption, and greater democratic accountability—particularly in relation to the future of the southeast—have become increasingly apparent (Jalali 2002).

The third element has its roots in the Helsinki meeting of the European Council in December 1999, where it was agreed to extend the accession stipulations for full EU membership for Turkey. The political criteria for this, previously agreed at Copenhagen in 1993, were based on the presence "of institutions guaranteeing democracy, the rule of law, human rights and the protection of minorities" (Bozarslan 2001). In an effort to harmonize its laws with those of the EU members, the Turkish parliament adopted eight major reform packages between October 2001 and May 2004. While it is clear, that major problems persist in the implementation of this new legislation, the very fact that the state has acknowledged that improvements in its human rights regime are necessary, suggests an emerging political will to institutionalize a more democratic future for Turkey and to end human rights abuses in the southeast (Bozarslan 2001). Issues such as minority rights, which have remained a taboo subject in Turkey since the establishment of the Republic in the 1920s, have now started to be debated in a more open manner. In the future, further integration of Turkey into the institutions of the EU may mean an improved position for all types of minorities—including ethnic, religious, and linguistic groups. This is particularly important as the state currently recognizes only non-Muslim minorities identified in the 1923 Treaty of Lausanne. In all, it is clear that any extension of these rights to the country's main ethnic groups—the Kurds, the Circassians, and the Laz—cannot, as Baskin Oran's contribution to this volume points out, constitute a threat to the indivisibility of the state within the current climate.

So, as the UN's RSG underlines, the Turkish state now has a good opportunity to facilitate the unrestricted voluntary return and reintegration of IDPs from the southeast. Some of his preliminary proposals include

the need for the Government to formulate a clear policy on the issue, to make that policy and related programmes transparent to all concerned, to establish focal points within the Government, to improve co-ordination among the relevant Government institutions, including regional authorities, as well as with the international community and to convene a joint meeting in the near future to formulate programmes and strategies for co-operation with the international community in meeting the urgent needs of the affected populations. (UNHCR n.d.)

Furthermore, the RSG emphasizes the need for "an open and constructive partnership involving the Government, civil society, and international agencies" in this process (UNHCR n.d.). As such, organized sectors of civil society, from human rights and religious groups to professional associations and the media, are be seen as an integral component in the physical reconstruction and social reintegration of the southeast. In particular, civil society groups must be involved in the implementation of any national protection strategy for IDPs. This could also act as a nationwide catalyst between state and citizen not only providing public arenas for greater participation, but also promoting the accountability of the political class (Bratton and van de Walle 1997).

Conclusion

In conclusion, it is clear that a national IDP assistance and protection system needs to be holistic in character and closely linked to issues of social development. It should be a long-term commitment, which aims to implement policies guided by the needs of current IDPs in Turkey with the ultimate objective of moving from relief to reconstruction. Such a return to "normality" cannot be simply ensured by the provision of basic requirements such as food and housing assistance. Communities displaced from the southeast need to be self-sustaining upon their return home. This cannot be achieved, however, if the assistance is considered from a sequential perspective. The provision of humanitarian assistance should be conducted in conjunction with the planning of development programs as an integral part of an overall strategy for the southeast. This would not only use relief programs for laying foundations for development, but would also avoid displaced populations becoming dependent on state-led assistance. In other words, nongovernmental groups should not be coopted by a neoliberal agenda under which they become "a substitute for the state, taking over functions like welfare or humanitarian assistance" (Kaldor 1999).

Instead, quick impact projects, such as those recommended and deployed by the UNHCR, should be implemented. These prioritize the restoration of basic infrastructural utilities and establish assistance programs for rebuilding the agricultural and small business sectors as soon as possible after the return of displaced populations (Korn 1999). Such initiatives do, however, need to be linked to overall development plans in order to ensure that they become sustainable. The emphasis that the Turkish state placed on financial support in its Return to the Village Project was thus a beneficial step in this direction. It can, in our view, now be built upon through the implementation of employment development schemes that aim to provide both basic and advanced skills-training courses. In short, the national protection of IDPs should be a bottom-up approach aimed at livelihood sustainability and focused on locally appropriate coping mechanisms. As Mark Vincent and Refslund Sorensen point out, IDPs should not simply be regarded as victims of displacement and targets of humanitarian assistance, but as "human beings with various histories, ambitions and resources" (2001, 266). Based on lessons learned from a number of other displacement-affected countries, such as Afghanistan, Angola, Sri Lanka, Sudan, and the former Yugoslavia, it is clear that individuals retain "several axes of identity aside from being displaced, and these all influence the impact of displacement as well as the[ir] response strategies" (Vincent and Sorensen 2001, 266). In other words, national protection strategies need to be tailored to the complex combination of needs, expectations, and aspirations of the IDPs they are established to assist.

In order to facilitate this in the case of Turkey, considerable training and advocacy will need to be used to raise awareness of good practice within the public sector. Here, the impact of a closer relationship with the EU on the protection of minority rights and the institutionalization of more accountable government may be instrumental. According to the Global IDP Project,

The prospect of joining the European Union (EU) has been a strong incentive for European countries to implement durable solutions for IDPs, as compliance with European human rights standards, particularly with regard to the protection of minorities, is one of the key criteria to be fulfilled by candidates for EU membership. The EU Commission regularly monitors the applicants' human rights progress, including its record on the treatment of IDPs, as in the case of Turkey. (Global IDP Project c. 2005)[5]

In all, then, a balance must be struck "between effective international protection and assistance for the displaced while upholding state responsibilities" (Bennett 1998, 5). According to the RSG, sovereignty means responsibility. The third of his *Guiding Principles* states that "national authorities have the primary duty and responsibility to provide protection and humanitarian assistance to internally displaced persons within their jurisdiction." Furthermore, principle 28 allocates authorities "the primary duty and responsibility to establish conditions, as well as provide the means, which allow internally displaced persons to return voluntarily . . . or to resettle voluntarily in another part of the country. Such authorities shall [also] endeavor to facilitate the reintegration of returned or resettled internally displaced persons" (Reliefweb). So, while it may be that, in the absence of "responsible and effective national action," it is the international community that acts for the protection of IDPs, strengthening national capacities should be the primary priority (McLean 1998). Such an approach "would reduce the risk of dependence on external assistance and ease co-ordination difficulties between governments and international agencies" (McLean 1998, 11). The collaboration of the state is thus the principal way to ensure both the protection of IDPs internally and the monitoring of IDPs internationally; it is, of course, also the only "sound and lasting basis for prevention of internal displacement" in the first place (Korn 1999, 95).

Chapter 11

Turkish Asylum Policy and Human Rights

KEMAL KİRİŞÇİ

Turkey is not known to be a country of immigration, let alone a country of asylum, but it has a long record of receiving immigrants, asylum seekers, and refugees (Kirişçi 1991, 1996a).[1] It has received considerable number of asylum seekers from Nazi Germany and Nazi-occupied territories, the Soviet bloc during the Cold War and from neighboring countries since the end of the Cold War.

Turkey was also among the drafters as well as original signatories of the principal international legal instrument on refugees, the 1951 Geneva Convention Relating to the Status of Refugees. However, it is one of the few countries that continue to maintain a "geographical limitation" to the applicability of the convention. Hence, Turkey is not obligated to apply the convention to refugees coming from outside Europe. The European Union is putting pressure on Turkey to lift the limitation as one of the many preconditions that Turkey has to meet during the pre-accession period for membership.[2] Turkey has also been bitterly criticized by refugee advocacy groups as well as human rights groups for clinging to this "limitation." This policy has long had major implications in terms of the human rights of asylum seekers and refugees in Turkey. The opening of administrative decisions on asylum to judicial review and an expansion of cooperation between the United Nations High Commissioner for Refugees (UNHCR) and the Turkish government have engendered considerable improvement.

This chapter makes three arguments. First, over the last few years a vague and restrictive asylum policy has evolved into a system that is better defined and more sensitive toward the human rights of asylum seekers and refugees in Turkey. Second, training programs and seminars for Turkish officials supported by the UNHCR, as well as a body of national and European Court of Human Rights (ECHR) jurisprudence, have been instrumental in this process of change. Finally, Turkey's pre-accession strategy for European Union membership is creating the prospects of further improvement and the removal of the "geographical limitation."

Asylum and Human Rights

The issues of asylum and refuge are very closely linked to human rights. Invariably, it is the gross violation of human rights in a country that forces individuals to flee their homes and seek asylum elsewhere. Thus, like human rights, asylum and refugee issues have become subjects of international law, mainly after the Second World War (Goodwin-Gill 1986; *State of the World's Refugees* 2000; Loescher 2001). The Universal Declaration of Human Rights, adopted in December 1948 by the United Nations General Assembly, recognizes in Article 14 that "everyone has the right to seek and enjoy in other countries asylum from persecution" (UNHCR 1988, 101). However, this right is not automatically accompanied by a right to be granted asylum. States have jealously guarded their sovereign right to control entry into their respective territories (Goodwin-Gill 1986, 101–23). Hence, an individual asylum seeker can become a legally recognized refugee only after the competent authorities of a state, from which the individual is seeking asylum, can grant the person the status of a refugee.

It is the 1951 Geneva Convention Relating to the Status of Refugees and the accompanying 1967 protocol that codifies the rights of refugees. The convention provides also a definition of who a refugee is. It is not the purpose of this chapter to dwell on the rights of the refugees as defined in the convention. Instead, three important aspects of the convention will be stressed in respect to the human rights of refugees. First and most important, the convention aims to achieve effective protection for a refuge. The most important aspect of this is obviously personal security and the right to life. The Universal Declaration on Human Rights, as well as other international legal instruments, defines the right to life and personal security as fundamental human rights. In an Annex to the 1951 Geneva Convention, the UNHCR is entrusted with the task of providing international protection to refugees and assisting governments and other organizations to find permanent solutions. Permanent solutions to the status of a refugee can take the form of actual integration to the host country by eventually receiving citizenship. Alternatively, the refugee can be resettled not in the first country of refuge but in a third country, where he or she can be integrated into this new society and eventually become naturalized. Finally, a permanent solution may involve the voluntary return of the refugee to his or her country of origin, once the adverse conditions in the country cease to exist. In an effort to ensure effective protection, Article 33 of the convention prohibits the return of a refugee to the country of origin or to a country where the person's life and freedom would be at risk. This is known as the principle of non-refoulement and is considered to be a pillar of the convention (Goodwin-Gill 1986, 69–100). Furthermore, Article 31 also provides that if a refugee has had to enter his or her country of asylum by irregular means or without authorization, this cannot be held against the person. Beside these basic rights, the convention also provides for a range of social and economic rights for refugees.

The 1951 Geneva Convention, while clear on the rights of refugees, does not include explicit references to the rights of asylum seekers. Nevertheless, some rights of asylum seekers, implicit in the convention, have evolved as a result of the state practices. Accordingly, asylum seekers are expected to enjoy access to status-determination process, that is the process by which state authorities or the UNHCR officials decide whether the person is a refugee or not. Articles 31 and 33 of the convention are also generally accepted to apply to asylum seekers, too. In other words, states are expected to respect the basic human rights of life and security of asylum seekers by not deporting them until their cases are heard and a final decision about their status is reached. Furthermore, states are also expected not to hold the entry of asylum seekers into their territory without proper documentation or authorization against them. The common argument holds that asylum seekers, because of the persecution they may be facing, may not be able to leave their country of origin and enter the country of asylum in a regular manner.

There are also a number of international and regional legal instruments that have indirectly provided a basis for the human rights of asylum seekers (Plender and Mole 1999). Both the Universal Declaration of Human Rights and the International Covenant on Civil and Political Rights include articles that relate to asylum seekers. They include the basic right to life (as recognized in Article 3 and Article 6 of the instruments, respectively), the right not to be subjected to torture or cruel, inhuman or degrading treatment (Articles 5 and 7, respectively), and the right to judicial protection and review against criminal charges (Articles 10 and 13 respectively). At a regional level, there is also the European Convention for the Protection of Human Rights and Fundamental Freedoms, of November 1950. Although this convention does not define any specific rights for asylum seekers or refugees, the European Court of Human Rights has developed a case law and jurisprudence that actually has applied some of the general human rights to both asylum seekers and refugees. In 1991, the court, in the cases of *Cruz Varas v. Sweden* and *Vivarajah v. United Kingdom,* established the rule that asylum seekers could not be returned to a country where they risked facing torture or ill treatment.[3]

Turkish Asylum Policy and Practice

Turkey has long been a country of immigration, especially for Muslim ethnic groups, ranging from Bosnians to Pomaks and Tatars, as well as

Turks from the Balkans and to a lesser extent from the Caucasus and central Asia (Kirişçi 1996a). Between 1923 and 1997, more than 1.6 million immigrants came and settled in Turkey. Furthermore, after the Nazi takeover in Germany and then during the Second World War, there were many Jews who fled to Turkey and then resettled in Palestine. There were also many who fled German-occupied Balkans for Turkey and returned to their homelands after the war had ended. Since the collapse of the Soviet Union, Turkey has also become a country receiving an increasing number of irregular workers and immigrants from Balkan countries and the former Soviet republics, as well as from Iran, northern Iraq, and some African countries. These often include people that overstay their visa and work illegally. There are no reliable figures but there were claims in 2000 that put their numbers to more than a million.[4]

Turkey has also been a country of asylum, and is among the original signatories of the 1951 Convention Relating to the Status of Refugees. However, as mentioned above, Turkey is among a very small number of countries that still maintain a "geographical limitation" to the agreement's applicability as defined in Article 1.B(1)(a) of the convention. Accordingly, Turkey does not grant refugee status to asylum seekers coming from outside Europe, and maintains a two-tiered asylum policy.

The first tier of this policy is centered on Europe and is deeply rooted in Turkey's role as a Western ally neighboring the Soviet Union during the Cold War. During that period, in close cooperation with the UNHCR, Turkey received refugees from the Eastern bloc countries in Europe, including the Soviet Union. Such refugees, during their stay in Turkey, enjoyed all the rights provided for in the 1951 Convention Relating to the Status of Refugees. Only a small number were allowed to stay on in Turkey, often as a result of marriages with Turkish nationals. The others were resettled outside Turkey. Although it is difficult to obtain accurate statistics on their numbers, the Ministry of Interior (MOI) has indicated that some 13,500 asylum seekers benefited from the protection of the 1951 convention between 1970 and 1996. Statistics for previous years are not available.

In addition, approximately 20,000 Bosnians were granted temporary asylum in Turkey during hostilities in the former Yugoslavia, between 1992 and 1995. Some of the refugees were housed in a refugee camp near the Bulgarian border, while many went on to stay with relatives in large cities such as İstanbul and Bursa. Since the signing of the Dayton Peace Plan in 1995, many of these refugees have been steadily returning to Bosnia. In addition, in 1998 and 1999, approximately 17,000 Kosovars came to Turkey to seek protection from the strife in their ancestral homeland. The majority have returned.

The second tier of Turkey's asylum policy deals with people from outside Europe. The new policy emerged in 1980 in the wake of the Iranian

Revolution, and subsequent instability in the Middle East, Africa, and Southeast Asia. Upheaval in these areas led to a steady increase in the number of asylum seekers coming from outside Europe. For a long time, the government allowed the UNHCR considerable leeway to temporarily shelter these asylum seekers with the tacit understanding that they would be resettled outside Turkey if the UNHCR recognized them as refugees, and that those whose claims were rejected would be deported. However, the growth in the number of illegal entries into Turkey and in the number of rejected asylum seekers stranded in Turkey strained this practice. The situation was also aggravated by the 1988 and 1991 mass influxes of Kurdish refugees from Iraq, amounting to almost half a million. Officials were also concerned that among these asylum seekers were militants of the Kurdistan Workers' Party (Partia Karkaren Kürdistan, PKK) trying to enter Turkey from northern Iraq.

It was against such a background that the government introduced a decree, the Asylum Regulation, in November 1994.[5] The regulation aimed at bringing the status determination under the control of the Turkish government and also introducing strict regulations governing access to asylum procedures (Kirişçi 1996b). The practice that evolved in the first few years of the application of the regulation attracted serious and concerted criticism from Western governments, as well as major international human rights advocacy groups (U.S. Department of State 1997; Frelick 1997a, b). Critics argued that Turkey was violating the rights of asylum seekers and refugees by denying them access to asylum procedures or failing to provide them adequate protection by violating the principle of non-refoulement. The following section will examine the recent policy, as well as the impact that above criticisms and the EU accession process has had on the evolution of the Turkish policy and practice.

Human Rights and Asylum Seekers in Turkey

The Asylum Regulation was prepared with national security considerations rather than humanitarian or human rights in mind. The emphasis was mainly placed on enhancing the control over entries into Turkey and limiting the access to asylum procedures. The system that was put into place was one that replaced the close cooperation with the UNHCR. The new system changed the status determination from being the standard and well-recognized process of determining whether an asylum seeker fulfilled the criteria for refugee status into one whereby Turkish authorities would screen the applicants to determine whether an applicant is a "genuine" asylum seeker or not. Depending on the outcome of the screening process, the person would then be permitted to approach the UNHCR or be deported. At the same time, the regulation relegated the role of the UNHCR simply to arranging resettlement of asylum seekers whose applications were accepted by the Turkish authorities. This was in stark contrast to the earlier system in which the UNHCR was central to the process of status determination. In other words, the new system severely curtailed the access of individuals who would be considered by the international community as asylum seekers, to the proper, internationally recognized status-determination process. Consequentially, it also curtailed the effective protection for asylum seekers who could otherwise be duly recognized as refugees. Such a practice brought about a situation that created a risk that fundamental human rights, such as the right to life and security, would be violated, not to mention the violation of the principles of non-refoulement and protection from the risk of torture and inhuman treatment.

Furthermore, the regulation also had an inbuilt bias in favor of asylum seekers' entering the country legally as opposed to by illegal means. While asylum seekers in the first group could file an asylum application anywhere in the country, the second group had to do it at their point of entry into Turkey. This situation often required people to make trips from the big cities of Turkey in the west to the eastern border regions of the country. Additionally, the regulation introduced a five-day limit for filing an application. This gave the authorities the possibility of rejecting those who failed to meet this time limit, often without addressing the actual substance of an application. The rejection was accompanied by swift deportation procedures that left no room for appeal or review possibilities, to which asylum seekers could resort. The spirit of the regulation seemed more concerned about deterring applications for asylum than ensuring protection for asylum seekers and refugees.

The human rights violations that resulted from the implementation of the 1994 regulation are best captured by the July 2000 ECHR ruling on *Jabari v. Turkey*. Hoda Jabari, an Iranian woman, applied to the ECHR in February 1998 claiming that she would be subjected to a real risk of ill-treatment and death by stoning if expelled from Turkey and that she had been denied an effective remedy to challenge her expulsion decision. She invoked Articles 3 and 13 of the convention with respect to these two complaints. Jabari had entered Turkey illegally in November 1997, fearing that she would be punished by death for having entered into sexual relationship with a married man in Iran. She subsequently acquired a forged Canadian passport and tried to travel to Canada via France. In France, she was apprehended and deported back to Turkey. The Turkish authorities turned down her asylum application and informed her that she would be deported. She was informed that under the Asylum Regulation of 1994 she should have lodged her application for asylum within five days of her initial arrival in Turkey. In the meantime, while under custody, she was given access to the UNHCR officials. The UNHCR concluded that she had a well-founded fear of persecution if sent back to Iran, as she risked being subjected to inhuman punishment, such as death by stoning, or being whipped or flogged, and hence they granted her refugee status. Jabari also applied to an administrative court to seek a review of the police decision and asked a stay of execution on the deportation order. The court ruled against Jabari, in April 1998, and concluded that the police decision was not illegal and that the implementation of the deportation would not cause irreparable harm to the applicant. However, in the meantime Jabari had also applied to the ECHR and the court had issued a stay of execution on the deportation order. The police granted her a temporary residence permit.

Eventually, the ECHR did rule that if Jabari were to be deported to Iran there was a serious risk that Article 3 of the European Human Rights Convention would be violated and that by failing to provide Jabari with effective judicial protection, Turkey had also failed to satisfy the requirements of Article 13. More important in terms of Turkish asylum policy and practice, the court announced:

The Court is not persuaded that the authorities of the respondent State conducted any meaningful assessment of the applicant's claim, including its arguability. It would appear that her failure to comply with the five-day registration requirement under the Asylum Regulation 1994 denied her any scrutiny of the factual basis of her fears about being removed to Iran. In the Court's opinion, the automatic and mechanical application of such a short time-limit for submitting an asylum application must be considered at variance with the protection of the fundamental value embodied in Article 3 of the Convention.[6]

Accordingly, this meant that Turkish authorities could not raise the violation of the time limit defined in the 1994 regulation for filing an asylum application, as a pretext for issuing a deportation order, without addressing the actual substance of an asylum claim (Çiçekli 2003a, 14; 2003b, 135–36). Subsequently, Jabari was resettled outside Turkey by the UNHCR.

The *Jabari v. Turkey* ruling of the ECHR turned out to be a critical decision that reinforced a nascent practice of judicial review of the MOI's negative asylum decisions. The Turkish Constitution provides that "All acts or decisions of the authorities are subject to judicial review" (Article 125), and does not make any distinction between Turkish nationals and aliens. As a military judge argued before, Article 125 makes it possible for administrative decision to receive judicial appeal including those by foreigners (Odman 1995, 187). Actually, as early as 1980, a Turkish legal scholar had argued that it was possible for a foreign national to challenge in court an administrative decision preventing the entry or calling for the expulsion of a foreigner. In 1978 the Council of State (Danıştay) had actually ruled against the state for expelling a Swedish TV crew without providing clear evidence of a violation of the law demanding such an expulsion.[7]

Despite this precedence and a general legal opinion that asylum seekers and refugees can appeal a decision of the Turkish state, such a course of action had never been tried by disenchanted asylum seekers. A lack of confidence in the Turkish police and appeal system, coupled with a fear that challenging authorities in court might adversely affect their case, had deterred asylum seekers or refugees from going to court to challenge the authorities. The opportunity to break this apprehension occurred in July and October 1997, when two administrative courts (*idari mahkeme*) ruled in support of two Iranian asylum seekers and UNHCR recognized refugees against the MOI decisions calling for their deportations for violating the time limit clause of the 1994 Asylum Regulation.[8] In both cases the Iranian asylum seekers had been recognized as refugees by the UNHCR in Ankara, and their resettlement to third countries had been arranged. The problem had arisen when the UNHCR sought the cooperation of the Turkish government to assist the Iranians to leave the country. The MOI not only rejected the UNHCR request, it started proceedings against the refugees arguing that they were in violation of the 1994 regulation, for having entered the country illegally and failed to apply for asylum within the required time limit (Tarhanlı 2000, 21).

The UNHCR branch office in Ankara saw this as an opportunity to test the judicial appeal system. Both refugees were encouraged to take their cases to court. In both cases the courts ruled that the interpretation of the regulation by the MOI was at fault and that what was critical was the actual substance of the cases and not the time limit. The courts argued that international law that had been duly ratified was part of Turkish law and hence the 1951 convention needed to be respected. The courts argued that the MOI had failed to cite any evidence to show that these persons were not actually refugees and hence canceled the deportation orders. This initial decision encouraged other judicial review cases. Many of the cases were settled in favor of the applicants, with a few exceptions. One such exception was the decision of an administrative court in Ankara that rejected an appeal for suspension of an MOI deportation order by a UNHCR-recognized Iranian refugee waiting to be resettled outside Turkey. Subsequently, this decision was appealed by the Iranian refugee to the Ankara Regional Administrative Court, a higher court. The court, in January 2000, overruled the lower court's decision and granted the suspension of the deportation order. The court in its rulings, inter alia, cited Article 3 of the United Nations Convention against Torture and Other Cruel, Inhuman, or Humiliating Treatment and Punishment as the basis for overturning the decision of the lower court that had upheld the deportation order of the police. The higher court also ruled, in a manner very similar to the ECHR's *Jabari v. Turkey* ruling, that the time limit in the 1994 regulation "shall not be grounds for their deportation without examining their situation" (UNHCR 2000b, 154–55).

There were two additional critical developments in respect to judicial review and effective remedy. First, the MOI appealed against one of the administrative court rulings suspending its deportation orders to the Council of State, the highest appeal body in Turkey for administrative decisions. After a long period of deliberations, the Council of State ruled in January 2000 against the MOI appeal and supported the initial lower court decision suspending the deportation order.[9] The ruling justified the rejection of the MOI appeal on the grounds that the authorities should have acted in pursuant of Article 31 of the 1951 Geneva Convention, which states that illegal entry into a country by a refugee should not be held against the person. Second, the government introduced an amendment to the 1994 regulation in 1999 to increase the five-day time limit for filing an asylum application to ten days.[10] This helped to alleviate to some degree the problems arising from asylum seekers failing to reach Turkish authorities within the initial time limit.

There is no doubt that these judicial rulings have deeply affected the practice of the MOI and are contributing positively to a better protection of the rights of asylum seekers and refugees in Turkey. The court cases have soundly established the practice that decisions of the MOI are open to judicial review and appeal. Furthermore, the administrative court rulings, together with the one by the European Court of Human Rights, constitute an important source of jurisprudence that is likely to influence future court cases, as well as the practice of the MOI. Third, the court rulings in an unequivocal manner draw attention to the need not to interpret the time-limit clause in the regulation in a mechanical and technical manner. In any event the courts seem unanimous that this clause should not be held against an actual evaluation of the substance of an asylum application. All of these developments would have the added effect of strengthening the non-refoulement principle in comparison to the past.

It would be unrealistic to argue that the problem of refoulement and effective remedy in Turkey has been completely overcome. However, a survey of the 1994–2002 U.S. Department of State *Country Reports on Human Rights Practices* shows that there has been a steady improvement in the implementation of the principle of non-refoulement. The problem peaked in 1995 and 1996, and since then the cases of refoulement demonstrated a falling trend (U.S. Department of State n.d.). Furthermore, the MOI officials have become much more conscious about the need to respect the right to effective remedy. The UNHCR has played an important role in this regard. After long negotiations the UNHCR was able to convince

Turkish authorities to organize training conferences and seminars on refugee law and status determination for Turkish officials. The first of these took place in September 1998 and involved officials that directly dealt with asylum seekers and refugees. These seminars organized by the UNHCR were often the first of their kind that many of the officials had attended. No doubt they contributed to a major improvement in the officials' understanding of the issues involved, and helped to change the attitudes of many of these officials toward asylum seekers and refugees. For example, there was a medium-rank official who, during the early stages of one of the seminars, naively blurted out that he thought asylum seekers were basically people who had betrayed their country; by the end of the seminar, however, he was able to express empathy for asylum seekers and refugees.[11]

The training programs were gradually expanded to include other officials such as judges, prosecutors, and gendarmes. Gendarmes are usually the first people that asylum seekers encounter in border areas. Awareness programs to differentiate between illegal immigrants and asylum seekers were introduced to the training of the gendarmerie. Programs were also held with the bar associations for prosecutors and judges focusing on refugee law. The police and gendarmes normally have to report immigrants or foreigners illegally present in Turkey to the local courts. Hence, prosecutors and judges play a critical role in deportation decisions. The seminars in these respects were critical in raising awareness of a body of law and practice to help distinguish between illegal immigrants and asylum seekers and Turkey's legal obligations under international law.

By 2003, the close cooperation between the UNHCR and the Turkish authorities has culminated in a situation that leaves the refugee status determination in Turkey to the UNHCR. It is possible to argue that there has been a return to the practice prior to the adoption of the 1994 Asylum Regulation. Though the regulation identifies the MOI as the body responsible for status determination, the MOI officials have come to rely increasingly on the judgment of the UNHCR. They are quite content to go along with the UNHCR decisions, as long as the asylum seekers are also registered with them and eventually those who are recognized as refugees resettle outside Turkey. The occasional differences are usually sorted out through informal consultations. Training seminars and close cooperation have also enabled the UNHCR to gain access to groups of irregular migrants that get apprehended by the Turkish authorities, particularly in border regions of Turkey. During 1995–2002, there were approximately 4,000 to 4,500 asylum applicants filed annually.[12]

In spite of significant improvements in Turkey's asylum system, there are also persistent problems. An important problem involves the cases of individuals who file asylum application with only the UNHCR, refusing to register an application with the Turkish authorities. The cooperation between the MOI and the UNHCR, however, is based on an understanding that all asylum seekers applying to the UNHCR must also be encouraged to register with the police. The number of cases in violation of this situation was quite large in the mid-1990s, and many of the judicial appeal cases were about this problem, since Turkish authorities refused the UNHCR-recognized refugees to leave the country for resettlement on the grounds that their presence in the country had been illegal in the first place. However, this close cooperation, which was supported by a systematic campaign to inform asylum seekers reaching Turkey, resulted in a significant drop in the number of such cases. Nevertheless, as of June 2003, more than 100 refugees fell into this category and faced the risk of having their right to effective protection undermined. Another problem results from the Turkish governmental practice of not accepting applications from asylum seekers, mostly Iranian nationals, who reach Turkey via third countries, in particular from northern Iraq. The authorities argue that such cases should be dealt with in the first country of asylum. A precarious understanding between the Turkish government and the UNHCR has enabled such persons to informally remain in Turkey. However, refugee advocacy groups see this as falling short of ensuring protection for such asylum seekers, since occasionally the Turkish authorities try to deport them back to Iran or northern Iraq.

The EU, too, has played an important role in helping to improve the human rights of asylum seekers and refugees. The European Commission and some member states of the EU have provided funding for the UNHCR to run training seminars. Moreover, the EU's conditions and criteria for Turkey's membership also include the development of reception centers for asylum seekers, the signing of readmission agreements with third countries, and the development of an institutional capacity for national status determination. The EU also expects Turkey to lift the "geographical limitation" to the 1951 Geneva Convention. The Turkish National Program (NP) for the Adoption of the Acquis responded quite favourably to these demands. Most striking was the apparent willingness to consider the lifting of the geographical limitation. Even if an eventual decision to lift it is made conditional to the introduction of "legislative and infra-structural measures" and "the attitudes of the EU Member States on the issue of burden-sharing" (Secretariat-General for the EU Affairs 2001), it must be viewed as no short of a revolutionary departure from the previous practice. In the past, it was almost taboo to bring up the idea of lifting the geographical limitation.

However, it should be noted that lifting the geographical limitation in practice will not be easy. The inclusion of the existing formulation into the NP was the result of considerable negotiation and careful wording to appease the concerns of the advocates of the traditional policy. The military and other security agencies still remain very reluctant and afraid of the possibility of a mass influx from neighboring Middle Eastern countries. Additionally, there are still many officials who continue to be apprehensive about the possibility of Turkey becoming a buffer zone where asylum seekers and refugees congregate but eventually fail to enter their destination country in Europe. In any event, the lifting of the geographical limitation will be a function of a long bargaining process between the EU and Turkish authorities, who will try to extract from their counterparts a commitment to share the burden. For the Turkish authorities the continuation of the present resettlement commitments would be regarded as an important element of burden-sharing expectations. Furthermore, the issue will also be intricately linked to the legal and political reforms in Turkey and the way the EU responds to these reforms. A critical factor in the lifting of the limitation will be whether the EU can engender confidence among officials that the EU is serious about Turkey's membership and that Turkey has the prospect of becoming a member. The worst-case scenario for Turkish officials is a situation where a decision to lift the geographical limitation would not eventually be accompanied by EU membership.

The EU, since it adopted a revised version of the Accession Partnership in April 2003, has also made funding available for "twinning projects." Twinning projects enable the bureaucracy of candidate countries to pair up with their EU counterparts to prepare projects allowing for an exchange of experiences and institutional capacity building programs. This applies to the Turkish MOI. One of the twinning projects is actually assisting Turkey to develop an action plan for meeting the EU conditions and to prepare a draft asylum law. Finally, the EU has helped to improve the climate for asylum seekers and refugees also by supporting nongovernmental organizations that are concerned about asylum issues. A growing number of nongovernmental organizations are taking an interest in various ways of assisting asylum seekers and refugees.[13] Although limited in scale, this effort constitutes an important beginning. Bar associations in big cities such as Ankara, İstanbul and İzmir, as well as in some border towns, have developed various programs geared to providing legal assistance for asylum seekers, as well as training programs for their members, on asylum law and human rights of asylum seekers.

These are clearly positive contributions resulting from Turkey's engagement with the EU. However, the EU is also putting massive pressure on Turkey to combat irregular transit migration. It is estimated that approximately half a million irregular migrants enter the EU. Some of these migrants come through Turkey. The number of irregular migrants apprehended in Turkey increased from 11,362 in 1995 to 94,514 in 2000, although it fell to 82,825 in 2002 and 56,219 in 2003. Officials recognize this as a sign that Turkey is becoming a much more difficult country to transit. In August 2002 the government introduced new articles to the Penal Code criminalizing human smuggling and trafficking. This, along with stricter controls at borders and ports, has had a deterring effect against irregular transit migration through Turkey. It is reported that human smugglers have redirected their routes elsewhere. However, this "Turkish success" involves the risk of mistaking asylum seekers as illegal migrants and deporting them, which of course would be a denial of access for asylum seekers to make their claim.[14] Furthermore, such vigilance also runs the risk of deterring potential bona fide refugees from attempting to enter Turkey.

In an effort to meet the Copenhagen criteria, Turkey recently went through a major reform process, and a significant improvement has been noted in addressing human rights issues. This improvement was also acknowledged by the EU at its December 2004 summit, when it took the historic decision to start accession negotiations with Turkey in October 2005. Hence, a thorough improvement in the implementation of the human rights of asylum seekers and refugees in Turkey will be closely linked to the completion of the ongoing reform process of the Turkish political and legal system to meet the criteria for membership. This reform process is going to be critical to the development of the institutional and legal frameworks, as well as the political culture, that will make Turkey more sensitive toward human rights, in general, and the rights of asylum seekers and refugees, in particular.

Conclusion

During the course of the last few decades international legal instruments ranging from the 1951 Geneva Convention to the Universal Declaration on Human Rights, as well as the Covenant on Civil and Political Rights have made a string of human rights applicable to asylum seekers and refugees. These rights, ranging from the principle of non-refoulement to the right to life and security, from the right to effective remedy to the freedom from torture and cruel and degrading punishment, have also been reinforced by the case law and jurisprudence of the European Court of Human Rights.

Compared to the 1990s (Kirişçi 1992), contemporary Turkey has an asylum system that is much more attentive to human rights. The cooperation between Turkish authorities and the UNHCR is well established. This cooperation has enabled hundreds of Turkish officials and members of the gendarmerie to receive training on asylum law. Compared to the early 1990s, civil society is much more developed in Turkey, and a modest section of it is actually taking interest in assisting asylum seekers and refugees. These improvements were actually acknowledged by an official of Amnesty International (Graf 2002).

Turkey's aspiration to become an EU member also created a momentum and a public resolve to further improve the asylum system and develop the institutional capacity to undertake directly the task of status determination. This will undoubtedly mean the lifting of the "geographical limitation" to the 1951 Geneva Convention. This is a major challenge that requires the development of Turkey's confidence in the EU. Only then would it be possible to talk of a system that respects and guarantees the principle of non-refoulement and the asylum seeker's right to effective protection, access to proper status determination, and right to judicial review. Now that the EU has actually taken the decision to start membership talks, putting into place such a system should become easier. Turkish decision makers will feel much more confident in cooperating with the EU. However, it should not be overlooked that Turkey's efforts to harmonize its law and practice with the EU will be taking place at a time when the European asylum system is increasingly under pressure from conservative and anti-immigrant circles. The steady "securitization" of immigration issues in the EU is occurring, ironically, at a time when the Turkish asylum system is being successfully nudged out of a national security-dominated agenda to a human rights-focused one.

Part IV
Women's Rights

Chapter 12
Women's Rights, Women's Organizations, and the State

Yıldız Ecevit

In Turkey, the state has been one of the most powerful actors affecting women's rights. The position of the state, however, has been volatile and appears to be self-contradictory. On the one hand, the state has taken a parafeminist stance and opened up new opportunities for women through legislative and administrative reforms. On the other hand, it has supported the traditional role of women within the family, pursued pro-natalist policies, and maintained women's dependency on men.

Until recently, it was largely accepted that the state initiated and carried out reforms that granted women some rights, while there were no political demands or organized efforts by women. Women, of course, fight for their rights, even though their struggle may not be steady or always effective. Contrary to the common belief, women in Turkey have been involved in politics to advocate their rights or address other issues. Zehra Arat notes that "Turkish women's search for identity and their expression of demands and contention have taken different forms. They are usually characterized as complacent or resilient, but defiance has not been a stranger to them either" (1998, 2).

In this chapter, I examine the policies and discourses related to women's rights in Turkey since the establishment of the Republic of Turkey in 1923, in an effort to understand the factors that contributed to the policy changes in favor of women. Thus, I explore the role of women's organizations in demanding, defending, and promoting women's rights, their interaction with the state, and the methods employed by the officials in responding to women's demands and activism. I contend that the state followed alternative strategies of co-optation and repression in dealing with women's organizations; co-optation is pursued, if women's demands were relevant to the regime's goals, but repression was employed if the organization was seen as a threat to the regime.

In order to show the shifts in the state's strategies, I will examine the development of women's organizations and state policies in four periods, 1920–40, 1940–60, 1960–80, and since 1980.

The Formative Years of the Republic of Turkey, 1920–40

Under the Kemalist regime, the educational, professional, and legal opportunities of women were expanded. The principle of free education was adopted at all levels, and primary education was made mandatory for both sexes. In 1926, the new regime replaced the Islamic civil code. Polygamy was outlawed, equality in inheritance as well as equal rights in divorce was granted, and the marriage age for girls was lowered. Marriage by proxy was abolished. In the case of divorce, child custody could be awarded to either parent with a judge determining which parent would gain custody. The Turkish Grand National Assembly granted women's political rights in the 1930s. A careful examination of this period reveals women's determination to achieve suffrage, despite the consistent discouragement experienced in every stage of their campaign. Women's demand for civil and political rights dates back to the late Ottoman period (Abadan-Unat 1986; Kandiyoti 1991; S. Çakır 1996), and their emphasis on political participation and representation resurfaced in 1923, when women came together to establish the Turkish Women's Party. The founder was Nezihe Muhiddin, who had argued even before the establishment of the Republic that women must be "independent" and active in public life (Baykan 1999, 25–31). The establishment of the Turkish Women's Party was criticized by the media for diverting the attention from major issues faced by the country and creating political divisions (Toprak 1998, 31). The governor of İstanbul did not respond to the women's application, and the national government withheld its consent and advised women to establish an association. Nezihe Muhiddin and her associates, determined to form a women's organization, established the Woman's Union (Kadın Birliği) on 7 February 1924.[1] However, as required by law, the association bylaws had to include a statement declaring that the association would have no relation to politics.

Between 1925 and 1926, the union mainly carried out educational activities and support for destitute women. However, women's rights continued to be an important issue and remained on its agenda. The issue was discussed in the articles published in its journal, *Women's Path* (Yaraman 1999, 47). The union also established international links and became a member of the International Women's League. It nominated Halide Edib and Nezihe Muhiddin as candidates in the 1925 elections. Although women did not have the right to run for office, by nominating these two prominent women, the organization tried to influence public opinion and create a favorable climate for women's enfranchisement. However, the motion was harshly criticized by the media and was regarded as a "non-serious" engagement at a time when the rebellion of the Kurdish groups was threatening the development of the Republic.

In 1926, the union launched a campaign for women's political rights. In 1927, at its annual convention, members of the union voted to add a new article into the bylaws of the organization, which would enable them to promote women's political rights.[2] The amendment was rejected by the governor of İstanbul, who argued that the primary duty of women was to give birth to children and raise them. However, the national government gave its consent, and the new bylaws were approved by the Directorate of Legal Affairs of the İstanbul Province (Caporal 1982, 691). In July 1927, Nezihe Muhiddin declared in a speech: "We have not given up our goal to obtain our electoral rights. Because if we give up, there will be no raison d'etre for our union to exist. We shall work for our cause until our death. If our life span is not sufficient, we will nevertheless pave the way for the next generation" (693).

Although Nezihe Muhiddin was determined to pursue her aim and demand political rights, she faced opposition. Some members of the union, as well as other critics, argued that demanding enfranchisement was not timely and the union should be more involved in philanthropic matters regarding women's health and children. She was accused of misusing her authority during the elections of the administrative board; and as a result of this and other accusations she was discredited and isolated. After the annual convention, debates on women's suffrage started to take place in the media, parliament, and cabinet meetings. Although there was some supportive talk on behalf of women, neither the government nor the Republican People's Party supported the union, and it was argued that public was not ready to accept the idea (Bozkır 2000, 22–23). The government not only completely withdrew its support but also openly opposed the union. Nezihe Muhiddin was warned to refrain from demanding political rights for women, but she refused. The office of the union was searched, and its documents were confiscated by the police. The official justification of this government intrusion was listed as "infraction of rules" by the union. However, the later analysts noted that the real reason was "the extreme demands of the union" (Caporal 1982, 694).

Between 1927 and 1934, the union mainly focused on philanthropic work, but it did not completely drop its demand for women's suffrage. It organized a series of conferences to explore the relationship between women and municipalities, in an effort to prepare the public for women's participation in municipal elections. However, the union stopped playing the leading role on the question of enfranchisement; it followed the initiatives taken by the national leaders rather passively. Mustafa Kemal brought together a group of experts to examine women's political rights in other countries. The discussions, directed by him, led to a favorable proposal, and the Grand National Assembly unanimously amended the Municipal Law on 3 May 1930, to allow women to vote in municipal elections. The union organized a mass meeting to celebrate this occasion. Ironically, more men than women participated in the meeting (Bozkır 2000, 24).

As the union was coopted by the state, Nezihe Muhiddin was silenced. The pacification of the other women leaders led to the emergence of a period, later to be referred to in feminist literature as "state feminism," in which the advocates of westernization, nationalism, and secularism became the advocates of women's rights. Afet İnan, the adopted daughter of Mustafa Kemal, who was designated by him to serve as the new symbol of Turkish womanhood (Kırkpınar 1998, 13), gave a speech in April 1931 on the merits of granting full electoral rights to women (Taşkıran 1973, 131–35). After the idea was debated and accepted by Mustafa Kemal's inner circle, on 5 December, Prime Minister İnönü presented the draft bill for women's suffrage to the Grand National Assembly, which adopted the bill by amending the Articles 5, 11, 16, 23, and 58 of the Constitution.

In December 1934, the union issued a written announcement and organized a mass meeting at the Beyazıd Square to celebrate the adoption of the draft bill for women's suffrage. One of the members, Saadet Rafet, made a speech to declare the gratitude of women to Turkish men. A day before, the president, Latife Bekir, had given an interview to a journalist from the newspaper *Zaman*. In her response to the journalist's question about the role that the union played in achieving the right to vote, she noted: "The Women's Union did nothing on this issue. Nevertheless, the Turkish woman carried out her duty to her nation, served unobtrusively and self-sacrificingly for her nation. The Turkish woman deserved to become enfranchised and to stand for election, this right was given to her without her requesting it" (Doyran 1997, 30).

Nevertheless, women's enfranchisement in Turkey stirred international excitement. Several countries congratulated Turkey. On 18 May 1935, the Twelfth Congress of the International Women's League, organized by the Women's Union, was held in İstanbul, with participants representing 42 countries. In her opening speech to the Congress, Latife Bekir repeated her earlier sentiment and words: "There is no woman's question in Turkey anymore. Women can work as well as men, under the management of a single leader for the good of the country" (Ökten 2002, 59). A few days after the international congress, the union decided to dissolve itself. Latife Bekir explained the decision in a speech: "The Woman's Union reached its goal. Women have been granted all their rights. We have been working for twelve years. There is no more need for this union and no need for a separate women's organization. Therefore I propose to close down the union" (Kaplan 1998, 159; Bozkır 2000, 26).

After the union was closed down, its members were encouraged to take on philanthropic work in the women's auxiliary of the Republican People's Party (Cumhuriyet Halk Partisi, CHP).

The struggle of the Woman's Union for suffrage is illuminating, because it shows how the union was forced to become a passive advocate of women's rights and comply with the government directives. The hegemonic party rule and authoritarian policies did not allow women, or other segments of the society, to voice their demands. The state dominated the public sphere. Although it had a parafeminist tone, its approach to women's issues remained patriarchal. The regime tried to mold and control "the new woman" according to its own purposes and prevented the development of autonomous women's movements. Therefore it would not be erroneous to conclude that during the 1930s the government granted women some rights not in support of their activism but to pacify and coopt them.

The Period of Stagnation, 1940–60

After women were enfranchised in 1934 and the Woman's Union was dissolved in 1936, women's activism dwindled to a near halt (Yaraman 1999, 54). It is important to explore the causes of the lack of feminist discourse and activity in this period, to which Tekeli refers as "the barren years" (1998, 337).

Kemalist intellectuals idealized "a new woman," someone who internalizes her familial, social, and national duties and lives for others' well-being (Berktay 1999, 275). The image of the "new woman" was also used by the cadres of the new republican elite eager to present a picture of a civilized society. Urban women were presented as the agents of transformation for modernization. Carrying the responsibility of being the markers of modernization and "the guardians of the reforms, progress, modernization and enlightenment" (Durakbaşa 1998, 142), women could not attempt to challenge this new assigned identity. On the contrary, they accepted it and internalized its discourse (Y. Arat 2000a, 112). Moreover, as aptly put by Deniz Kandiyoti, "authoritarian nature of the single-party state and its attempt to harness the 'new woman' to the creation and reproduction of a uniform citizenry, aborted the possibility for autonomous women's movements" (1991, 43).

The early 1940s also correspond to the one-party rule, during which freedoms and associations were highly restricted. When the Law of Associations was amended in 1948, the Woman's Union was reestablished, albeit with different goals, including the following: the protection of women's rights provided by Kemalist reforms; the promotion of Turkish women in the cultural sphere; and contributing to the raising of Turkish mothers who would serve their husbands and children with self-sacrifice and loyalty (Kılıç 1998, 349).

Women's associations proliferated during the late 1940s and the 1950s. Professional women founded their own associations such as the Association of Soroptimists (1948) and the Association of Women University Graduates (1949). In 1953, the Association for Investigating Women's Social Life was established, with the objectives of organizing public conferences on women's issues and conducting research on several aspects of women's lives. Other women's organizations formed at this time included: the Association for Helping Poor (1952); the Association for Protecting Women (1954); the Association for Empowering Women (1955); and the Association of Turkish Mothers (1959) (Ardıç 1983, 198–201). They were initially formed in major cities such as İstanbul, Ankara, and İzmir but they later opened branches in other cities.

These associations were mostly apolitical, philanthropic organizations that promoted voluntarism among women. Members were usually well-educated upper-middle- or upper-class women who enjoyed high social status and eminent family backgrounds. They subscribed to the notion that already having obtained their rights, Turkish women had no need to work for new rights; instead, they should strive to protect and use these rights properly. With the mission of contributing to the progress of the country, they were primarily preoccupied with educational and social welfare issues, such as providing scholarships to poor but talented young girls for their education. Some of these associations are still active and work in similar areas, without a major change in their gender approach or philosophies.

The Restless Years, 1960–80

In the 1960s, in addition to the philanthropic organizations, professional women established new professional associations such as the Association of Turkish Jurist Women (1968) and the Association of Women Pharmacists (1968) (Kılıç 1998, 351). An exception to this general trend was the Turkish Association of Progressive Women. Founded in 1965, this association had an ideological stance that included goals such as "guiding women to realize their social and political rights" and "working for the promotion of working women's rights and demanding further rights for them" (Talay 2002, 213). These goals were translated into demands, including longer maternity leaves and child care services in workplaces. Its president, Beria Önger, wrote extensively about women's issues from a feminist perspective: "for women's emancipation, remnants of feudal order that hinder the advancement of women, conservative obstacles and wicked traditions should be eradicated by comprehensive reforms" (Talay 2002, 215). She argued that problems of women should be reconsidered and debated with a new approach that would put women in the *center*. She saw as futile the approach that made women's emancipation depend on a socialist revolution, since women's problems could not wait until after the establishment of a new social order (Talay 1999, 198). Önger argued that single women were subject to sexual exploitation and married women were deprived of their independence. She criticized the regulations and practices through which women registered as prostitutes, claiming that these health regulations infringed on women's rights. She raised issues with the Civil Code, for assigning the role of representing the family to the husband and making the wife's ability to work outside the home depend on his permission. She also criticized women intellectuals for wasting their time in collecting donations and helping the destitute, instead of concentrating on gaining political power, which she saw as the only way of influencing policy makers in the government and the parliament (Talay 2002, 215).

However, the association remained active for only about five years, dissolving in 1970 due to declining membership (Kılıç 1998, 351). In the 1970s, parallel to the proliferation of left-wing organizations, which involved many women activists, a number of women's organizations were established by leftist women, including the Association of Democratic Women, the Union of Laboring Women, and the Association of Revolutionary Women. The first socialist and women-only organization, the Union of Revolutionary Women, was established in April 1971 (Paker and Toska 1997, 16) and chaired by a well-known socialist woman writer, Suat Derviş. But the restrictive policies that followed the military coup of 12 March 1971 cut short the life of the union.

The most notable women's organization of this period was the Association of Progressive Women, established in 1975. With more than 15,000 members and 33 branches, it is the largest and most widely organized women's organization in Turkey's history.

The Association of Progressive Women (APW) was a product of the heightened mass activism and radical politics that emerged after the 1971 military coup. It was conceived by the Communist Party leaders as a women's organization that would support the party. However, the women of the APW managed to stay relatively detached from the Communist Party. Members were not required to belong to the party, carry out the party propaganda, or to distribute party publications (Akal 1996, 97–98). Consequently, the membership of the APW was drawn from a wider political spectrum. Its founders defined the APW as "a mass movement of all women who work in fields, factories, offices and houses," and they declared it to be "an active supporter of women's struggle for their everyday economic demands and their struggle for equality, democracy, progress and peace" (97). The APW adopted a Marxist-feminist discourse (180), since the members believed that women were doubly oppressed and their liberation could be achieved only by women's participation in social production and through the socialization of child care and housework. It was actively engaged in promoting women's rights, with a particular emphasis on the rights of women workers. It addressed a wide variety of issues, including maternity leave, social security coverage for domestic workers, early retirement for women, equal pay for equal work, and recognition of motherhood as a social contribution. Although some of its publications included other issues such as women's subordination within family and reproductive rights, it fell short of pressing for them.

The AWP organized campaigns, prepared various petitions to be submitted to the parliament, the cabinet, and the municipal government, and initiated rallies and demonstrations. It tried to raise the consciousness of women in factories and of women living in the outskirts of big cities, by organizing training workshops, teach-ins, forums, seminars, and panels. Its newspaper, *Women's Voice*, was distributed widely from 1975 to 1980 and reached a circulation of 30,000. In the late 1970s, heightened battles between radical groups became a prime concern, and the APW organized antifascism campaigns to alert the public and stop the killings carried out by the right-wing militants.

Women working in the APW called other women to join democratic mass organizations, persuaded women workers to play an active role in trade unions, and encouraged teachers, nurses, engineers, doctors, and lawyers to be active in their professional organizations and assume leadership positions. It can be argued that the politicization and training experienced in the APW, prepared many women to play leading roles in the feminist movements of the post-1980 period.

The governments showed no interest in women's issues and rights in the 1960s and 1970s. The only exception to this indifferent attitude was the enactment of the Family Planning Law (No. 557) on 10 April 1965 (E. Arat et al. 1983, 145), but even that was not legislated with a concern over women's rights but was conceived as a population control policy.[3] Women's civil organizations were not treated as sources of democratization but responded with hostility. The Union of Revolutionary Women and the APW, along with other left-wing organizations and political parties, were kept under surveillance. The APW headquarter and several of its branches were raided, some branches were closed down, and its members were arrested. The organization was ultimately banned on 28 April 1979, after the Kahramanmaraş massacres, by the İstanbul Martial Law administration. Nevertheless, the organization continued as an underground one until the next military coup on 12 September 1980.

Arguably, the APW was banned and its members were persecuted not because it was a women's organization but because it was governed by socialist ideas and the mission of establishing a new social order. Since the APW threatened the state and challenged its ideological base, it was repressed.

Since 1980: The Autonomous Women's Movement

The scope and strength of women's movement in the post-1980s period cannot be compared with women's activism in previous periods. The new women's movement has all the hallmarks of feminist thinking and developed as an independent and autonomous movement. Thus, it has included a variety of groups and organizations. In addition to associations and foundations, which held legal person status, several initiatives and ad hoc or informal groups emerged.

Although the formation of small consciousness raising groups by feminist women dates back to 1983, their first public appearance occurred on March 1986, when they initiated a petition drive to press for the implementation of the CEDAW (the Convention on the Elimination of All Forms of Discrimination against Women), to which Turkey had became a party by ratifying it in 1985 (see Yasemin Çelik in this volume, Chapter 13). Approximately 7,000 signatures were collected. Later, they launched a campaign against domestic violence and made it a public issue. Almost all women's groups started to celebrate women's day (8 March) every year by organizing rallies, conferences, and exhibitions that would use the occasion to spread their message and to raise gender consciousness among different classes of women. Similar activities have been carried out through out the year, and some groups started to publish books, newspapers, and journals that questioned women's status, challenged patriarchal discourses, and initiated provocative debates (Tekeli 1986, 1990; Sirman 1989; Y. Arat 1991).

The main concerns of these relatively recent women's groups and organizations center on domestic violence, rape, sexual harassment, body politics, and unequal treatment by laws and courts. As their provocative and radical actions such as protest marches, rallies, and campaigns slowed down in the second half of the 1990s, many people believed that the women's movement was withering away. However, at the dawn of the new century, the dramatic rise of independent feminist groups, their countrywide organization, their highly sophisticated discourse, and their accumulated experience and wisdom based on twenty years of activism, all signify the increasing strength and dynamism of women's movement.

The relationship between women's groups and the state has been also complicated. Since this relationship took different forms in the 1980s and 1990s, it is necessary to evaluate these two decades separately. In the 1980s, the state did not take women's activism seriously and did not deal with women's organizations on equal terms. The state bureaucrats were typically not interested in getting engaged in a dialogue with women's organizations. Historically, the state played a paternalistic role and women expressed their gratitude to the state for their "granted rights." Feminist women were not eager to work with the state, either. They were concerned that establishing alliances or cooperating with the state would diminish the radicalism of women's movement and would, ultimately, result in the "institutionalization" of women's movement. Thus, they did not try to obtain political power or representation in the current system. In fact, arguing that the state was essentially patriarchal, with all its institutions and laws, and incapable of protecting women's rights or pursuing gender equality, they detached themselves from the state.

In the early 1990s, however, the state started to become more attentive to women's issues. A national "women's machinery," called the Directorate General on the Status and Problems of Women, was established in October 1990, to oversee the implementation of the CEDAW and the "Forward-Looking Strategies for the Advancement of Women," adopted at the 1985 UN Conference in Nairobi. The bill was not welcomed by women's organizations that were suspicious about the intentions of the directorate. First, they were concerned that the creation of a state agency would be an instrument of the hegemonic state and would control the gender discourse. Second, they found the phrase that defined the mission of the directorate as "directing the activities of women's organizations in accordance with the national viewpoint to be formulated" as an indication of the state's effort to control women's organizations (Kardam 1994). As a response to the serious opposition by women's groups, the bill was revised and the directorate was placed under the Ministry of Labor and Social Welfare and later was attached to one of the state ministries. At the beginning, women, especially those from the radical strands of the movement, refused to recognize the directorate, asserting that its actions and policies could only reflect the dominant patriarchal ideology and gender discourse of the state. Nevertheless, the directorate gradually gained the support of some groups that held liberal feminist views and sought women's emancipation through legal reforms, as well as the secularist, Kemalist women who were uneasy about and threatened by the rise of the Islamic movement.

During the 1980s and early 1990s, women's groups drew attention to the laws and regulations that discriminate against women and reinforce their dependent and secondary status. The Civil Code and the Penal Code became the main targets. Various protests and lobbying efforts of women resulted in some amendments in these laws (see Yasemin Çelik in this volume, Chapter 13).

In time, the Directorate General managed to gain the trust of women's organizations, and the subsequent state ministers responsible for women's affairs felt the need to collaborate with women's organizations. The first significant attempt in that direction was the conference organized by the directorate on November 1993. The purpose of the conference was to bring together women's organizations and discuss the establishment of an interministerial advisory group in which women's organizations would be represented (Atauz 1993). Although such an *official* advisory group was not actualized, the directorate started to seek input and collaboration of women's organizations regularly. For example, in preparing the country report for the Fourth World Congress, which was to take place in Beijing in 1995, the directorate called many organizations to contribute to the report. Similarly, the drafts of the National Plan of Action after the Beijing conference and the draft CEDAW reports for the second and third terms were prepared in 1997 by incorporating proposals of women's organizations and revised according to their suggestions.

While collaborating with the directorate, women's organizations continued with their criticisms of the discriminatory laws and practices of the state. The dual position of women's groups was clearly demonstrated at the 1995 Sinop meeting, which was called by the directorate and included major women's organizations. During this well-attended two-day meeting, women raised all their qualms with the state practices. Representatives of various women's organizations raised some issues as responsibilities of the state (KA-DER 2002, 42):

1. An Equal Opportunities law should be passed, laying down specific legislation against discrimination.
2. Equal opportunity commissions should be established.
3. The state ministry responsible for women's affairs and its Directorate General for Women's Status and Problems should coordinate other ministries for the realization of gender equality policies.

In recent years the directorate has not played an active role either in the realization of these demands or in the development of a comprehensive national women's policy. This was because the original law establishing the directorate had been repealed and the new law did not come into force until November 2004. In this period, with very limited personnel and financial resources, the directorate was virtually voiceless and the relationship with women's groups deteriorated.

It can be argued that women's groups have also made a distinction between the directorate and the rest of the state apparatus. While the former was seen as aware and concerned about women's subordinate position, and appreciated for taking action to improve women's status, the state, as the overarching institution, has been viewed as hostile to women. The direct actions of the state that violated women's human rights, including virginity tests used in recruiting personnel for state offices and carried out in girls' boarding schools and dormitories (Y. Arat 2000b, 280), became targets of criticisms and protests. A campaign, launched on June 1992 and lasting for six months, employed the slogan, "No to Virginity Tests, Our Bodies Belong to Us," and criticized all who participated in carrying out the tests, along with the state. The purpose of the campaign was to raise public awareness about the issue and to present it as a violation of human rights that should be politicized.

Violence against women was assigned a priority, and a wide range of feminist groups worked in different ways to draw the attention of the public and the media to domestic violence. They organized large rallies and opened shelters to protect women from their violent male partners and relatives.[4] They directed attention to the fact that acts of sexual violence within family, although very widespread, were not punishable by law, and rape within marriage was not recognized in the Penal Code as a crime. They problematized the separation of public and private domains and criticized the state for being indifferent to all forms of violence in the family, including rape, incest, and beating. Consequently, the Law on the Protection of the Family was enacted in 1998, addressing for the first time the question of domestic violence.

While very critical of the state, women also realized the need to work with the state to achieve some changes. Thus, they have been engaged in uneasy collaboration with the state. Pursuing changes in the Civil Code constitutes an illustrative example.

The concerns over the discriminatory aspects of the Civil Code had been raised by women earlier, but an actual attempt to revise it began in 1981, when the first draft was prepared by a commission appointed by the Ministry of Justice. Women called for a change, because the code reinforced men's domination over women, but they also argued that the amendments for a partial improvement would not be sufficient. Yet, they diligently worked for the amendments. They signed petitions and lobbied extensively. Women from İstanbul, Ankara, and İzmir launched a national campaign in 1992 to publicize the issues pertaining to the code (Ekren 1993, 10). Later, representatives from various women's organizations participated in the working group formed by the Directorate General to work on the draft bill. Women lawyers from the bar associations in major cities discussed and assessed the implications of the articles in the draft bill. The Women's Research Center in İstanbul University prepared an alternative draft bill. The intensified efforts continued in the early 2000s. Women paid visits to the deputies and rallied protests against the conservative members of the parliament who opposed the draft, and 101 women's groups and organizations made an appeal to the parliament to pass the bill (Kadınlar Dünyası 2001, 2). Consequently, the parliament enacted the new law on 22 November 2002. The new Civil Code assured women's rights and equality between women and men in marriage—except recognizing the husband's last name as the family name.

In the late 1990s, demands by women's organizations were diversified and became more sophisticated. In 1997, the organization KA-DER was established to encourage, train, and support women in seeking public office and acquire equal representation of women. KA-DER urged the state to adopt a policy that would encourage women to participate in politics and take measures to guarantee increases in women's representation. It devised a National Plan of Action for Gender Equality to be proposed by the cabinet and ratified by the parliament. KA-DER also demanded the establishment of a "permanent commission for gender equality" within parliament, noting that the association would have its own committee for gender equality that would work as a government and parliament watchdog.[5]

According to a 2003 study, the number of women's organizations and autonomous groups, including their branches, had reached about 300—74 percent of them established after 1990.[6] These organizations and groups also have played a significant role in pressing the state to implement CEDAW. They also assisted the state to meet its obligations, including the preparation of the country reports. Yet, they continue to monitor the conduct of the state. For example, in May 2003, more than four hundred representatives of women's NGOs throughout the country gathered in Ankara, at the initiative of a women's organization, Flying Broom, to discuss the content of a "*shadow* country report" to complement the Turkey's official report of CEDAW for the fourth and fifth terms.

The state agencies learned to appreciate the value of and contributions by women's groups and started to follow up on women's work, although they did it rather clumsily. Some projects carried out by women's organizations have inspired state institutions to work. For example, after the establishment of the shelters for battered women by feminist NGOs, the Directorate General for Social Work and Social Services created "guest houses" for such women. A very effective project developed by the Women's Human Rights group in İstanbul, which focused on teaching women about their rights, was put into practice in the community centers that are run by the same directorate. Municipalities also sought input from women's organizations, when they established consultancy services for women (Ecevit 2001, 247–52).

Being a candidate to the European Union, Turkey has recently proposed some policy changes regarding women's issues, mostly in the legal sphere. In addition to strengthening its commitment to the CEDAW, by withdrawing all reservations and ratifying the Optional Protocol (see Yasemin Çelik in this volume, Chapter 13), the parliament enacted a new Labor Code in 2003, which includes provisions prohibiting discrimination on the basis of gender, and eliminating discriminatory practices against women, including those relating to one's marital status or family responsibilities. The new Penal Code, enacted in 2004, defines sexual crimes as crimes committed against the individual rather than against public decency. For the first time, the code covers marital rape and sexual harassment in the workplace, as well as human trafficking.

Among the most important of these changes is the amendment of Article 10 of the Constitution in May 2004, making the state responsible not only for ensuring nondiscrimination between women and men, but also for taking the necessary measures to implement equal rights and create opportunities in practice for women in every field. However, it falls short of including an affirmative action clause.

It is clear that these developments in the legal field are partly related to Turkey's status as a candidate EU country and the Copenhagen political criteria. However, it cannot be denied that the impetus for these changes has been attained through the persistent successful advocacy and lobbying efforts of the women's movement in Turkey. Improving women's rights is among the prerequisites of EU membership, and women's organizations in Turkey are aware of the positive impact that the candidacy process has on women's rights. Many of the legal changes that the women's movement campaigned for over decades have finally been implemented as a result of the pressure to comply with the Copenhagen criteria. Most recently, women's organizations have increased their contact and collaboration with European women's organizations and networks, and started to participate in the European Women's Lobby.

Conclusion

In this chapter I analyzed the women's movement in Turkey in terms of its historical development and its relationship with the state. I tried to show that while women's organizations were subject to cooptation and repression by the state, a more complex relationship between the state and women's groups emerged after 1980.

The new women's movement that originated in metropolitan centers such as İstanbul, Ankara, and İzmir gave way to the mushrooming of women's organizations in all regions. In many provinces, women's organizations that carry out mainly philanthropic and charitable activities exist side-by-side with more radical women's groups and organizations that function as advocates of women's rights. It is possible to distinguish them as those that serve women's practical and basic needs and those that focus on strategic (feminist) interests. The international conferences of the 1990s under the auspices of the United Nations have also allowed women to become acquainted with global feminism. Women from different NGOs participated in the Fourth World Women's Conference in Beijing in 1995. Particularly important in this respect was the Habitat Conference held in İstanbul in 1996. This conference allowed many women's organizations to acquire pro-feminist perspectives, revise their agendas, and strengthen their resolve. The rapid increase in the number of other civil society organizations working on human rights, good governance, development, and environment also contributed to the expansion of women's organizations.

Women's work since 1980 has been fruitful in yielding significant changes in favor of women. The most important developments included the revision of the Civil Code and the ratification of CEDAW. Also significant to note is the collaboration between the women's groups and the state. However, their alliance is far from being complete, and is subject to some tension and ambivalence. Women are skeptical of the deeply rooted patriarchal norms and male-dominated institutions, and the state has yet to prove its genuine commitment to human rights, in general, and women's rights, in particular. The state's indifference to honor killings, the repression of protests by groups such as the "Saturday Mothers,"[7] and the repressive policies toward Islamist women students' and teachers' demand to wear head scarves in schools and universities are a few examples of pending issues.

Two tasks await women's organizations in the future. First, there is a need to closely observe the state's approach to the "women's question." Women's organizations will continue with their advocacy and lobbying efforts and press for the implementation of these changes. Second, gender inequality, violations of women's rights, patriarchal discourse, and antifeminism are subjects about which women's organizations must continue to forge a common platform for the years ahead.

In their shadow report to the CEDAW committee, women's organizations demanded that the state take special temporary measures and affirmative action, adopt an Equality Framework Law, establish a Gender Equality Monitoring Commission in the Turkish Parliament, and create a Gender Equality Ombuds office

Chapter 13

The Effect of CEDAW on Women's Rights

Yasemin Çelik Levin

After years of work by various governmental and nongovernmental organizations, the UN General Assembly adopted the Convention on the Elimination of All Forms of Discrimination against Women (CEDAW) in 1979 as an international bill of rights for women. CEDAW defines discrimination against women as "any distinction, exclusion or restriction made on the basis of sex which has the effect or purpose of impairing or nullifying the recognition, enjoyment or exercise by women, irrespective of their marital status, on a basis of equality of men and women, of human rights and fundamental freedoms in the political, economic, social, cultural, civil or any other field" (Article 1).

Nation-states that accept the Convention pledge to adopt laws, policies, and other measures to end discrimination against women. And those that have ratified it are bound to put into practice the various provisions of the Convention. The CEDAW seeks to achieve equality for women in the political and public spheres, in education, health, and employment. It affirms the reproductive rights of women, women's rights to acquire, change, or retain their nationality (and the nationalities of their children), and seeks to stop all forms of exploitation of women. The CEDAW entered into force on 3 September 1981 and as of October 2004, 179 countries were party to the Convention. This makes up over 90 percent of countries that are members of the UN.

Article 28 of CEDAW allows countries to ratify the Convention subject to reservations, "provided that the reservations are not incompatible with the object and purpose of the Convention." States are permitted to enter reservations to specific articles of the Convention that contradict their national laws, traditions, religion, or culture. The General Assembly of the UN also adopted an Optional Protocol to the CEDAW, on 6 October 1999, that entered into force on 22 December, 2000. By ratifying the Optional Protocol, states "(recognize) the competence of the Committee on the Elimination of Discrimination against Women—the body that monitors states parties' compliance with the Convention—to receive and

consider complaints from individuals or groups within its jurisdiction."
The CEDAW is a living document and its scope changes according to the
general comments of this committee. Some important issues which were
not discussed in the original document have been added to it over time.

Turkey ratified CEDAW in 1985, and assumed its obligations after the
document was submitted to the UN on 19 January 1986. It signed the
Optional Protocol on 8 September 2000, and ratified it on 29 October
2002. This chapter explores Turkey's implementation of the CEDAW, with
an emphasis on the laws and policies that were changed to bring them
into compliance with the Convention, and the tangible changes that have,
or have not, occurred as a result. Despite Turkey's poor human rights
record, the Turkish government supported the CEDAW from the early
stages of its inception. It voted yes to the UN General Assembly Resolution No. 3521, on 15 January 1975, which requested the drafting of the
Convention, as well as to Resolution No. 34/180 on 18 January 1979,
which announced it (Acar 2000). Turkey had shown some commitment
to the issue of women's rights in the international arena prior to the
CEDAW, as on 22 December 1966, when it ratified the International Labor
Organization Equal Remuneration Convention (dated 1951), which stipulated equal pay, for men and women, for equal work (State Institute of
Statistics c. 2003). Turkey signed and ratified the CEDAW soon after it
came into force, but significant changes in laws were not initiated until the
late 1990s. The reforms made by Turkish legislators to improve women's
rights in Turkey prior to the 1990s were limited in nature. There was also
a significant lack of enforcement. However, the women's organizations
that emerged and became active in the 1980s have used the CEDAW and
other means to push for tangible changes.

Women's Rights in Turkey

Turkish governments have espoused support for women's rights since the
beginning of the Republic in 1923. The overriding objective of Mustafa
Kemal Atatürk was to modernize and westernize Turkey. Women's rights
were thought to be an integral part of this process. Ziya Gökalp, an intellectual who set the tone for the modernization of Turkey in his extensive
writings, argued that women's rights were actually indigenous to Turkish
culture because pre-Islamic Turks in Central Asia had considered men
and women equal. He contended that "women could become a ruler, a
commander of a fort, a governor and an ambassador" (Y. Arat 2000a,
107). Gökalp argued that the emancipation of women should be thorough,
including socioeconomic life, education, and legal treatment (Fleming
1998, 128). As a result of such attitudes, there were revolutionary changes
regarding women's rights in Turkey.

Islamic law was abolished in 1926 and replaced by a new civil code derived from the Swiss system. Religious marriages were made illegal, civil marriage became compulsory, and polygamy was abolished. Men and women were given equal shares in inheritance and equal rights in custody over children. Women gained the right to vote first in municipal elections in 1930, and then the right to vote and run in parliamentary elections as a constitutional right in 1934. Consequently, Turkey was championed as a model of a secular Muslim country in which women could have many of the same rights as men. However, as noted by some scholars, this perception might have harmed women's rights and activism by giving the impression that they are not needed (Müftüler-Baç 1999; and see Yıldız Ecevit in this volume, Chapter 12).

Despite several pro-women declarations and legislation, women in Turkey have been far from equal to their male counterparts. There are several factors that act as the agents of women's oppression in Turkey. A highly sexist and patriarchal family structure has remained in place. As a result, the importance of *namus* (sexual purity) is used by society as a control mechanism over women's freedom (Müftüler-Baç 1999). Gender biases disadvantage girls in educational access. Most rural and urban lower-class women are not educated beyond primary school. Despite significant improvements in the past few decades, 28 percent of women still cannot read and write.[1] Women are underrepresented in decision-making posts and politics. During the 1935 elections—the first in which women were allowed to run for the parliament—18 women were elected into the Grand National Assembly, comprising 4.6 percent of the entire parliamentary body. By the 1995 general election, however, this percentage had dropped to 2.4 percent, with only 13 women out of 550 members of parliament. The proportion of female parliamentarians in 2002 was a mere 4.4 percent (Population and Development Indicators). More disturbing is the female electorate's position on this issue: while 73 percent believe that a woman can act as a successful mayor, and 64 percent believe that a woman could be a successful prime minister, 79 percent do not want their daughters to be politically active (Abadan-Unat and Tokgöz 1994, 713).

Gender segregation exists in the workplace as well as in family life. The majority of housework is still performed by women. Although women have advanced in some professions as physicians, university professors, and public civil servants, only 15.5 percent of Turkish women (and 23.1 percent of men) were enrolled in institutions of higher education in 1996–97, and women's labor participation rate in 1998 was 27.9 percent.[2] According to the official labor statistics, 70 percent of the female workforce in Turkey is employed in the agricultural sector, 10.6 percent in industry, and 19.4 percent in services (*Women in Turkey* 1999). However, these figures underestimate women's work in the informal sector and in rural areas, where women work as unpaid family workers, and the female participation rate in the labor force is 43.7 percent (*Women in Turkey* 1999). Women who migrate to the cities from the countryside are also usually employed in the informal sector as domestic help.

The life expectancy rate for women in Turkey is 71.5 years (for men, it is 66.9), which is significantly less than that in most developed countries (Population and Development Indicators). According to the Gender Empowerment Index—a composite index measuring gender inequality based on three dimensions of empowerment – Turkey ranks 63rd of 70 countries (UNDP 2001). Compounding the inequalities and challenges, as discussed above, is the fact that there is a high degree of inequity among different segments of women—urban/rural, upper/lower income—in terms of access to education, health, and employment.

Implementation of the CEDAW

There are many aspects of women's lives that could be significantly improved by bringing Turkish laws and policies more in line with the stipulations of the CEDAW. Turkey ratified the Convention with reservations placed on Article 15 (par. 2 and 4) and Article 16 (par. 1 c, d, f, g). As such, Turkey was one of the 69 countries that adopted CEDAW with reservations. Paragraph 2 in Article 15 of the CEDAW stipulates: "States Parties shall accord to women, in civil matters, a legal capacity identical to that of men and the some opportunities to exercise that capacity. In particular, they shall give women equal rights to conclude contracts and to administer property and shall treat them equally in all stages of procedure in courts and tribunals." Paragraph 4 assigns women equality "with regard to the law relating to the movement of persons and the freedom to choose their residence and domicile." The paragraphs of Article 16, on which Turkey placed reservations, grant women equal rights "during marriage and at its dissolution," in matters related to children, and "same personal rights as husband and wife, including the right to choosing a family name, a profession and an occupation."

The Turkish government expressed concern that certain aspects of the Convention contradicted relevant clauses of the Turkish Civil Code regulating marriage and family life. The Turkish Civil Code of 1926, which was still in effect, stated the following:

1. The husband has the legal standing to represent the conjugal union (Article 154).
2. The husband chooses the domicile and duly provides for the maintenance of wife and children (Article 152/2).
3. The wife acquires the husband's surname (Article 153/1).

4. The wife, to the extent of her ability, must assist the husband by word and deed in his effort to maintain the home. The wife is responsible for household management (Article 153/2).
5. Both parents share parental authority over children but in the case of dispute, the husband's view prevails (Articles 263) (Introductory Statement 1997).

Yet, the ratification document noted that "the Turkish State did not refute its obligation or intention to fully implement the Convention with regard to substantive issues and at no instance attempted to invoke its reservations as an argument or excuse to implement any article of the Convention" (Acar 2000, 4). Thus, all reservations were removed on 20 September 1999, and a number of important steps were taken toward the full implementation of the Convention. The work of various governmental agencies has been urged and advanced by numerous nongovernmental organizations that became active during the last few decades. The CEDAW has contributed to improving the status of women in Turkey and will continue to do so because of the institutions, laws, and policies that have been adopted within the framework of the Convention.

Programs and Institutions

After the discussion of women's issues as an independent and planning problem for the first time in the Fifth Five-Year Development Plan (1985–90), the Directorate General on the Status and Problems of Women (DGSPW) was established as the national mechanism on women's affairs on 25 October 1990 (Law No. 3670). The establishment of this body was necessary to fulfill the requirements of the CEDAW. The DGSPW became a part of the Ministry of Labor and Social Security on 27 November 2002, and was subsequently placed under the state ministry responsible for women and family that was attached to the prime minister's office. The General Directorate's objectives include improving the status of women in Turkey in social, political, economic, and cultural spheres of life. Despite its broad mission, the DGSPW has a small budget and limited resources. Its work is also constrained by its institutional organization. Being under a state ministry, it cannot influence government policies in a direct manner. The DGSPW works in close cooperation with NGOs on policy formulation, research activities, and project implementation (Replies of the Turkish Delegation 1997). It is the body that coordinates the activities of various governmental and nongovernmental agencies working toward women's equality. There are no provincial agencies of the DGSPW; thus Women's Status Units were established in 10 provinces to offer women consulting services. Some basic laws are reviewed by the DGSPW, and although its considerations are not always taken into account, the Directorate General has played an important role in "institutionalizing gender issues" (Southeastern European Women's Legal Initiative).

In 1987, the Committee for Policies for Women was established within the State Planning Organization, and a Women's Unit was established at the premises of the Ministry of Labor in 1989. Under the aegis of the DGSPW, and co-sponsored by the United Nations Development Program (UNDP), the National Program for the Enhancement of Women's Integration in Development Project was launched in 1992 and extended until the end of 1998. The objectives of this program were to change the negative images of women in all fields of life and to integrate women's issues into development plans.

At the same time, universities started to pay more attention to women's issues, and women's studies centers initiated a variety of innovative projects. The Ankara University's Women's Studies Center, for example, has conducted short-term training programs to establish gender sensitivity in institutions and organizations that offer public services to women such as political parties and trade unions. It has also carried out programs aimed at supporting women's organizations to increase solidarity among women and to empower women to fight sexism. In addition, Middle East Technical University, Aegean University, and İstanbul University also have women's studies graduate programs. There are also 12 Women's Research Centers, in Ankara (4), İstanbul (2), Adana, Mersin, Gaziantep, Diyarbakır, Van, and İzmir.[3] The Turkish government proudly publicizes the fact that Turkey participated in the Fourth World Women's Conference in Beijing in 1995 with an all-women delegation and adopted the Beijing Platform of Action without any reservations. The Beijing Platform "is an agenda for women's empowerment (that) aims . . . at removing all the obstacles to women's active participation in all spheres of public and private life through a full and equal share in economic, social, cultural and political decision-making" (*Beijing Declaration and Platform for Action* 2001). Furthermore, in December 1997, a parliamentary commission was convened to ascertain the steps needed in order to ensure full implementation of the CEDAW.

Legal and Constitutional Reforms

According to Article 10 of the Constitution, everyone is equal before the law, regardless of their race, gender, religion, or ethnicity. Acknowledging that this does not guarantee equality for women, the Directorate General on the Status and Problems of Women proposed adding a paragraph to Article 10 that would make the equality clause stronger. Although the initial attempts to amend Article 10 failed, it was finally changed in May

2004 to add a paragraph stating, "Women and men have equal rights. The state is obliged to realize this equality in life" (Z. F. Arat 2004, 21). Article 90 was also amended to have international human rights treaties supersede Turkish laws in case of conflict. An equality clause was also added to Article 41 of the Constitution on 3 October 2001. Referring to family as the foundation of the Turkish society, Article 41 now specifies that family is based on equality between the husband and wife.

The Constitutional Court has also assumed a progressive stand. Two verdicts of the court on the legal equality of men and women actually referred to the CEDAW (Acar 2000, 4). On 19 November 1990 (Constitutional Court Decision No. 1990/31) the provision of the Civil Code, Article 159, which necessitated a husband's permission for his wife's professional activity, was annulled. In 1996, the court also annulled Articles 440 and 441 of the Turkish Penal Code on the grounds that they defined the adultery of married men and women differently, thus violating the principle of equality before the law and the principles outlined in the CEDAW.[4] Moreover, as a result of these annulments, adultery is no longer defined as a crime under the law.[5] Article 438 of the Turkish Penal Code, which reduced the sentence of a rapist by one-third if the victim was a prostitute, was also annulled by the Grand National Assembly in 1990 for violating the equality principle.

Some legislative amendments followed the court decisions. A change in Article 153 of the Civil Code passed in May 1997, allowed women to retain their maiden names along with their husband's names if they wish to do so. An amendment to the Tax Law in 1998 permitted women to declare their income independently of their husband's.

A significant development for women's rights in Turkey was the adoption of the new Turkish Civil Code on 22 November 2001. Women's struggle to change the Civil Code had a long history. Finally, as a response to the demands by the women's movement of the 1980s, the Ministry of Justice set up a commission composed of civil law professors to draft a gender-sensitive bill to bring Turkish laws in closer alignment with those in European countries. The bill was also expected to improve Turkey's prospect to join the European Union as a member and address Turkey's obligations to meet the gender equality provisions in international treaties, including the CEDAW. Thus, the draft bill for the new civil law, announced on 17 February 1998, included several progressive changes.

Article 152 of the 1926 Civil Code had deemed the "the head of the conjugal union" to be the husband. While on the one hand obligating the husband to perform certain responsibilities (such as providing for the requirements of the spouse and children), this clause placed the wife in a subordinate position in the marriage contract (*NGO Report on the Implementation of CEDAW* 1997). The new Civil Code eliminated the entire concept of "the head of the conjugal union." It also raised and equalized the minimum age of marriage for men and women and introduced a more egalitarian matrimonial property regime (Statement by Prof. Yakın Ertürk 2002). The new Civil Code stipulates that each spouse represents the conjugal union and that each shares an equal part in determining the conjugal home. Women are granted the right to use the maiden name before the husband's name, as well as the right to work without seeking any permission from the husband. Furthermore, husband and wife share equally the property acquired during marriage.

In the early days of the Republic, when the Turkish Civil Code was adopted on 17 February 1926, the concept of "separate ownership" was accepted as the legal property regime. Meanwhile, "united ownership" was accepted as a choice. However, since this option was never publicized, it was never applied. According to the "separate ownership" regime, each spouse kept the property they previously owned or those they acquired during marriage. In the case of divorce, the spouse who did not have his/her name on the property (account/deed, etc.) had no right to the property. Since tradition dictated that most property would be registered in the husband's name, wives could not have any legal claim over property in the case of divorce. According to the new regime, the unpaid work of women at home is recognized by stating that the added value of all property acquired during marriage shall be shared equally if the marriage is terminated. This new regime is based on a German law (Equal Rights Law, 1957), in that it is a "partnership in gain" regime. Accordingly, spouses are considered to be partners in the property they acquired during their marriage. They cannot claim ownership to property owned prior to the marriage or that acquired by inheritance. The objective is to have equal access to the property acquired by joint labor. According to the Turkish government's statement to the Forty-Sixth Session of the Commission on the Status of Women at the UN, "the national machinery for women's affairs is actively disseminating information about the new law and sponsoring nation-wide debates to ensure that women become informed of their new rights and other actors in society become sensitized to these changes" (Statement by Prof. Yakın Ertürk 2002).

Turkey's National Action Plan, published in 1997, highlighted eight out of the twelve critical areas of concern stated in the Platform of Action of the Fourth World Conference on Women: (1) education and training of women; (2) the rights of the girl-child; (3) women and health; (4) violence against women; (5) women and the economy; (6) women in power and decision making; (7) institutional mechanisms for the advancement of women; and (8) women and the media.[6] In line with the Action Plan, in 1998 the Grand National Assembly formed a special parliamentary investigative commission for gender discrimination. It was the report of this commission that "recommended that Turkey withdraw its reservations to CEDAW; that gender mainstreaming be integrated in all policies; that temporary special measures be taken in education, labor and politics to ensure equality" (Acar, Acuner, and Şenol 1999).

The violence against women became a priority issue for the women's groups in the 1990s and led to the legislation of a new law. The Law on the Protection of the Family (Law No. 4320), which entered into force on 17 January 1998, was the first legislation that addresses the issue of domestic violence in Turkey. This act requires the state to take action to protect women from human rights abuses committed by family members. It regulates the punishments for domestic abusers and seeks protection for the women and children who are victims of domestic abuse. The law states that the perpetrators of the violence should be removed from their homes for a certain period of time and, if the law is violated again, there should be a jail sentence imposed. This law, however, was not sufficient to address many types of violence against women.

Significant progress on this issue came with the drastic alteration of the 1926 Turkish Penal Code on 26 September 2004. The Turkish Penal Code had been in violation of several paragraphs in Article 2 of the CEDAW (*Shadow NGO Report* 2004). The new Penal Code includes more than thirty amendments to advance gender equality and protection of sexual and bodily rights of women and girls in Turkey (İkkaracan and Amado). Article 102/2 of the new Penal Code, for example, criminalizes marital rape and broadens the definition of rape (Z. F. Arat 2004, 22). Rapists will no longer get reduced sentences for offering to marry their victims. Various forms of domestic violence are addressed. The new Penal Code recognizes domestic violence as a crime that should be penalized by incarceration (Article 96/2). It also increases sentences for sexual crimes. It attempts to root out patriarchal concepts embedded in Turkish society that threaten the well-being of Turkish women and girls, such as chastity, honor, and morality, and "abolishes previously existing discriminations against non-virgin and unmarried women" (İkkaracan and Amado).

In addition to the changes in laws, some new programs have been developed to assist women. Starting in 1993, there have been special programs that grant small credits to women and promote women's entrepreneurship. Recognizing the illiteracy problem and educational gaps, the Turkish government made a pledge at the Beijing Women's Conference of 1995 to bring about equality in literacy rates by the year 2000. Although this objective has not been reached, due to the "Project for the Improvement of Women's Education," 231,000 women had taken part in literacy training courses by the end of 1999. Moreover, the Eight-Year Compulsory Basic Education Law, which was passed in 1997 and extended primary education from five to eight years, is also expected to improve the literacy rate over time. The secondary school enrollment statistics for girls have been lower than those for boys, mostly as a result of economic and cultural factors (see Gök and Ilgaz in this volume, Chapter 8). The new law will provide parents with greater incentives to keep their daughters in school beyond the primary level. It is also noted that this new education law is "expected to raise the marriage and child birth ages by keeping the girl child in the education system for a longer period of time."[7]

While all of these are significant developments, perhaps even more important is the fact that the CEDAW contributed to bringing the topic of women's rights to the forefront. Starting in the 1980s, feminist authors, journalists, academicians, and politicians became vocal about championing women's rights and publicized issues such as discriminatory articles in laws, sexual harassment, and bride price. The term "sexual harassment" entered the Turkish lexicon for the first time, and the attention to the issue has been sustained through public protests and mass campaigns. In 1996, the World Bank sponsored a project by the DGSPW to research gender-based discrimination and sexual harassment in the workplace. Also in 1996, the Confederation of Turkish Labor Unions (Türkiye İşçi Sendikaları Konfederasyonu, TÜRK-İŞ), the largest labor union in Turkey, published a guidebook on sexual harassment.[8] Due to the sustained attention by women's NGOs, the new Turkish Penal Code of September 2004 has made sexual harassment at the work place a crime punishable by law. It should be noted, however, that significant shifts in cultural norms and attitudes must also occur to end sexual harassment in Turkey.

Challenges for the Future

Despite the significant improvements that have been made toward the implementation of the CEDAW in Turkey, there are certain areas that have not been addressed, or are in need of further attention. In 1997, the *NGO Report on the Implementation of CEDAW in Turkey* noted that "the main obstacle in the way of women's human rights is the lack of women's awareness of what their rights are and the absence of effective means for their enforcement. A meaningful implementation of CEDAW in Turkey requires widespread, concrete action-programs to support and empower women in dealing with the discrimination they face in their everyday lives." Women for Women's Human Rights, a Turkish women's NGO, thus cites raising awareness of women's rights and "(supporting) women in developing effective strategies for the implementation of these rights" as one of its most important goals (*NGO Report on the Implementation of CEDAW in Turkey* 1997). Furthermore, the *Consideration of Turkish Combined Second and Third Periodic Reports by the Committee on the Elimination of Discrimination against Women* (1997) identified the following challenges: "the disparities in status and opportunities for urban middle-class and rural women; violence against women in the private domain; a strengthening of the contribution of the media to the advancement of women, including through an increase in the number of female professionals . . . ; and the revision of educational materials, which continued to portray women in their traditional roles as mothers and wives; and the low participation by women in politics and parliament."

One way to achieve these goals is to make women a more integral part of the decision-making process. In fact, the Association for the Support and Training of Women Candidates (KA-DER) was formed in 1997, to promote greater representation by women in politics. Some other pending issues include citizenship, property ownership, violence against women, and women's reproductive rights.

According to Article 19 of the Turkish Citizenship Law, "a Turkish woman married to an alien, if her husband's national law permits and if she notifies the relevant authorities that she decides to choose her husband's citizenship, loses her Turkish citizenship."[9] This law is based on the assumption that women often choose to live in their husband's home countries. Article 9 of the CEDAW, however, says, "State Parties of the Convention should ensure that neither marriage to an alien nor change of nationality by the husband shall automatically change the nationality, render her stateless, or force upon her the nationality of her husband."[10] Although the Turkish law does not make the woman stateless or change her nationality automatically (the woman has to voluntarily notify the authorities), the contradiction with the CEDAW stems from the fact that this only applies to women.

In addition, although women have equal rights of ownership over property, there is a clause in the Civil Code (Article 597) which states that "in cases of agricultural enterprises that are run as a single unit, to prevent the fragmentation of agricultural land, the judge is given the right to allocate property to the inheritor which has the capability to run the enterprise."[11] The next article maintains that local customs as well as the standing of the inheritors in the community shall be taken into account when making a decision. Turkish customs see men as the provider and more qualified to run agricultural ventures. Furthermore, a high percentage of women in rural areas work in family enterprises as unpaid or informal workers. As such their labor does not entitle them to the benefits of work in the formal sector such as social security and healthcare.

Another significant violation of the CEDAW is the practice of "honor killings," in which girls and women are killed by male relatives if their actions are deemed to bring shame to a family's honor. This practice is more common in eastern and southeastern Turkey, but it occasionally occurs in the large cities as well. Since this practice follows a belief in the inequality of men and women, it violates the CEDAW's preamble as well as Articles 1f (on discrimination) and 14 (on rural women). The new Penal Code does not recognize honor killings as a separate category of crimes. It does, however, include "custom killings" and murder of a parent, child, or spouse as "special cases" that should be punished with life imprisonment with hard labor (Z. F. Arat 2004, 22). It remains to be seen whether the new measures will reduce the number of honor killings in Turkey.

Another area of contention concerns women's reproductive rights, which are addressed in Article 15 of the CEDAW, but without referring to the word "abortion." Although abortion during the first 10 weeks of gestation became legal in Turkey, provided it is not used as a method of birth control, the law requires a married woman to seek the consent of her husband and a minor must get parental permission. The inadequate access to contraceptives and the lack of sex education continue to jeopardize women's reproductive health and control over their bodies.

Strengthening of NGOs, such as the Women for Women's Human Rights, the Equality-Watch Committee, the Purple Roof Women's Shelter Foundation, and KA-DER may reinforce the progress. The *NGO Report on the Implementation of CEDAW in Turkey* (1997) cites some other measures to bring about a "meaningful and effective implementation of the Convention": legal aid services for women; more shelters and hotlines for victims of domestic abuse; gender-sensitivity training of judges, prosecutors, lawyers, and the police; programs to train women entering the labor force; and programs that would make the public more aware of discriminations against women in education, the workplace, public life, and family.

Conclusion

Successive governments since the inception of the Turkish Republic claimed to have championed women's rights. A highly patriarchal culture and male-dominated public sphere, however, have prevented women's rights from becoming a part of the national agenda until the 1980s, when a new feminist movement began to challenge laws and practices that had been accepted for generations. By signing and ratifying the CEDAW, the state committed itself to bringing about gender equality. The recent legislation and institutional arrangements have created a formal framework that can lead to important changes toward advancing women's rights in Turkey. In addition to the legislative reforms, however, actual improvements in women's lives require major shifts in public attitudes and values.

Part V
Civic and Educational Efforts

Human Rights Discourse and Domestic Human Rights NGOs

BAŞAK ÇALI

Turkish domestic human rights organizations (HROs) have played a major role in developing a human rights discourse by using human rights as an interpretive framework to criticize, resist, and reform domestic political, social, and economic arrangements. This chapter contends that since 1986, domestic Turkish HROs have been major actors in the development of a domestically grown human rights perspective in Turkish politics. They have introduced framing issues as *human rights issues* and paved the way in fostering a culture of minimum guarantees and protections that any individual ought to enjoy within the Turkish political community.

For the purposes of this study, I define domestic HROs as nongovernmental organizations that intervene in the *political* and the *social* arrangements of their localities through an interpretation and appropriation of domestic political, social, and economic practices from a universal standpoint of human rights claims.[1] Human rights claims act as showing the nonnegotiable limits of commission and omission in political decision making. HROs take their cue from human rights ideals, principles, and law, in order to assess, criticize, and resist domestic legal frameworks and exercise of power (Donnelly 1995, 236; Freeman 2002; Wilson 1997). The chapter primarily focuses on four main human rights NGOs in Turkey to analyze the *emergence* of domestic human rights activism: Human Rights Association (İnsan Hakları Derneği, İHD), Human Rights Foundation of Turkey (Türkiye İnsan Hakları Vakfı, TİHV), Association for Human Rights and the Oppressed (İnsan Hakları ve Mazlumlar için Dayanışma Derneği, Mazlum-Der), and Human Rights Institution of Turkey (Türkiye İnsan Hakları Kurumu, TİHAK).[2]

Literature on the conditions under which domestic HROs emerge has been limited.[3] Existing theoretical models point to the importance of the interaction between domestic and international actors and their mobilization of support for a human rights-based struggle in the country in question (Risse, Ropp, and Sikkink 1999; Bugerman 1998, 905). The model developed by Keck and Sikkink further point to, what they call as the "boomerang effect," the role played by transnational advocacy networks in putting pressure on foreign governments and the host state by using the information they receive from domestic HROs (1998). This model identifies domestic human rights activists as strategic information providers. They contribute to monitoring, transmission of cases and factual situations to transnational advocacy networks and international organizations. Domestic human rights groups are conceptualized as instrumental agents constituting an essential part of the international human rights regime. HROs are analyzed from the perspective of making human rights violations in their country known to the "outside world" in order to receive support, protest, and ultimately pressure the host government for policy change.

This chapter supports the contention that the relation between domestic and international actors for HROs is dialectical, in that domestic activism can create HROs and international support can confer them legitimacy, recognition, and support internationally. However, it aims to contribute to a theoretical mapping of the conditions under which domestic political groups emerge by identifying themselves as human rights activists, prior to engaging with international human rights actors. In this respect, instrumentalist models of studying HROs are a consequence rather than a cause of the emergence of domestic HROs. Domestic HROs with a domestic support base are often born out of "traumas," with direct consequences for the persons involved, for example as a reaction to systematic oppression affecting many (such as military dictatorships), or the disowning, neglecting, or victimizing of a particular group by the political community (such as ethnic minorities, sexual minorities, terrorist suspects, immigrants). However, the continuity of HROs often depends on their ability to apply human rights principles to new struggles over new issues when the immediacy of their original cause has ceased. In this respect, HROs must constantly adapt themselves to the new and emerging issues of marginalization, oppression, or victimization in order to be sustainable over time,[4] and so must engage with transnational advocacy networks and follow the international developments of human rights activism and policy. This chapter shows that the domestic sociopolitical environment in Turkey contributed *more* to the emergence and initial diversification of a HRO-led domestic human rights discourse than the interaction of HROs with international human rights regimes or transnational advocacy networks. This has prepared the conditions for a domestically grown human rights activism. The proliferation of domestic human rights activism in the aftermath of the popularization and normalization of human rights discourse, however, has taken place in an ongoing interaction between international, European, and domestic dynamics of human rights policy.

Human Rights Organizations in Turkish History

It is not a coincidence that the first two organizations in Turkey with the words "human rights" in their titles were established by a small group of diplomats, academics, and state elites in 1946, following the advent of the United Nations in 1945. The first HRO, the Association for Human Rights and Fundamental Rights and Freedoms (İnsan Hakları ve Temel Hak ve Özgürlükler Derneği) was established by the members of the ruling party, the Republican People's Party (Cumhuriyet Halk Partisi, CHP), which had been the hegemonic party between 1925 and 1945. As a response to the CHP initiative, the newly established opposition, the Democrat Party (DP), pushed for the establishment of Association for the Protection of Human Rights (İnsan Haklarını Koruma Cemiyeti), whose president was the War of Independence hero Marshall Fevzi Çakmak, a political figure known for his conservative views (Bora, Peker, and Sancar 2002).

In the immediate aftermath of World War II, Turkey was keen to be a part of the emerging international order. The UN Charter made vague normative references to the importance of the promotion of human rights for peace and security. Plagemann notes that the UN Commission on Human Rights was instrumental in encouraging the formation of domestic HROs at the time (2001, 361). The first HROs in Turkey were established as a response to this undemanding international incentive. These organizations were primarily products of the corresponding instrumental motives of the government and opposition parties to *conform* to the new international order. While the Association for Human Rights and Fundamental Rights and Freedoms had paid lip service to the importance of human rights internationally, during its short tenure, it had not attempted to formulate the relevance of human rights as principles regulating the relations between the individuals and Turkish state. The Association for the Protection of Human Rights, on the other hand, had made references to the freedom of political activism and freedom of expression for religious identity. This position corresponded to that of the DP, which criticized the aggressive secular policies of the CHP. However, it collapsed in the same year as a result of accusations that it had relations with a group of "leftist intelligentsia." In 1960, a military coup d'état was carried out against the populist majoritarian rule of the DP, which had come to power in 1950 and maintained its parliamentary majority in the 1954 and 1957 elections. Since the ten-year rule of the DP was characterized by authoritarian and antipluralist policies, the postmilitary coup constitution aimed to curb the absolutist tendencies of the future governments. The 1961 Constitution made a strong reference to human rights by suggesting that the Turkish state was "based on human rights." Detailed definitions and safeguards for the protection of civil and political rights as well as economic and social rights were introduced (Tanör 1998, 364–431; Soysal 1986).

The progressive rights framework of the 1961 Constitution enabled civil and political expression of demands for economic equality and social justice by a wide range of groups. A new HRO, the İnsan Hakları Derneği, was established in 1962, led by Mehmet Ali Aybar, a prominent academic and political figure. This organization had a short life and became redundant when Aybar became the president of the newly found Turkish Labor Party in 1962.

In the late 1960s and the 1970s, the Turkish political landscape was occupied by the grand political narratives of class politics (Samim 1981, 60; Aydınoğlu 1992). This narrative placed more emphasis on the notions of social justice, equality, emancipation for the masses, redistribution of wealth, and democratization. The dominant understanding of "human rights" by the Turkish left regarded this concept as an instrument for the advancement of class struggle; they were skeptical about a human rights discourse that was not based on class politics.[5] Trade unions, student unions, associations, as well as outlaw leftist organizations, pursued revolutionary politics, using both violent and nonviolent forms of action. Political activism of this period was primarily directed toward systemic and structural transformation of the society. The activists' demands reforms for freedom of association, free education, and land distribution. It was social justice (activism for maximization of human well-being) and not human rights (activism for maintenance of minimum standards for all) that was central to the political platforms advancing demands for equality and freedom (Z. F. Arat 2002). Human rights-based political discourse also did not sit comfortably with the "anti-imperialist" stand of the Turkish revolutionary left in the 1960s and 1970s, which regarded human rights as a "Western bourgeois construct" imposed on "Third World" peoples as a diversion tactic from real issues.

In the aftermath of the 1971 military intervention, many left-wing activists were detained and imprisoned. Torture in prisons and detention centers was systematically carried out. The London-based Amnesty International (AI) in this period decided to focus and raise awareness for the increasing number of Turkish political prisoners and practices of torture in the international arena. To this end, the AI sent foreign researchers to Turkey to investigate the situation, and publicized the violations. The interactions of the Turkish left intelligentsia—which also faced political prosecution—with the AI led to the establishment of the small Turkish branch of Amnesty International in 1974.[6] In line with the general policy of the AI at the time, the mandate of its Turkish branch was limited to investigating and disseminating human rights violations of civil and political rights in other countries. Neither the AI nor its Turkish branch was able to create the sufficient conditions for a domestic human rights discourse in the 1970s. Interactions of the AI were limited to reporting the situation of (leftist) political prisoners and the leftist intelligentsia saw no need to express themselves through human rights claims. Other human rights-oriented organizations, such as the Peace Association (Barış Derneği) and Association of Contemporary Lawyers (Çağdaş Hukukçular Derneği), also fell short of shaping the political discourse. Yavuz Önen, the president of an HRO and a former left-wing activist, comments on this period:

In late 1960s and 70s, we had a multiplicity of tools of emancipatory politics in Turkey. Establishing an HRO at the time sounded almost ironic to many. When human rights issues were discussed by people who were involved in revolutionary class politics, they would regard human rights discourse as being "too humanist," "too soft," "too bourgeois." There was no need for a human rights-based struggle for the revolutionary/communist/socialist left. These groups were very powerful at the time and they did not need a human rights discourse or an HRO to engage in domestic political struggle.[7]

Within the right-wing groups, the notion of human rights had even less relevance to the political agenda. The nationalist and religious right tried to mobilize the workers and students by resorting to the elimination of "social injustices," attempting to stop "communists" threatening the nation and religion (Z. F. Arat 2002; Bora 2003).

The 1980 Coup d'État and the Aftermath

The 1980 coup involved an unprecedented degree of state violence, especially toward the political activity of all left-wing groups, and can be marked as a turning point in the development of a domestic human rights discourse. The establishment of the İHD in 1986 did not emanate from a theoretical or intellectual conviction, but as a practical response to the mass detention, torture, and disappearances primarily of "left-wingers" under the the military regime and the civilian governments that followed it after 1983. The estimated numbers of 650,000 detentions and more than 100,000 torture cases reveal the sociopolitical trauma informing the formation of the İHD.[8] No matter how fractured the left-wing parties and groups had been in the 1970s, the extreme brutality of the military regime toward these groups encouraged them to join forces within the auspices of an HRO.[9]

The military rule banned all political or civic organizations that had been involved in left-wing activism. This included all student unions and associations as well as trade unions and professional associations established by civil servants. Later, the 1982 Constitution imposed extensive restrictions on all civil and political liberties. The formation of the İHD was a practical measure that intended to help families whose children were in prison or detained, and to organize the left-wing journalists, intellectuals, lawyers, and academics who had no other legitimate means of participation in political life. Within this repressive political structure, human rights discourse emerged as one of the few available ways of criticizing and resisting the state violence. Hüsnü Öndül, a founding member and the former president of the İHD, comments on the unifying effect of the repression: "The primary reason for human rights to enter into our domestic agenda was the junta. All who joined under the İHD banner were victims of the junta in one way or another. Even though the founders of the organization were left-wing, the İHD was not established with a political purpose. Our common concern was human rights violations."[10]

By the end of 1980, domestic NGOs were able to enter into networks that included international governmental agencies, nongovernmental organizations, and reporting and monitoring methods of addressing violations of civil and political human rights. The considerable numbers of asylum seekers that fled from Turkey to Europe were instrumental in establishing contacts.[11] Since the Turkish state elite had considered participation in international human rights regimes as useful to strengthening alliances with the Western world in the 1980s, Turkey was already a party to several international human rights treaties. Most significantly, Turkey's entry to the jurisdiction of the European Court of Human Rights, in 1987, allowed the articulation of the state oppression and violence within the medium of international human rights law and language. The human rights language has not only enabled international alliances, but also legitimized the İHD and unified its otherwise politically fractured membership. Hence, the founders of the İHD have stated the organization's mission as "conducting activities in the field of human rights and freedoms."[12]

Nevertheless, the emergence of HROs and a domestic discourse on "human rights violations" irritated the state officials. The state authorities have started to characterize human rights movement as the marriage of "internal traitors" with "international enemies," and maintained a skeptical and suspicious attitude toward HROs.[13]

Diversification Within and Among HROs in the 1990s

By the end of 1980s, the İHD had become the most prominent voice in reporting the violations of civil and political rights in Turkey. The public started to identify the addressing of issues such as arbitrary killings, torture, unlawful detention, disappearances, freedom of expression, and political prisoners as the sphere of an HRO, despite the continuous legal and political pressure put on this organization. Since its establishment in 1986, more than 400 court cases were brought against the İHD by the public prosecutors, and through these cases over 300 active members of İHD have been brought to trial. The local offices of İHD were shut down more than 30 times by the governors of various provinces, and 14 members of the İHD were extrajudicially killed (Kuruluşundan Bugüne İHD 2001).

Nevertheless, the 1990s also witnessed the diversification and proliferation of human rights activism in Turkey, partially due to the success of the İHD. Since the initial activities of the association focused on helping the victims of the military coup, a decade after the coup most of the victims and their families considered the mission fulfilled and lost interest in the activities of the organization. At the same time, however, the heightening of the armed conflict between the state security forces and the Kurdistan Workers' Party (Partia Karkaren Kürdistan, PKK), the Kurdish separatist guerrilla group, raised new concerns. The measures taken by the state security forces to combat the guerrillas in southeast Turkey, as well as PKK's terrorist activities in other parts of the country, involved serious abuses. In addition to torture, arbitrary killings, and disappearances, perpetrated by both the state and the PKK militia, the military forcibly evicted villagers and villages were destroyed as a security measure in provinces that were declared in a state of emergency (see Jacoby and Özerdem in this volume, Chapter 10).

Although, human rights discourse has an important role to play in addressing the sufferings of civilians in times of conflict, neutrality vis-à-vis the parties to the conflict is a difficult line to maintain. This very issue led to deep divisions within the organization. While some held that the situation in southeast Turkey could be reported without jeopardizing neutrality, others disagreed. The İHD members, who had concerns about maintaining strict impartiality, shied away from active involvement of the organization. In its 1992 General Council meeting, the İHD defined the armed conflict in the regions in a state of emergency as an internal armed conflict and demanded both parties to comply with the Common Article 3 of the Geneva Conventions (1949). Since the PKK had also demanded compliance with the Geneva Conventions (but not specifying which provisions) and the state maintained that it was conducting counterterrorism operations under a state of emergency, many regarded the İHD as supporting the PKK. Consequently, while some members of the İHD distanced themselves from the organization,14 southeast Turkey became a new pool of membership, leading to a strong organizational and membership base in Diyarbakır.

Despite the internal splits and increasing state pressure on the İHD, the commitment to addressing the Kurdish question as a human rights issue was firmly established in the İHD by the mid-1990s. Initially, the İHD dealt with violations of civil and political rights toward the Kurdish population. The international support from foreign governments and nongovernmental organizations, which usually articulated the issue as "human rights violations in southeast Turkey," also aided the consolidation of the İHD's position on the issue. Hundreds of cases, involving arbitrary killings, torture, disappearances, and burnings of villages in southeast Turkey, were taken to the European Court of Human Rights. The Diyarbakır branch of İHD has functioned as the main source of legal aid to victims who wanted to bring cases before the European Court of Human Rights.[15]

The inclusion of the Kurdish question in the scope and activities of the İHD has led to the expansion of the Turkish human rights discourse. While the original starting point for the İHD was the state's repression of the broadly defined "left," a new issue has emerged, more attuned to the ethnic and cultural identities of Turkish citizens. During the heyday of the conflict between the state security forces and the PKK, the human rights activism of the İHD was pointing to two different forms of human rights violations. In addition to highlighting the fact that the most fundamental human rights of people in those regions under the state of emergency were being violated, the İHD also argued that the Kurdish citizens were punished twice due to their ethnic origin. Thus, discrimination based on ethnic, cultural, and linguistic origins has become an integral part of the human rights discourse of the İHD. In the late 1990s, the İHD was campaigning not only for freedom from discrimination, but also for the positive enjoyment of cultural rights for citizens of Kurdish ethnic origin.

In 1990, the İHD led the initiative that resulted in the establishment of a human rights foundation Türkiye İnsan Hakları Vakfı (TİHV). This foundation was established by the İHD and 32 individuals, with the principal purpose of addressing the rehabilitation of torture victims and their families. Unlike the İHD, the foundation was legally allowed to receive donations from private persons. The networks of diasporas, which primarily included those who had sought asylum in Scandinavian countries in the aftermath of the coup, were instrumental in providing the financial support in establishing the foundation.

The TİHV represents the specialization and institutionalization of human rights advocacy in Turkey. Even though the initial project was conceived as providing medical and financial help to the postcoup victims of torture, the TİHV has transformed itself into an organization that also carries out projects on the prevention and investigation of torture. The

TİHV has evolved into an expert institution in the field of torture and a crucial awareness-raising force that mobilized other human rights organizations, medical associations, social workers, bar associations, trade unions, and political parties to combat torture.

While the establishment of the TİHV was sponsored by the İHD, it could be argued that the formation of Mazlum-Der in 1991 was a reaction to the İHD's inadequate attention to the problems of the "conservative/ nationalist/religious/right-wing" prisoners. Although, the human rights discourse itself promised human rights for all, the İHD primarily emerged as a natural coalition of the left-wing segments of the society. The founders of the Mazlum-Der primarily belonged to a Sunni-Muslim conservative political elite. The 1991 program of the Mazlum-Der specified the mission of the organization as the "indiscriminate defense of human rights of all persons both inside and outside Turkey without any double standards" (*Statute of the Mazlum-Der* 1990). Even though the goals and objectives, as well as the working methods, of the Mazlum-Der are similar to those of the İHD, this organization has attracted members from a completely different segment of the society.

In the same vein as the İHD, the Mazlum-Der initially focused on issues related to civil and political rights such as torture, police brutality, prison conditions, and fair trial, and provided reports, as well as legal aid, to the victims and their families. People applying to the Mazlum-Der were mainly prisoners or detainees who were members of conservative religious groups, but it also received complaints from people who were convicted of ordinary crimes. Thus, it was instrumental in pointing out that violations such as ill treatment, torture, or unfair trials were not exclusively problems faced by leftists; anyone could be subject to such abuses. In fact, the Mazlum-Der joined the İHD in its petition campaigns and protests of poor prison conditions.[16]

The Mazlum-Der is mostly known for its work on discrimination on religious grounds. It diversified the profile of rights-based societal activism in Turkey by framing the strict regulation of the public space vis-à-vis manifestation of religious beliefs as a human rights issue. The Mazlum-Der articulated religious freedoms and the right to be free from religious discrimination by employing a liberal conception of state neutrality, which supports the accommodation of manifestations of religious beliefs in the public sphere.[17] In practice, Mazlum-Der has become a leading voice in framing the practices of the state toward Sunni Muslims as discriminatory and interventionist, and has advocated a change from republican secularism to liberal state neutrality. The Mazlum-Der also focused on "Muslims" as a victimized and marginalized category in all parts of the world, where Islam is regarded as a potential bedrock of fundamentalism. The Mazlum-Der's international campaigns to collect money for the victims of war in Bosnia-Herzegovina and later on for Iraq, Kosovo, and Chechnya show that the organization tries to have a broader activity domain concerning protection of Muslims all around the world.[18]

The Mazlum-Der does not define itself in opposition to or in competition with the İHD or the TİHV, even though it argues that the human rights violations faced by the Sunni Muslims in Turkey were undermined or insufficiently addressed by these organizations (Ensaroğlu 2001). In fact, it shows solidarity with and supports the work of the İHD and the TİHV, especially in regard to their work on torture, arbitrary detention, and problems faced by the citizens of Kurdish ethnic origin in Turkey. The Mazlum-Der, therefore, sees itself not as an alternative, but as filling a gap in the human rights discourse of the post-1980 Turkey.

The ban on head scarves worn by university students and women employed as civil servants, and likewise the expulsion of servicemen from the army on charges of religious fundamentalism, have become one of its key activity areas. The association frames these issues as violation of freedom of religion and discrimination based on religious grounds. The president of the Mazlum-Der states:

It is not only because we think that discrimination on religious grounds is a serious source of human rights violations in Turkey. It is also the case that we have become the first port of call for people who think that their human rights are infringed on religious grounds. Especially our İstanbul branch cannot literally deal with any other human rights issue, due to the overwhelming number of complaints they are receiving from the public every single day. We are not an HRO claiming to be specialized on the head scarf problem, even though in practice we are being obliged to deal with it daily.[19]

When the İHD characterized the state approach to the "Kurdish problem" as a set of human rights violations, İHD members were portrayed as separatists or partisans of ethno-political Kurdish separatists by the state. In a similar vein, the Mazlum-Der has been regarded as being a pro-Islamic fundamentalist organization in disguise or an organization that supports such political activism. Legal proceedings have also been brought against the Mazlum-Der by public prosecutors, and the organization has been subject to surveillance, searches, and closures of its branches.

A fourth domestic organization that included the term "human rights" in its name was established in 1999, when 93 men and women, some of them also members and founders of the İHD, established TİHAK. The founders were primarily motivated by the "overpoliticization" of the human rights discourse in Turkey.[20] The vice president of TİHAK expresses this common sentiment: "the human rights discourse in Turkey is faced with the hegemony of Kurdish chauvinism and religionization of politics. I protest the use of human rights discourse for specific ideologies and political aims."[21]

The foundation assumed the goal of "working for the acquisition, enjoyment, protection, and development of human rights and fundamental freedoms and working toward embedding a human rights conscience and culture in individuals and society."[22] Human rights education, supporting and encouraging academic research on human rights, raising awareness for economic and social rights as much as civil and political rights are included among the TİHAK priorities. This organization reacts to the current order of priorities in the domestic human rights field, which favors claims based on identity politics at the expense of the socioeconomic rights and entitlements or the negative consequences of neoliberal economic policies and globalization. TİHAK does not define itself in opposition to the existing HROs, but emphasizes that underdevelopment, poverty, and lack of access to education are also crucial human rights issues in Turkey. Likewise, the other three HROs also do not deny the importance of economic and social rights, even though their work and advocacy in these spheres were limited.

Proliferation of Domestic HROs: A "Human Rights Culture" in Turkey?

There are now several viable HROs, including a new branch of the Amnesty International, that keep human rights on the civil society agenda in Turkey. The number of organizations indicating an interest in "human rights issues" is also on the rise (see Table 14.1). The four human rights organizations, however, can be seen as representing of the progression of domestic *human rights activism* as advocacy of minimum universal standards in Turkey. In principle, all four HROs declare commitment to human rights per se. In practice, however, their order of priorities has been different. Until recently, this prioritization privileged arbitrary use of coercive force, civil and political rights, and definition and scope of citizenship, similar to the trend that has been evident in the international human rights movement.[23] Domestic human rights activism gave voice to sufferings of specific groups and had a grassroots base of victims within the political community.

The emergence of the HROs after 1980 has called for a "human rights perspective" in relation to three traditional binary divides in Turkish politics: left/right, Turkish/Kurdish, and Islamist/secular. Human rights activism has initiated a dialogue among groups and individuals with diverging political views by focusing on human rights as *the minimum non-negotiable standards* of the existence of a political community. Human rights activism was mostly about systematic practices of torture, arbitrary arrest, detention, arbitrary killings, freedom of expression and association, in times when such standards themselves were in danger. In the late

TABLE 14.1. NONGOVERNMENTAL ORGANIZATIONS WITH CONSULTATIVE STATUS WITH THE PRIME MINISTER'S HUMAN RIGHTS DIRECTORATE

Associations

Adli Tıp Uzmanları Derneği (Forensic Experts Association)
Çağdaş Gazeteciler Derneği (Association of Contemporary Journalists)
Çağdaş Hukukçular Derneği (Association of Contemporary Lawyers)
Çağdaş Yaşamı Destekleme Derneği (Association for the Support for Modern Living)
Çocuk İhmalini ve İstismarını Önleme Derneği (Association for the Prevention of Child Neglect and Abuse)
Cumhuriyet Kadınları Derneği (Association of the Women of the Republic)
Helsinki Yurttaşları Derneği (Helsinki Citizens Association)
Hukukun Egemenliği Derneği (Rule of Law Association)
İnsan Hakları Derneği (Human Rights Association)
İnsan Hakları ve Mazlumlar için Dayanışma Derneği (Association for Human Rights and the Oppressed)
Kadın Adayları Destekleme ve Eğitme Derneği (Association for the Support and Training of Women Candidates)
Liberal Düşünce Topluluğu (Society for Liberal Thought)
Pir Sultan Abdal Kültür Derneği (Pir Sultan Abdal Cultural Association)
Toplumsal Düşünce Derneği (Association for Social Thought)
Türk Dünyası İnsan Hakları Derneği (Association for Human Rights in the Turkish World)
Türk Sanayici ve İşadamları Derneği (Turkish Industrialists' and Businessmen's Association)
Türkiye Barolar Birligi İnsan Hakları Araştırma ve Uygulama Merkezi (Human Rights Research and Practice Centre of the Turkish Bar Union)
Türkiye Dernekler ve Vakıflar Topluluğu (Society of Turkish Associations and Foundations)
Türkiye Felsefe Kurumu (Turkish Philosophy Institute)
Umut Çocukları Derneği (Association of Hope for Children)

Foundations

Beyaz Nokta Vakfı (White Point Foundation)
Cumhuriyetçi Eğitim ve Kültür Merkezi Vakfı (Republican Education and Culture Center Foundation)
Hacı Bektaş Veli Anadolu Kültür Vakfı (Hacı Bektaş Veli Anatolia Cultural Foundation)
İktisadi Kalkınma Vakfı (Economic Development Foundation)
Kadın Dayanışma Vakfı (Women's Solidarity Foundation)
Kadının İnsan Hakları—Yeni Çözümler Vakfı (Women's Human Rights—New Solutions Foundation)
Kadının İnsan Hakları Projesi (Women's Human Rights Project)
Türk Demokrasi Vakfı (Turkish Democracy Foundation)
Türkiye Çocuklara Yeniden Özgürlük Vakfı (Turkish Freedom Again for Children Foundation)
Türkiye Ekonomik ve Sosyal Etüdler Vakfı (Turkish Foundation for Economic and Social Studies)
Türkiye İnsan Hakları Kurumu Vakfı (Human Rights Institute Foundation of Turkey)
Türkiye İnsan Hakları Vakfı (Human Rights Foundation of Turkey)

Source: Prime Minister's Human Rights Directorate.

1990s, following a relative normalization of Turkish politics, HROs also broadened their spheres of activity and issues of concern. The İHD, for example, started a program on gender discrimination, including the subordination of women and ill-treatment of transsexuals and homosexuals by the police. Similarly, the Mazlum-Der has brought to its agenda the discriminatory practices relating to non-Muslims and asylum seekers. By reaching out beyond their immediate clientele, the post-coup HROs in Turkey have shown that the struggle for the human rights of "others" is both possible and necessary.[24] The practices of these HROs point to their potential of transcending their original causes for establishment. However, their ability to influence a change in public policies and public opinion depends on the extent to which both the HROs and other societal and state actors join the human rights debate in a sustainable way. The president of the İHD acknowledges the limited achievements: "Let alone initiating change in the attitudes of government authorities toward human rights, we are still struggling to have consensus among our members that human rights principles apply to all. As soon as we secure some funding, our first project will be to train our members about human rights. Without a proper understanding of human rights among the human rights advocates, we cannot move forward."[25]

The development and sustainability of a human rights culture depends on three factors: (1) HROs' ability to generate increasing number of human rights advocates, who are not just self-interested political activists; (2) HROs' likelihood of avoiding bureaucratization and project funding-driven NGO culture, which is a likely outcome of professionalization of human rights (Çalı and Ergun forthcoming); and (3) state authorities' willingness to end antagonism and engage in an effective dialogue with HROs.

The human rights capital and experience of HROs in Turkey have steadily expanded through their interaction with a range of actors, including the victims, state authorities, other segments of the civil society, and international governmental and nongovernmental organizations. The bureaucrats or elected officials in Turkey, on the other hand, have not had such experiences. The attitude of the state toward HROs and their activities has included suspicion and imposition of legal prosecution and political repression. Instead of engaging in a principled dialogue with these organizations, the state officials have, for the most part, preferred to promote an argument that these organizations serve personal or group interests rather than a common public good.

The establishment of a parliamentary Human Rights Investigation Commission in 1990 marked the first official human rights monitoring mandate. With Turkey's declared aim to be a member of the European Union and the EU's own human rights conditionality requirements, institutionalization of human rights has become a government policy. There now also exists a number of governmental agencies with a complex and over-lapping set of human rights protection, promotion, monitoring, and train-ing mandates set up by the executive (see Table 14.2). However, HROs observe that such human rights institution-building efforts are means to satisfy the EU demands rather than ends in themselves ("İnsan Haklarında Neredeyiz?" 2004).

The work of the Grand National Assembly Human Rights Investiga-tion Commission is regarded to be the most impartial and independent by the HROs in Turkey, although this commission lacks an effective en-forcement mandate. HROs maintain contact with it and contribute to its fact-finding missions. The human rights institution-building undertaken by the executive, on the other hand, has failed to meet the expectations of HROs.[26] HROs note that they were not consulted in the drafting of the statutes and mandates of the governmental human rights agencies. The structure and mandate of local human rights councils have particu-larly sparked a debate. The mandate of these councils gives the power to investigate human rights violations to the same agencies that allegedly violate them, and therefore raises serious questions about the impartiality of these agencies. The participation at the human rights councils by the representatives of the civil society is also upon invitation by the governor of the province or the borough in question. All four HROs discussed here have protested the structure and mandate of human rights councils.[27] The tension between governmental human rights agencies and HROs point to an emergence of a parallel and not necessarily overlapping set of "human rights projects" in Turkey. HROs complain that despite a con-siderable amount of legal reforms, primarily in the spheres of administra-tion of justice, criminal law and laws of associations, and cultural rights to comply with the EU requirements, such reforms follow a patchwork pattern rather than a holistic approach and therefore the implementation

TABLE 14.2. RECENTLY ESTABLISHED STATE AGENCIES ON HUMAN RIGHTS

Legislative

Turkish Grand National Assembly Human Rights Investigation Commission (1990)

Executive

State Ministry Responsible for Human Rights (1994)
Committee on the Decade of Human Rights Education (1998)
Provincial and Borough Human Rights Councils (2000)
Advisory Committee on Human Rights (2001)
Committees for the Investigation of Alleged Human Rights Violations (2001)
Directorate of Human Rights at the Prime Ministry (2001)
High Commission of Human Rights (2001)

of these reforms is still the most important and inadequately addressed problem. The joint press release of 10 December 2004 of İHD and TİHV states: "We are neither for nor against the EU membership. We look at this from the perspective of human rights, fundamental freedoms, and democratization. We support the Turkey EU membership process to the extent to which it contributes to human rights, fundamental freedoms, and democracy." These HROs point out that the EU-driven human rights agenda not only fails to encompass all international human rights standards, but it also disregards the fact that same legal reforms have been persistently called for by domestic civil society actors, even before the EU has requested them.[28] HROs, therefore, recognize the contribution of EU membership criteria to legal reform, but do not regard human rights protections in Turkey as an EU-led process.

The human rights advocacy in the world has increasingly become a professional sector, resulting in important differences and gaps between international and national NGOs (including grassroots-based HROs). None of the Turkish HROs discussed here are born out of project-based initiatives funded by international donors. They also invariably refuse to receive any funding from foreign governments. The financial support that they receive from international organizations has also been limited. It could be argued that not depending on major sponsors is what enabled them to be independent actors and maintain amateur and voluntary structures.

The amateur structures of HROs may work both to the advantage and disadvantage of the future of the human rights struggle in Turkey. On the positive side, these organizations are not obliged to follow any human rights agenda that is internationally designed. Their amateur character allows them to be critical of not only the human rights policies in Turkey, but also those of international governmental and nongovernmental human rights organizations.[29] In this respect the HROs in Turkey can evolve to resist the power structures within the human rights field. On the other hand, the amateur status limits the scope and activities of HROs in an increasingly specialized and professionalized field of human rights. Working with professional experts on human rights issues can increase the effectiveness of these organizations and enable them to be closer to where decisions are made. This, however, causes concerns over moving away from the grassroots toward a technical policy approach to human rights advocacy.

Conclusion

The role of domestic HROs in shaping the human discourse and policies is still in the making. Domestic HROs in Turkey have emerged as a domestically grown movement out of a political trauma caused by the oppressive policies of the 1980 military coup. It has over the last twenty-five years followed the changing political, social, and economic conditions and agenda in Turkey. The establishment of HROs does not, in itself, suggest that a human rights culture will take root in a country. As HROs change their priorities, they are also changed by the human rights discourse itself. In Turkey, we see a move from human rights activism based on the advocacy of particular group's rights toward a more encompassing deliberation of human rights theory and praxis. However, this evolution in the human rights discourse remains to be limited to the realm of HROs. Public authorities as well as the mainstream media do not address human rights issues in a comprehensive way, mostly due to the pervasive public policy that barred any principled engagement with human rights and regarded the domestic human rights actors as potential outlaws and human rights standards as foreign interventionism. While the EU has been crucial in initiating and following up a speedy legal reform process, its human rights agenda is set—and therefore limited—by political decision-making processes of the EU, and its funding structures are prone to create project funding-driven professional HROs detached from societal roots of human rights activism. The new challenge for domestic HROs in Turkey is to remain an authentic, but popular voice of human rights amid the cacophony of human rights agendas of the state and international donors and organizations.

Chapter 15

Tensions and Dilemmas in Human Rights Education

Kenan Çayir

The second half of the twentieth century was characterized by the proliferation of human rights conventions, covenants, and standards. However, serious human rights violations still continue. A glaring gap still exists between "texts and contexts" (Yeban 1995). One of the reasons for this is the fact that human rights as an ethical tradition have limited channels for becoming embedded in a community, in contrast, for instance, to religiously grounded ethical traditions (Osler and Starkey 1994). Studies demonstrate that almost sixty years after the Universal Declaration of Human Rights was adopted by the United Nations, people knew very little about human rights (Ross and Gupta 1998). Creating an awareness of human rights through education, therefore, has appeared on the international agenda to make human rights accessible to all people. There is currently an international consensus on the importance of human rights education (HRE) to raise people's awareness about human rights, to make them act in defense of human rights, and to promote tolerance and combat all forms of discrimination at a global scale (Andreopoulos and Claude 1997; Starkey 1991).

HRE can be defined as the process whereby individuals learn the body of knowledge, values, and action skills of human rights.[1] Basic notions of HRE have been developed in several international conferences on human rights since the 1970s (Baxi 1997). In 1993, at the World Conference on Human Rights in Vienna, the participants reaffirmed the importance of HRE by declaring it "essential for the promotion and achievement of stable and harmonious relations among communities and for fostering mutual understanding, tolerance and peace."[2] Along with this declaration, all countries were called upon to introduce human rights education in all sectors of society. In response, the UN General Assembly proclaimed the years 1995–2004 as the UN Decade for Human Rights Education and prepared the Action Plan, encouraging member states to establish a ten-year national plan of action to promote education and training in human rights.

Turkey is one of the first countries in Europe that established a National Committee on the Decade for Human Rights Education (1998) and formulated a National Program (1999) (National Committee 1999). The National Committee prepared an inventory of ongoing HRE works, identified priorities and primary target groups, and developed short-term and long-term plans to implement HRE in Turkey. The formation of the National Committee has been a catalyst for the systematization of the HRE works that have been provided at various levels and for the initiation of new ones for different sectors of the society. The most important and comprehensive step in regard to the HRE in Turkey has been taken by the introduction of Citizenship and Human Rights Education courses in primary schools in 1998 and a Democracy and Human Rights course in high schools in 1999.

This chapter examines the HRE both at schools and aimed at selected professional groups, but it focuses on the curricula and textbooks for the two HRE courses, since students form the largest target group (currently there are about 10 million students in primary and high schools) and represent the future. The first part of the chapter reviews the normative and institutional regulations regarding HRE and provides basic information on the state of HRE for civil servants and the curriculum of HRE courses. The second part involves a critical evaluation of HRE efforts in Turkey and offers suggestions for further action. I contend that the major shortcomings of the HRE program in Turkey stem from the persistent étatist/nationalist political culture, the educational policy that prioritize duties over rights, and the pedagogical approaches employed in formal education and training seminars that remain at cognitive level rather than being transformative.

Normative and Institutional Regulations on Human Rights Education

Since the late1990s, Turkey has implemented several reforms in order to bring its legal structure in conformity with international agreements. All government cabinets included a minister of state in charge of human rights issues and various agencies and organizations have been established as administrative and consultative bodies on human rights in order to protect and improve human rights standards. In response to the appeal by the UN for the implementation of HRE at the national level, the High Coordination Board for Human Rights established the National Committee on the Decade for Human Rights Education in 1998. This committee is attached to the Prime Ministry and includes representatives from:

the Prime Ministry; the Ministries of Justice, Internal Affairs, Foreign Affairs, National Education, Health, and Culture; and NGOs active in the field of human rights. It also includes four academicians expert in the field of human rights. the chair of the committee is Professor İonna Kuçuradi, a prominent philosopher with many publications on human rights.

The committee stated its goals as evaluating the existing programs on human rights, making recommendations, preparing educational programs in collaboration with interested parties, assisting the implementation of these programs, and monitoring the work done. The main target groups have been identified as teachers who teach or will teach HRE courses in primary and high schools, law enforcement officers (judges, public prosecutors, police, gendarmerie, and penitentiary personnel), members of the mass media, members of NGOs active in human rights, and social workers at community centers who will provide HRE for underprivileged sections of society (National Committee 1999, 14–16). The National Committee has established twelve working groups to evaluate, make recommendations for, assist, and monitor HRE programs for target groups. The prior objectives of the committee have been stated as the revision of the curriculum of HRE courses for pupils in formal education and civil servants, assistance in preparation of written and visual material for HRE, and preparation of a plan for training the trainers to provide HRE for various professions.

The mid-report of the committee (İnsan Hakları Eğitimi On Yılı Ulusal Komitesi 2001), issued at the end of 2000, notes progress in several areas: HRE had become part of the agenda of educational branches of several ministries; the number of civil servants such as police, gendarmerie, and judges and prosecutors who received HRE had dramatically increased for the previous few years; new human rights centers and graduate programs had been established in universities; several projects were developed by the National Committee and by several NGOs to increase the quality of HRE in primary and high schools.

Human Rights Education in Primary and High Schools

An important step toward the institutionalization of HRE in Turkey has been the introduction of Human Rights Education courses to the primary and high schools curricula, as a result of a protocol agreement between the Ministry of National Education and the Ministry of State in charge of human rights in 1995. In 1998, Citizenship and Human Rights Education was incorporated as a required civics course, and offered for one hour per week in grades 7 and 8 in primary schools. In 1999, Democracy and Human Rights was introduced to the curricula of high schools as an elective course that would be taught for one hour per week.

Turkey has a highly centralized education system. The Board of Education under the Ministry of National Education prepares the curricula for all subjects, and its approval of the textbooks is required for adoption. The board identifies the basic principles, general objectives, and outlines of the courses that should be followed by textbook authors. The Ministry of National Education itself prepares textbooks, but private publishing companies are allowed to produce textbooks, if their content is approved by the board. For the 2004–5 academic year, thirteen seventh and eighth grade textbooks were available for the Citizenship and Human Rights Education courses, and two for the Democracy and Human Rights course. Since the textbooks have to follow the detailed curricula guidelines of the board, they are more or less identical. Nevertheless, the authors can differ on their emphasis of some themes.

Major objectives of the Citizenship and Human Rights Education course, as defined by the board can be summarized as follows: providing an awareness of being human; providing a consciousness of being a citizen; teaching citizenship rights and responsibilities; informing students on the responsibilities of a democratic government toward its citizens; teaching students about their duties and responsibilities toward the state; teaching students about the relations between the principles of Atatürk and human rights.[3] The outline of the course for grade 7 includes

- basic concepts on the common heritage of humanity;
- the development of the notion of human rights;
- ethics and human rights;
- basic rights and freedoms.

The outline for grade 8 is as follows:

- basic concepts on state, democracy, citizenship, and rights and responsibilities of citizens;
- the protection of human rights;
- the elements of national security and national power;
- basic problems concerning the protection of human rights.

The curriculum for grade 7 focuses more on human rights part of the course title, emphasizing the history, ethical foundations, and content of basic human rights. Topics covered in grade 7 include ones like the universality of human rights, relationship between ethics and human rights, and the state's role in instrumentalization of human rights. Grade 8 topics, on the other hand, are more extensive on the responsibility of citizens, the national security issues, the role and significance of the Turkish Army, and internal and external threats to Turkey's national security.

The board defines the objectives of the high school level Democracy and Human Rights Education course, as providing students with knowledge of human rights and democratic principles that will enable them to suggest solutions to national and international problems.[4] It provides the following outline:

- human rights, law, and state;
- basic concepts of democracy as a lifestyle;
- the protection and implementation of human rights;
- the Atatürk revolution, human rights, and democracy.

All approved books include a simplified version of the Universal Declaration of Human Rights and of the Convention on the Rights of the Child as appendix. Besides these three courses, human rights themes are also covered in primary school fourth grade social studies and high school sociology and philosophy courses.

The Present State of Human Rights Education for Civil Servants

The HRE of civil servants, especially those of law enforcement officers, has been essential for meeting the standard set by the European Convention on Human Rights, the jurisprudence of the European Court of Human Rights, and the National Programme for the Adoption of the Acquis. The HRE of law enforcement officers seems to be intensified when the training department of the Ministry of Justice began to cooperate with the National Committee after 2000. The Ministry of Justice reports that from 1996 to the end of 2002, 7,206 of a total of 9,000 judges and public prosecutors were trained in human rights. The number of penitentiary personnel that received HRE was 17,351 (Eğitim Dairesi Başkanlığı 1996–2004).

The Ministry of Justice has recently initiated joint projects to train the trainers among judges and prosecutors with the National Committee on the Decade for Human Rights Education, the Council of Europe, the British Council, and the European Union. A joint project with the British Council involved a five-day seminar to educate 225 trainers, who trained 9,266 judges and prosecutors in 206 different seminars in 2004. Some joint projects provide short probationary programs for a group of judges in European Court of Human Rights. The Ministry of Justice also informs judges and prosecutors about the jurisprudence of the European Court of Human Rights by distributing booklets (Kaboğlu 2002a).

The HRE for law enforcement officers is provided through conferences and seminars organized by the training department of the Ministry of Justice. Seminars are generally led by professors of law or trainers from the ministry who lecture on recent legal amendments. They tend to focus on the European Convention on Human Rights and its implementation and on the analysis of the decisions of the European Court of Human Rights.

Gendarmerie constitutes a significant component of the security forces in Turkey. It is active over 93 percent of the country where 41 percent of the population live (National Committee 1999, 15). A human rights course, as a separate subject, was added to the curricula in gendarmerie schools in 1992. The textbook for this course has been reviewed by and revised according to the recommendations of the National Committee, and the new text began to be used in the 1999–2000 academic year. Moreover, in-service training on human rights was received by 29,713 gendarmerie personnel (1,967 officers, 8,804 noncommissioned officers, and 18,942 sergeants) between 1992 and 2002. The Gendarmerie General Command reports that during the 2000–2001 academic year, 230 officers were trained as trainers in one-week seminars, and they trained 5,500 officers by 2003 (Jandarma Genel Komutanlığı n.d.). In-service education of the gendarmerie is generally provided by one-day seminars that are consisted of lectures by academicians and gendarmerie officers on several subjects. For example, a seminar offered on 26 April 2001 included the following topics:

- the evaluation of the effects of the applications made to the European Human Rights Court and their influence on Turkish domestic law;
- international dimensions of the right to live without being exposed to torture and unfair treatment;
- the role played by the European Human Rights Accord on Turkish criminal law;
- the importance of ethics of gendarmerie in human rights education;
- the rules pertaining to the treatment of civilians in their application to police and security centers (Jandarma Genel Komutanlığı 2001)

The Ministry of Internal Affairs also provides programs for HRE. On 23 June 1999, it announced that all governors, provincial governors, and police chiefs have attended the human rights seminars organized by the education department of the ministry. Since these seminars were held before the formation of the National Committee in 2001, the ministry began a new series of seminar for the implementation of the National Program with the cooperation of the committee. The new program divided Turkey into ten districts and offered one-week human rights seminars on a monthly basis between September 2001 and July 2002. Each seminar had approximately 50 participants (mainly assistant governors, who serve as presidents of human rights provincial boards, and lieutenant governors who were the presidents of human rights county boards). The content of the seminars consisted of the historical development of human rights, fundamental rights, institutionalization of human rights, and the role of NGOs in the field of human rights (Kaboğlu 2002a, 106).

The police force was also involved in various programs in cooperation with the National Committee. The Directorate General of Security organized a series of in-service training programs in 2000; 81 percent of the police personnel (127,389 total) attended these seminars. Moreover, in a project conducted under the auspices of the Council of Europe, entitled Police and Human Rights Beyond 2000, a small group of police officers were trained as trainers in three-week courses offered in Turkey. The second part of the project will be completed in various EU countries (Körezlioğlu 2002, 114–15). In 2002, the directorate launched a new training of trainers seminar, in which about 150 police officers were issued trainer's certificates. Furthermore, upon the recommendation of the committee in the National Program, the police schools, which recruited lower-rank officers and trained them only for a period of nine months, were converted into two-year vocational schools in 2001. The textbook for the human rights course was also updated to include references to the decisions of the European Court of Human Rights, and new subjects such as psychology, sociology, and behavioral sciences were added to the curriculum (İnsan Hakları Eğitimi On Yılı Ulusal Komitesi 2001, 219–235; Erdoğan 2002).

Implementation of Human Rights Education: A Critical Evaluation

The Political Culture and Philosophy of Education in Turkey

In all societies, incorporating human rights themes into school curricula is challenging for the dominant political culture. As noted by Misgeld, fundamental rights like the freedom of expression or freedom of thought are treated as undermining the authority of the state (1994). This is especially valid for Turkey, where the 1920s policies of prioritizing stability, unity, security, and order still define the political culture. This culture is shaped by a strong state tradition, which leans on a "transcendentalist polity" that endorses a moral community in which public interest transcends particularistic group interests and defines the scope of individual interests (Heper 1985). The state tradition is very sensitive about the principles of "unity and indivisibility," and involves a military bureaucracy that interfered in political life repeatedly to "safeguard" the Republic, whenever *it felt* that the territorial unity or secularist tenets of the regime were in danger. Human rights in such a context have not been translated into popular language (Cizre 2001). Instead, violations are often justified by political (and even civil) actors, by referring to the "special circumstances" of Turkey.

Such a political culture breeds a particular philosophy of education. For the republican elite that launched the modernization process in the 1920s, education was the most important institution in forming a nation, "one and indivisible." It would work toward erasing all ethnic and linguistic differences of the Ottoman subjects, creating a homogenous community of Turks (Mardin 1997; Kasaba 1997). Ziya Gökalp, who was an influential nationalist thinker on education at the beginning of the twentieth century, endorsed an education system geared toward yielding unselfish, patriotic, and self-sacrificing people for the national unity.[5]

Maintaining a "nation of order" is still an ideal and such principles articulated in the Constitution, as well as by the Basic Law on National Education. Article 11 of the Basic Law reads:

In order to establish and maintain a stable, strong and free social order, the knowledge of democracy that citizens need to possess, in addition to the knowledge pertaining to the governance of the nation-state and the sense of responsibility regarding the understanding of and respect to the traditions, should be taught to and advanced among the students in the national education system. *However, in the aforementioned institutions of education, ideological discussions and debates that relate to daily political developments and conflicts, or, those that are critical of Kemalist (Atatürkçü) nationalism, could not be allowed to take place.* (emphasis added)[6]

Consequently, state institutions such as the Ministry of National Education and the Council of Higher Education tightly control the curricula for all levels.

THE LANGUAGE OF TEXTBOOKS AND HRE

A recent study shows that the textbooks in Turkey are still imbued with essentialist and nationalist precepts that form an obstacle to the development of a critical mind (Çotuksöken, Erzan, and Silier 2003; Ceylan and Irzık 2004). Many textbooks present Turkish culture and identity with an essentialist language that promotes an ethnocentric vision of the world. Such a perspective is reflected, for instance, in a high school human relations course as "interacting with other cultures sometimes may affect Turkish culture negatively" (Yamanlar 2002, 33). This essentialism is widespread especially in history, geography, and national security courses, in which students are constantly warned against "expansionist" foreign powers and encouraged to sacrifice themselves for national unity (Bora 2004; Altınay 2004).

The Citizenship and Human Rights curricula and textbooks also reflect this perspective. The eighth grade curriculum is particularly problematic. It defines citizenship responsibilities as "performing military service," having "the mindset that would not allow activities of divisive or destructive nature," "the sustenance of an education for the securing of national unity and (social and political) harmony," and holding "pride in Turkish national identity."

One of the eighth grade textbooks describes Turkey as "always under threat because of its geopolitical situation. Those foreign powers that have their eyes set on the prize of Turkey are not willing to allow it to become a significant power" (Bilgen et al. 2001, 81). This perspective, which appears in other textbooks in similar words, obviously contradicts the basic premises of HRE, which aims to promote international peace and order.

The Article 26 of the Universal Declaration of Human Rights, which endorses the right to education, conceptualizes education not merely in terms of development of individual personality or even in terms of good citizenship of a nation-state. It promotes that education has a global orientation of producing true citizens of the world, imbued with civic virtues or respect for pluralism, peace, dignity, and rights (Baxi 1997, 144). In Turkey, however, education is used as a tool to develop self-sacrificing "good citizens" who should always "be alert" about foreign entities' intentions and be ready to protect the unity of the nation. Providing HRE with the same approach is, of course, not conducive to creating a universal culture of human rights.

THE PRESENTATION OF STATE-INDIVIDUAL RELATIONS AND HUMAN RIGHTS

The primary problem in textbooks prepared for the seventh grade involves the definition of fundamental rights. Most of the authors (who are not human rights experts), define them from an étatist perspective, justifying the inclusion of a right by the fact that it is included in the 1982 Constitution (e.g., "this right or freedom exist in current Turkish Constitution as such"), and then present the current constitutional limitations (most of which are in conflict with universal human rights) without taking a critical stance. The authors, thus, privilege the state and define the status quo as the ideal, and some of them reinforce it with an explicit statement such as, "During the Republican period, our people . . . have an ideal state protecting human rights" (Yamanlar 2001, 43). Although it may not be easy to be critical of the status quo in formal education, the presentation of the existing situation as perfect conflicts with the transformative purpose of HRE. Moreover, the state and national interests are always assigned priority over individual rights as illustrated by the following quotation from a textbook: "The citizens should believe in the superiority of the national interests over their individual interests. If individuals do not behave in a responsible way, this would lead to a situation that is harmful for all citizens. The security of the country would fall into danger, and order and unity would be damaged" (Kapulu et al. 2001, 36).

Collective interests based on democratic participation, mutual understanding, and solidarity are, of course, important to human rights. However, when concerns over national security are presented in sentences like "criticizing state policies and state officials are the strategies of terrorists and separatists" (Bilgen et al. 2001, 81), the scope of human rights claims against state is limited. Then, HRE becomes a means of sustaining an obedient society, rather than a way to introduce democratic values, toleration of diversity, or promotion of human rights.

CITIZENSHIP EDUCATION AND HRE

Suggesting that a Turkish citizen is always expected to embrace "certain truths and conducts" and be socialized to assume "appropriate roles" based on the patriotic notions described above, the textbooks promote a duty-based social order rather than a rights-based one. A duty-based social order, as Steiner and Alston note, seems to be inherently less subject to universalization since the content of duties (toward community, God) can be very specific, bound to a given context (2000, 374). The textbooks' emphasis on the duties and responsibilities of citizens that stem from "special circumstances" of Turkey also undermines the universality of human rights and leads students to adopt a particularistic vision of rights and responsibilities (Gök 2004).

The textbooks also fail to address the importance of citizens' participation in the policy processes and reduce democracy to voting. Moreover, through their selective references to NGOs, they undermine human rights activism. In Citizenship and Human Rights textbooks, for example, the authors do not name NGOs working in the field of human rights in Turkey, which are often subjected to state repression, but mention more "benign" NGOs such as those that work on environmental issues.

PEDAGOGICAL PROBLEMS

In addition to the content, the method of instruction sets an obstacle to effective HRE in Turkey; the information introduced in textbooks basically remains at the cognitive level. Although any exposure to human rights is important, pouring information is not enough. Educators note that HRE should involve attitudinal and behavioral dimensions, beside the cognitive one, and emphasize skill development (Tibbitts 1994; Meintjes 1997). They find the traditional teacher-centered techniques inadequate for providing a transformative HRE, and suggest activity-based techniques that involve teamwork, role playing, or drama (Brander et al. 2002). The textbooks in Turkey are particularly short on such material. Although a few authors include hypothetical scenarios dealing with conflict resolution, almost all textbooks assess learning through multiple choice questions and fill-in-the blank exercises that emphasize memorization. They do not stress developing the skills that would help students accept differences, identify prejudice, stereotypes, or discrimination, and respect others' rights or advocate their own.

Problems in HRE Aimed at Civil Servants

Training of civil servants typically involves one- or two-day seminars, which are basically lectures on recent legal amendments, or the decisions of the European Court of Human Rights, given by academicians, who are experts in human rights law. Although important, depending solely on legal information limits seminars to a legalistic discourse on human rights. In fact, this legalistic approach and the emphasis on the connection to the EU send the message that human rights constitute a legal body of knowledge that civil servants must know for the process of EU *acquis*—it does not require any attitudinal or behavioral changes.

The number of civil servants who have already participated in HRE seminars is impressive. However, this quantitative measure does not assure that governors, law enforcement officers, including police officers, are now committed to respect human rights or have learned how to change their behaviors. Educators lecturing in these seminars note that governors, for instance, often adopt a nationalistic/militarist vision and display a defensive attitude by invoking "special circumstances" of Turkey. They subscribe to the notion that respecting human rights would serve the interests of terrorists and separatists, and would endanger national unity (Kaboğlu 2002a, 109). The following comment by a police chief, who participated in a seminar organized by the Gendarmerie General Command on 26 April 2001 reveals that these deep-rooted attitudes remain unchanged:

The members of terrorist organizations receive military, as well as ideological, training. Those who come from the European Court of Human Rights or several NGOs seem to know whom to meet. They either talk to those in prison or to those who are active members of terrorist organizations. What would I say if I were in prison? I would tell them that I was tortured. In any case, the members of the terrorist organizations are already trained to give such statements. (Jandarma Genel Komutanlığı 2001, 4–1-16)

Given this "they versus us" attitude embedded within the culture and particularly prevalent among law enforcement officers, two-day seminars that remain at cognitive level cannot be enough to change the outlook and behavior of the personnel. Although important, seminars can be only an initial step and should be enhanced by incorporating interactive pedagogical approaches.

Conclusion: Future Prospects

Turkey has taken an important step by acknowledging the need for HRE and introducing HRE courses for students and the law enforcement personnel. The formation of various bodies pertaining to human rights, and especially of a National Committee on the Decade for Human Rights Education, has provided an impetus for HRE aimed at different sectors of society. There seems to be, however, several impediments in the organization of HRE at the national level. First of all, as pointed out by a member of the National Committee, most of the agencies that work on human rights hold a consultative status and lack their own budget (Kaboğlu 2002a, 109). The coordination of HRE efforts is difficult because the state agencies lack the commitment and the appreciation of the importance of HRE and the function of the committee.[7]

The shortage of trainers constitutes another obstacle to the development of serious and effective HRE programs. Several ministries state that they organized one-week training-the-trainers seminars lasting. A one-week seminar, however, as the National Committee notes, is not enough to create a competent trainer who can adopt proper content and methodology (İnsan Hakları Eğitimi On Yılı Ulusal Komitesi 2001, 267). More comprehensive and longer series of seminars are needed to train trainers for professional groups. Existing joint projects with the Council of Europe are promising in this respect. Increasing cooperation may improve both the quality and quantity of trainers.

The Ministry of National Education recently launched studies geared toward revising the current curricula and textbooks. The aim was to introduce new programs and textbooks that involve activity-based materials and allow a student-centered education. However, the ministry later announced that the new curricula would not include a separate human rights education course, instead the themes of existing Citizenship and Human Rights courses would be infused into other course curricula. Integration of human rights themes into several courses is supported by many human rights educationalists, since several issues such as tolerance and conflict resolution can be linked to many subjects of study and respect for human rights can be promoted as a way of life.[8] However, covering human rights in a separate course has the advantage of drawing attention to the importance of human rights at schools. Thus, discontinuing the Citizenship and Human Rights courses will have a negative consequence, and the loss can be compensated for only if the incorporation of human rights theme in a wide range of courses is done effectively. The impact of this change can be assessed after 2008, when new curricula will start for grades 7 and 8. Also important is the training of teachers for transmitting knowledge and skills necessary for the development of a human rights culture. Some in-service training programs for teachers have been initiated by the National Committee to meet this purpose, but so far they have not been satisfactory in terms of both quality and quantity. Preservice and in-service education of teachers need to be improved, with an emphasis on activity-based instructional techniques that have been alien to most of the teachers in Turkey.

Of course an effective HRE requires proper teaching tools, including textbooks that promote human rights and related values such as tolerance and peace. Fortunately, there have been a few promising efforts to that end. A project, conducted by the History Foundation, entitled "Promoting Human Rights in Primary and Secondary School Textbooks," is a notable example.[9] Undertaken between March 2001 and December 2004, the project involved the assessment of about 200 textbooks in every subject in terms of their human rights content, making recommendations for improvement, and providing guidelines and to carry out workshops and seminars on HRE. The project has recently yielded three edited volumes: (1) on the analysis of textbooks (Çotuksöken, Erzan, and Silier 2003; Ceylan and Irzık 2004); (2) the guidelines for textbook authors (Bağlı and Esen 2003); and (3) on the HRE methodology for teachers (Gök and Şahin 2003). Incorporating the project's findings and following its recommendations would result in major improvements in HRE.

NGOs are also active in developing appropriate instructional materials on HRE. Two books (a students' version and a teachers' version of the same book), entitled *Yurttaş Olmak İçin* (To Be a Citizen) and prepared by a team of scholars of law and education under the sponsorship of the Umut Foundation, are the first to employ interactive methodologies in teaching the Citizenship and Human Rights courses (Gürkaynak et al. 1998). The same team has also provided a series for training teachers in interactive methodologies for HRE (Bağlı 2003). In another project, funded by the British Council and the Ministry of National Education, the same team has drafted HRE booklets for grades 1–6, the curricula of which have not yet included HRE courses. The booklets are being reviewed the Ministry of National Education; should they be approved, but incorporation of these new tools into the curricula would definitely improve the quality of HRE at schools.

Finally, it should be noted that the effectiveness of HRE in Turkey also depends on economic and social conditions. Inadequate teacher salaries, poor physical conditions of many schools, overcrowding, and an undemocratic school ethos have to be addressed, along with the similar problems faced by the law enforcement personnel.

Part VI
International Affairs and Interactions

Turkey's Participation in Global and Regional Human Rights Regimes

Füsun Türkmen

Turkey has been part of the United Nations-led global human rights regime since its beginnings, and joined the European one by ratifying the European Convention on Human Rights and Fundamental Freedoms in 1954. Turkey's involvement in these two regimes has been shaped by factors both exogenous and endogenous to Turkish politics. The exogenous factors involve the very nature of these respective regimes, and the endogenous ones stem from Turkey's 200 year-old aspiration for westernization (i.e., Europeanization).

It is largely accepted that the United Nations system in general has not been particularly efficacious, especially in the field of human rights. This is attributed to the heterogeneous membership of the organization, which includes a mixture of democracies and authoritarian regimes, as well as to its heavy bureaucratic machinery, characterized by a lack of coordination and enforcement power. Jack Donnelly classifies the UN regime as a "strong promotional" one that has "weak monitoring procedures" (1986, 634). This was especially valid throughout the Cold War when human rights also fell prey to interbloc ideological struggle, relentlessly waged in the UN fora. Thus, Turkey could, for a long time, justify its highly selective treaty ratification record at the UN, without any significant commitment to human rights at home.

On the other hand, Turkey had been nurturing a prolonged dream of westernization, by taking Europe as its reference. The centralized state and Islam-dominated Ottoman system marked by the absence of individualist values was indeed first "infiltrated" by European concepts back in the eighteenth century through military reforms, diplomatic missions, and the works of an emerging intelligentsia. And it was back then that Europe, in turn, focused its attention on the values and practices prevailing in this old autocratic empire. Already in 1856, the British foreign secretary, the earl of Clarendon, was writing Lord Stratford de Redcliffe, then ambassador in İstanbul, "the continued neglect of the Porte in human rights matters must lead to constant interference by foreign powers in the internal affairs of Turkey, which will be detrimental to her independence, and which it is alike the duty and the interest of the Porte to prevent."[1] Today, Turkey aspires to join the European Union as a member, and the membership criteria include meeting certain human rights standards. This time, Turkey attempts to reshape its economic, political, and social systems to formally belong to Europe, and it inevitably embraces the human rights criteria imposed by the EU.

From a theoretical point of view, this can be explained by referring to recently formulated ideas on the influence of international human rights pressure on state behavior (Cardenas 2004). Analyses regarding the impact of international human rights pressure are divided into three categories: (1) the ideational-sociological (or constructivist) approach emphasizing the strength and influence of the international normative context within a given society; (2) the materialist-rationalist approach emphasizing the influence of the state's self-interest in complying with human rights norms through international legal regimes; and (3) the latest approach, emphasizing, when appropriate, the role of power in obtaining compliance with human rights norms. This chapter argues that the timing, speed, and scope of the human rights reforms undertaken by Turkey in recent years demonstrates the link between the reforms and the national interest perceived as embodied in an eventual membership of the EU. In other words, I contend that Turkey's participation in international human rights regimes has been based on concerns of realpolitik. It has been noncommittal where there were no immediate interests involved, as it has been the case with the UN, but willing to commit itself to secure concrete returns in the future, as in the European context. I also contend that this dual and utilitarian approach has been an important obstacle to the progress of human rights in Turkey.

The Human Rights Regimes of the UN and Europe

A comprehensive comparison of the UN and European human rights regimes is beyond the scope of this study. However, I will highlight a few differences, in order to be able to trace Turkey's path within both contexts.

The framework used by Philip Alston in his critical appraisal of the UN program as a whole proves a useful tool in assessing human rights regimes (1996, 21). Alston's framework includes standard-setting, promotion of international norms, and establishment of accountability through various means. Judged against these criteria, the UN has certainly been effective in setting standards and norms but not as successful in promoting human rights at the national level or establishing accountability through dissuasive measures. The weakness of the regime, on the latter points, is as much due to the political nature of the organization as to the unplanned and random growth of its various human rights bodies and their lack of enforcement mechanisms. Some of these institutions have been created by treaties that, while adopted within the UN context, possess autonomous implementation machinery. An example is the International Covenant on Civil and Political Rights, drafted and adopted within the UN organization: it stands as a separate treaty with an autonomous supervisory body in the Human Rights Committee. Other institutions and supervisory mechanisms have been created by the UN Charter with specific mandates or because they have evolved under the charter on an ad hoc basis (Davidson 1997, 63). Nevertheless, both the charter-based and treaty-based organs are not very effective because of their inability to employ dissuasive sanctions against the violators. The violator states are aware that all they risk is negative publicity, mainly achieved through the reports drafted by these organs. Moreover, during the Cold War period, the bipolar bloc politics determined much of the behind-the-scenes bargaining among the member states and allowed the superpowers to avoid explicit references to their allies in human rights reports. The few that could not escape criticism were consoled by the fact that a mere paragraph in a UN report was not the end of the world. Although the post-Cold war era is marked by a growing tendency within the UN system to set up an effective sanctions mechanism—for example, by adopting additional protocols to the existing conventions and the recent creation of the International Criminal Court—the UN still cannot be considered nearly as effective as the European human rights regime, which has been by far the most successful regional system in promoting and enforcing human rights.

The European Convention for the Protection of Human Rights and Fundamental Freedoms, the first regional human rights instrument, was adopted in 1950, and fulfilled the Council of Europe's desire to move faster than the UN in drafting a legally binding human rights instrument (Davidson 1997, 101). The preamble of the Convention states that the parties resolve "to take the first steps for the collective enforcement of certain of the rights stated in the Universal Declaration of Human Rights." Thus, by creating the European Commission on Human Rights and the European Court of Human Rights, two enforcement mechanisms were established under the Convention: (1) an interstate complaint system, and (2) the right to file an individual application. Through these mechanisms, member states are judged, and when appropriate, condemned to pay indemnities to the victims, and pushed into taking the necessary measures to prevent violations, which is subsequently monitored by the Council's Committee of Ministers. Given the growing number of cases, the Commission and the Court were merged in 1999 to form a permanent court.

The human rights system set up by the Council of Europe has been gradually moving toward a further integration with the EU, especially since the Maastricht Treaty of 1992 has recognized the Convention as a general principle of law. Following the end of the Cold War, as the newly emerging democracies of Central and Eastern Europe became EU candidates, certain criteria, known as the Copenhagen criteria, were adopted at the 1993 summit meeting of the EU, as conditions to be fulfilled by the candidates to join the EU. The criteria include maintaining the rule of law, respect for human rights, protection of minorities, and the application of the market economy rules. In 1997, these criteria were formally incorporated into the Amsterdam Treaty. A further step was taken in 2000, when the EU Charter of Fundamental Rights was adopted. The 2003 draft constitution of the EU foresees to incorporate the charter, as well as to make the EU a party to the Convention.

Turkey's Human Rights Policy in Multilateral Contexts

As a founding member of the UN since the San Francisco conference in 1945, and a member of the Council of Europe since 1950, Turkey has committed itself to promote human rights. However, it did not include human rights on its policy agenda until the 1980s. This can be partially explained by the slow evolution of international human rights regimes in the aftermath of World War II. Although the norms were defined, effective monitoring and enforcement mechanisms have proven difficult in the presence of the sacrosanct concept of state sovereignty, staunchly defended by the main actors of the Cold War. Consequently, Turkey's geostrategic priorities could prevail and override human rights efforts, both at the domestic and international levels, without much criticism from the international community until the 1980s, the decade that became a turning point for Turkey as well as for the global politics.

In Turkey, the military takeover on 12 September 1980 and the ensuing human rights violations triggered some reactions. Globally, as a consequence of its diminishing apprehension toward a faltering Soviet bloc, a bolder approach to human rights by Europe became possible. In other words, the approaching end of the Cold War was at the same time a forewarning of the internationalization of Turkey's human rights problems. The process was further institutionalized by Turkey's formal application to the EU in 1987.

TURKEY'S PARTICIPATION IN THE UN HUMAN RIGHTS REGIME

The treaty ratification record and diplomatic activity patterns of Turkey show that Turkey's participation in the UN regime was initially marked by great enthusiasm. As a founding member of the UN, Turkey actively participated in the seven drafting stages of the Universal Declaration of Human Rights. In addition to the inner core of drafters, a long list of second-tier drafters made significant contributions at various points, and Adnan Kural of Turkey is cited among them (Morsink 1999, 32). Turkey was eager to join the international institutions after the Second World War, especially since the country had been somewhat marginalized by the international community due to its neutral stance during the war. Thus, it did not hesitate to embrace the first human rights conventions of the UN system. Moreover, the UN human rights instruments of the 1940s and 1950s were more humanitarian than political in nature, which reduced the risk in ratifying them.

Turkey's hesitancy in ratification or practice of placing reservations began when the two international covenants were adopted by the General Assembly in 1966. The International Covenant on Civil and Political Rights (ICCPR) was not signed by Ankara until 2000, on the grounds that Article 27 of the covenant recognized the rights of the ethnic minorities in a manner incompatible with Turkish legislation. Similarly, the International Covenant on Economic, Social, and Cultural Rights (ICESCR) was not signed until the same date, on the grounds that Article 13 granted educational and cultural rights incompatible with the Turkish Constitution. Both covenants were finally ratified in 2003. The aforementioned reservations remain, however. The Convention on the Elimination of All Forms of Racial Discrimination (CERD) was signed in 1972 but not ratified until 2002, for the same reasons related to reservations about the ICCPR.

Within this general context, the ratification of the Convention against Torture and Other Cruel, Inhuman or Degrading Treatment or Punishment (CAT) in 1988 can only be explained by then Prime Minister Turgut Özal's grand strategy of liberalization, which was pursued with the conviction that it would render his country eligible for EU membership. The same year, and for the same reason, Turkey became a party to the Council of Europe's Convention against Torture.

In 1985, in a manner consistent with Turkey's parafeminist Kemalist view on women's rights, the Convention on the Elimination of All Forms of Discrimination against Women (CEDAW) had been ratified with reservations, which were to be removed later (see Yasemin Çelik in this volume, Chapter 13). Later, in 1995, the Convention on the Rights of the Child (CRC) was treated similarly and ratified with reservations placed on Articles 17, 29, and 30 (see Marylou O'Neill in this volume, Chapter 5).

Turkey's record of treaty ratification can be characterized as a reserved and timid one, until December 1999, when the EU officially recognized Turkey as "a candidate State destined to join the Union on the basis of the same criteria as applied to the other candidate States" (European Council 1999, Part I, par. 12). Since then, not only the ratification process of certain UN conventions was accelerated and reservations removed, but Turkey's diplomatic stance on human rights has been shifted to become more consistent with its EU candidacy, admitting its shortcomings in the area of human rights, and adopting the EU line on most issues. In response, perhaps in a tacit agreement, the EU members stopped confronting their candidate in the UN fora.[2] Moreover, Turkey has invited, in recent years, the UN's special rapporteurs to visit the country, and allowed them to draft their reports freely.[3] The irregularity of the reports submitted by Turkey to various treaty bodies, such as the CAT, CEDAW, or CRC committees, has been remedied as well.[4]

TURKEY'S PARTICIPATION IN THE EUROPEAN HUMAN RIGHTS REGIME

Turkey's aspiration to join the EU has also influenced its stance toward the Council of Europe's mechanism of protection of human rights. For example, although Turkey had ratified the Convention back in 1954, it accepted Article 25 of the Convention, which allows individuals to file complaints against the state, only in 1987, when it formally applied for EU membership. Toward the same end, Turkey recognized the jurisdiction of the European Court of Human Rights on 26 December 1989.

Before the EU Candidacy. Although Turkey signed the Association Agreement with the European Community—as the union was then called—in 1963 during the early phases of its candidacy, it had remained distant toward integration with Europe. The relationship involved mainly some economic cooperation. The relationship inevitably turned political with the 1980 military coup in Turkey.

Although the EC considered the military takeover as disturbing, there was no immediate rupture in the Turkish-EC relations, and the ongoing negotiations on the Fourth Financial Protocol were not suspended (European Communities 1981, 5) until a year later. Until the mid-1980s, the EC displayed a dual attitude toward Turkey. On the one hand, there was the highly critical standpoint of the European Parliament (EP), led for the most part by the socialist deputies from Germany and the Nordic countries. On the other hand, a milder and more cautious posture was adopted by the European Commission and the European Council. The EP members, free from governmental concerns and motivated by their respective ideologies and constituencies, and sometimes influenced by Turkish political exiles, could ignore the period of violence that preceded the military takeover, and concentrate on the state repression that followed the coup. Moreover, Turkey, not being a member, had no deputies

in the EP who could inform the members about the situation in the country. This was not the case with the commission and the council. As executive bodies, they were more inclined to take the Turkish political crisis
into account within the enduring Cold War context, and unlike the EP,
they had direct communication with Ankara.[5]

The dichotomy in the EC's approach toward Turkey continued until
the restoration of civilian rule in 1983, when the EP, which had been the
primary source of criticism against human rights violations in Turkey,
started to influence the other institutions (Dağı 2000, 128). In 1985, on
the basis of a report by the EC representative in Turkey, the EP set five
conditions for the normalization of relations with Turkey: abolition of the
death penalty, prohibition of torture, ending of collective trials, recognition of the right of individual application to the European Court of
Human Rights, abolition of all laws restricting the freedom of thought.[6]
This was a sign that the EC agencies were now more united and Turkey
could no longer count on the "understanding" of some European governments. Parallel to the EC's own evolution toward the institutionalization
and unification of human rights policies, a demand-compliance pattern
settled in between the European Community and Turkey.

The return to civilian rule and the accession of the liberal Motherland
Party to power, under the leadership of Turgut Özal, in November 1983,
did not alter the position of the EC—and in particular, of the EP—and
the improvement in the realm of human rights continued to be a sine
qua non for the revival of relations with Turkey. Thus, the 600 million
ECU aid envisaged in the Fourth Financial Protocol was not released by
the EP upon Turkey's return to civilian rule, despite British and German
support in favor of it (Dağı 2000, 189). (Blocked by Greece, this fund
was not released until 1999, when Turkey's candidacy was recognized by
the EU.)

In spite of his weltanschauung primarily focused on economic liberalization, Özal was aware of the irreversible process of the internationalization of the human rights issue. He realized that he had "to do something"
in order to revive the Association Agreement with the EC and integrate
Turkey into the European economic sphere. The only solution was an
official application for the EC membership, which he filed on 14 April
1987. In fact, Turkey had already recognized the right to individual application before the European Court of Human Rights in January 1987. In
1988, both the UN and European conventions against torture were ratified by Turkey, in an effort to strengthen Turkish candidacy to the EU
membership. On 15 September 1988, the European Parliament recommended the revival of the Association Agreement.

Nevertheless, two years after the submission of the application, the EC
Commission rejected it in December 1989. Wrapped up in diplomatic

language, the reasons for the rejection were first linked to the EC's own integration process, temporarily focused on the implementation of the European Single Act, ratified in 1986.[7] The commission then stated that it would not recommend the start of full membership negotiations with any candidate state before 1993.[8] But the real reasons behind the decision are articulated in the conclusion of the commission report: Turkey's problems with political pluralism and human rights, the Turkish-Greek rift, and the unresolved Cyprus question.[9]

The rejection did not deter Turkey, and it continued with its democratization process by expanding its international commitments. Turkey recognized the jurisdiction of the European Court of Human Rights, and Özal himself signed the CSCE Charter for a New Europe at the Paris Summit in 1990.[10] On the domestic front, a State Ministry for Human Rights was created in 1991. Articles 141, 142, and 163 of the Turkish Penal Code were abolished because of their incompatibility with the Convention. This was followed by a partial reform of the Criminal Procedure Code.

The politics in the 1990s were marked by the Kurdish question. The EU, along with the Council of Europe and the Organization for Security and Cooperation in Europe (OSCE), increasingly pressed the successive governments in Turkey to recognize the Kurdish identity and improve the conditions of this large ethnic group. This pressure increased Turkish officials' suspicions of political foul play against the country's territorial integrity and led them to question the credibility of the European human rights policy.[11]

Another stumbling block on Turkey's long road to Europe was the Customs Union, which was to enter into force in 1996, according to the 1992 decision of the Council of Association. The European Parliament started to press for specific reforms in the field of human rights as a precondition for its approval of the Customs Union. In the light of these "suggestions," Ankara proceeded to amend Article 8 of the Antiterrorism Law and undertook the revision of some constitutional provisions in favor of a broader political participation. In what can be considered an immediate result, the Customs Union decision was adopted on 6 March 1995, and approved by the EP on 13 December 1995, with 343 votes in favor, 149 against, and 113 abstentions. At the same time, a resolution calling for democratization, respect for human rights, and, for the first time, a political solution to the Kurdish problem, was put to vote. It generated 395 favorable, and only 19 opposing votes (European Communities 1996). The EP's action was also supported by the commission, which addressed the issues of democratization and human rights in its October 1996 report on the functioning of the Customs Union, although these issues were irrelevant in that context (European Union 1996–97, 63).

On the eve of the April 1997 meeting of the Council of Association, the Turkish Parliament undertook a substantive legislative reform by adopting laws on the political rights of state employees, freedom of expression, and improvement of the conditions of detention. At the same time, a Supreme Board of Coordination for Human Rights was established in Ankara with members representing various ministries. During the Council of Association meeting held in Luxembourg, consensus was reached on evaluating Turkey's candidacy through the "same objective standards and criteria" as for other candidates (European Union 1996–97, 84).

Subsequently, and despite a crisis at the Luxembourg EU Summit around the issue of human rights, Turkey stepped up its efforts in reforming human rights legislation and practice.[12] In the fall of 1999, the Supreme Board of Coordination for Human Rights presented a report to which the representatives of some 50 Turkish universities and 18 NGOs had contributed. It proposed several constitutional and legal amendments, including, inter alia, the abolition of Article 13 of the Constitution (which limited rights and liberties), of the State Security Courts, and of the death penalty. In October 1999, the state minister on human rights, Mehmet Ali İrtemçelik, convened, for the first time, state and civil society representatives together to create a Consultative Council on Human Rights. This was an important step toward reconciling the state with civil society in a country where the latter had traditionally been subject to state repression and unable to defend its interests. The council designed an eleven-point "Short-Term Democratization Program" to be proclaimed after the EU Helsinki Summit in December 1999.[13] Turkey had never appeared so serious in its efforts of democratization and promotion of human rights. This clearly contributed to the EU's decision to confirm Turkish candidacy on 11 December 1999, at the Helsinki Summit.

Since the EU Candidacy. After the recognition of Turkey as an accession candidate in 1999, the EU launched a process that primarily focused on human rights. It first presented Turkey with an Accession Partnership document setting out practical short and medium-term priorities in the political and economic fields that ought to be implemented in order to satisfy the Copenhagen criteria.[14] Shortly after the document was made public, a statement by Günther Verheugen, the European commissioner responsible for the enlargement, indicated that "the crucial point here is the fact that Turkey is now taking the decisions needed in order to give practical expression to its intentions regarding respect for human rights" (Verheugen 2000, 3).

The short-term political criteria set out in the Accession Partnership document emphasized the strengthening of legal and constitutional guarantees in various areas: freedom of expression, freedom of association, prohibition of torture, alignment of Turkish legal procedures with the European Convention on Human Rights, training of officials about the EU legislation, maintaining a de facto moratorium on capital punishment, and removing all kinds of language restrictions in broadcasting. These measures were expected to be in place and effective by the year 2001. Although the deadline could not be respected, as they will be discussed in the following pages, most of the legislative changes were made by the end of 2004.

The medium-term political criteria had a larger scope and were expected to be completed in more than one year, while the work would begin in 2001. Emphasizing implementation as a logical follow-up to legislation, they called for the ratification of major international human rights instruments not yet ratified by Turkey, underlined the right to cultural diversity, proposed the lifting of the state of emergency in the southeast, and recommended the transformation of the National Security Council into a purely advisory body.

Once the Accession Partnership was adopted by the EU Council of Ministers on 4 December 2000, it was Turkey's turn to take the necessary steps toward full membership. To this effect, the Turkish government proclaimed the National Programme for Adoption of the Acquis (NPAA) in March 2001.[15] Judicially speaking, this was a unilateral declaration of will, outlining the calendar and process of adoption of the *acquis communautaire*, along with the structural changes to be undertaken. Consisting of six main parts, the first part of the program focused on the political criteria set out by the Accession Partnership document.[16] The introduction contained a solemn declaration that Turkey would fulfill the Copenhagen criteria and "accede to all relevant international conventions and take the necessary measures for their effective implementation for further alignment with universal norms manifest in the EU *acquis* and the practices in EU member States, particularly in the areas of democracy and human rights" (Turkish Ministry of Foreign Affairs 2001, 2). It also indicated that as of 2001, the government would speed up its ongoing work on political, administrative, and judicial reforms and duly convey its legislative proposals to the Turkish Grand National Assembly.

Expected reservations set aside—that is, the Cyprus issue upon which no calendar was fixed; or the right to broadcast in non-Turkish mother tongues; the abolition of the death penalty; and the role of the National Security Council (all "to be considered in mid-term")—the program was, in general, in accordance with the criteria set forth in the Accession Partnership document.[17] Turkey also committed itself to accede, in the medium term, to Protocol Nos. 4, 7, and 12 of the Convention, to the revised version of the European Social Charter, and to the Additional Protocol for a System of Collective Complaints.

To fulfill these commitments, the Turkish Grand National Assembly adopted in 2001, one of the most comprehensive packages of constitutional amendments, since the adoption of the 1982 Constitution. During the nineteen-year period since its adoption, the Constitution had been amended about five times, but never substantially. The 34 amendments adopted on 3 October 2001, in line with the priorities put forward by the EU, included: freedom of thought and expression; prevention of torture; strengthening of democracy and civilian authority; freedom and security of the individual; privacy of the individual life; inviolability of the domicile; freedom of communication; freedom of residence and movement; freedom of association; and gender equality. Most of the articles were amended with specific references to the relevant articles of the Convention and/or its protocols, as well as to the relevant sections of the National Programme.[18]

The constitutional amendments were followed by other legislative reforms. By December 2004, eight reform packages including a second series of constitutional amendments—in total 490 laws—were adopted and/or amended by the parliament. The death penalty was abolished in accordance with the 13th Additional Protocol to the European Convention on Human Rights, and changes in laws included the improvement of the legal situation of non-Muslim religious minorities and the liberalization of civil and political rights in general. In addition to amendments to the Preamble and Article 26 of the Constitution, the first, third and sixth reform packages of 2002 and 2003 broadened significantly the scope of the freedom of expression by permitting the use of local languages other than Turkish in radio and TV broadcasts or eliminating the so-called "thought crimes" (Özbudun and Yazıcı, 2004). The Law on Associations was progressively liberalized through the second, third, fourth and fifth reform packages. In July 2004, the parliament passed an entirely new law on associations that is characterized as "the most progressive Law on Associations in over 20 years," by a leading Turkish NGO, the Third Sector Foundation of Turkey (TÜSEV,Türkiye Üçüncü Sektör Vakfı, see Özbudun and Yazıcı 2004, 21).

Moreover, there has been a considerable improvement in Turkey's stance before the European Court of Human Rights, where a qualitative change took place in cases related to Turkey. They no longer concern overt violations of physical integrity of person, such as the violation of the right to life or prohibition of torture, but involve various issues of repression, such as, the freedom of expression or right to property.

As a result, the EU Council, "welcoming the decisive progress made by Turkey in its far-reaching reform process" (European Council 2004, par. 18), has concluded that Turkey sufficiently fulfilled the political criteria and decided, on 17 December 2004, to open the accession negotiations

on 3 October 2005. On the basis of the EU commission's recommendations, a new strategy consisting of three pillars has been pursued.[19] The
first pillar concerns cooperation to reinforce and support the reform
process in Turkey. In order to guarantee the sustainability and irreversi-
bility of the political reform process, the EU will continue to monitor
progress of these reforms closely. This will be done on a yearly basis
through a revised Accession Partnership and the commission may recommend the suspension of the negotiations in case of a serious and persistent breach of fundamental rights and freedoms, in accordance with
the EU law.

The second pillar concerns the specific way of approaching accession
negotiations with Turkey under 31 headings aiming at implementing the
acquis. The third pillar entails a substantially strengthened political and
cultural dialogue bringing people together from EU member states and
Turkey. The latter one is important in two respects: for overcoming mutual
prejudices and misperceptions that seem to be running high, especially
in Europe, toward Turkey; and for inculcating further the international
human rights norms with Turkish society—a process that has been under-
way for some time, especially since civil society in Turkey appeared responsive to and supportive of the reforms.

Conclusion

The internationalization of the human rights issues of Turkey first started
in the aftermath of the 1980 military coup d'état (see Başak Çalı in this
volume, Chapter 14). A second development, Turkey's candidacy to the
EU, enhanced the internationalization pattern and stimulated Turkish
participation in international human rights regimes. Eager to realize its
objective of integration with the West as a member of the EU, Turkey has
become more actively involved in both global and European human rights
regimes. Although what happened during the last decade are serious improvements, there are problems inherent to the process. First, Turkey's
utilitarian approach to human rights appears to be a tool of realpolitik
rather than an end in itself. Second, as consequence to the first, the system is apt to suffer from deficiencies in implementation. Implementation,
of course, is crucial; as pointed out by the Commission of European
Communities, "the extent to which individuals in Turkey will enjoy a real
improvement in the exercise of fundamental freedoms in practice will
depend on the details of implementing legislation and the practical application of law" (Commission of European Communities 2001, 20).

Democratization and respect for human rights cannot be limited to the
State's participation in international human rights regimes, with a narrow objective of self-interest, in this case joining the EU. Whatever the

outcome of the negotiation process, the primary responsibility of the Turkish state is to its people. This responsibility can be fulfilled only if the state approaches human rights as a moral commitment, irrespective of the requirements of realpolitik. Once this transformation is completed—that is, international human rights norms are fully applied by the state and internalized by society—then the so-called materialist-rationalist perspective can be replaced by the constructivist approach in explaining Turkey's behavior with regard to international human rights norms. In other words, human rights will be on solid ground in Turkey when "the Copenhagen criteria" are turned into "the Ankara criteria"—as Prime Minister Recep Tayyip Erdoğan often claims it to be the case.

Chapter 17

Leveraging Norms: The ECHR and Turkey's Human Rights Reforms

Thomas W. Smith

Of the many international influences on human rights in Turkey, none are more important than the rules and norms that make up the European human rights regime. The regime is founded on the European Convention for the Protection of Human Rights and Fundamental Freedoms (from here on, the Convention), which entered into law in 1953. Enforcement is provided by the European Court of Human Rights (ECHR), which opened its doors in 1959. Turkey ratified the Convention in 1954. But it was not until 1989, when Ankara accepted the binding jurisdiction of the ECHR, did Turkey become a full participant in the European regime.[1]

Since then, more than 5,000 applications from Turkey have flooded the court's docket.[2] For much of the 1990s, the ECHR received more petitions from Turkey than from any other country. The number of new cases has ebbed, but the judgments continue to mount. Since 1999, Turkey has been the respondent in more cases involving the right to life (Article 2), torture (Article 3), liberty and security (Article 5), fair trials (Article 6), free expression (Article 10), free association (Article 11), and the right to an effective remedy before a national authority (Article 13), than any other country. It has been a stream of almost exclusively adverse rulings; Turkey has won only about 10 percent of the cases in which it was the respondent.

This chapter argues that despite the often rocky relations between Ankara and the ECHR, the court has taken a key role in reforming Turkey's legal system. A review of the rulings against Ankara, together with the reforms that often followed, suggests that the ECHR has helped to legitimize a wider array of rights than those guaranteed under Kemalism. The ECHR has prompted reforms in pretrial detention, trial procedures, freedom of expression, and freedom of assembly and association. The influence of the ECHR has been mixed with regard to political party closures and religious freedom, and may have been counterproductive on the question of a divided Cyprus. Its compliance with the ECHR rulings has been a material condition for Turkey's future membership in the European Union, but the court has also provided a blueprint for real normative change.

The chapter proceeds first with an overview of the ECHR as an arbiter of European human rights norms. Next is a discussion of the clash between the liberal norms articulated by the ECHR and Turkey's Kemalist legal culture. This is followed by a review of the politics and perceptions of the ECHR's role in the Kurdish issue. The lengthiest section of the chapter is then devoted to Turkey's compliance with ECHR rulings and the effect the court's judgments have had on Turkish law and practice. The chapter ends with some reflections on the political and normative dynamics between Turkey and the European regime.

Establishing Supranational Norms

International lawyers generally regard the ECHR system as the "most effective and advanced" human rights regime in the world, "a striking example of what a well-conceived instrument can accomplish in a propitious environment" (Drzemczewski 1983, 3; Merrills 1988, 2). Compliance has been so consistent that the court's decisions are considered "as effective as those of any domestic court" (Helfer and Slaughter 1997, 283). Even jaded political scientists confirm that the ECHR is "a rare success story in the international arena."[3]

The Convention and the court promote human rights and political development. But the regime has also successfully articulated European norms. Although national governments may invite a torrent of petitions and public shaming by allowing the court to hear cases brought against them, this is offset by the legitimacy showered on countries that join the court. In this way, the court has helped to consolidate democratic institutions and anchor liberal reforms (Moravcsik 2000).

Governments almost always comply with ECHR rulings. The court is designed to complement rather than replace national courts; before petitioning the tribunal, applicants must first exhaust local remedies. When the court finds violations, it orders the offending state to compensate the victim or retry the case. The court also insists on "positive integration" of its rulings into national law in order to prevent future violations. The ECHR tracked the effect of its rulings on 18 member states between 1960 and 1994, and found that adverse judgments produced legislative, administrative, judicial, or constitutional reforms about 80 percent of the time. The data also suggested that compliance rose as the ECHR matured as an institution (Zorn and Van Winkle 2002, 9–11).

Kemalist Jurisprudence and Clashing Conceptions of Rights

Turkey has locked horns with the ECHR over questions of jurisdiction, but the sharpest exchanges have centered on theories of jurisprudence concerning the nature and limits of rights. The Convention enshrines the liberal, individual model of rights, while granting states discretion to decide when individual freedoms threaten the common good. This clashes with the hard-communitarian Kemalist model of civic nationalism. The court has legitimized critics who see the "spirit of authority" represented by Kemalism as hostile to civil, political, and minority rights (Rumpf 1993, 395–96).

Kemalists have responded that rights are central to Turkey's European identity as reflected in the country's rights-based Constitution and Civil and Penal Codes. But European identity has not always led to European practice. Those who have identified most strongly with the European tradition—the military, the courts, and the civil service—historically have resisted liberal European mores. Judges have guarded Kemalism with their strict reading of the Constitution and the rigid application of the restrictive clauses of civil and penal codes. Nonetheless, the European human rights regime has begun to erode Turkey's jurisprudence of civic nationalism. The Turkish Constitutional Court (Türk Anayasa Mahkemesi) ruled in 1992 that Turkey was obliged to bring domestic law into conformity with the Convention and other international agreements (Özdek 1992, 28–29).

From a legal standpoint this was entirely proper. Under Article 90 of the Constitution, "international agreements duly put into effect carry the force of law." This generally has been interpreted to mean that international law binds domestic law, although in practice the relationship is unsettled. Prior to 1990, the Constitutional Court consistently held that international agreements enjoy equal status with domestic law. But it was vague on whether or not international law would trump domestic law when the two came into conflict. Although the Constitutional Court has made occasional references to the Convention since the 1960s, it treated international human rights instruments as "supporting norms," not as applicable, stand-alone law.

In 1990, the Constitutional Court began to recognize what it called "supra-constitutional norms" of the European Convention (Özdek 1992, 29). The Council of State (Danıştay), the country's highest administrative court, also affirmed that the Convention was effectively incorporated into Turkish law upon its ratification. Conflicts are not resolved automatically in favor of the Convention, although the Constitutional Court has applied it directly in striking down a number of antiquated provisions related to family law and women's rights (see Yasemin Çelik in this volume, Chapter 13). Yet even as Turkey aligned itself with the EU, many Turkish judges seemed skeptical about applying the Convention to linguistic, religious, and expressive freedoms, citing concerns over maintaining national unity (see Baskin Oran in this volume, Chapter 3). Lower courts almost never cite international law.

Still, the Convention and the court have served as benchmarks for Turkey's legal reformers. Prominent jurists have publicly contrasted the libertarian Convention with Turkey's own democratically cramped Constitution. In 2001, Sami Selçuk, then president of the Court of Appeals, called the Constitution "a set of police regulations" rather than an expression of fundamental rights.[4] Selçuk's successor Eraslan Özkaya called for reforms in line with the Convention. In September 2002, chair of the Constitutional Court Mustafa Bumin called for greater tolerance in the country's political parties law, noting that because "Turkey accepted the jurisdiction of the European Court of Human Rights, Turkey must adjust its laws."[5] A month later, arguing that "the aim is to form a common law," the justice minister Aysel Çelikel called on the application of ECHR law to Turkey.[6] Following the November 2002 elections, the new minister of justice Cemil Çiçek pledged to align Turkish law with the Convention.

The Convention and the ECHR figured prominently in the countdown to December 2004, when the EU officially invited Turkey to begin membership talks. Progressive reforms were enacted. The Ministry of Justice trained judges in European law, sponsored public forums on the ECHR, and even distributed pamphlets explaining how a citizen may bring a case. The ministry also led a public accounting of Turkey's failings before the court, reciting the number of cases filed, the win-loss statistics, and the mounting fines.

Of course, states are not the only violators of human rights. A crucial subtext to the debate about Turkey's participation in the ECHR concerns the degree to which "separatist Kurds" and "fundamentalist Islamists" may hijack the court's rhetoric of rights and turn it to illiberal ends. Human rights lawyers who funnel cases to the ECHR are often assumed to be sympathetic to the Kurdistan Workers' Party (Partia Karkaren Kürdistan, PKK) or other illegal organizations, and have frequently been harassed by state officials. Some Kurds who had lodged petitions with the court were singled out and hounded by security officials. Local NGOs that have cooperated with the court have faced a Kafka-esque onslaught of investigations and prosecutions (see Başak Çalı in this volume, Chapter 14).

Law and Politics: The Kurdish Issue

Turkey joined the ECHR just as the country's conflict escalated with the PKK, the Kurdish separatist organization headed by Abdullah Öcalan. Most of the applications filed against Turkey have originated in the largely

Kurdish southeast of the country. Civil rights were suspended in the southeast beginning in 1987. The controversial State Security Courts (Devlet Güvenlik Mahkemeleri), which combined military and civilian judges, were established in 1973 with left-wing militants in mind, but were used predominantly to try Kurdish separatists and sympathizers. The 1991 Antiterrorism Law further constricted civil rights. As the war waned, Turkey took broad strides in repealing repressive statutes and restoring civil liberties. The state of emergency was lifted in the final two provinces in November 2002. Despite some progress, the southeast remains the main site of illegal detentions, torture, disappearances, and extrajudicial killings. PKK violence has also increased since June 2004, when the rebels ended an earlier ceasefire.

The ECHR and Turkey were often at loggerheads throughout the 1990s. At low points, Ankara threatened to withdraw recognition of the ECHR altogether. Beginning in 1995, the ECHR began to function as a court of first instance for many cases from Turkey, as Kurdish applicants argued that Turkish tribunals did not offer them effective remedies. The ECHR tended to agree. As the number of filings soared, Ankara grew defensive, viewing the court as moralistic and unappreciative of the separatist threat. Aslan Gündüz (2001), who represented Turkey before the ECHR at the time, suggests that in many cases originating in the southeast he bore the burden of proving the government's innocence. The court "seem[ed] to have formed an *a priori* opinion of Turkish culpability . . . [and] thus to have politicized what ought to be judicial functions." Gündüz writes that "the ECHR continues to exercise an intrusive and deep-penetrating influence on the Turkish political and legal system," and that the court's "decisions might lead to the erosion of the Turkish constitution" where it departs from the Convention (Gündüz 2001, 9).

The eagerness with which the ECHR took up the Öcalan case was seen by many as further evidence of a pro-Kurdish agenda at the court. Turkish agents arrested the PKK leader in Nairobi on 16 February 1999. Later the same day, the court heard a petition from Öcalan's lawyers concerning the conditions of his detention and his access to legal aid. The ECHR ruled on the motion two days later—before Öcalan had been arraigned in Turkey. Many Turks were dismayed to see the court seeming to side with Turkey's number one enemy. A special State Security Court later convicted Öcalan of treason and sentenced him to death, though his life was spared thanks to EU pressure backed by Article 6 of the Convention, which bans capital punishment. Nationalist fervor resurfaced in March 2003, when the ECHR ruled that Öcalan had not received a fair trial. The court ruled that the proceedings were flawed because Öcalan's access to his lawyers had been curbed and because a military judge had presided over the opening of the trial.[7]

Although it raised nationalist hackles, the court did bend in the face of Turkey's national security needs. In 1992, during the war, Turkey followed the Convention and stated publicly its departure from Article 5 regarding arrest, arraignment, and pretrial detention. Although the court continued to uncover violations of Article 5, elsewhere the court found that "the particular extent and impact of PKK terrorist activity in South-East Turkey has undoubtedly created, in the region concerned, a 'public emergency threatening the life of the nation.'" Still, the court ruled that the government had failed to make the case "as to why the fight against terrorism in South-East Turkey rendered judicial intervention impracticable."[8]

In addition, the ECHR has demanded high standards of evidence from Kurdish applicants who claimed that they were mistreated because of their ethnicity. Indeed, it has proved almost impossible for Turkish applicants to prevail in discrimination (Article 14) cases. The court has strictly enforced time limitations on filing applications and has rejected many cases because national remedies were not exhausted. The court has avoided blanket condemnations of Turkey. In freedom of expression cases, it has carefully weighed the threat posed by "separatist" language against applicants' free speech rights as guaranteed under Article 10. In cases that alleged incitement to violence or threats to national security, the court has granted a wide "margin of appreciation" to the Turkish government. Noting that "national authorities are in principle better placed than the international judge to appreciate what is 'in the public interest,'" the ECHR tends to grant governments the benefit of the doubt in intrastate conflicts.[9] The court has *always* sided with the Turkish government against applicants who have alleged that Turkey has overstepped the legitimate limitations on rights recognized under Article 18 of the Convention. With the exception of its criticism of the State Security Courts, the ECHR has been soft-spoken on the role of the military in Turkish politics.

Compliance with and Effects of ECHR Judgments

Many observers remain unimpressed by Turkey's record of compliance with the ECHR. The Council of Europe has cited Turkey's "manifest disregard" for its obligations under the Convention, including problems in payment of fines and satisfaction of judgments; retrial and other redress for applicants convicted after an unfair trial; and the restoration of civil and political rights to people whose criminal convictions had been reached in violation of the Convention (Council of Europe Committee on Legal Affairs and Human Rights). In an overview of issues facing Turkey in 2005, Human Rights Watch noted that torture and ill-treatment in police custody are common, and that there has been little progress on the return of internally displaced Kurds to their homes (Human Rights Watch 2005). Amnesty International noted in November 2004 that judicial remedies against torture remained "insufficient and inadequate" (Amnesty International 2004).

My own analysis of ECHR judgments in cases from Turkey, along with that of recent legal and administrative reforms, highlights several areas of marked improvement as well as some persistent shortcomings. Many of the judgments, tabulated in Table 17.1, were in cases lodged by Kurdish applicants seeking compensation under Protocol I for homes wrecked by Turkish security forces during the war. But most judgments dealt with core areas of the Convention.

Since 2000, there has been a sharp increase in the number of "friendly settlements." In these cases, the respondent government files a declaration with the ECHR accepting responsibility for the violations alleged and outlines measures taken to prevent future abuses. The government typically compensates the victim or the victim's family as well. If the court is satisfied with the settlement and is convinced that the "positive integration" of legal and administrative reforms will prevent future violations, it strikes the case from the docket. (Turkey's declarations invariably stress

TABLE 17.1. ECHR JUDGMENTS IN CASES FROM TURKEY, 1995–2004

Nature of violation / Convention article	Total number of judgments	Number of adverse judgments
Protection of property (Protocol, Article 1)	216	211
Right to a fair trial (Article 6)	203	194
Right to an effective remedy (Article 13)	64	58
Prohibition on torture (Article 3)	76	51
Freedom of expression (Article 10)	56	50
Right to liberty and security (Article 5)	56	44
Right to life (Article 2)	54	44
Respect for family and private life (Article 8)	27	18
Freedom of assembly and association (Article 11)	9	7
No punishment without law (Article 7)	6	3
Prohibition of discrimination (Article 14)	34	1
Freedom of thought, conscience, and religion (Article 9)	5	1
Right to free elections (Article 3)	1	1
Abuse of legitimate limitations on rights (Article 18)	19	0

Source: Database of the Case-Law of the European Court of Human Rights (HUDOC).

Data cover all judgments in which Turkey was the respondent from 23 March 1995, when the ECHR first ruled in a case from Turkey, through 31 December 2004. Some cases involve multiple applicants. In cases that examine multiple articles of the Convention, judgments are disaggregated by article.

the "occasional and individual" character of violations, thus avoiding any suggestion that there might be a pattern of abuse.) Between January 2000 and December 2004, the ECHR approved 167 friendly settlements from Turkey. Turkey had reached only one such settlement before 2000. Many of these agreements covered Protocol No. 1 property claims, but the government also settled scores of right to life, torture, detention, fair trial, effective remedy, and freedom of expression cases. Turkey has paid several million dollars in settlements to victims.

Although Ankara does not call attention to this part of its legal strategy, the cumulative effect of these cases and the subsequent changes in Turkey's law and practice suggest that the country has gone from being a nation on trial to actively working to resolve cases and craft reforms in line with the Convention. In many instances a virtuous cycle has emerged. The ECHR spotlights areas that need improvement; Ankara undertakes reforms to comply with the Convention; reforms help resolve pending cases and prevent further violations.

PRE-TRIAL DETENTION

Improvements in pretrial detention have been guided by a confluence of Article 3 (torture) and Article 5 (unlawful arrest or detention) cases, with added impetus from *Denmark v. Turkey,* a rare States Parties case in which a Danish citizen was detained and tortured by Turkish authorities and eventually convicted by a State Security Court of aiding the PKK.[10] The Turkish National Program for the Adoption of the Acquis pledged to align pretrial detention with the Convention. Turkey's new Penal Code, adopted in September 2004 and due to take effect in April 2005, defines torture and ill-treatment in accordance with international conventions. Doctors who draft false medical reports used to whitewash torture cases may now be prosecuted. The practice of blindfolding detainees was banned. A detainee's relatives must now be informed of the arrest "without delay," though still "by decision of the prosecutor." Members of security forces may now be held personally liable for judgments of torture or ill-treatment by the ECHR. Reforms to the Law on the Duties and Competencies of the Police have limited the discretionary authority of officers. A new judicial bench will review claims by prisoners that their rights have been violated.

The Interior Ministry now publishes ECHR rulings in Police Academy publications and circulates outlines of cases and compliance warnings to police bureaus across the country. The time from arrest to arraignment has been shortened. People detained for "collective offenses" may be held incommunicado and without access to a lawyer for up to 48 hours. While this practice still seems tailored to extract confessions, it improves on the two-week detentions previously allowed under emergency rule. Allegations of police torture have declined markedly over the past few years, although abuses are still common, particularly in "political" cases. More than a thousand cases charging abuses by police or Jandarma are forwarded to Turkish prosecutors each year. Growing numbers end in conviction, often for mistreatment rather than the more serious crime of torture. Several human rights NGOs along with the Committee for the Prevention of Torture are urging immediate access to a lawyer as the most effective deterrent to ill-treatment and torture.

STATE SECURITY COURTS

Responding to a combination of political pressure and ECHR rulings, Turkey dismantled its State Security Courts (SSCs) in June 2004. The courts, long at the center of the debate about judicial independence, heard cases involving persons accused of "offenses against the Republic . . . against the indivisible unity of the State . . . or against the free, democratic system of government and offences directly affecting the State's internal or external security."[11] Three civilian and two military judges were empaneled for each trial. The SSCs often held closed hearings and admitted evidence obtained through secret interrogations. They could be transformed into martial law courts under emergency rule. Appeals were limited. The ECHR's decisions in 1998 in *İncal v. Turkey* and *Çıraklar v. Turkey* held that the presence of military judges on the courts violated the right to a fair trial before an independent and impartial tribunal guaranteed under Article 6.[12] Those precedents became the basis for a string of adverse rulings. With the EU contemplating opening accession talks with Turkey, it became increasingly clear that the SSCs could not be reconciled with European norms.

RETRIALS IN TURKISH COURTS

A major package of reforms passed by the Turkish Parliament in August 2002 cleared the way for Turkish courts to retry cases remanded to them by the ECHR. When the court finds violations of the Convention as the result of an unfair trial, the defendant shall now have the automatic right to a retrial. This decision was spurred by the case of Leyla Zana, the celebrated Kurdish human rights activist who was jailed in 1994. Zana was elected to the Turkish Parliament in 1991 on the Kurdish-based Democracy Party (DEP) ticket. Along with several other DEP members, she sparked a furor by making a statement in Kurdish during the swearing-in ceremony. Convicted by the Ankara SSC of belonging to an illegal armed gang, Zana and her colleagues successfully sued at the ECHR. In

Sadak, Zana, Dicle, and Doğan v. Turkey the court found violations of Article 6(1) regarding the independence and impartiality of the Ankara tribunal; Article 6(3)(a), the right to be informed of the charges being brought; Article 6(3)(b), which guarantees an adequate defense; and Article 6(3)(d), the right to present and examine witnesses at trial.

When the ECHR ordered that the applicants be given a new trial in Turkey, it was rebuffed by Ankara. In August 2002, however, the parliament amended the law to allow retrials. In January 2003, under EU pressure, the amendments were made retroactive. In a new trial, Zana and her colleagues were reconvicted, but in June 2004 were freed on appeal. In July, an appeals court ordered a third trial, but with the case threatening to derail Turkey's drive for EU membership, and in light of the new liberalization of Kurdish rights, Turkish authorities agreed to halt the prosecution. Zana's case showed that hundreds of SSC and other convictions conceivably could be overturned by the ECHR. (The court has received more than 1,000 applications from Turkey involving the right to a fair trial.) The prospect of ECHR-mandated retrials has prompted closer vigilance of due process and has strengthened the independence of the judiciary; it also has accelerated amnesties for Kurds convicted of low-level political offenses.

PARTY CLOSINGS

Turkey's Constitutional Court has closed 18 political parties since the return to civilian rule in 1983. Four Kurdish and two Islamist parties were shuttered in the past decade. Despite the liberalization of the Law on Political Parties (No. 2820) in 1999, the Islamist-oriented Virtue (Fazilet) Party was closed by the Constitutional Court in June 2001 on grounds that it was a hotbed of "Islamic and antisecular activities." In 1998, its predecessor, the Welfare (Refah) Party had been dissolved for "conspiring against the secular order." As recently as March 2003, the Turkish court banned the Kurdish-based People's Democracy Party (Halkın Demokrasi Partisi, HADEP). Chief prosecutor Sabih Kanadoğlu petitioned to close HADEP's successor, the Democratic People's Party (DEHAP), as well. Legal challenges are also pending against the pro-Kurdish Party of Rights and Freedoms (Hak ve Özgürlükler Partisi).

These closure cases may represent the last stand of Kemalist prosecutors against the encroachments of electoral liberalism. With only one exception—the Refah Party case discussed below—the ECHR has found Turkey's party closings to be in violation of Article 11. The court ruled in *United Communist Party of Turkey and Others v. Turkey* that the government could not dissolve a political party that had engaged in no illegal activities. In *Freedom and Democracy Party (ÖZDEP) v. Turkey*, it held that the party's interest in self-determination for national or religious minorities did not undermine democracy.[13] Although Turkish law on political parties has been refashioned and the Constitution amended to liberalize political association, the rules remain cumbersome (Hakyemez and Akgün 2002). The charters of NGOs, ironically, still require government approval. Plans to free labor unions from official meddling, and to ease restrictions on public meetings and demonstrations, are still awaiting action.

Freedom of Expression

Much of the ECHR's case load on the freedom of expression has come from Turkey, most of it related to the Kurdish issue. Although the court takes Turkey's concerns over terrorism and separatism seriously, it frequently finds the government's response disproportionate to the threat. The absolutism of the war years has waned, however, and the government is now settling a large share of Article 10 cases. Prosecutors have tried to silence scores of publishers and writers, though this has been balanced by a wave of high-profile acquittals. Still, barriers to free speech, including vague press laws, remain in place. Local officials also act as extrajudicial censors, seizing offensive materials and muzzling free speech on their own initiative.

The new Penal Code edges Turkey's free speech laws closer to the Convention. New Article 301 regarding criticism of the state or state institutions was restricted to speech intended to "insult" or "deride" those institutions. The statute against "mocking and insulting government ministers" was repealed, but other defamation laws in the new code may yet dampen public discourse. New Article 216 replaces the notorious Article 312 regarding "incitement to hatred on the basis of differences of social class, race, religion sect, or region." The new article is amended to read "in a way that may be dangerous for public order," thus mirroring the Convention's focus on the *ordre publique*. In providing a rationale for new Article 305 prohibiting "acting against fundamental national interests" the Parliamentary Committee of Justice noted illustratively that the law would apply to a citizen who called for the withdrawal of Turkish troops from Cyprus or who declared that the Armenian genocide took place (International Publishers Association).

The liberalization of Kurdish language instruction and television broadcasts has been driven as much by political pressures as by the ECHR. One of the most challenging cases involved *Özgür Gündem*, a pro-Kurdish newspaper known popularly as the "PKK Daily," that was closed by the government in 1994. The paper sued and won under Article 10. The judgment noted, "the public enjoys the right to be informed of different perspectives on the situation in southeast Turkey, however unpalatable they might be to the authorities." The pioneering part of the ruling was that the Convention demanded not simply government laissez-faire, but that freedom of expression "may require positive measures of protection," thus turning a negative right into a positive duty.[14]

Religious Freedom

The ECHR has been a tepid promoter of religious freedom in Turkey, ruling only once, in the *Cyprus* case discussed below, that Turkey had abridged religious freedom. In *Kalaç v. Turkey* the court upheld the Supreme Military Council's decision to dismiss a judge advocate in the Turkish Air Force who allegedly, through his conduct and attitude, "revealed that he had adopted unlawful fundamentalist opinions." The application was denied in *Tepeli et al v. Turkey*, in which 41 former members of the armed forces claimed they were purged for their religious beliefs.[15] The court has blocked about 20 petitions involving military life and religious observance and dress. The court ruled inadmissible a challenge to state-sanctioned religious education in public lycées (Erdem), and barred the Article 9 elements of a Greek Cypriot application which argued that the division of the island blocked access to particular religious sites (Josephides). The court admitted a case dealing with the expropriation of a Christian place of veneration under the law, on pious foundations (Institute of French Priests).[16] The law at issue, rooted in Ottoman jurisprudence, was amended in August 2002 to help safeguard minority religious property from government seizure. Leaders of Turkey's Alevis—a 10-million-member heterodox Shiite sect—have threatened to sue Ankara over compulsory religious classes, which they claim reflect the Sunni mainstream of the Directorate of Religious Affairs.

In a rare affirmation of Turkey's Constitutional Court, the ECHR upheld the closure of the Refah Party and the seizure of its assets by the state. The Constitutional Court had feared that Refah might attempt to undermine the secular order. Some party leaders had advocated a "pluralistic" legal system that would include Quranic law alongside Turkish law. Citing the European Court's precedent of granting ample discretion to states in electoral matters, a divided ECHR concluded that "it was reasonable on the part of the authorities to act as they did in order to protect the electoral system of the state."[17] In June 2004, in the *Şahin* case, the court ruled against a woman who was barred from attending medical school at İstanbul University because she wore an Islamic head scarf. The court held that "Article 9 does not protect every act motivated or inspired by a religion or belief," and indeed, found that the university ban on head scarves "pursued the legitimate aims of protecting the rights and freedoms of others and of protecting public order."[18]

CYPRUS

Turkish officials have vigorously resisted the ECHR judgments regarding Cyprus.[19] In the *Loizidou* case, a divided court held that Turkey exercised effective control over the Turkish Republic of Northern Cyprus (TRNC), and awarded Greek Cypriot Titina Loizidou U.S.$600,000 in damages for being deprived of her property in the north. The justices ruled that the deprivation was a "continuing violation," given the division of the island, though Turkish lawyers had argued that the partition was "spontaneous." *Loizidou* seemed designed to open the gates to hundreds of similar applications against Turkey, as indeed has happened. In *Cyprus v. Turkey*, the court ruled that Turkey had violated 14 different articles of the Convention during the occupation of northern Cyprus. The *Loizidou* decision was rendered in 1996, *Cyprus* in 2001, yet only recently did Ankara agree to honor the judgments. If anything, the judgments hardened the Turkish military's position on the impasse and steeled the resistance of Rauf Denktaş, the nominal president of the TRNC, to a settlement based on confederation.

Conclusion

The effects of normative regimes are usually subtle—coloring debate and cajoling compliance. In the Turkish case, however, the European human rights regime has given concrete direction and definition to human rights reforms. Major ECHR rulings receive wide publicity, and specific cases are often cited by reformers. Human rights NGOs, Kurds, Alevis, labor organizers, Islamists, and others have drawn inspiration—and sometimes formal protection—from the court. The Convention has become the country's standard on many human rights issues.

Of course, on the most pressing issues—the right to life, torture, illegal detention—legal remedies come too late. Though even in these cases the ECHR can render justice and expose violations as a way to prevent future abuses. Turkey will no doubt continue to be a regular respondent before the court. Even if some rulings are met with dismay in some quarters in Turkey, the legitimacy of the Convention and the court is gaining ground as the European human rights regime becomes a normal part of Turkish politics.

Chapter 18
Conclusion: Turkey's Prospects and Broader Implications

Zehra F. Kabasakal Arat

The chapters in this volume are primarily concerned with disentangling human rights practices in Turkey and assessing their prospects. Examining a range of human rights issues over time, however, enables us to derive some generalizable conclusions. Thus, the cumulative findings of the chapters can be discussed both for the case of Turkey and in terms of their broader theoretical relevance and implications.

Patterns and Prospects

Despite their critical assessment of the practice of human rights in Turkey, all chapters in the volume, with the exception of the one on the right to education, conclude on an optimistic note, typically with a reference to the recent legislative reforms as a positive and promising step. However, this is a cautioned or conditioned optimism. There is an implicit consensus that the authoritarian past is still haunting the country, and authors underscore the importance of implementation, which face institutional and cultural resistance. The history of Turkey dictates prudential predictions. After all, most human rights were articulated and protected by law, but their recognition on paper did not ensure citizens' enjoyment of those rights. Laws in general safeguarded the state's security at the expense of human security and rights. Consequently, real-life experience has obscured the content of law and legal recognition of human rights. A 1997 survey of the university students, for example, finds the awareness about the existence or absence of internationally recognized human rights in Turkey's laws as quite low (at 53 percent), but notes that the students from the southeastern Anatolia region, where the repression and violations were more profound, scored the lowest (48 percent) (Payaslıoğlu and İçduygu 1999).

In fact, the effective implementation of the new legislation is yet to be noted. Cases of violation of the due process rights and torture are still reported in daily papers and reports of human rights organizations, despite the changes in law and the government's claim of "zero tolerance on torture" (Amnesty International, Turkey Report 2005). The ban on speaking and publishing in Kurdish was removed, and broadcasting in Kurdish, along with some other local languages, are now allowed, but citizens are still prosecuted for using *q, x,* and *w*—letters that do not exist in the Turkish alphabet but are used in Kurdish—in spelling names. Political candidates are fined for greeting the public in Kurdish during their election campaigns. Article 42 of the Constitution, which prevents the education of children in their mother tongues, remains intact. Violations of the freedoms of speech and expression are rampant. Even the advocacy of human rights can be subject to stringent legal action, as demonstrated by the court decisions that ordered the closing of Eğitim-Sen, one of the largest labor unions in the education sector, for including the advocacy of education in one's mother tongue as a goal in its bylaws.[1]

The death penalty was abolished, as well as the military-led State Security Courts; but the latter has been replaced by Special Felony Courts, which intend to perform the same function, albeit without including military personnel on the bench. Repeatedly amended Civil and Penal Codes were finally supplanted by noticeably improved new ones in 2001 and 2004 respectively. A draft for a new law that will replace the Antiterrorism Law—which was enacted in 1991 and continues to be notorious in restricting freedoms despite several amendments that relaxed its worst provisions—is in process.[2] However, these new laws still entail provisions that restrict individual freedom and rights or permit discrimination, especially against women and advocates of muliticulturalism.

In addition to various structural and institutional obstacles that slow down the progress, the advancement of human rights encounters attitudinal resistance. In reference to the repression of minority rights, Baskın Oran labels this obstructive mindset as the Sèvres syndrome or paranoia—the fear that the recognition of diversity and granting rights and freedoms would result in the collapse of the Republic, disintegration of the state, and partitioning of the country. The continuation of terrorist acts, the end of ceasefire by the People's Defense Force, the hard-line militant wing of the PKK (now Kurdistan People's Congress, or Kongra-Gel) in June 2004, and the resurgence of military clashes in the Southeast, which claim a few lives on daily basis and caused 147 deaths during first five months of 2005,[3] rekindle such fears and nationalistic fervors. The city of Diyarbakır has been already redrawn into the chaos and militarism of the 1990s on 29 March 2006, when the demonstrators at the funeral of PKK guerillas were responded by unrestrained military and police forces, and several people, including children, were killed.

Economic liberalization, especially privatization, is also brought up as an impediment to the improvement of human rights conditions. Privatization of the state-owned economic enterprises (SEEs) is the most obvious, and its negative consequences for labor rights are addressed by Weisband and Öner, in Chapter 7. Since the Turkish privatization program has largely lacked regulatory mechanisms (Ercan and Öniş 2001, 117), and the regulation of economic enterprises, public or private, has been generally weak and inconsistent, further deterioration of labor and environmental rights is a likely outcome of privatization. Most important point about the privatization process in Turkey, however, is the fact that it has gone beyond the SEEs and included media sources, education, and even social services. The negative human rights implications of the corporate takeover of the news media and the privatization of education are discussed in Chapters 2 and 8 respectively. The increasing cost of living, high unemployment, declining real wages, combined with a decline in social services, have increased the out-of-pocket expenses and need for assistance, especially for the urban poor. The result has been de facto privatization of social services. In fact, it is often pointed out that by capitalizing on this phenomenon and organizing charity networks in urban slums, Islamist parties have been able to expand their constituencies (White 2002; Pope and Pope 1999, 327–37; Mango 1994, 80–82; Kalaycıoğlu 2001).

Ironically, even the human rights organizations that were established and peopled by left-wing activists have been mostly mute on the continuous violations of social and economic rights. Most prominent human rights NGOs have focused on the issues of torture, arbitrary arrests and imprisonment, violation of due process and prisoners' rights, and the repression of the freedom of thought, speech, and religion. Labor unions, although relentless in bringing up declining wages and increasing poverty in press releases and conferences, have been ineffective in reaching beyond their immediate constituencies and reluctant (or unable) to formulate their demands in human rights terms.

The authors also agree that Turkey's candidacy to European Union membership has been a facilitator, if not the engine, of the desire to amend laws in favor of civil and political rights. However, the internalization of the "European" human rights standards both by the state officials and the public will be crucial. Human rights organizations and advocates continue to experience harassment and prosecution by the state and various forms of attacks by private actors. The resentment and backlash were already evident in public protests that reportedly included slogans such as "damned with human rights" (*kahrolsun insan hakları*), in the early 1990s (Bozarslan 2001, 50). The Justice and Development Party (AKP, Adalet ve Kalkınma Partisi, AKP) government, while eager to make Turkey an

EU member, has been hesitant on some issues, especially on gender equality and sexual freedom, and seems to be interested in pushing for change in some areas only when it feels the EU pressure.

The impact of the EU on social and economic rights is more dubious. While the European Social Charter and the EU's labor standards require Turkey to pay attention to and seek improvement in economic and labor rights as well, other factors, also stemming from Europe, would pull the country in the opposite direction. First, the current EU members' economic and social policies reveal a shift from commitment to social welfare and security to increasing productivity and trade competitiveness. Second, the EU membership also demands and encourages the privatization and liberalization of the candidate state's economy. In fact a less known aspect of the famous Copenhagen criteria is "the existence of a functioning market economy as well as the capacity to cope with competitive pressure and market forces within the Union," and the economic requirements of the EU are noticeably in tune with the International Monetary Fund prescriptions (Eder 2003) that have been guiding the Turkish economy since the beginning of 1980. Finally, and very important for a country like Turkey, is the unambiguous decline in financial assistance from the EU to the recent candidates. In sum, the rising tide of neoliberalism, which is neither rebuked nor fought back by the EU governance, does not promise a bright prospect for social and economic rights in Turkey (or in other EU states).

Although on the rise, the human rights discourse in Turkey seems to be limited to the classical liberal, or Lockean, understanding of human rights, which defines rights narrowly and as individual claims against the state (Z. F. Arat 1999). Thus, human rights debates and struggles focus on the elimination of violations that are ordered or directly and deliberately carried out by state officials. The comment of a prominent male human rights leader is illustrative: campaigning against capital punishment in the 1990s, he complained about the media attention devoted to the honor killings for "exaggerating this women thing to the level of a human rights violation and therefore diminishing the power of human rights" (as reported by Pervizat 2003). If not blatant sexism and assigning a lesser value to women's lives, it is the narrow conceptualization of human rights that prevents this human rights activist from grasping the fact that honor killings, too, constitute a form of capital punishment and summary execution. His state-centric approach also misplaces the urgency: while at least 200 women and girls have been killed every year by their families for "violating the family honor" (World Organization against Torture 2003), there was a de facto moratorium on court-ordered death sentences for more than 20 years!

Nevertheless, the increase in human rights activism, the recent changes in laws, at least a rhetorical commitment to human rights by state officials, and the influence of the EU promise improvements at least with regard to civil and political rights. The sustainability and expansion of the progress to cover the full spectrum of human rights, however, demand more from all actors. Among other things, it requires the currently fragmented social movements—labor movement, women's movement, environmentalist movement, and human rights movement—to see the *common* thread of human rights in their *overlapping* goals and to collaborate with each other in promoting human rights as an indivisible whole—and continue to put pressure on policy makers and state officials.

The Turkish Case in International and Theoretical Contexts

INTERDEPENDENCY AND INDIVISIBILITY OF HUMAN RIGHTS

Although this book project was undertaken with a clear division of labor among the authors and each author focuses on a specific human rights issue, some issues keep surfacing in several chapters. The most notable cluster is around the Kurdish identity and on the rights of Kurdish citizens. Practically all chapters touch upon the human rights violations experienced by this ethnic group. In addition to the O'Neil chapter that focuses on the importance of language rights for the national identity of Kurds, Oran's chapter argues that the Lausanne Treaty actually protects those rights, among others. Gök and Ilgaz point to the discrimination in access to education in predominantly Kurdish populated areas and note the denial of the right to education in one's mother tongue. Çatalbaş examines the removal of the ban on publishing and broadcasting in Kurdish, along with other issues related to the freedom of press. As documented by Özerdem and Jacoby, Kurds have faced further repression and hardship as internally displaced people. Çalı addresses how the advocacy of the rights of Kurds has worked against some human rights NGOs, which have been attempted to be discredited by the state for being partial and "ethnic." Finally, again Oran's historical and interpretive piece allows us to understand why the talk of ethnicity, the acknowledgment of diversity, and the advocacy of nondiscrimination are still touchy subjects, and how they are used by state officials to justify the repression of rights in general. These intersecting themes and observations not only underscore the multiple jeopardy faced by Kurds but also corroborate that the human rights issues pertaining to this particular group (or others) are not isolated from other human rights issues.

What may appear to be an element of redundancy in this case denotes and confirms a normative foundation of the International Bill of Rights: *human rights are not separable but interdependent and indivisible.* The principles of interdependency and indivisibility of human rights were recognized in several international forums. They were explicitly asserted first in the final document of the International Human Rights Conference, held in Teheran in 1963, and then reiterated at the Vienna Conference in 1993 (Alston 1993).

The overlapping human rights references in this volume reveal the complex connections among human rights, as echoed in the principles of interdependency and indivisibility. They show that individuals who face one type of repression or discrimination are subject to other types of violations (e.g., lacking freedom of expression, many Kurdish citizens are also subject to political repression, forced migration/displacement, lack of education). They also demonstrate that the denial of some rights to some groups or individuals would trigger further violations for other segments of the population (e.g., the repression of Kurdish identity prompts the repression of the freedom of expression and press for many non-Kurds who attempt to address the "Kurdish question"; or, the denial of employment or livable wages to adults (parents) bring about the violations of children's rights, as children lose access to education and/or become child laborers).

THE TOLERANCE/DISCRIMINATION AND RECOGNITION/ASSIMILATION NEXUS

Tolerance and discrimination tend to be treated as opposites. Most dictionaries define *discrimination* as "unfair treatment of one person or group, usually because of *prejudice* about race, ethnic group, age group, religion, or gender" (*Encarta World English Dictionary*, North American ed.), or as "*prejudiced* or *prejudicial* outlook, action, or treatment" (*Merriam-Webster's Online Dictionary*, 10th ed.; emphasis added), and list *tolerance* as an antonym of *prejudice*.

Similarly, when state policies toward different groups are considered, *recognition* of a group and its distinct identity and *assimilation* are regarded as opposites, and recognition is associated with tolerance, thus expected to involve no discrimination. Contrary to this assumption, recognition can go hand in hand with discrimination, and Turkey constitutes an excellent case to illustrate that recognition maybe more discriminatory than assimilation, if the recognized "others" are tolerated to exist but *not* accepted (as equals).

The Lausanne Treaty forced the Turkish state to recognize non-Muslims as minorities and protect their rights and cultural-religious identity. As noted by Baskın Oran in this book, the Republic of Turkey recognized Armenians, Greek Orthodox, and Jews as "distinct" groups and allowed them to speak and study their languages, practice their religion, and preserve other cultural practices.[4] Muslims, on the other hand, were assumed to be homogenous; there was no recognition of the diversity in terms of ethnicity, language, or religious beliefs. The expectation or plan was to blend all into a Turkish nationality, the demarcation of which would be mainly the language.

The state's approach to the Greek Orthodox and Kurdish populations—two groups that are explicitly discussed in this volume—has exhibited two contrasting policies, recognition and assimilation, respectively. While Greeks were recognized, thus tolerated to exist as a distinct group and allowed to maintain their religion, language, schools, press, and so on, they were considered as non-Turkish, and sometimes treated as foreigners. As such, they were subjected to discrimination through the denial of access to important military, bureaucratic, and political posts, and at times in other areas such as taxation. Treated with suspicion, their religious and educational institutions were not allowed to operate freely. Kurds, on the other hand, were denied forming or claiming a distinct ethnic identity, and, by the same token, they were not subject to official discrimination in the form of exclusion, either. They were considered "mountain Turks" to be taught "proper Turkish," "civilized," and incorporated into the "modern" Turkish life. Assimilated Kurds could move on the social and political ladder and occupy top positions in public office. As aptly noted by Will Kymlicka, "The problem is not that Turkey refuses to accept Kurds as Turkish citizens. The problem is precisely its attempt to force Kurds to see themselves as Turks" (2001, 247). The juxtaposition of the Greek Orthodox and Kurdish experience show that while tolerance (recognition) was accompanied by discrimination, intolerance in the form of assimilation appeared with nondiscrimination. What has been consistent in this dualistic approach was granting full citizenship rights only to those who were willing to become "Turks," both linguistically and religiously (at least nominally).[5]

Repressing ethnic, linguistic, or other identities or consenting to differences through discrimination has not been unique to Turkey. In fact, in some other societies, particularly where racism is prevalent, discrimination could reach the level of rejecting even those who are willing to assimilate or taking measures (e.g., official segregation) to prevent assimilation and integration efforts by the "other" (Kymlicka 2001). "Universalism" of human rights, however, objects to both forced assimilation and mere tolerance. Equality in dignity calls for the acceptance of differences without discrimination.

THE RULE OF LAW AND HUMAN RIGHTS ADVOCACY

Due process rights have been frequently violated in Turkey, and abuse in detention or prison, including torture, have been endemic (*Prison*

Conditions in Turkey 1989; *Turkey: End Sexual Violence against Women in Custody!* 2003; *Turkey: Torture and Medical Neglect of Prisoners* 1988). Especially since the late 1980s, all governments would speak against torture, but none has acknowledged its scope and systematic use. Only for a brief period, between 1998 and 2000, the Human Rights Investigation Commission of the parliament attempted to document prison conditions and abuse, issued several reports, and even displayed instruments of torture used by officials in front of the parliament building. However, the progression of such work was interrupted when Sema Pişkinsüt, the chair of the committee, was pushed out (Pişkinsüt 2001).

The commission's reports revealed that ill-treatment and torture were not exclusively used for political prisoners, and even juvenile delinquents were subject to cruelty and abuse. However, isolation and solitary confinement were reportedly employed more frequently for those who were incarcerated under the Antiterrorism Law. That is why, when F-type prisons, which involved one-person cells, were introduced by the government as an alternative to and an improvement over the dormitory-type cells (which had been subject to criticisms for overcrowding, violating privacy rights, and permitting interprisoner abuse), they immediately became target of criticisms by human rights advocates, who have seen them as a dangerous venue that would permit isolation and further violations. Also perceived as a scheme to prevent the development of solidarity or support systems among the inmates, F-type prisons have been protested by some prisoners, their families, and left-wing groups, in various forms, including hunger strikes (*Turkey: Call for Immediate Steps Against Isolation in "F-type"* 2002).

Even the harshest critics of these practices, however, cannot not characterize Turkey as a country that has totally lacked the rule of law. Although biases and arbitrariness appear to be higher compared to the countries to which it would like to relate, Turkey has largely maintained a legalistic system and relatively autonomous judiciary. For human rights, the aggravating factor in Turkey has been the content of the law, rather than its arbitrary implementation, manipulation by the government, or lawlessness. It is often overlooked that the rule of law is not necessarily liberating or protective of individual rights; if the law is discriminatory, unjust, and repressive, it does not buttress democracy but reinforces authoritarian rule (Rajagopal 2006).[6]

In Turkey, laws have been restrictive and allowed the interpretation of almost any act of opposition, advocacy of pluralism and diversity, demand for religious freedom, or criticism directed at the government or the military as a security threat, and permitted the criminalization of a wide range of thoughts and acts. Consequently, they condensed the political space and hampered political activism. Those who were not deterred were pushed to the margins of political life.

In industrial democracies, human rights organizations tend to be criticized for being bureaucratized—an ailment demonstrated in their over-reliance on litigation and lobbying—and for not being able to connect to political movements and grassroots activism. In Turkey and other developing countries, on the other hand, restrictive laws tend to push all who seek to change social and political conditions to political activism that is more adversarial and inclined to employ more contentious strategies, such as protest marches and demonstrations. As the state enforces repressive laws to silence protest and opposition groups, it radicalizes the activists; now, advocacy groups would have no option but to assume an antistate or antiregime posture. For example, if the law does not make a distinction between an act of terrorism and the advocacy of a terrorism suspect's right to fair trial, human rights advocates can find little room for lobbying for preventive measures or to redress violations through litigation. The self-perpetuating cycle of state repression and antigovernment protests is common in "illiberal democracies"—a termed coined by Fareed Zakaria (1997) to describe the political systems of new democracies that function as a procedural democracy with periodic, multiparty, and competitive elections, but that fall short of guaranteeing basic liberties and protecting the constitutional rights of citizens.

In Turkey, dissident voices, especially those that have been followers of or sympathetic to the leftist ideologies, Kurdish nationalism, and Islamist politics, have constituted a significant segment of the prison population. For most of the years through the 1990s, Turkey was placed at the top of the lists that ranked countries according to the number of journalists in prison (Yurdatapan 1998; Freedom House 2001), and both the print and broadcasting media have been subject to frequent charges of fines, bans, and closings. The fear of state sanctions often led to self-censorship. Human rights activists and organizations, being subject to discrediting and persecution by the state, have concentrated on antigovernment protest, publicizing violations, and shaming strategies.

Legislative reforms, which entail new laws that allow more freedoms and room for criticisms and opposition, can change the political culture, broaden the venues of activism, and facilitate a *liberal* rule of law. If laws are protective of human rights, then the breach of them by the state or other entities can be subject to litigation by the affected individuals or human rights groups. By using these favorable laws, human rights activists can expand their lobbying and litigation efforts for further improvements, both in legislation and implementation of laws. In other words, reforming repressive legislation may also change the character of human rights activism and enhance its effectiveness.

Liberalization of law would also allow removing the protective shield surrounding state officials, including the military. Reducing the political role of the military and making it accountable constitute the toughest challenge, but recently there have been a few promising cases of litigation for corruption (e.g., retired officers were individually held accountable, at least for their engagement in self-serving financial deals).

Liberal laws, however, do not generate liberal minds. The public outrage of some intellectuals, government officials, and parliamentary deputies from both the ruling and opposition parties about an international academic conference on the predicament of Ottoman Armenians is a telling episode. The conference was canceled the night before its scheduled opening on 25 May 2005, due to pressure from the minister of justice, Cemil Çiçek, who referred to the Turkish participants as "traitors."[7]

INTERNATIONAL NORM ADAPTABILITY AND STATE-CIVIL SOCIETY INTERACTION

A theoretical question that preoccupies most of the recent work in the bourgeoning human rights literature involves the conditions under which international human rights norms are adopted (Coicaud, Doyle, and Gardner 2003; Risse, Ropp, and Sikkink 1999; Katzenstein 1996; Goldstein and Keohane 1993). How can the violator states, and more recently nonstate actors (Andreopoulos, Arat, and Juviler 2006), be turned around to respect, or even to protect, human rights? Would shaming and imposing sanctions on the violator or engaging and rewarding the improved conduct be more effective? The longitudinal analysis of Turkey offers some clues to the norm adoptability and helps assessing the relative merits of the alternative "carrots" and "sticks" strategies.

First, on the impact of the formal recognition of human rights in legal documents, the case of Turkey tilts the balance in favor of the argument that incorporating rights in constitutional law or limiting participation in an international human rights regime by ratifying some human rights instruments does not necessarily yield a human rights-respecting system. Turkey has signed on to both the United Nations and the European human rights regimes since their beginnings, but without a major commitment to revise its own internal mechanisms and priorities.

Yet, we have already noted that some progress has taken place in most human rights areas (at least in the form of legal reforms) after Turkey's long-time aspiration to join the EU turned into a concrete effort in the late 1980s. This change shows that international human rights norms are more likely to be adopted by a country when there are anticipated gains. In the case of Turkey, EU membership has been the reward; it is expected to provide some further benefits, albeit the expected benefits are not clear or not likely to be the same for different segments of the society.

Various surveys conducted since the 1990s place the level of public support for Turkey's EU membership at 54–72 percent. A 2002 study by the Turkish Economic and Social Studies Foundation (TESEV) indicates that 64 percent of Turkish citizens would vote for EU membership and 30 percent against; 53 percent see the improvement of the economy and decline in unemployment as the most important benefits expected from membership ("TESEV Anketi" 2002). The business elite may concur on economic benefits and favor membership for its potential to boost the business investment and trade opportunities. A study of the members of the parliament (MP), conducted in 2000, finds that 33 percent of the MPs saw the improvements with regard to human rights violations and democracy as the "major benefit" of acquiring EU membership; and other advantages are listed as follows: socioeconomic development (27 percent), becoming part of Europe/West (13 percent), free movement of goods, services, and people (5 percent), legal reform (5 percent), and various other benefits such as cultural development, globalization, and integration into the world system, the development of universal values, and an increase of state power (McLaren and Müftüler-Baç 2003).

Even the military has been in favor of EU membership, despite its reservations on some of the EU demands, such as political liberalization, concessions on the Cyprus issue, removing the extraordinary security measures in the southeast region, recognition of Kurdish identity and rights and, of course, reducing the military's influence over the country's political affairs. As noted by William Hale, "the military broadly supported the goal of eventual EU accession as a natural extension of Turkey's NATO membership, which would further cement its relationship with the western powers" (Hale 2003, 110). Although there have been occasional expressions of frustration with the increasing European demands, the top leadership reiterated the military's commitment to the accession process. For example, in March 2002, when General Tuncer Kılıç, the secretary of the National Security Council caused a commotion by suggesting that Turkey should abandon its membership bid, the chief of the General Staff, General Hüseyin Kıvrıkoğlu, stepped in immediately to define the EU membership as a "geostrategic" need for Turkey, diminishing Kılıç's view as a personal one that was not representative of the military's (Hale 2003, 124, n. 12).

While some people and organizations desire the EU membership for the sake of improving human rights, various other expectations, including that of the military leaders, show that the goal of the EU membership combines security issues and the promotion of human rights—two goals that are usually seen as irreconcilable and that call for a trade-off. Moreover, the changes that took place around the EU membership bid suggest that adopting international human rights norms does not necessarily stem from an "idealist" approach, but, as argued by Türkmen in Chapter 16, it can be a function of policies based on realpolitik as well.

The experience of Turkey also corroborates the importance of the institutional structure of international human rights regimes in advancing human rights. As demonstrated by the Türkmen and Smith chapters, if the regime includes some enforcement mechanisms, for example, the European Court of Human Rights, it can be more successful in stirring the country toward adopting international human rights norms.

Finally, in order to be able to trigger change, the acceptance and advocacy of international human rights norms have to encompass a broad cross-section of the society. Viable and autonomous (independent from the state, political parties, and international agencies) domestic human rights organizations are necessary but not sufficient to achieve change; a variety of civil society organizations has to come on board, and some state offcials and agencies have to be willing to promote human rights and collaborate with national NGOs.

Turkey has recorded significant progress on these critical conditions. In addition to the emergence of human rights organizations and the rise of women's rights movement in the 1980s, various other different, and perhaps unexpected, components of the society started to take pro-human rights stance. Powerful business groups, such as the Turkish Industrialists' and Businessmen's Association (TÜSİAD), which applauded and supported repressive military takeovers and regimes in the past, started to call for respect for human rights and democracy. Also particularly important is the change in the discourse of Kurdish nationalist leaders and Islamist groups. The recent official acknowledgment of the existence of Kurds as an ethnic and linguistic group and the state's consent to address their cultural claims can be largely attributed to the ability of the Kurdish diaspora in Europe and its leadership to reframe their plight in human rights terms and carry out a successful campaign in EU member states to rally support for their cause. Similarly, the moderation in the attitude of Islamist groups, now best demonstrated by the AKP, can be traced back to Necmettin Erbakan's resort to the ECHR to acquire justice, when his Welfare (Refah) Party was closed down by the Constitutional Court of Turkey.

Yet, changes in favor of human rights cannot be accomplished by pressure from the civil society and a few desperate or opportunist politicians alone. State agencies, at least a critical number among them, need to be willing to change their postures as well. However, pursuing pro-human rights reforms as a strategic maneuver toward the EU membership can be perilous. As reforms carried out to please some outsiders may cause nationalist backlash, shifts in the EU politics and collisions in negotiations can retard the human rights agenda. Changes in favor of human rights are not irreversible. After the 11 September attacks, we have already witnessed many democratic countries adopting antiterrorism laws and executive orders that undermine their long-lasting tradition of respect for individual liberties and the right to privacy. Reversals are likely to be more common and severe in societies that have not established institutional mechanisms to protect human rights.

Summary

This volume finds the root causes of human rights violations in Turkey in the authoritarian, nationalist, patriarchal, and assimilationist history and political culture of the country, which were shaped by the national security and modernization concerns raised in the 1920s. The authors tend to approve the recent trend of change and hold an optimistic view about the prospect of human rights in Turkey. Turkey's aspiration to acquire full membership in the EU is seen as a catalyst for change, if not the main reason, and various nongovernmental organizations are credited for changing the discourse and influencing the content of the reforms. Nevertheless, some cautionary tales have accumulated in the country's journey toward establishing democracy and respect for human rights, and the possibility of a significant backlash cannot be ruled out.

Although its current condition includes some desirable elements, given its painful history and still mounting problems, Turkey presents a model that can be hardly recommended for wholesale emulation. Nevertheless, when examined at the intersection of domestic and international politics, the Turkish experience provides valuable policy lessons, as well as propositions for normative and empirical theories of human rights. It confirms and stresses the interdependency of human rights, the danger of the coexistence of tolerance for difference with discrimination, and the importance of strong enforcement mechanisms and rewards for norm adoptability. The implicit strategic guidelines for human rights advocates include cooperation with different rights-oriented groups and establishing a delicate balance between maintaining autonomy and collaborating with the state.

A topic not addressed in this book is the role of Turkey's allies in influencing the successive governments' human rights approach and policies. The subject is critical and deserves to be examined in a separate comprehensive volume. Nevertheless, it should be noted that European countries have been largely indifferent to the human right violations in Turkey until the 1980s, and the United States kept its silence much longer. The impact of this complicit inaction is reinforced by their competition in the arms market, where Turkey has been courted as a significant buyer.[8]

Notes

Chapter 1. Collision and Crossroads: Introducing Human Rights in Turkey

I am grateful to Hasan Can Arat for his comments on a draft of this chapter. With his love for the country and concern about its people, he could approach my findings and arguments with a different sensibility and keep me cognizant of the human dimension and implications of social research.

1. The UNDP *Human Development Report 2000* indicates that "the distance between the incomes of the richest and poorest country was about 3 to 1 in 1820, 35 to 1 in 1950, 44 to 1 in 1973, and 72 to 1 in 1992"; a "study of worldwide income distribution among households shows a sharp rise in inequality—with the Gini coefficient deteriorating from 0.63 in 1988 to 0.66 in 1993"; and the "gaps between rich and poor are widening in many countries," industrial and developing (6).

2. The trend was set before September 2001, at the end of the Cold War. S. Kuznetsov of ITAR-TASS (17 January 1992) noted: "The United States has launched an off-stage campaign to prompt the former Soviet Central Asian Republics to adhere to the Turkish Model of development, not to the example of Iranian Islamic fundamentalists." A. Nasibov of BBC (11 February 1992) repeats the same argument, adding, "Washington believes this is exactly that path of development on which Kazakhstan and Kyrgyzstan are now embarking." About a decade later, the model was seen as applicable to a larger geography. As reported by Sedat Ergin in the *Turkish Daily News* (21 January 2001), "Vice President Dick Cheney told [Turkish Prime Minister] Ecevit that with its sound Islamic traditions and democratic and secular system, Turkey constituted the best example not only for Afghanistan but for the entire Islamic world." For more on the "Turkish model," see Özkaleli and Özkaleli 2003.

3. In the absence of a better term, *Islamist* is employed in reference to individuals and groups that advocate a stronger role for religion in public life and use Islam as the main reference in shaping their political ideology or formulating public policy.

4. For a human rights theory of instability of democracy in developing countries and the application of the theory to explain the military interventions in Turkey, see Z. F. Arat 2003a.

5. Law No. 3686, dated 5 December 1990. It is announced in the official gazette, *Resmi Gazete*, no. 20719, 8 December 1990.

Chapter 2. Freedom of Press and Broadcasting

1. In 1994, 45 of 96 private radio stations and 19 of 71 television channels were controlled by various Islamist groups. See Atabey 1998, 78.

Chapter 3. The Minority Concept and Rights in Turkey: The Lausanne Peace Treaty and Current Issues

This chapter is a summary of parts of a book by the author, *Türkiye'de Azınlıklar: Kavramlar—teori—Lozan—iç mevzuat—içtihat—uygulama* (İstanbul: İletişim, 2004). A different version was also published in France, "National Sovereignty Concept: Turkey and Its Internal Minorities," *Cahiers d'Études sur la Mediterranée Orientale et le Monde Turco-Iranien (CEMOTI)* 36 (2003): 33–62.

1. The criterion in question is mentioned in Articles 8, 9/2, and 12. For the full text of the Treaty, see Thornberry 1994, 299–403.
2. Supreme Court of Appeals, First Legislative Branch, ruling dated 24 June 1975, no. 3648-6594. See Reyna and Şen 1994, 91–92.
3. Dated 11 December 1975, no. E:975/11168, K:975/12352; see Reyna and Şen 1994, 93.
4. Interview with Professor Turgut Tarhanlı, 10 February 2003, İstanbul.
5. See "Draft Resolution Submitted by the Turkish Delegation," in *Lozan Barış Konferansı*, 167.
6. This review is mainly based on Ayzit (2002).
7. Unless otherwise is indicated, information on this subject is mainly based on a study by Aliefendioğlu (2002), a former member of the Turkish Constitutional Court.
8. After the declaration of the republic in October 1923, M. Kemal started to use "Türk" instead of "Türkiye"; had he not done so, he would have enhanced the cultural integration in Turkey. For a content analysis of his five-volume speeches for these two terms, see Oran 1999, 209–11.
9. *Agos* (İstanbul weekly published by the Armenian community in Turkey), no. 361, 28 February 2003. Interestingly "The Subcommittee for Minorities" does not take place in the formal state apparatus, nor is there any information about it, but its decisions on behalf of protecting "national security" are cited in official documents presented to the courts. On 24 February 2004 it was announced that the subcommittee was abolished on 5 January 2004 by a government secret decree. *Hürriyet*, 24 February 2004.
10. *Partie civile* is someone whose main interests are directly and badly hurt, and who can therefore take part in the case with powers similar to the prosecutor: questioning the witnesses, calling for new ones, appealing to a higher judicial authority, and so on. For example, a fifteen-year-old boy whose schooling expenses are paid by his father can apply to become a *partie civile* against the killer of his father.

Chapter 4. The Human Rights Condition of the Rum Orthodox

The author would like to thank Athanasios Bourtsos, Anastasia Piperi, and Sofia Ntornta for their library assistance. The responsibility for the content of the chapter rests entirely with the author.

1. I use the term *Rum Orthodox* instead of *Greeks*—which is used in the 1923 Convention concerning the Exchange of Greek and Turkish Populations, signed at Lausanne on 30 January 1923—to underline the fact that members of the minority think of themselves as Romii, an identity that emphasizes the Orthodox Christian tradition. The Rum Orthodox trace their lineage back to the Byzantine tradition and the Rum millet within the millet system of the Ottoman Empire. The emphasis on the religious dimension is maintained to include references to the Muslim minority in Western Thrace, Greece, which is composed of predominantly ethnic Turks.

2. I owe this argument to the comments by Zehra Arat on an earlier draft of this chapter.

3. An important study that views the population exchange as ethnic cleansing in the context of nation building is Preece 1998. For a recent appraisal of the 1923 compulsory population exchange see Hirschon 2003. I thank Vassiliki Chryssanthopoulou for introducing me to the work of Hirschon.

4. The Convention concerning the Exchange of Greek and Turkish Populations, signed at Lausanne in 1923, specifically refers to Greek inhabitants of Constantinople and Muslim inhabitants of Western Thrace. Turkish nationals of Greek Orthodox religion are mentioned as Greeks and Greek nationals of the Muslim religion as Muslims. For the full text of the Convention, see Psomiades 1968. It was upon Turkey's insistence that the Convention adopted a religious instead of a linguistic demarcation of groups. See Rozakis 1966, 116; Heraclides 2001, 306.

5. Foreign Minister Fatin Zorlu sent a telegram from London on the eve of the conference to Menderes, asking him to take active measures that would exhibit forcefully Turkish resentment over Greek demands for self-determination in Cyprus (Linardatos 1978, 334–35); indicating that "a little activity would be useful," Zorlu meant a demonstration that would aid his bargaining position in London (Weiker 1963, 34). Turkish officials reasoned that by pointing to street demonstrations in Turkey, they could strengthen the government's hand over Cyprus at the London conference (Hale 1994, 95). Reşat Kasaba (1997, 28) argues that the September events did not happen in a vacuum, but the Cyprus issue was manipulated by Turkish officials to incite nationalist passions among a mob that rallied against the Rum Orthodox in Turkey.

6. It is ironic that as early as May 1963, Greek Foreign Minister Evangelos Averoff-Tositsas had conveyed to Greek Cypriot leaders his strong reservations that any unilateral action on Cyprus would have adverse effects on the Rum Orthodox community and the Ecumenical Patriarchate (Vlachos 1980, 276).

7. Patriarch Demetrios raised the issue of reopening in his meetings with President Clinton on 17 November 1999 and with President George W. Bush on 5 March 2002.

8. Turkey and minority members in Western Thrace charge Greek authorities with violations of the agreements. Greeks, in response, use the reciprocity principle to limit the number of exchange teachers from Turkey (Human Rights Watch, Greece 1999, 10–11) and maintain that the two protocols issued recommendations and were not legally binding upon the parties (Blatsiotis 1997, 321–23. Penelope Stathi (1997, 67) states that the 1968 Educational Protocol was not ratified by Greece and was not published anywhere. Irini Sarioglou (2004, 201–28) uses declassified documents to shed more light on the 1968 Education Protocol.

Chapter 5. Linguistic Human Rights and the Rights of Kurds

1. Kurds demanded education in Kurdish long before the establishment of the Republic of Turkey. In 1906, Sayyid Nursi wrote to the sultan of the Ottoman Empire and requested that Kurdish-speaking teachers be sent to the east of what is now Turkey in order to provide Kurds with a secular education, arguing that this would help produce "good Ottoman citizens." See McDowell 2000, 93.

2. General Comment no. 23 of the monitoring committee recognized the negative nature of the rights provided for in Article 27. However, the committee also pointed out that a right does exist and that it cannot be denied.

3. There are numerous agreements from all regions of the world but my focus here remains on Europe, as the agreements concluded by European states are the most germane to the situation of the Kurds in Turkey. For a discussion of agreements impacting linguistic rights not limited to Europe, see de Varennes 1996.

Chapter 6. Freedom of Religion: Secularist Policies and Islamic Challenges

1. The principle put forward in the UDHR is reiterated in the International Covenant for Civil and Political Rights (ICCPR) and further elaborated on in the 1981 UN Declaration on the Elimination of All Forms of Intolerance and Discrimination Based on Religion or Belief. ICCPR uses a slightly different expression and does not explicitly mention the freedom to change one's religion or belief.

2. The principle of equal dignity and rights is put forward in Article 1 of the UDHR. Article 2 protects individuals against discrimination on the basis of religion or belief, and Article 7 provides for equality before the law, also beyond the scope of religious liberty. Similarly, the general limitations applicable to the rights and freedoms, allowed by Articles 29 and 30, are themselves consistent with the principle of nondiscrimination.

3. The ulema, the class of religious scholars, belonged to the ruling elite and were in charge of most institutions of education and justice. In addition, regulations promulgated by the Ottoman sultans were approved by the Sheik al-Islam, the foremost religious dignitary of the empire. Members of the religious institutions were appointed and could be dismissed by the sultan. Theoretically, ulema had the right to invalidate any act of the sultan, if they felt it was in conflict with the Islamic jurisprudence, but they rarely did so. Furthermore, the invalidation could only take the form of contrary opinions formulated by the Sheik al-Islam who had no right to interfere directly in the government or in legal administration.

4. Under the 1961 Constitution, even proposing obligatory religious education in a party program could be reason for outlawing the party.

5. Article 19 and Article 24 of the Constitutions of 1961 and 1924 respectively.

6. This constitutional stipulation prohibits the exploitation of religion or religious feelings for the purpose of political and personal benefit. Corresponding laws in the Turkish Penal Code provide implementation for the constitutional provisions concerning secularism. See Özbudun 1996, 31.

7. Audi and Wolterstorff (1997) contend that liberal democracy need not protect, in the name of religious freedom, practices that violate basic human rights, but they also admit the difficulty in determining the range of these rights or the appropriate state sanctions that can be imposed on violators.

8. Although the Constitution specifies that no individual shall be compelled

to reveal his religious faith and belief (Article 19, 1962), the religious and sectarian identity of every Turkish citizen is stated in his or her birth certificate.

9. This right had been de facto taken away since 1936. See Özbudun and Yazıcı 2005, 9.

10. This is what John Rawls argues when discussing the possible dynamics of transition toward an overlapping consensus. See Rawls 1993, 165.

11. The underlying principle here is *tawhid*, or the Quranic doctrine of monotheism that lies at the heart of the Muslim religion. The doctrine of *tawhid* establishes the absolute centrality of God in the entire system of existence as the sole locus of creation, preservation, guidance, and judgment. See Rahman 1979. In the social realm, the doctrine of *tawhid* is interpreted in a way that claims relevance for Islamic values in all spheres of life. The idea of a moral or political space that is left entirely to the requirements of prudence or any other secular logic is not considered acceptable.

12. The divine will expressing itself in the realm of beings as well as through revelation.

13. İlyas Üzüm notes: "The fundamental sources of Islam do not provide doctrinal material for a total sociopolitical project or a specific model of political organization. Quranic references to *imamat* (imamate, or religious leadership), *khalifat* (caliphate, the office of Muhammad's successor), *hakimiya* (sovereignty), etc. neither specify institutions of power nor amount to a model. There is almost a total silence on the rules of succession and specific institutional arrangements. In the area of government, Quran merely lays down general precepts such as not violating the rights of others, the principles of consultation and agreement, giving everyone his due, and embracing justice" (1997, 58).

14. For example, Ali Bulaç (1992, 110) advocates a social contract theory, depicting unforced consent of contracting parties as the basis of a legitimate political organization in a pluralist society.

15. Here I define the term *liberal* in the sense of "political liberalism" as elaborated by Rawls (1993). This theoretical framework limits the relevance of liberal values to basic social and political institutions, and to the fundamental procedures of decision making in the public sphere. Aspects of life not pertaining to the basic structure of society can be legitimately organized according to nonliberal principles.

Chapter 7. So Near, Yet So Far: Freedom of Association and Workers' Rights

1. Also Sera Öner's interviews at Center for Improvement of State Owned Enterprises (Kamu İşletmeciliğini Geliştirme Merkezi Vakfı, KİGEM), Ankara, 27 May 2002.

2. KİGEM, interview by Sera Öner, Ankara, 27 May 2002.

3. For suggested solutions, see Karadeniz 1999, 428.

4. The implications were outlined by Yıldırım Koç in an interview at TÜRK-İŞ headquarters, Ankara, 20 December 2004.

5. These issues have appeared in various Benchmark and Recommendation Drafts presented to governments over the last two decades by various unions and confederations, including TÜRK-İŞ, DİSK, METAL-İŞ, and PETROL-İŞ.

6. The information on issues on complaints are gathered from the following sources: Koç 2000; Report on Complaints of the Confederation of Turkish Labor Unions (TÜRK-İŞ) and the Confederation of Revolutionary Workers' Trade

Unions of Turkey (DİSK), 1948, no. 87; Complaint against the Government of Turkey presented by DİSK; interviews conducted between 21 May–4 June 2002 and in February 2005 with the representatives and lawyers of PETROL-İŞ (İstanbul), EĞİTİM-SEN (Ankara), TÜRK-İŞ (Ankara), TİSK (Türkiye İşverenler Sendikaları Konfederasyonu), KİGEM (Kamu İşletmeciliğini Geliştirme Merkezi-Ankara); and interviews with Professors Metin Kutal (Galatasaray University), Adnan Güriz (Ankara University), Erinç Yeldan (Bilkent University), and Mesut Gülmez (TODAİE).

7. Interview with Yıldırım Koç, headquarters of TÜRK-İŞ, Ankara, 12 December 2004.

8. Köstekli 2002, 181–82; interview with İlyas Köstekli, by Sera Öner, Ankara, 20 May 2002.

9. Sera Öner's interview with EĞİTİM-SEN representatives and lawyers, 27 May 2002.

Chapter 8. The Right to Education

1. This did not mean that the Turkish state and the governing Republican People's Party (Cumhuriyet Halk Partisi, CHP) were opposed to private education. For example, in his 1925 opening speech of the Grand National Assembly, Atatürk asked wealthy people to establish private educational institutions (Ministry of National Education 1991).

2. Among the OECD countries, the level of public investment in education in Turkey is the lowest (3.5 percent,compared with OECD average of 5.7 percent of GDP). See Tomasevski (2002), par. 25.

3. Daily papers: *Star*, 29 July 2003 and 31 July 2003; *Yarın*, 18 July 2003; *Radikal*, 17 July 2003.

4. The wealthiest 6 percent avail themselves of 33 percent of the national income. The poorest 40 percent, comprising the lowest income groups, benefit from 11 to 12 percent of the national income. The top 1 percent of the income groups receive 16.6 percent of the national income. The rate of unemployment was 15.5 percent (3.5 million) in 2002. The gender gap is also wide: 76 percent of those employed are men and only 24 percent are women; women's labor force participation rate is 23 percent. See Sönmez (2003b, 2002, 15).

Chapter 9. Environmental Protection and Rights

1. The new bill (no. 5491) eliminated LECs.

2. For example, the Act on National Parks No. 2871 (1983) allows construction, mineral/petroleum exploration, and extraction in areas reserved as national and natural parks; and the Act on the Protection of Natural and Cultural Assets No. 2863 (1983) asserts the need to preserve assets, but then defines ownership and responsibility in conflicting terms.

3. The concept of "third-generation human rights" was coined by French jurist Karel Vasak, former director of the UNESCO Division of Human Rights and Peace. In a November 1977 speech, Vasak pointed to the three normative themes of the French Revolution—freedom, equality, and fraternity—as analogous to the basic values embodied by three different generations of human rights. Arguing that the third-generation human rights focus on fraternity, or solidarity, Vasak

identified five related rights: the right to development, the right to peace, *the right to environment*, the right to the ownership of the common heritage of humankind, and the right to communication. See Tseng 2003; Ksentini.

4. Dated 21 November 1986, Decree No. 1985/11 main, Decree No. 1986/29. See Aksoy 1999, 69.

Chapter 10. Conflict-Induced Internal Displacement

1. Article 2.7 of the UN Charter states that "nothing contained in the present Charter shall authorize the United Nations to intervene in matters which are essentially within the domestic jurisdiction of any state or shall require the Members to submit such matters to settlement under the present Charter." Adelman 2001, 8.

2. GAP stands for Güneydoğu Anadolu Projesi. It is a multisectoral, integrated regional development project carried out in nine provinces (Adıyaman, Batman, Diyarbakır, Gaziantep, Kilis, Mardin, Siirt, Şanlıurfa, Şırnak) in southeastern Anatolia—currently the least developed region in Turkey. It is not only limited to dams, hydroelectric power plants and irrigation systems. It also contains a significant investment program for the development of socioeconomic sectors such as agriculture, industry, urban and rural infrastructure, communication, education, health, culture, tourism, and other social services.

3. It is rightly argued that, at the national level, internal displacement is closely linked with the shortcomings of governance and ineffective cooperation between civil society and state with regard to promoting "respect for human rights—understood as the entire spectrum of universal norms, ranging from civil and political rights to economic, social, and cultural rights to minority rights" (Korn 1999, 99).

4. *Los Angeles Times*, 10 January 2000.

5. Cohen and Deng suggest that the EU role could be bolstered by international organizations with a more explicitly reformist remit. They advocate, for instance, "a more vigorous OSCE role with regard to forced displacement and Kurdish minority rights" (1998, 26).

Chapter 11. Turkish Asylum Policy and Human Rights

1. On recent immigration to Turkey, see Erder (2000); İçduygu and Keyman (2000); on emigration from Turkey, see Abadan-Unat (1995, 2002); Böcker (1996).

2. *Accession Partnership Document: 2000* adopted by the General Affairs Council of the European Union in December 2000. This document was updated in *Accession Partnership Document: 2003* in April 2003. Both documents can be accessed at: http://www.deltur.cec.eu.int (accessed 4 November 2004).

3. *Cruz Varas v. Sweden*, 20 March 1991, European Court of Human Rights, ser. A, no. 201; and *Vivarajah v. United Kingdom*, 30 October 1991, ser. A, no. 215. A similar ruling had also been announced in *Soering v. United Kingdom*, 7 July 1989, ser. A, no. 161.

4. In 2000, the Ministry for Labor Affairs and Social Welfare announced that there were approximately 1 million illegal immigrant workers in Turkey (*Radikal*, 30 December 2000). A few days later, the Ministry of Foreign Affairs put their numbers at 1.2 million (*Radikal*, 4 January 2001).

5. *Official Gazette*, no. 22127, 30 November 1994.

6. European Human Rights Court (Fourth Section), *Case of Jabari v. Turkey* (application no. 40035/98), Judgment, Strasbourg (11 July 2000): 7–8, http://www.echr.coe.int/Default.htm (accessed 7 July 2003).

7. For the ruling, see *Danıştay Dergisi* 8, nos. 30–31 (1978): 50.

8. For the cases and the court rulings, see UNHCR (2000b, 156–59).

9. For the case, see UNHCR (2000b, 120–24).

10. *Official Gazette*, no. 23582, 13 January 1999.

11. İltica ve Mülteci Konusunda Seminer (Seminar on Asylum and Refuge), held at Neva Palas Oteli, Ankara, 28 September–2 October 1998.

12. According to the MOI, between 1995 and 2002 there were more than 32,200 applications. About 16,000 of them were accepted by the Turkish authorities and approximately 12,000 were resettled outside Turkey with the assistance of the UNHCR.

13. On 28–29 December 2004, the Ankara branch office of the UNHCR held its third annual consultation meeting. More than 65 participants from Turkish nongovernmental organizations joined the meeting, along with the representatives from government agencies and universities.

14. For the tension between "combating irregular migration" and the protection of asylum in Turkey, see Kirişçi 2004.

Chapter 12. Women's Rights, Women's Organizations, and the State

1. I translate "Kadın Birliği" as "Woman's Union." Other sources use "Women's Federation" and "Women's League" for the same name.

2. According to the new article, the Woman's Union would work for promoting women to the level at which they could prove all kinds of responsibilities and interest regarding their social and political rights. Bozkır 2000, 22.

3. The extent of women's participation in the pre-parliamentary discussions of this law is not clear and can be revealed only after a detailed study of the relevant archival documents.

4. Women activists launched a campaign in 1987 against the battering of women in the home. In May, about 3000 women marched to protest domestic violence. Sirman 1989, 1.

5. Press release by KA-DER, 12 December 2002.

6. Survey research conducted by the author in February 2003.

7. The name of the group is derived from the fact that every Saturday they meet and protest for their "lost" sons and relatives who disappeared after being taken into police custody.

Chapter 13. The Effect of CEDAW on Women's Rights

1. Women Information Network in Turkey, http://www.die.gov.tr/tkba/English_TKBA/kadin_haklari.htm (accessed 9 March 2003).

2. The statistics are from the combined DGSPW and UNDP Report. See *Women in Turkey* 1999.

3. Information obtained from Yıldız Ecevit by e-mail in January 2004.

4. Article 440 defined adultery for woman as a married woman's involvement in a sexual act with a man who is not her husband. Article 441 defined an adulterous man as a married man who is involved with another woman in a continuous

relationship that resembles the one between a husband and wife. These different definitions allowed men and women to be punished differently for committing the same offense—adultery.

5. It is, however, considered to establish a ground for divorce for both men and women.

6. The four areas left out of the National Action Plan: women and poverty; women and armed conflict; human rights of women; and women and the environment.

7. Prepared by A. Feride Acar, Selma Acuner, and Nevin Şenol, for the General Directorate on the Status and Problems of Women, Response of the Republic of Turkey to the Questionnaire on Implementation of the Beijing Platform for Action, Ankara, May 1999.

8. Replies of the Turkish Delegation, Article 7.

9. Replies of the Turkish Delegation, Article 9.

10. Replies of the Turkish Delegation, Article 9.

11. Replies of the Turkish Delegation, Articles 15 and 16.

Chapter 14. Human Rights Discourse and Domestic Human Rights NGOs

1. On local appropriation of human rights, see Wilson 1997.

2. The data on these organizations were gathered through in-depth interviews conducted in Ankara in December 2001–January 2002 and July–August 2002 with the heads and members of HROs, human rights activists, and academics. The questions for the interviewees were unstructured and open-ended. All interviews were tape recorded and lasted from one and a half to three hours.

3. For the relationship between social movements and human rights, see Stammers 1999. On a comparative study of the emergence of social movements seeking civil and political rights in Brazil, Chile, Mexico, and Spain, see Forewaker and Landman 1997; on the emergence of human rights networks, see Sikkink 1996, 59.

4. This argument also holds for international human rights organizations. For example, Amnesty International initially defined its mandate as advocating amnesty to political prisoners but recently broadened its activities to include business conduct, women's rights, and so on.

5. Interview with Amnesty International, Turkey, desk officer (1972–86), Ankara, 18 April 2003, İstanbul.

6. Interview with Amnesty International, Turkey, desk officer (1972–86), Ankara, 18 April 2003.

7. Interview with the director of TİHV, Ankara, 3 June 2002.

8. Interview with former director of the İHD (1986–93), current director of TİHAK, Ankara, 4 January 2002; interview with director of the İHD, Ankara, 6 June 2002.

9. It should be noted that, in 1986, another association was established to assist the families of the detained and imprisoned left-wing victims of the coup, Solidarity Association of the Families of the Detained and Imprisoned (Tutuklu ve Hükümlü Aileleri Dayanışma Derneği, TAYAD). TAYAD was immediately banned, like a few other organizations, including Association for Rights and Freedoms (Haklar ve Özgürlükler Derneği) and Platform of Solidarity for the Revolutionary Prisoners (Devrimci Tutsaklarla Dayanışma Platformu), which did not affiliate themselves with a universal human rights discourse but emphasized their solidarity with the leftist/revolutionary political prisoners.

10. Interview with the director of the İHD, Ankara, 6 June 2002.

11. Interview with the deputy director of TİHV, Ankara, 1 June 2002.

12. The İHD statute (1986), par. 1.

13. On 6 May 2003, for example, the police raided and confiscated all the archives, documents, and computer equipment of the İHD, following a warrant by the State Security Court. The State Security Court charged the organization with a breach of Article 312 of the Turkish Penal Code, for "assisting and abetting illegal organizations."

14. Interview with the former director of the İHD (1986–93), Ankara, 4 January 2002.

15. For example, *Akdıvar and Others v. Turkey* (Application No. 2189393), judgment of the European Court of Human Rights (ECHR), (16 September1996); *Kurt v. Turkey* (Application No. 24276/94), judgment of the ECHR (28 May 1998); *Çakıcı v. Turkey* (Application No. 23657/94), judgment of the ECHR (8 July 1999); *Timurtaş v. Turkey* (Applica(tion No. 25531/94), judgment of the ECHR (13 June 2000); *Dulaş v. Turkey* (Application No. 25801/94), judgment of the ECHR (30 January 2001); *Bilgin v. Turkey* (Application No. 25659/94), judgment of the ECHR (17 July 2001); *Akdeniz and Others v. Turkey* (Application No. 23954/94), judgment of the ECHR (31 May 2001): database of the Case Law of the European Court of Human Rights (HUDOC), http://cmiskp.echr.coe.int/tkp197/search.asp?skin=hudoc-en (accessed 6 June 2005).

16. Interview with the director of the Mazlum-Der, Ankara, 6 June 2002.

17. Gottfried Plagemann argues that the Mazlum-Der was originally interested in formulating an Islamic understanding of human rights, but it has later chosen to embrace the internationally recognized norms, without presenting an Islamic interpretation of their meaning (2001, 377–85).

18. The director of the Mazlum-Der states that one of their future plans involves the formation of a network of human rights organizations extending from the Central Asia to the Middle East and the Balkans, but he admits that they face financial and other difficulties to realize this project. The Mazlum-Der's relations with HROs in these regions are limited compared to its relations with several NGOs based in western Europe. They also find the Muslim human rights organizations based in the West to be fragmented and disinterested in formulating global policies that would address the problems of Muslims in a comprehensive and consistent manner. Interview with the director of the Mazlum Der, Ankara, June 2002.

19. Interview with the director of the Mazlum Der, Ankara, 6 June 2002.

20. Interview with the director of TİHAK , Ankara, 5 January 2002.

21. Interview with the deputy director of TİHAK, Ankara, 6 January 2002.

22. The statute of the TİHAK, Article 3, published in *Türkiye İnsan Hakları Kurumu Kuruluş Bildirgesi* 2000.

23. Despite the proclamations that human rights are "independent, indivisible and interdependent," as confirmed in the United Nations Vienna Programme of Action (1993), civil and political rights, and to some extent minority and cultural rights, receive more attention and enjoy closer monitoring mechanisms than do economic and social rights. The Copenhagen human rights criteria of the EU also set a similar order of priorities for accession to the EU.

24. The lack of professionally trained personnel and other resources is identified as serious impediments to the development of a multifaceted human rights policy and activism, both by the İHD and the Mazlum-Der.

25. Interview with the director of the İHD, Ankara, 6 June 2002. The president of the Mazlum-Der also points to the need of overcoming internal disagreements

within the organization about human rights principles. Interview with the director of the Mazlum-Der, Ankara, 6 June 2002.

26. The National Human Rights Institutions set up by the executive also do not conform to the principles of independence and impartiality set out by the Paris Principles on National Human Rights Institutions. *National Human Rights Institutions* 1995. The Parliamentary Human Rights Commission reports also indicate the shortcomings and the ineffectiveness of the human rights bodies established by the executive. For example, see the commission reports of 17–20 January 2003 in relation to Batman and Diyarbakır Human Rights Councils, at http://www.tbmm.gov.tr/komisyon/insanhak/insanhaklari.htm (accessed 1 February 2003).

27. For example, Mazlum-Der press release, 13 July 2001, Mazlum-Der, Ankara.

28. Joint press release of TİHV and İHD, 10 December 2004; www.ihd.org.tr/ (accessed 20 December 2004).

29. Interview with the director of the TİHV, Ankara, 3 January 2001.

Chapter 15. Tensions and Dilemmas in Human Rights Education

I would like to thank Nergis Canefe for her support in writing this paper.

1. See Flowers et al. 2000. The Plan of Action of the UN Decade for Human Rights Education provides a more comprehensive definition of HRE as "training, dissemination and information efforts aimed at the building of a universal culture of human rights through the imparting of knowledge and skills and the molding of attitudes which are directed to the strengthening of human rights and fundamental freedoms . . . and the promotion of understanding, tolerance, gender equality, and friendship among all nations, indigenous peoples and racial, national, ethnic, religious and linguistic groups." General Assembly Resolution No. 49/184, 23 December 1994.

2. United Nations Vienna Programme of Action, par. 33–34.

3. *Tebliğler Dergisi* (May1998).

4. *Tebliğler Dergisi* (April 1999).

5. For the history of education in the process of modernization in Turkey, see Kazamias 1966.

6. Milli Eğitim Temel Kanunu (1), http://www.hukuki.net/kanun/1739.15.text.asp (accessed 7 June 2005).

7. For instance, although the National Committee's program indicates that Citizenship and Human Rights course textbooks should be revised by the committee before their approval, the Ministry of National Education did not submit any books to the committee until 2000. See İnsan Hakları Eğitimi On Yılı Ulusal Komitesi 2001, 271.

8. On different ways of incorporating human rights themes into school curricula see Tibbitts (n.d.).

9. The project has been conducted in cooperation with the Human Rights Committee of the Turkish Academy of Sciences, the Human Rights Foundation of Turkey, and the National Committee on the Decade for Human Rights Education.

Chapter 16. Turkey's Participation in Global and Regional Human Rights Regimes

1. Letter dated 23 September 1856 in "Instructions Respecting Financial and Administrative Reforms and the Protection of Christians in Turkey: 1856–75," *Turkey No. 17*, House of Lords, 1877, as quoted Barchard 2000, 41.

2. This information was gathered through a series of interviews with the officials at the Turkish Ministry of Foreign Affairs, Ankara, on 3 December 2001.

3. For example, special rapporteurs on torture, religious intolerance, arbitrary executions and disappearances, internally displaced people, and the right to education in the mother tongue traveled in different regions of the country and interviewed state and civil society representatives.

4. UN Document No. CRC/C/51/Add.4 of 8 August 2000.

5. As indicated by the visit of Turkish foreign minister İlter Türkmen to the president of the commission Gaston Thorn, on 12 January 1982. By disclosing his government's agenda on the return to democracy, the foreign minister had underlined the importance attached by Turkey to the EC's adequate perception of the political situation in the country, as commented by Baç 2001, 137.

6. Resolution on the Human Rights Situation in Turkey, Document No. A2–117/85, the European Parliament, 23 October 1985, in *Official Journal of the European Communities* C 343/60 (31 December 1985).

7. This act aimed at redefining the common policies of the community including foreign policy, and enlarging the functions of various organs, with particular emphasis on the EP.

8. Bulletin of the EC, 12 December 1989, 88.

9. Commission Report on Turkish Application, Brussels, 18 December 1989.

10. The charter consecrated democracy as the sole legitimate type of government, in the aftermath of the collapse of Soviet rule in Eastern Europe.

11. During this period, the European Parliament has passed numerous resolutions condemning Turkey's human rights policy; it awarded Ms. Leyla Zana, an imprisoned DEP deputy of Kurdish origin, the Sakharov Peace Prize; and Germany suspended its arms transfers to Turkey in order to prevent the use of German-made weapons against Kurds in the southeast.

12. At the Luxembourg Summit, Turkey's eligibility was made conditional upon the improvement of its human rights record, with a special emphasis on minority rights. Moreover, the commission report issued before the summit, "Agenda 2000," for the first time criticized the political role of the military in Turkey. Ankara reacted strongly, but the crisis was rapidly defused by mutual diplomatic efforts.

13. The program had the following objectives: ratification of the two UN covenants; implementation of the new human rights mechanisms; creation of an ombudsman post; decentralization; application of the Penal Procedure Code to those judged by the state security courts; independence of the High Council of Judges and Prosecutors from governmental authority; improvement of the legislation in favor of the freedom of expression; improvement of the rights of the non-Muslim minorities; abrogation of the state of emergency in the southeast and return of the evacuees to the region; legislation on the indemnity of victims of terror and antiterror measures; activation of the constitutional amendment project.

14. (a) "Proposal for a Council Decision on an Accession Partnership with Turkey," European Commission, Brussels, 8 November 2000; (b) the Copenhagen criteria: "Membership requires that the candidate country has achieved stability of institutions guaranteeing democracy, the rule of law, human rights, and respect for the protection of minorities, the existence of a functioning market economy as well as the capacity to cope with competitive pressure and market forces within the Union"(Excerpt from the Copenhagen Presidency Conclusions, 1993).

15. *Official Gazette*, 24 March 2001, no. 24352 bis.

16. The six parts are "Introduction," "Political Criteria," "Economic Criteria," "Capacity to Assume Membership Requirements," "Administrative Capacity for

Implementing the *Acquis Communautaire*," and "Evaluation of the Reforms from the Financial Perspective."

17. See "Political Criteria" in Turkish Ministry of Foreign Affairs 2001, 1–9.

18. For example, Article 1 on freedom of thought and expression has been amended in the light of Article 10 of the ECHR and the introductory part of "Political Criteria," sec. 2.1. See "Analytical Note on Constitutional Amendments from the Perspective of European Union Standards," Prime Ministry, Secretariat General for EU Affairs (Ankara, 4 October 2001).

19. Commission of European Communities, "2004 Regular Report on Turkey's Progress Toward Accession," Brussels, 6 October 2004, Press Release IP/04/1180.

Chapter 17. Leveraging Norms: The ECHR and Turkey's Human Rights Reforms

1. See "Turkey Accepted" 1990. Turkey recognized the jurisdiction of the Court only within "the boundaries of the national territory of the Republic of Turkey," thus eliding the issue of whether or not Ankara exercised control over northern Cyprus.

2. The Convention and a trove of ECHR case law and statistical information are available at http://www.echr.coe.int. The European Commission on Human Rights was established in 1954. Based in Strasbourg, France, the Commission and the Court comprised the "Strasbourg Institutions." Applications were lodged with the Commission, which would screen them before forwarding them to the Court. In 1998 the Commission and its functions were folded into the Court.

3. Quoted in Zorn and Van Winkle 2002, 2.

4. *Turkish Daily News* (8 September 2001).

5. "Turkish Constitutional Court President Says Political Bans to Harm Ties with EU." BBC Worldwide Monitoring (26 September 2002). Last accessed via Lexis-Nexis on 6 August 2006.

6. *Turkish Daily News* (15 October 2002).

7. See *Öcalan v. Turkey* (Application no. 46221/99), Judgment, 12 March 2003.

8. See *Aksoy v. Turkey* (Application no. 100/1995/606/694), Judgment, 26 November 1996, § 70 and § 78.

9. Quoted in Merrills 1988, 141–44.

10. See *Denmark v. Turkey* (Application no. 34382/97), Judgment, 5 April 2000.

11. Turkish Law No. 2845 on the Creation and Rules of Procedure of the National Security Courts.

12. See *Incal v. Turkey* (Application no. 41/1997/825/1031), Judgment, 9 June 1998; and *Çıraklar v. Turkey* (Application no. 70/1997/854/1061), Judgment, 28 October 1998.

13. *United Communist Party of Turkey* (Application no. 133/1996/752/951), Judgment, 30 January 1998; and *Freedom and Democracy Party v. Turkey* (Application no. 23885/94), Judgment, 8 December 1999.

14. See *Özgür Gündem v. Turkey* (Application no. 23144/93), Judgment, 16 March 2000, §§ 40, 42.

15. *Kalaç v. Turkey* (Application no. 20704/92), Judgment, 1 July 1997, § 8; and *Tepeli et Autres contre la Turquie* (Application no. 31876/96), Decision on Admissibility, 11 September 2001.

16. *Erdem contre la Turquie* (Application no. 26328/95) Decision as to Admissibility, 11 September 2001; *Josephides v. Turkey* (Application no. 21887/93) Decision as to Admissibility, 24 August 1999; and *Institute of French Priests and Others v. Turkey* (Application no. 00026308/95) Decision as to Admissibility, 14 December 2000.

17. See *Affaire Refah Partisi (Parti de la Prospérité) et Autres c. Turquie* (Application nos. 41340/98, 41342/98, 41343/98, 41344/98), Judgment, 31 July 2001, § 58 and § 66.

18. See *Şahin v. Turkey* (Application no. 44774/98), Judgment, 29 June 2004, § 66 and § 84.

19. See *Loizidou v. Turkey* (Application no. 40/1993/435/514), Judgment, 28 November 1996 and Judgment (just satisfaction) 28 July 1998; and *Cyprus v. Turkey* (Application no. 25781/94), Judgment, 10 May 2001.

Chapter 18. Conclusion: Turkey's Prospects and Broader Implications

1. The attempt to close down Eğitim-Sen was initiated by the military. A "confidential" memo, issued by General Köksal Karabay on behalf of the General Staff of the Turkish Armed Forces and sent to the Ministry of Labor and Social Security on 27 June 2003, indicated that Article 2, paragraph b, of the Eğitim-Sen bylaws, which spelled "[the union] advocates individuals' education in their mother tongue and development of their culture," was in violation of Articles 3 and 42 of the Constitution and thus that measures should be taken to change it. *Milliyet*, 4 September 2004.

2. *Turkey: Torture and Mistreatment in Pre-Trial Detention by Anti-Terror Police* 1997. As of April 2006, the draft of the new law, being short on provisions that would protect the right of the accused, appeared unpromising and bleak.

3. Press release by the Diyarbakır branch of the Human Rights Association, 9 June 2005.

4. The cultural-religious differences were already largely recognized and tolerated within the context of the Ottoman millet system, which was the institutionalized form of the earlier Muslim tradition that had recognized Jews and Christians (and later Buddhists and Hindus) as the people of the book who deserved protection under the Muslim rule. While these groups were allowed to practice their religions and customs, they were subject to various forms of discrimination. For a brief review of the Ottoman policies, see Aral 2004; Senturk 2005.

5. The current phase of the Sèvres syndrome, however, endangers even the acceptance of the assimilated, since the rising nationalist sentiments tend to question the sincerity and commitment of the converted and assimilated. A recent public preoccupation involves the identification of Sabateyists/Sabataists and exposing the "Jewish heritage of supposed Muslims." The label "Sabateyist" is driven form Sebatay Sevi (Sabbatai Sevi), an Ottoman rabbi who came forward with messianic claims in 1648 in İzmir. Encountered with death threats (or sentence) by the Jewish Orthodox leaders, he converted to Islam and assumed the name of Mehmet Efendi but secretly continued with his Jewish believes and teachings, which came to be known as Sabbatianism, a mystic Judaism.

6. It should be noted that advocates and leaders of passive resistance, or civil disobedience, such as Mahatma Gandhi and Martin Luther King, Jr., formulated their philosophy on the basis of making a distinction between "just" and "unjust" laws.

7. *Radikal*, 25 May 2005. The conference was eventually held in September 2005. Yet, it still stirred protests by ultranationalist groups and led to the prosecution of some journalists who reported the conference discussions.

8. See Tirman 1997; also numerous articles by Burak E. Bekdil and Ümit Engingsoy published in *Defense News*.

References

Abadan-Unat, Nermin. "Movements of Women and National Liberation." In *Women in the Developing World: Evidence from Turkey*, ed. Nermin Abadan-Unat. Monograph Series in World Affairs 22. Denver: Graduate School of International Studies, University of Denver, 1986. 11–25.

———. "Market Research and Public Opinion Polling in Turkey as an Agent of Social Change." In *Structural Change in Turkish Society*, ed. Mübeccel Kıray. Bloomington: Indiana University Press, 1991.

———. "Turkish Migration to Europe." In *The Cambridge Survey of World Migration*, ed. Robin Cohen. Cambridge: Cambridge University Press, 1995. 279–84.

———. *Bitmeyen Göç: Konuk İşçilikten Ulus-Ötesi Yurttaşlığa*. Istanbul: Bilgi University Publishing House, 2000.

Abadan-Unat, Nermin and Oya Tokgöz. "Turkish Women as Agents of Change in a Pluralistic Democracy." In *Women and Politics Worldwide*, ed. Barbara J. Nelson and Najma Chowdhury. New Haven, Conn.: Yale University Press, 1994. 705–20.

Acar, Feride. "Turkey." In *The First CEDAW Impact Study: Final Report*, ed. Marilou McPhedran, Susan Brazilli, Moana Erickson, and Andrew Byrnes. Toronto: Centre for Feminist Research, York University and International Women's Rights Project, 2000.

Acar, Feride, Selma Acuner, and Nevin Şenol. *Response of the Republic of Turkey to the Questionnaire on Implementation of the Beijing Platform for Action*. Ankara: General Directorate on the Status and Problems of Women, May 1999.

Adelman, Howard. "From Refugees to Forced Migration: The UNHCR and Human Security." *International Migration Review* 35, no. 1 (2001): 7–32.

Ahmad, Feroz. "The Transition to Democracy in Turkey." *Third World Quarterly* 7, no. 2 (1985): 221–27.

———. *The Making of Modern Turkey*. London: Routledge, 1994a.

———. "The Development of Working Class Consciousness in Turkey." In *Workers and Working Classes in the Middle East: Struggles, Histories, Historiographies*, ed. Zachary Lockman. Albany, N.Y.: SUNY Press, 1994b.133–63.

"Aitimata ton Christianon tis Tourkias" [Demands of Christians of Turkey]. *Anatoli* [Orient], November–December 2003.

Akal, Emel. "Women and Socialism in Turkey: The Case of Progressive Women's Organisation." M.S. thesis, Department of Sociology, Middle East Technical University, 1996.

Akar, Rıdvan. "If Only They Hadn't Left. If Only They Were Here . . . " In *Constantinople: City of Cities*. Athens: Ephesus, 2003. 235–50

Akıncı, Müslim. *The Formation and the Construction Period of Turkish Environmental Law*. Kocaeli: Kocaeli Book Club, 1996.

Aksoy, Selma. "Environmental Law in European Union and Turkey." M.S. thesis, University of Ankara, Social Sciences Institute, 1999.

Aktay, Yasin. *Türk Dininin Sosyolojik İmkanı*. Istanbul: İletişim Yayınları, 2000.

Akyüz, Yahya. *Türk Eğitim Tarihi*. Istanbul: Kültür Koleji Yayınları, 1994.

Alemdar, Korkmaz. "The Early Years of the Republican Press (1920–1950)." *Boğaziçi Journal* 18, nos. 1–2 (2004): 35–41.

Alert: Coordinating Committee of Press Freedom Organizations Calls on Turkey to Remove Criminal Defamation and Insult Laws. International Freedom of Expression Exchange. http://www.ifex.org/en/content/view/full/62743/ (accessed March 2005).

Alexandris, Alexis. *The Greek Minority of Istanbul and Greek-Turkish Relations, 1918–1974*. Athens: Center for Asia Minor Studies, 1983.

———. "To istoriko plaisio ton ellinotourkikon sxeseon, 1923–1954" [The Historical Framework of Greek-Turkish Relations, 1923–1954]. In *Oi ellinotourkikes sxesis, 1923–1987* [Greek-Turkish Relations 1923–1987], ed. A. Alexandris et al. Athens: Gnosi, 1988. 31–172.

Aliefendioğlu, Yılmaz. "Azınlık Hakları ve Türk Anayasa Mahkemesinin Azınlık Konusuna Bakışı." In *Ulusal, Ulusalüstü ve Uluslararası Hukukta Azınlık Hakları: Birleşmiş Milletler, Avrupa Birliği, Avrupa Konseyi, Lozan Antlaşması*, ed. İbrahim Kaboğlu. Istanbul: Istanbul Bar Association Human Rights Center Publications, 2002. 218–41.

Alpay, Şahin. "Journalists: Cautious Democrats." In *Turkey and the West, Changing Political and Cultural Identities*, ed. Metin Heper and Ayşe Öncü. London: Heinz Kramer, I.B Tauris, 1993. 69–91.

Alston, Philip. "The Importance of the Inter-Play Between Economic, Social and Cultural Rights, and Civil and Political Rights." In *Human Rights at the Dawn of the 21st Century: Proceedings of the Interregional Meeting Organized by the Council of Europe in Advance of the World Conference on Human Rights, Palais de l'Europe, Strasbourg, 28–30 January 1993*. Strasbourg: Council of Europe Press, 1993. 59–74.

———. *The United Nations and Human Rights: A Critical Appraisal*. New York: Oxford University Press, 1996.

Altınay, Ayşe Gül. "Human Rights or Militarist Ideals? Teaching National Security in High Schools." In *Human Rights Issues in Textbooks: The Turkish Case*, ed. Deniz T. Ceylan and Gürol Irzık. Istanbul: History Foundation of Turkey, 2004. 76–91.

Amnesty International. *Turkey: Selective Protection: Discriminatory Treatment of Non-European Refugees and Asylum Seekers*. London: International Secretariat, March 1994.

———. *Turkey: No Security Without Human Rights*. New York: Amnesty International, 1996.

———. "Turkey: Insufficient and Inadequate: Judicial Remedies Against Torturers and Killers." November 2004. AI Index: EUR 44/037/2004. http://web.amnesty.org/library/print/ENGEUR440372004 (accessed 16 November 2004).

———. "Turkey Report, 2005." http://web.amnesty.org/report2005/tur-summary-eng (accessed 21 March 2006).

Anastasiadou-Dumont, Meropi. "Apo to pathos ke apo to chreos gia ti diatirisi enos Romeikou pirina stin poli: Sizitisi me ton Dimitri Frangopoulo" [Out of Passion and Fear for the Preservation of the Rum Nucleus in the City: Interview with Dimitris Frangopoulos]. *Sychrona Themata* [Current Issues] 22 (2000): 88–113.

Andreopoulos, George J., Zehra F. Kabasakal Arat, and Peter Juviler, eds. *Non-State Actors in the Human Rights Universe*. New York: Kumarian Press, 2006.

Andreopoulos, George J. and Richard P. Claude, eds. *Human Rights Education for the Twenty-First Century*. Philadelphia: University of Pennsylvania Press, 1997.

Arabacı, Caner. "Basın ve Siyaset Üzerine." In *Medyada Yeni Yaklaşımlar*, ed. Metin Işık. Konya: Eğitim Kitabevi, 2004. 105–28.

Aral, Berdal. "The Idea of Human Rights as Perceived in the Ottoman Empire." *Human Rights Quarterly* 26, no. 2 (2004): 454–82.

Arat, Enise et al. "Türk Kadınının Hukuki Durumu." In *Atatürk ve Kadın Hakları: Kadın Dernekleri Federasyonu ve Gönüllü Kuruluşlar*, ed. Kadın Dernekleri Federasyonu. Ankara: Türk Ticaret Bankası Yayınları, 1983. 54–154.

Arat, Yeşim. "1980'ler Türkiyesi'nde Kadın Hareketi." *Toplum ve Bilim* 53 (Spring 1991): 7–19.

———. "From Emancipation to Liberation: The Changing Role of Women in Turkey in Turkey's Public Realm." *Journal of International Affairs* 54, no. 1 (2000a): 106–23.

———. "Gender and Citizenship in Turkey." In *Gender and Citizenship in the Middle East*, ed. Suad Joseph. Syracuse, N.Y: Syracuse University Press, 2000b. 275–86.

Arat, Zehra F. Kabasakal. "Introduction: Politics of Representation and Identity." In *Deconstructing Images of " The Turkish Woman"*, ed. Zehra F. Kabasakal Arat. New York: St. Martin's Press, 1998. 1–34.

———. "Human Rights and Democracy: Expanding or Contracting." *Polity* 32, no. 1 (Fall 1999): 119–44.

———. "Human Rights and Identity Politics in Turkey." Paper prepared for the Special Convention on Nationalism, Identities and Regional Cooperation: Compatibilities and Incompatibilities, organized by Centro per l'Europa Orentale e Balcanica (CECOB), in association with Association for the Study of Nationalities (ASN), University of Bologna, Forlì campus, Italy, 4–9 June 2002.

———. *Democracy and Human Rights in Developing Countries*. Authors Guild Backprint.com ed. Lincoln, Neb.: Universe, 2003a.

———. "Promoting Identities, Human Rights, and Democracy Within Cycles of Politics: The Case of Turkey." Paper prepared for the 99th Annual Meeting of the American Political Science Association, Philadelphia, 27–31 August 2003b.

———. "Institutions and Women's Rights: The State, Religion, and Family in Turkey." Paper prepared for the Symposium on Family, Gender, and Law in a Globalizing Middle East and South Asia, University of Illinois at Urbana-Champaign, 7–9 October 2004.

———. *Human Rights Worldwide: A Reference Handbook*. 3rd ed. Santa Barbara, Calif.: ABC-CLIO, 2006.

Ardıç, Nimet. "Cumhuriyet'ten Sonra Kurulan Kadın Dernekleri." In *Atatürk ve Kadın Hakları: Kadın Dernekleri Federasyonu ve Gönüllü Kuruluşlar*, ed. Kadın Dernekleri Federasyonu. Ankara:Türk Ticaret Bankası Yayınları, 1983.194–204.

Atabey, Melek. "Television News Broadcasting and Journalism in Turkey: The Impact of Political, Economic, and Socio-Cultural Change in the 1990s." Ph.D. dissertation, University of London, 1998.

Atauz, Akın. "Research and Pilot Projects and NGOs Final Report." Prepared for

Directorate General on the Status and Problems of Women. Ankara, December 1993.

Audi, Robert, and Nicholas Wolterstorff. *Religion in the Public Square: The Place of Religious Convictions in Political Debate.* Lanham, Md.: Rowman and Littlefield, 1997.

Ayata, Ayşe. "The Emergence of Identity Politics in Turkey." *New Perspectives in Turkey* 17 (Fall 1997): 67–69.

Aydemir, Şinasi. "Türkiye'de Kayıt Dışı Ekonomi." Istanbul: Maliye Hesap Uzmanları Derneği Yayını, 1995.

Aydın, Mustafa. "Determinants of Turkish Foreign Policy: Historical Frameworks and Traditional Inputs." In *Seventy Five Years of the Turkish Republic*, ed. Sylvia Kedourie. London: Frank Cass, 2000. 152–86.

Aydınoğlu, Ergun. *Türk Solu: Eleştirel Bir Tarih Denemesi 1960–1971.* Istanbul: Belge Yayınları, 1992.

Ayzit, Aynur. "Mevzuatın Görünümü." In *Ulusal, Ulusalüstü ve Uluslararası Hukukta Azınlık Hakları: Birleşmiş Milletler, Avrupa Birliği, Avrupa Konseyi, Lozan Antlaşması*, ed. İbrahim Kaboğlu. Istanbul: Istanbul Bar Association Human Rights Center Publications, 2002. 242–61.

Baç, Meltem Müftüler. *Türkiye ve AB: Soğuk Savaş Sonrası İlişkiler.* Istanbul: Alfa Yayınları, 2001.

Bağlı, Melike T. "A Report on 1st Regional Human Rights Education Training for Teachers and Activists from South Eastern European Countries." In *Thematic Dossiers*, ed. A. Bregant et al. Maribor: EIP, 2003a. 83–86.

Bağlı, Melike T. and Yasemin Esen, eds. *Ders Kitaplarında İnsan Hakları: İnsan Haklarına Duyarlı Ders Kitapları İçin.* Istanbul: Tarih Vakfı Yayınları, 2003.

Bahçeli, Tözün. *Greek-Turkish Relations Since 1955.* Boulder, Colo.: Westview Press, 1990.

Balım, Çiğdem et al., eds. *Turkey: Political, Social and Economic Challenges in the 1990s.* Leiden: E.J. Brill, 1995.

Barchard, David. *Building a Partnership: Turkey and the European Union.* Istanbul: TESEV, 2000.

Barkey, Henri J. and Graham E. Fuller. *Turkey's Kurdish Question: Carnegie Commission on Preventing Deadly Conflict, Carnegie Corporation of New York.* Lanham, Md.: Rowman and Littlefield, 1998.

Baxi, Upendra. "Human Rights Education: The Promise of the Third Millennium?" In *Human Rights Education for the Twenty-First Century*, ed. George J. Andreopoulos and Richard Pierre Claude. Philadelphia: University of Pennsylvania Press, 1997. 142–55.

———. *The Future of Human Rights.* Delhi: Oxford University Press, 2001.

Baydar, Oya. *Türkiye'de Sendikacılık Hareketi.* Istanbul: Friedrich Ebert Foundation, 1998.

Baykan, Ayşegül. "Nezihe Muhiddin'de Feminizmin Düşünsel Kökenleri." In *Nezihe Muhiddin ve Türk Kadını 1931*, ed. A. Baykan and B. Ötüş-Basket. Istanbul: İletişim Yayınları, 1999. 15–38.

Beijing Declaration and Platform for Action with the Beijing +5 Political Declaration and Outcome Document. New York: United Nations Department of Public Information, August 2001. http://www.un.org/womenwatch/daw/followup/beijing+5.htm (accessed February 2002).

Bell, Lynda S., Andrew J. Nathan, and Ilan Peleg, eds. *Negotiating Culture and Human Rights.* New York: Columbia University Press, 2001.

Bennett, Jon. "Forced Migration Within National Borders: The IDP Agenda." *Forced Migration Review* 1 (1998): 4–6.

"Bergama Villagers Worry That International Arbitration Could Lead to the Resumption of Controversial Gold Mining." *Turkish Daily News*, 19 July 1999. http://www.turkishdailynews.com/old_editions/07_19_99/dom.htm (accessed 12 November 2003).

Berkan, İsmet. "İki Kilise Öyküsü."*Radikal*, 29 November 2004. http://www.radikal.com.tr (accessed 17 February 2004 İki Kilise Öyküsü 5).

Berkes, Niyazi. *Teokrasi ve Laiklik*. Istanbul: Adam Yayıncılık, 1997.

———. *The Development of Secularism in Turkey*. London: Hurst, 1998.

Berktay, Fatmagül. "Yeni Kimlik Arayışı, Eski Cinsel Düalism: Peyami Safa'nın Romanlarında Toplumsal Cinsiyet." In *Bilanço 1923–1998: Türkiye Cumhuriyeti'nin 75 Yılına Toplu Bakış*. Istanbul: Tarih Vakfı, 1999. 267–76.

Bilgen, H. Nihat et al. *8. Sınıf için Vatandaşlık ve İnsan Hakları Eğitimi*. Ankara: Milli Eğitim Bakanlığı Yayınları, 2001.

Birtek, Faruk and Binnaz Toprak. "The Conflictual Agendas of Neo-Liberal Reconstruction and the Rise of Islamic Politics in Turkey." *Praxis International* 13, no. 2 (July 1993): 192–210.

Bitsios, Dimitri S. *Cyprus: The Vulnerable Republic*. Thessaloniki: Institute for Balkan Studies, 1975.

Blatsiotis, Lambros. "Elliniki diikisi ke mionotiki ekpedeusi sti dytiki Thraki" [Greek Administration and Minority Education in Western Thrace]. In *To mionotiko phenomenostin ellada* [The Minority Phenomenon in Greece], ed. Konstantinos Tsitselikis and Dimitris Christopoulos. Athens: Kritiki, 1997. 315–48.

Böcker, Anita. "Refugee and Asylum-Seeking Migration from Turkey to Europe." *Boğaziçi Journal* 10, nos. 1–2 (1996): 55–75.

Bora, Tanıl. *Türk Sağının Üç Hali: Milliyetçilik, Muhafazarlık ve İslam*. Istanbul: İletişim Yayınları, 2003.

———. "Nationalism in Textbooks." In *Human Rights Issues in Textbooks: The Turkish Case*, ed. Deniz T. Ceylan and Gürol Irzık, trans. İ. Akça. Istanbul: History Foundation of Turkey, 2004. 49–76.

Bora, Tanıl, Y. Bülent Peker, and Mithat Sancar. "Hakim İdeolojiler, Batı, Batılılaşma ve İnsan Hakları." In *Modernleşme ve Batıcılık*, ed. Uygur Kocabaşoğlu. Istanbul: İletişim Yayınları, 2002. 302–3.

Bozarslan, Hamit. "Political Aspects of the Kurdish Problem in Contemporary Turkey." In *The Kurds: A Contemporary Overview*, ed. Philip G. Kreyenbroek and Stephan Speri. New York: Routledge, 1992. 95–114.

———. "Human Rights and the Kurdish Issue in Turkey, 1984–1999." *Human Rights Review* 3, no. 1 (October–December 2001): 45–54.

Bozdağ, İsmet. *Dünyada ve Türkiye'de Basın İstibdadı*. Istanbul: Emre Yayınları, 1992.

Bozkır, Gürcan. "Türk Kadınının Siyasi Hakları Kazanması ve Türk Kadınlar Birliği." *Toplumsal Tarih* 13, no. 75 (March 2000): 21–26.

Brander, Patricia et al. *Compass: A Manual on Human Rights Education with Young People*. Strasbourg: Council of Europe Publishing, 2002.

Bratton, Michael and Nicolas van de Walle. *Democratic Experiments in Africa: Regime Transitions in Comparative Perspective*. Cambridge: Cambridge University Press, 1997.

Braude, Benjamin and Bernard Lewis, eds. *Christians and Jews in the Ottoman Empire*. New York: Holmes, 1982.

Brown, David. "Foreword." In Faik Ökte, *The Tragedy of the Turkish Capital Tax*. London: Croom Helm, 1987.

Bugerman, Susan D. "Mobilising Principles: The Role of Transnational Activists in Promoting Human Rights Principles." *Human Rights Quarterly* 20, no. 4 (November 1998): 905–23.

Bulaç, Ali. "Medine Vesikası Hakkında Genel Bilgiler." *Birikim* 38–39 (June/July 1992): 102–11.

———. "Medine Vesikası Üzerine Tartışmalar I." *Birikim* 47 (March 1993a): 40–46.

———. "Medine Vesikası Üzerine Tartışmalar II. " *Birikim* 48 (April 1993b): 48–58.

Bulutay, Tuncer. *Türkiye'de Çalışan Çocuklar.* Ankara: DİE, 1999.

Çakır, Hamza. *Osmanlı'da Basın ve İktidar İlişkileri.* Ankara: Siyasal Kitabevi, 2002.

Çakır, Serpil. *Osmanlı Kadın Hareketi.* Istanbul: Metis, 1996.

Çalı, Başak and Ayça Ergun. "Domestic Politics and Human Rights: Fragmented Visions." In *Criticizing Global Governance,* ed. Markus Lederer and Phillipp S. Müller. New York: Palgrave Macmillan, 2005.

Çalışma ve Sosyal Güvenlik Bakanlığı. Yıllara Göre Grev Sayısı. October 2002a. http://www.calisma.gov.tr/istatistik/grev.htm (accessed February 2005).

———. Sendika Üye İstatistikleri. October 2002b. http://www.calisma.gov.tr/istatistik/sendika_uye070.htm (accessed February 2005).

———. Yıllara Göre Sendika Sayısı. 2002c. http://www.calisma.gov.tr (accessed February 2005).

———. Number of Workers and Unionization Rate. October 2003. http://www.calisma.gov.tr (accessed February 2005).

Canatan, Kadir. "Toplum Tasarımları ve Birlikte Yaşama." *Bilgi ve Hikmet* 5 (Winter 1994): 98–108.

———. *Din ve Laiklik.* Istanbul: İnsan Yayınları, 1997.

Çaplı, Bülent. "Turkey." In *Television and the Viewer Interest,* ed. Jeremy Mitchell, Jay G. Blumler, Philippe Mounier, and Anja Bundschuh. London: John Libbey, 1994. 135–46.

Caporal, Bernard. *Kemalizmde ve Kemalizm Sonrasında Türk Kadını: 1919–1970.* Ankara: Türkiye İş Bankası Kültür Yayınları, 1982.

Capotorti, Francesco. "Are Minorities Entitled to Collective International Rights?" In *The Protection of Minorities and Human Rights,* ed.Yoram Dinstein and Mala Tabory. The Hague: Nijhoff, 1992.

Cardenas, Sonia. "Norm Collision: Explaining the Effects of International Human Rights Pressure on State Behavior." *International Studies Review* 6, no. 4 (December 2004): 213–31.

Casanova, Jose. *Public Religions in the Modern World.* Chicago: University of Chicago Press, 1994.

Çatalbaş, Dilruba. "Broadcasting Deregulation in Turkey: Uniformity Within Diversity." In *Media Organisations in Society,* ed. James Curran. London: Arnold, 2000. 126–48.

Çavuşoğlu, Naz. "Azınlık Hakları: Avrupa Standartları ve Türkiye-Bir Karşılaştırma." In *Ulusal, Ulusalüstü ve Uluslararası Hukukta Azınlık Hakları: Birleşmiş Milletler, Avrupa Birliği, Avrupa Konseyi, Lozan Antlaşması,* ed. İbrahim Kaboğlu. Istanbul: Istanbul Bar Association Human Rights Center Publications, 2002. 124–46.

Çetik, Mete and Yüksel Akkaya. *Türkiye'de Endüstri İlişkileri.* Istanbul: Friedrich Ebert Stiftung & Türkiye Ekonomik ve Toplumsal Tarih Vakfı, 1999.

Çetin, Fethiye. "Yerli Yabancılar!" In *Ulusal, Ulusalüstü ve Uluslararası Hukukta Azınlık Hakları—Birleşmiş Milletler, Avrupa Birliği, Avrupa Konseyi, Lozan Antlaşması,* ed. İbrahim Kaboğlu. Istanbul: Istanbul Bar Association Human Rights Center Publications, 2002. 70–81.

Ceylan, Deniz T. and Gürol Irzık, eds. *Human Rights Issues in Textbooks: The Turkish Case.* Istanbul: History Foundation of Turkey, 2004.

Chomsky, Noam. *Rogue States: The Rule of Force in World Affairs.* London: Pluto Press, 2000.

Christides, Christophoros. *Ta Septembriana* [The September Events]. Athens: Center for Asia Minor Studies, 2000.

Christophoridis, Chrisostomos. "Tenedos—Imbros, i martiriki poria dio nision" [Imbros—Tenedos, the Tormented Course of Two Islands]. In *I lismonimeni Tenedos* [The Forgotten Tenedos]. Athens: Anatoli Publications, 1996. 71–77.

———. *Ta Septembriana* [The September Events]. Athens: Center for Asia Minor Studies, 2000.

Çiçekli, Bülent. "Yorum: Jabari v. Türkiye." *Avrupa İnsan Hakları Mahkemesi Kararları Dergisi* 1, no. 4 (January 2003a): 14–15. http://www.pa.edu.tr/tr/baskanlik/menu/dergi2/sayi4/1–105.pdf.

———. *Yabancılar ve Polis.* Ankara: Seçkin, 2003b.

Ciment, James. *The Kurds: State and Minority in Turkey, Iraq, and Iran.* New York: Facts on File, 1996.

Cizre, Ümit. "The Truth and Fiction About (Turkey's) Human Rights Politics." *Human Rights Review* 3, no. 1 (October–December 2001): 55–77.

Cleveland, William L. *A Modern History of the Middle East.* Boulder, Colo.: Westview Press, 1994.

Cohen, Roberta. "Hard Cases: Internal Displacement in Turkey, Burma, and Algeria." *Forced Migration Review* 6 (December 1999): 25–28.

Cohen, Roberta and Francis M. Deng. *Masses in Flight: The Global Crisis of Internal Displacement.* Washington, D.C.: Brookings Institution Press, 1998.

Coicaud, Jean-Marc, Michael W. Doyle, and Anne-Marie Gardner, eds. *The Globalization of Human Rights.* Tokyo: United Nations University Press, 2003.

Combined 2nd and 3rd Periodic Country Report of Turkey to the Committee on the Elimination of Discrimination against Women. Turkish Republic Prime Ministry Directorate General on the Status and Problems of Women. Presented at the Periodic Review of Turkey. New York, January 1997.

Commission of European Communities. *Proposal for a Council Decision on an Accession Partnership with Turkey.* Brussels, 8 November 2000.

———. *2001 Regular Report on Turkey's Progress Toward Accession.* Brussels, 13 November 2001.

———. *2002 Regular Report on Turkey's Progress Toward Accession.* http://europa.eu.int/comm/enlargement/report 2002/tu_en.pdf (accessed 19 February 2003).

———. *2004 Regular Report on Turkey's Progress Toward Accession.* Brussels, 6 October 2004.

Committee on the Rights of the Child. *Initial Report of Turkey.* UN Doc. CRC/C/51/Add. 4 of 8 August 2000. Concluding Observations of 8 June 2001.

Consideration of Turkish Combined Second and Third Periodic Reports by the Committee on the Elimination of Discrimination against Women. United Nations. 17 January 1997.

Constitutional Court, E. 1989/1, K. 1989/12. 3 July 1989.

Cornell, Erik. *Turkey in the 21st Century: Opportunities, Challenges, Threats.* Richmond, England: Curzon, 2001.

Cornell, Svante E. "The Kurdish Question in Turkish Politics." *Orbis* 45 (2001): 31–40.

Çotuksöken, B., A. Erzan, and O. Silier, eds. *Ders Kitaplarında İnsan Hakları: Tarama Sonuçları.* Istanbul: Tarih Vakfı Yayınları, 2003.

Council of Europe. .European Union Progress Report, 2002. COM, 2002, 700 final, Brussels.

Council of Europe Committee on Legal Affairs and Human Rights. *Implementation of Decisions of the European Court of Human Rights by Turkey.* COE Document 9537, 5 September 2002.

Courbage, Youssef and Philippe Fargues. *Christians and Jews Under Islam.* London: I.B. Tauris, 1998.

Dağı, İhsan D. *İnsan Hakları, Küresel Siyaset ve Türkiye.* Istanbul: Boyut Kitapları, 2000.

Danıştay Dergisi. Year 8, nos. 30–31 (1978).

Davenport, David. "The New Diplomacy." *Policy Review* 116 (December 2002–January 2003).

Davidson, Scott. *Human Rights.* Buckingham: Open University Press, 1997.

Davison, Andrew. *Secularism and Revivalism in Turkey: A Hermeneutic Reconsideration.* New Haven, Conn.: Yale University Press, 1998.

Davison, Roderic. *Reform in the Ottoman Empire, 1851–1876.* 2nd ed. New York: Gordian, 1973.

Declarations and Reservations to the Convention on the Rights of the Child. Office of the United Nations High Commissioner of Human Rights. http://www.ohchr.org/english/law/crc-reserve.htm (accessed 1 August 2006)

Demir, Hülya and Rıdvan Akar. *İstanbul'un Son Sürgünleri.* Istanbul: Belge Yayınları, 1999.

Document of the Copenhagen Meeting of the CSCE. Adopted 29 June 1990. http://www.unesco.org/most/lnlaw6.htm (accessed 5 April 2002).

Donnelly, Jack. "International Human Rights: A Regime Analysis." *International Organization* 40, no. 3 (Summer 1986): 599–642.

———. "Post Cold War Reflections on the Study of International Human Rights." In *Ethics and International Affairs: A Reader*, ed. Joel H. Rosenthal. Washington D.C.: Georgetown University Press, 1995.

———. *International Human Rights.* 2nd ed. Boulder, Colo.: Westview Press, 1998.

Dositheos. *Thelo na pio olo ton Vosporo* [I Want to Drink All of Bosphorus]. Euritania: Holy Monastery of Tartani, 2000.

———. *Mia gorgona ston Keratio* [A Mermaid on the Golden Horn]. Euritania: Holy Monastery of Tartani, 2002.

Doyran, Ayşe. "1934'de Basındaki Tartışmalar: Kadınlar Milletvekili Seçilirken." *Toplumsal Tarih* 39 (March 1997): 27–34.

Drinan, Robert F. *The Mobilization of Shame: A World View of Human Rights.* New Haven, Conn.: Yale University Press, 2001.

Drzemczewski, Andrew Z. *European Human Rights Convention in Domestic Law: A Comparative Study.* Oxford: Clarendon Press, 1983.

Dumont, Paul. "Disciples of the Light: The Nurcu Movement in Turkey." *Central Asian Survey* 5, no. 2 (1986): 33–60.

Dündar, Fuat. *Oi mionotites sti Tourkia* [Minorities in Turkey]. Athens: Infognomon, 2003.

Dunér, Bertil and Edward Deverell. "Country Cousin: Turkey, the European Union, and Human Rights." *Turkish Studies* 2, no. 1 (Spring 2001): 1–24.

Durakbaşa, Ayşe. "Kemalism as Identity Politics in Turkey." In *Deconstructing Images of "the Turkish Woman"*, ed. Zehra F. Kabasakal Arat. New York: St. Martin's Press, 1998. 39–156.

Ecevit, Yıldız. "Yerel Yönetimler ve Kadın Örgütleri İlişkisine Eleştirel bir Yaklaşım." In *Yerli bir Feminizme Doğru*, ed. A. İlyasoğlu and N. Akgökçe. Istanbul: Sel Yayıncılık, 2001. 227–58.

Eder, Mine. "Implementing the Economic Criteria of EU Membership: How Difficult Is It for Turkey?" In *Turkey and the European Union: Domestic Politics,*

Economic Integration and International Dynamics, ed. Ali Çarkoğlu and Barry Rubin. London: Frank Cass, 2003, 219–245.

Eğitim Dairesi Başkanlığı. Faaliyet Raporu (1996–2004). http://www.edb.adalet. gov.tr/faalinsan.htm (accessed 1 February 2005).

Eğitim ve Bilim Emekçileri Sendikası. http://egitimsen.org.tr (accessed 5 November 2003).

Ekren, Fahrünnisa Akbatur. "Medeni Kanun Değişikliği: Kadın Aleyhine Hükümler." In *Hukuk ve Kadın Hakları.* Çağdaş Hukukçular Derneği Kadın Komisyonu. Ankara: Makro Print, 1993. 10–22.

Ekşi, Oktay. "Bilgi Edinme Bayramı." *Hürriyet*, 12 October 2003.

Energy Information Administration (EIA). *Turkey Environmental Issues.* "Renewable Energy" section. http://www.eia.doe.gov/emeu/cabs/turkenv (accessed 25 February 2004).

Ensaroğlu, Yılmaz. "AB-Türkiye İlişkilerinde İnsan Hakları." In *Türkiye'de Sivil Toplum ve Milliyetçilik,* ed. Stefanos Yerasimos. Istanbul: İletişim Yayınları, 2001, 397.

"Environmental Accountability in Africa (EAA): Environmental Procedural Rights." World Resources Institute. http://www.wri.org/index.html (accessed 10 February 2004).

Environment Foundation of Turkey (EFT). http://www.cevre.org (accessed 3 November 2003).

Ercan, Metin R. and Ziya Öniş. "Turkish Privatization: Institutions and Dilemmas." *Turkish Studies* 2, no. 1 (Spring 2001): 109–34.

Erder, Sema. "Uluslararası Göçte Yeni Eğilimler: Türkiye 'Göç Alan' Ülke mi?" [New Trends in International Migration: Is Turkey an Immigration Country?]. In *Mübeccel Kıray için Yazılar.* Istanbul: Bağlam Yayınları, 2000. 235–59.

Erdoğan, Fevzi "An Evaluation of the Training Activities of the Turkish National Police in View of Organizational and Behavioral Changes." In *Human Rights Education and Practice in Turkey in the Process of Candidacy to the EU,* ed. Muzaffer Dartan and Münevver Cebeci.: Marmara University European Community Institute, 2002. 117–37.

Ergin, Sedat. "Milli Güvenlik Siyaset Belgesi Değiştiriliyor." *Hürriyet*, 24 November 2004. http://www.hurriyetim.com.tr (accessed 17 February 2005).

European Communities. *Bulletin of the EC.* Brussels, 1981.

———. *Official Journal of the European Communities.* Brussels, 1996.

European Council. *Presidency Conclusions.* Helsinki, 1999.

———. *Presidency Conclusions.* Copenhagen, 2002.

———. *Presidency Conclusions.* Brussels, 2004.

European Parliament. Strategy Paper, Accession Partnership with Turkey and Progress Reports. Brussels, 8 November 2000.

European Union. *Bulletin of the European Union.* Brussels, 1996–97.

Eurostat Yearbook 2004. Luxemburg: Office for Official Publications of the European Communities, 2004. http://epp.eurostat.cec.eu.int/cache/ITY_OFFPUB/KS-CD-04–001–2/EN/KS-CD-04–001–2-EN.PDF (accessed 8 June 2005).

Evans, Tony, ed. *Human Rights Fifty Years On: A Reappraisal.* Manchester: Manchester University Press, 1998.

Evren, Kemal Öcal. "Dünya'da ve Ülkemizde Sosyal Diyaloğun Artan Önemi ve Üçlü Yapı Mekanizması." *Çalışma ve Sosyal Güvenlik Bakanlığı Dergisi* 2 (January–March 1999): 36–43.

Falk, Richard A. *Human Rights Horizons: The Pursuit of Justice in a Globalizing World.* New York: Routledge, 2000.

Finkel, Andrew. "Who Guards the Turkish Press? A Perspective on Press Corruption in Turkey." *Journal of International Affairs* 54, no. 1 (Fall 2000): 147–68.

Fleming, K. E. "Women as Preservers of the Past: Ziya Gökalp and Women's Reform." *Deconstructing Images of " The Turkish Woman"*, ed. Zehra F. Kabasakal Arat. New York: St. Martin's Press, 1998. 127–38.

Flowers, Nancy et al. *The Human Rights Education Handbook*. Minneapolis: University of Minnesota Press, 2000.

Forewaker, John and Todd Landman. *Citizenship Rights and Social Movements: A Comparative and Statistical Analysis*. Cambridge: Cambridge University Press, 1997.

Forsythe, David P. *American Exceptionalism and Global Human Rights*. Lincoln: University of Nebraska Distinguished Lecture Series, 1999.

Freedom House. *Freedom in the World Country Ratings, 1972–73 to 2000–01*. London: Freedom House, 2001. Electronic version at http://www.freedomhouse.org/uploads/FIWrank7305.xls (accessed 5 August 2003).

Freeman, Michael. *Human Rights: An Interdisciplinary Perspective*. London: Polity, 2002.

Frelick, Bill. *Barriers to Protection: Turkey's Asylum Regulations*. Washington D.C.: U.S. Committee for Refugees, 1997a.

———. *Turkey: Refoulement of Non-European Refugees—A Protection Crisis*. London: Amnesty International Secretariat, Document EUR 44/031/1997b.

Global Alliance of Performers. http://www.gap.org (accessed 30 July 2002).

Garr, Ted Robert and Barbara Harff, eds. *Ethnic Conflict in World Politics*. Boulder, Colo.: Westview Press, 1994.

Gemalmaz, Mehmet Semih, and Osman Doğru. *Türkiye'de Basın Özgürlüğü Mevzuatı*. Istanbul: Basın Konseyi, 1990.

General Directorate of Disaster Affairs, Earthquake Research Department http://www.deprem.gov.tr/kocaeli/info-izmit-1.htm (accessed 17 February 2004).

Geyikdağı, Mehmet Y. *Political Parties in Turkey: The Role of Islam*. New York: Preaeger, 1984.

Gillies, David. *Between Principle and Practice: Human Rights in North-South Relations*. Montreal: McGill-Queen's University Press, 1996.

Gilson, George. "Vatholomeos Demands Equal Rights." 2002. http://www.athensnews.gr/athweb/ (accessed 26 February 2003).

Global IDP Project. Internal Displacement Monitoring Centre. http://www.db.idpproject.org (accessed 30 July 2002).

———. "Despite Legislative Reforms, There Is Insufficient Implementation of 2002 Reforms (2000–2003)." Internal Displacement Monitoring Centre. http://www.db.idpproject.org/Sites/IdpProjectDb/idpSurvey.nsf/wViewCountries/5FCF59921E2DA872C1256AB200273437 (accessed 5 December 2004).

———. Internal Displacement Monitoring Centre. http://www.idpproject.org/regions/Europe_idps.htm (accessed 11 January 2005).

Global IDP Survey. *Internally Displaced People: A Global Survey*. 1998.

Gök, Fatma. "Educational Change and Politics in Turkey." Ph.D. dissertation, Columbia University, 1987.

———. "Türkiye'de Kadın ve Eğitim." In *Kadın Bakış Açısından 1980'ler Türkiye'sinde Kadın*, ed. Şirin Tekeli. Istanbul: İletişim Yayınları, 1990. 165–81.

———. "The Privatization of Education in Turkey." In *Ravages of Neo-Liberalism: Economy, Society and Gender in Turkey*, ed. Neşecan Balkan and Sungur Savran. New York: Nova Science Publishers, 2002. 93–104.

———. "Citizenship and Human Rights Education Textbooks." In *Human Rights*

Issues in Textbooks: The Turkish Case, ed. Deniz T. Ceylan and Gürol Irzık, trans. S. Eryiğit. Istanbul: History Foundation of Turkey, 2004. 108–23.

Gök, Fatma and Alper Şahin. *İnsan Haklarına Saygılı Bir Eğitim Ortamına Doğru.* Istanbul: Tarih Vakfı Yayınları, 2003.

Gök, Fatma et al. "An Analysis of the Turkish Primary Schools Textbook." Unpublished research paper. Istanbul, 1994.

———. "The Effect of Economic Crisis on the Parent's Educational Provision." Unpublished study based on research conducted in five shantytowns in Istanbul, 2002.

Goldstein, Judith, and Robert O. Keohane. *Ideas and Foreign Policy: Beliefs, Institutions, and Political Change.* Ithaca, N.Y.: Cornell University Press, 1993.

Goodwin-Gill, Guy. *The Refugee in International Law.* Oxford: Clarendon Press, 1986.

Graf, Denise. "İsviçre Örneğinde Mülteci Hukuku Avrupa Uygulaması." Paper presented at Mülteci Hukuku Eğitim Çalışması (Training Workshop on Refugee Law), organized by Amnesty International, Van, 19–20 October 2002.

Guide to Nongovernmental Organizations. Istanbul: Türkiye Çevre Vakfı, 1997.

Gülmez, Mesut. "Avrupa Sosyal Şartı'na Genel Bir Bakış ve Türkiye." *İnsan Hakları Yıllığı* 12 (Ankara: 1990): 91–121.

———. "Avrupa Sosyal Şartı Koruma Sistemi ve Türkiye." *Türk-İş Yıllığı* 2 (Ankara: 1999): 83–130.

Gündüz, Aslan. "Human Rights and Turkey's Future in Europe." *Orbis* 45, no. 1 (2001): 15–30.

Gunter, Michael M. *The Kurds in Turkey: A Political Dilemma.* Boulder, Colo.: Westview Press, 1990.

———. *The Kurds and the Future of Turkey.* London: Macmillan, 1997.

———. "The Continuing Kurdish Problem in Turkey After Öcalan's Capture." *Third World Quarterly* 21, no. 5 (October 2000): 849–70.

Gürkan Pazarcı, Nilgün. "Türkiye'de Medya-Siyaset Etkileşimi." In *Türkiye'de Kitle İletişimi*, ed. Nilgün Gürkan Pazarcı. Ankara: Turhan Kitabevi, 2004. 21–51.

Gürkaynak, İpek et al. *Yurttaş Olmak İçin: Öğretmen El Kitabı.* Istanbul: Umut Vakfı Yayınları, 1998.

Güvenir, O. Murat. *İkinci Dünya Savaşı'nda Türk Basını.* Istanbul: Gazeteciler Cemiyeti, 1991.

Hakyemez,Yusuf Şevki and Birol Akgün. "Limitation on the Freedom of Political Parties in Turkey and the Jurisdiction of the European Court of Human Rights." *Mediterranean Politics* 7, no. 2 (2002): 54–78.

Hale, William. *Turkish Politics and the Military.* London: Routledge, 1994.

———. "Human Rights, the European Union and the Turkish Accession Process." In *Turkey and the European Union: Domestic Politics, Economic Integration and International Dynamics*, ed. Ali Çarkoğlu and Barry Rubin. London: Frank Cass, 2003. 107–26.

Hallı, Reşat. *Türkiye Cumhuriyetinde Ayaklanmalar, 1924–38.* Ankara: General Staff Headquarters, 1972.

Hassanpour, Amir. "Kurdish Language Policy in Turkey." http://www.cogsci.edu. ac.uk/~siamakr/Kurdish/KURDICA/1999/JUL/policyunfilt.htm (accessed 13 November 2001).

Hathaway, James C. "Reconceiving Refugee Law as Human Rights Protection." *Journal of Refugee Studies* 4, no. 2 (1991): 113–31.

Helfer, Laurence R. and Anne-Marie Slaughter. "Toward a Theory of Effective Supranational Adjudication." *Yale Law Journal* 107, no. 2 (1997): 273–391.

Helicke, James. "Turkey's Policies on Minorities Spark Debate." 2004. http://www.archons.org/news/ (accessed 17 January 2005).

Helsinki Watch Report. *Denying Human Rights and Ethnic Identity: The Greeks of Turkey.* New York: Human Rights Watch, 1992.

Heper, Metin. *The State Tradition in Turkey.* Walkington: Eothen Press, 1985.

Heraclides, Alexis. *I Ellada ke o "ex Anatolon kindynos"* [Greece and the "Threat Emanating from the East"]. Athens: Polis, 2001.

Hicks, Neil. "Legislative Reform in Turkey and European Human Rights Mechanism." *Human Rights Review* 3, no. 1 (October–December 2001): 78–85. http://www.policyreview.org/dec02/ (accessed 4 April 2004).

Hirschon, Renee, ed. *Crossing the Aegean.* New York: Berghahn Books, 2003.

Holt, Sally and John Packer. "OSCE Developments and Linguistic Minorities." *International Journal on Multicultural Societies* 3, no. 2 (2001) http://www.unesco.org/most/vl3n2packer.htm (accessed 21 July 2001).

Houston, Christopher. *Islam, Kurds and the Turkish Nation State.* Oxford: Berg, 2001.

Human Rights Watch. *Turkey: Violations of Free Expression in Turkey.* February 1999. http://www.hrw.org/reports/1999/turkey/ (accessed March 2005).

———. *Displaced and Disregarded: Turkey's Failing Village Return Program.* New York: Human Rights Watch, 2002.

———. *A Crossroads for Human Rights? Human Rights Watch's Key Concerns on Turkey for 2005.* http://hrw.org/english/docs/2004/12/15/turkey9865.htm (accessed 15 December 2004).

Human Rights Watch, Greece. *The Turks of Western Thrace.* January 1999. http://www.hrw.org/reports/1999/greece/index.htm (accessed 17 December 2002).

Hürriyet, Vakfı. *Devlet ve Medya İlişkileri.* Istanbul: Hürriyet Ofset, 1988.

İçduygu, Ahmet. *Irregular Migration in Turkey.* Geneva: IOM, 2003.

İçduygu, Ahmet and Fuat Keyman. "Globalization, Security, and Migration: The Case of Turkey." *Global Governance* 6, no. 3 (2000): 383–98.

İkkaracan, Pınar and Liz Amado. *Reform of the Turkish Penal Code and Sexual Rights.* Challenging Fundamentalisms: A Web Resource for Women's Human Rights. www.whrnet.org/fundamentalisms (accessed December 2004).

Ilgaz, Deniz. "Köy Enstitüleri." In *75 Yılda Eğitim,* ed. Fatma Gök. Istanbul: Türkiye Ekonomik ve Toplumsal Tarih Vakfı, 1999, 311–344.

İmset, İsmet. *The PKK 1973–1992: A Report on Separatist Violence in Turkey, 1973–92.* Ankara: Turkish Daily News Publications, 1992.

İnsan Hakları Eğitimi On Yılı Ulusal Komitesi. *İnsan Hakları Eğitimi On Yılı Komitesi 2000 Yılı Çalışmaları.* Ankara: İnsan Hakları Eğitimi On Yılı Ulusal Komitesi Yayınları, 2001.

"İnsan Haklarında Neredeyiz?" *Radikal 2,* 5 December 2004.

International Association of Universities. "The Stockholm Declaration on the Human Environment." http://www.unesco.org/iau/sd/sd_declarations.html (accessed 5 November 2003).

International Federation of Journalists. "Media Rights in Turkey." http://www.ifj.org/default.asp?index=589&Language=EN (accessed 16 June 2001).

International Publishers Association. "New Turkish Penal Code: A Long Way to Freedom of Expression." http://www.ipa-uie.org/PressRelease/171204/COMMENTS.htm (accessed 17 December 2004).

Introductory Statement by Dr. Yakın Ertürk. Sixteenth Session of the Committee on the Elimination against Women, New York, 17 January 1997. http://www.die.gov.tr/CIN/women/cedawpr.htm#introductory (accessed 4 August 2006).

Ioannides, Christos P. *In Turkey's Image*. New York: Aristide D. Caratzas, 1991.

İnuğur, Nuri. *Türk Basın Tarihi (1919–1989)*. Istanbul: Gazeteciler Cemiyeti, 1992.

Jacoby, Tim. *Social Power and the Turkish State*. London: Frank Cass, 2004.

———. "Governance in the Ottoman Empire." *Journal of Peasant Studies* forthcoming.

Jalali, Rita. "Civil Society and the State: Turkey After the Earthquake." *Disasters* 26, no. 2 (2002): 120–39.

Jandarma Genel Komutanlığı. "İnsan Hakları Faaliyetleri." http://www.jandarma. tsk.mil.tr/uluslararasi/insanhaklari.htm (accessed 5 December 2004). n.d.

———. *İnsan Hakları Semineri*. Ankara: Jandarma Genel Komutanlığı Basımevi, 2001.

Jennings, Sir Robert and Sir Arthur Watts, eds. *Oppenheim's International Law*. Vol. 1. 9th ed. London: Longman, 1992.

Johannesburg Summit 2002: Turkey Country Profile. Turkey National Report. Ministry of Environment. n.p.: United Nations, 2002. http://europeandcis.undp. org/WaterWiki/images/8/86/TurkeyCP.pdf (accessed 6 August 2006).

Journalism and the Human Rights Challenge to Turkey: Putting Union Rights and Press Freedom on the Agenda. Report of the IFJ/EFJ (International Federation of Journalists/European Federation of Journalists) Mission to Turkey, 26–30 April 2002. http://www.tgs.org.tr/english/turkeyreport2002.pdf (accessed March 2005).

Jung, Dietrichand and Wolfango Piccoli. *Turkey at the Crossroads: Ottoman Legacies and a Greater Middle East*. London: Zed Books, 2001.

Kabacalı, Alpay. *Türkiye'de Basın Sansürü*. Istanbul: Gazeteciler Cemiyeti, 1990.

Kaboğlu, İbrahim Ö. "Human Rights Education in Turkey." In *Human Rights Education and Practice in Turkey in the Process of Candidacy to the EU*, ed. Muzaffer Dartan and Münevver Cebeci. Istanbul: Marmara University European Community Institute, 2002. 103–13.

Kaboğlu, İbrahim, ed. "Tartışmalar," *Ulusal, Ulusalüstü ve Uluslararası Hukukta Azınlık Hakları: Birleşmiş Milletler, Avrupa Birliği, Avrupa Konseyi, Lozan Antlaşması*. Istanbul: Istanbul Bar Association Human Rights Center Publications, 2002b.

KA-DER. *Kadın Siyasetçinin El Kitabı*. Istanbul, 2002.

———. Kadın ve Kız Çocuklarının Eğitimi Çalışma Grubu Raporu. Kadın Sorunlarına Çözüm Arayışı Kurultayı. Istanbul, 14–15 June 2003.

Kadınlar Dünyası. "101 Kuruluşun Ortak Açıklaması: TBMM Başkanlığına, Sayın Milletvekillerine." *Kadınlar Dünyası* 26 (November 2001): 2.

Kalaycıoğlu, Ersin. "Turkish Democracy: Patronage Versus Governance." *Turkish Studies* 2, no. 1 (Spring 2001): 54–70.

———. *The Political Criteria: Fair or Strict Conditionality?* St. Anthony's College, Oxford University. http://www.sant.ox.ac.edu/areastudies/lectures/Ersin.doc (accessed 15 February 2005).

Kaldor, Mary. "Transnational Civil Society." In *Human Rights in Global Politics*, ed. Timothy Dunne and Nicholas Wheeler. Cambridge: Cambridge University Press, 1999.

Kandiyoti, Deniz. "End of Empire: Islam, Nationalism, and Women in Turkey." In *Women, Islam, and the State*, ed. Deniz Kandiyoti. Philadelphia: Temple University Press, 1991. 22–47.

Kaplan, Leyla. *Cemiyetlerde ve Siyasi Teşkilatlarda Türk Kadını (1908–1960)*. Ankara: Atatürk Araştırma Merkezi, 1998.

Kapulu, Ahmet et al. *Vatandaşlık ve İnsan Hakları Eğitimi 7*. Ankara: Koza Yayınları, 2001.

Karadeniz, Oğuz. "Türkiye'de Yabancı Kaçak İşçilik." *Türk-İş Yıllığı* 99, 1999.

Karaelmas, Nilay. "Turks Get Some of the News, Not All." World Press Review Online. December 2001. http://www.worldpress.org/specials/press/turkey.htm (accessed March 2005).

Kardam, Nükhet. " The State, Gender Policy and Social Change: An Analysis from Turkey" In *Color, Class and Country*, ed. G. Young and B. Dickerson. London: Zed Press, 1994. 152–67.

Kardam, Nükhet and Yakın Ertürk. "Expanding Gender Accountability? Women's Organizations and the State in Turkey." *International Journal of Organizational Theory and Behavior* 2, nos. 1–2 (1999): 167–68.

Karmon, Ely. "Radical Islamic Groups in Turkey." *Meria: Middle East Review of International Affairs* 1, no. 4 (December 1997). http://meria.idc.ac.il/journal/1997/issue4/jv1n4a2.html (accessed 4 December 2004).

Karpat, Kemal. "The Ottoman Rule in Europe from the Perspective of 1994." In *Turkey Between East and West: New Challenges for a Rising Regional Power*, ed. Vojtech Mastny and Craig R. Nation. Boulder, Colo.: Westview Press, 1996. 1–44.

Kasaba, Reşat. "Kemalist Certainties and Modern Ambiguities." In *Rethinking Modernity and National Identity in Turkey*, ed. Sibel Bozdoğan and Reşat Kasaba. Seattle: University of Washington Press, 1997. 15–36.

Katzenstein, Peter J., ed. *The Culture of National Security: Norms and Identity in World Politics*. New York: Columbia University Press, 1996.

Kaya, Yahya Kemal. *İnsan Yetiştirme Düzenimize Yeni Bir Bakış: Eğitimde Model Arayışı.* Ankara: Bilim Yayınları, 1989.

Kaygusuz, Özlem. "Foreign Policy and the Reconstruction of Modern Turkish Citizenship During the National Struggle Period." Ph.D. dissertation, Bilkent University, 2003.

Kazamias, Andreas M. *Education and the Quest for Modernity in Turkey.* Chicago: University of Chicago Press, 1966.

Kazgan, Gülten. *Dışa Açık Ekonomik Büyüme.* Istanbul: Altın Kitaplar, 1988.

Keck, Margaret E. and Kathryn Sikkink. *Activists Beyond Borders: Advocacy Networks in International Politics.* Ithaca, N.Y.: Cornell University Press, 1998.

Kedourie, Sylvia, ed. *Turkey: Identity, Democracy, Politics.* London: Frank Cass, 1996.

Kejanlıoğlu, Beybin. "Türkiye'de Radyo Televizyon Yayıncılığı Siyasası." In *Habercinin El Kitabı: Radyo ve Radyoculuk*, ed. Sevda Alankuş. Istanbul: IPS İletişim Vakfı Yayınları, 2003. 139–70.

Keleş, Ruşen. "Urbanization and Environment Policies." *Urbanization and Environment Conference.* Ankara: Önder Press, 1997. 50.

Keyder, Çağlar. *State and Class in Turkey: A Study in Capitalist Development.* London: Verso, 1987.

———. "Class and State in the Transformation of Modern Turkey." In *State and Ideology in the Middle East and Pakistan*, ed. Fred Halliday and Hamza Alavi. London: Macmillan Education, 1988. 191–221.

———. "Whither the Project of Modernity? Turkey in the 1990s." In *Rethinking Modernity and National Identity in Turkey*, ed. Sibel Bozdoğan and Reşat Kasaba. Seattle: University of Washington Press, 1997. 37–51.

Kılıç, Zülal. "Cumhuriyet Türkiyesi'nde Kadın Hareketine Genel bir Bakış." In *75 Yılda Kadınlar ve Erkekler.* Istanbul: Tarih Vakfı Yayınları, 1998. 347–60.

Kirişci, Kemal. "The Legal Status of Asylum Seekers in Turkey: Problems and Prospects." *International Journal of Refugee Law* 3, no. 3 (1991): 509–28.

———. "Asylum Seekers and Human Rights in Turkey." *Netherlands Quarterly of Human Rights* 10, no. 4 (1992): 447–60.

————. "'Coerced Immigrants': Refugees of Turkish Origins since 1945." *International Migration* 34, no. 3 (1996a): 385–412.

————. "Is Turkey Lifting the 'Geographical Limitation'?: The November 1994 Regulation on Asylum in Turkey." *International Journal of Refugee Law* 8, no. 3 (1996b): 298–328.

————. "Turkey." In *Internally Displaced People: A Global Survey*, ed. Janie Hampton. London: Earthscan, 1998.

————. "UHNCR and Turkey: Cooperating Toward an Improved Implementation of the 1951 Convention." *International Journal of Refugee Law* 13, nos. 1–2 (2001): 71–97.

————. "Reconciling Refugee Rights with Efforts to Combat Irregular Migration: The Case of the European Union and Turkey." *Global Migration Perspectives* 11 (October 2004). Global Commission on International Migration. http://www.gcim.org/en/ir_gmp.html (accessed 1 November 2004).

Kirişci, Kemal and Gareth Winrow. *The Kurdish Question and Turkey: An Example of a Trans-State Ethnic Conflict.* London: Frank Cass, 1998.

Kırkpınar, Leyla. "Türkiye'de Toplumsal Değişme Sürecinde Kadın." In *75 Yılda Kadınlar ve Erkekler*, ed. A. B. Hacımirzaoğlu. Istanbul: Türkiye Ekonomik ve Toplumsal Tarih Vakfı, 1998. 13–28.

Koç, Yıldırım. *Türkiye'de Grev Hakkı.* Türk-İş Eğitim Yayınları 14. Ankara: Türk-İş, 1999.

————. *Türkiye'de Sendikalaşma Hakkı ve ILO Prensipleri.* Ankara: Türk-İş, 2000.

Köker, Levent. *Modernleşme, Kemalizm ve Demokrasi.* Istanbul: İletişim Yayınları, 1995.

Köktaş, Emin M. "Modern Zamanlarda İslam ve Siyasal Meşruiyet Sorunu." *Bilgi ve Hikmet* 12 (Fall 1995): 41–49.

Koloğlu, Orhan. *Osmanlı'dan Günümüze Türkiye'de Basın.* Istanbul: İletişim Yayınları, 1992.

Koray, Meryem. *The Industrial Relations System in Turkey: Developments, Problems and Expectations.* Economy and Society Series. Istanbul: Friedrich Ebert Foundation, 1992.

Korey, William. *NGOs and the Universal Declaration of Human Rights: "A Curious Grapevine".* New York: St. Martin's Press, 1998.

Körezlioğlu, Ulvi. "Human Rights in the Training of Turkish Police Forces." In *Human Rights Education and Practice in Turkey in the Process of Candidacy to the EU*, ed. Muzaffer Dartan and Münevver Cebeci. Istanbul: Marmara University European Community Institute, 2002. 113–17.

Korn, David. *Exodus Within Borders: An Introduction to the Crisis of Internal Displacement.* Washington, D.C.: Brookings Institution Press, 1999.

Köstekli, İlyas. "Sendikal Örgütlenme Stratejileri." *Petrol-İş* (1995–99) Labor Force Report. Istanbul, June 2002.

Kramer, Heinz. *A Changing Turkey: Challenges to Europe and the United States.* Washington, D.C.: Brookings Institution, 2000.

Kraut, Richard. "Politics, Neutrality, and the Good." *Social Philosophy and Policy* 16, no. 1 (1999): 315–32.

Krishnaswami, Arcot. "Study of Discrimination in the Matter of Religious Rights and Practices." (1960). Reprinted in *Religion and Human Rights: Basic Documents*, ed. Tad Stahnke and Paul J. Martin. New York: Columbia University Center for the Study of Human Rights, 1998. 2–52.

Ksentini, Fatma Z. "Review of Further Developments in Fields with Which the Sub-Commission Has Been or May Be Concerned." UN Economic and Social

Council, Commission on Human Rights. http://www.unhchr.ch/Huridocda/ Huridoca.nsf/(Symbol)/E.CN.4.Sub.2.2000.34.En?Opendocument (accessed 4 November 2003).

Kubicek, Paul. "The Earthquake, Civil Society, and Political Change in Turkey: Assessment and Comparison with Eastern Europe." *Political Studies*, 50, no. 4 (2002): 761–78.

Küçüker, Erdal, ed. *4. Demokratik Eğitim Kurultayı, Eğitim Hakkı*. Vol. 1. Ankara: Eğitim-Sen Yayınları, March 2005.

Kurban, Dilek. "Confronting Equality: The Need for Constitutional Protection of Minorities on Turkey's Path to the European Union." *Columbia Human Rights Law Review* 151, no. 35 (2003): 151–214.

"Kurdistan Workers' Party." International Policy Institute for Counter-Terrorism (ICT). http://www.ict.org.il/articles/articledet.cfm?articleid=74 (accessed 3 March 2005).

Kurdish Human Rights Project. *Surviving for a Living: Report on the Current Conditions of Kurds in Turkey*. London: Kurdish Human Rights Project, 1996.

"Kürtçe İsteyen 40 Öğrenciye Ceza." *Hürriyet*, 20 January 2002.

Kurubaş, Erol. *Asimilasyondan Tanımaya: Uluslararası Alanda Azınlık Sorunları ve Avrupa Yaklaşımı*. Ankara: Asil Yayın Dağıtım, 2004.

Kuruluşundan Bugüne İHD. Ankara: İHD, 2001.

Kymlicka, Will. *Politics in the Vernacular: Nationalism, Muliticulturalism and Citizenship*. Oxford: Oxford University Press, 2001.

Law Library of Congress. *Religious Liberty: The Legal Framework in Selected OSCE Countries*. Washington, D.C.: Library of Congress, 2000.

Lewis, Bernard. *The Emergence of Modern Turkey*. London: Oxford Unversity Press, 1968.

Libal, Kathryn. "Children's Rights in Turkey." *Human Rights Review* 3, no. 1 (October–December 2001): 35–44.

Linardatos, Spyros. *Apo ton Emphilio stin Chounta* [From the Civil War to the Junta], vol. B, *1952–1955*. Athens: Papazissis, 1978.

———. *Apo ton Emphilio stin Chounta* [From the Civil War to the Junta], vol. D, *1961–1964*. Athens: Papazissis, 1986.

Loescher, Gil. *The UNHCR and World Politics: A Perilous Path*. Oxford: Oxford University Press, 2001.

Lordoğlu, Kuvvet. "Avrupa Birliği, Türkiye ve Sendikal Hareket." *Petrol İş Sendikal Notlar* 5, no. 11 (October 2001a): 49–51.

———. "Enformel ve Yabancı Kaçak İstihdam Üzerine Notlar." *Sendikal Notlar* (Petrol İş Journal) 12, no. 11 (December 2001b). 114–117.

Lozan Barış Konferansı, Tutanaklar, Belgeler, Takım I, Cilt 1, Kitap 2. Trans. Seha L. Meray. Ankara: Faculty of Political Science, 1970.

Malksoo, Lauri. "Language Rights in International Law: Why the Phoenix Is Still in the Ashes." *Florida Journal of International Law* 12, no. 3 (Spring 2000): 431–67.

Mango, Andrew. *Turkey: The Challenge of a New Role*. Westport, Conn.: Praeger, 1994.

Manstry, Vojtech and Craig R. Nation, eds. *Turkey Between East and West: New Challenges for a Rising Regional Power*. Boulder, Colo.: Westview Press, 1996.

Mardin, Şerif. "Center-Periphery Relations: A Key to Turkish Politics." *Daedalus* (Winter 1972): 169–90.

———. "Religion and Politics in Modern Turkey." *Islam in the Political Process*. Cambridge: Cambridge University Press, 1989. 138–59.

———. *Türkiye'de Din ve Siyaset*. Istanbul: İletişim Yayınları, 1994.

———. *Türkiye'de Toplum ve Siyaset*. Istanbul: İletişim Yayınları, 1995.

———. "Projects as Methodology: Some Reflections on Modern Turkish Science." In *Rethinking Modernity and National Identity in Turkey*, ed. Reşat Kasaba and Sibel Bozdoğan. Seattle: University of Washington Press, 1997. 64–80.

Marulies, Ronnie and Ergin Yıldızoğlu. "Resurgence of Islam and the Welfare Party in Turkey." In *Political Islam: Essays from Middle East Report*, ed. Joel Beinin and Joe Stork. Berkeley: University of California Press, 1996. 144–53.

Mavridis, P. "Choris Antallagmata Anigi I Chalki" [Chalki Opens Without Reciprocal Offers]. *Express Daily*, 25 July 2004.

Mayall, Simon V. *Turkey: Thwarted Ambition*. McNair Paper 56. Washington, D.C.: Institute for National Strategic Studies, January 1997.

Mayer, Ann E. "A Critique of An-Na`im's Assessment of Islamic Criminal Justice." In *Islamic Rights Reform and Human Rights*, ed. Tore Lindholm and Kari Vogt. Oslo: Nordic Human Rights Publications, 1992.

Mazıcı, Nurşen. *A Modern History of the Kurds*. London: I.B. Tauris, 1992.

———. "1930'a Kadar Basının Durumu ve 1931 Matbuat Kanunu." *A.Ü. Türk İnkılap Tarihi Dergisi* 9, no. 18 (1996): 131–54.

———. *A Modern History of the Kurds*. London: I.B. Taurus, 2000.

McDowell, David. *A Modern History of the Kurds*. London: I.B. Taurus, 2000.

McLaren, Lauren M. and Meltem Müftüler-Baç. "Turkish Parliamentarians' Perspective on Turkey's Relations with the European Union." In *Turkey and the European Union: Domestic Politics, Economic Integration and International Dynamics*, ed. Ali Çarkoğlu and Barry Rubin London: Frank Cass, 2003. 195–218.

McLean, Jennifer. "National Responses to Internal Displacement." *Forced Migration Review* 1 (1998): 10–11.

Medeni Kanun Tasarısı: Mal Rejimleri. Turkish Republic Prime Ministry Directorate General on the Status and Problems of Women. http://www.kssgm.gov.tr (accessed July 2003).

Medico International and Kurdish Human Rights Project. *The Destruction of Villages in South East Turkey*. London: Medico International, 1996.

Meintjes, Garth. "Human Rights Education as Empowerment: Reflections on Pedagogy." In *Human Rights Education for the Twenty-First Century*, ed. George J. Andreopoulos and Richard P. Claude. Philadelphia: University of Pennsylvania Press, 1997. 64–80.

Merrills, J. G. *The Development of International Law by the European Court of Human Rights*. Manchester: Manchester University Press, 1988.

Ministry of National Education (Milli Eğitim Bakanlığı). *Geçmişten Günümüze Özel Eğitim Kurumları*. Ankara: Milli Eğitim Basımevi, 1991.

———. Board of Education. *15. Milli Eğitim Şurası: 2000'li yıllarda Türk Milli Eğitim Sistemi*. Ankara: Milli Eğitim Basımevi, 1996.

———. *2000 Yılında Milli Eğitim*. Ankara: Milli Eğitim Basımevi, 2000.

———. *Milli Eğitim Sayısal Veriler 2001*. Ankara: Milli Eğitim Basımevi, 2001.

———. *Milli Eğitim'de Sayısal Veriler 2003–2004*. Ankara: Milli Eğitim Basımevi, 2004. http://www.meb.gov.tr/Stats/ICINDEKILER1.html (accessed 6 June 2005).

———. *Milli Eğitim İstatistikleri 2004–2005*. Ankara: Milli Eğitim Basımevi, 2005.

Minority Rights Group International. "Turkey's EU Ambitions Are Failing to Produce Rights Reforms for Minorities," 15 March 2004. http://www.minorityrights.org/news_detail.asp?ID=234 (accessed 5 December 2004).

Misgeld, Dieter. "Human Rights Education: Conclusions from Some Latin American Experiences." *Journal of Moral Education* 23, no. 3 (1994): 239–50.

Moravcsik, Andrew. "The Origins of Human Rights Regimes: Democratic Delegation in Postwar Europe." *International Organization* 54, no. 2 (2000): 217–52.

Morsink, Johannes. *The Universal Declaration of Human Rights: Origins, Drafting, and Intent.* Philadelphia: University of Pennsylvania Press, 1999.

Müftüler-Baç, Meltem. "Turkish Women's Predicament." *Women's Studies International Forum* 22, no. 3 (May–June 1999): 303–15.

Muggah, Robert. "Conflict-Induced Displacement and Involuntary Resettlement in Colombia: Putting Cernea's IRLR Model to the Test." *Disasters* 24, no. 3 (2000): 198–216.

National Committee on the Decade for Human Rights Education. *Human Rights Education Programme of Turkey 1998–2007.* Ankara: National Committee on the Decade for Human Rights Education Publications, 1999.

National Human Rights Institutions: A Handbook on the Establishment and Strengthening of National Institutions for the Promotion and Protection of Human Rights. Geneva: United Nations Centre for Human Rights, 1995.

National Student Selection and Placement Centre. http://www.osym.gov.tr (accessed 5 November 2003).

Nebiler, Halil. *Medyanın Ekonomi Politiği: Türk Basınında Tekelleşme ve Basın Ahlakının Çöküşü.* Istanbul: Sarmal Yayınevi, 1995.

Nesin, Aziz. *Kremaste tous san ta ttsambia* [Hang Them like a Bunch of Grapes; Greek translation of *Salkım Salkım Asılacak Adamlar*]. Athens: Kastaniotis, 1999.

NGO Report on the Implementation of CEDAW in Turkey. Prepared by Women for Women's Human Rights and presented to the United Nations Committee for the Elimination of All Kinds of Discrimination against Women, at the Periodic Review of Turkey. New York, January 1997. http://www.wwhr.org (accessed February 2002).

Nur, Rıza. *Hayatım ve Hatıratım.* Vol. 3. Istanbul: Altındağ Publishing House, 1967.

Odman, Tevfik. *Mülteci Hukuku.* Ankara: AÜ. SBF. İnsan Hakları Merkezi Yayınları 15, 1995.

Okçabol, Rıfat. *Adult Education.* Istanbul: Der Yayınları, 1994.

Oktay, Ahmet. *Toplumsal Değişme ve Basın.* Istanbul: Bilim Felsefe ve Sanat Yayınları, 1987.

Ökte, Faik. *The Tragedy of the Turkish Capital Tax.* London: Croom Helm, 1987.

Ökten, Nazlı. "1935 Istanbul Uluslararası Kadınlar Birliği Kongresi: Otuz Yurdun Kadınları." *Tarih ve Toplum* 219 (2002): 55–60.

Öniş, Ziya. "The Political Economy of Islamic Resurgence in Turkey: The Rise of the Welfare Party in Perspective." *Third World Quarterly* 18, no. 4 (1997): 743–66.

Oran, Baskın. "The Sleeping Volcano in Turco-Greek Relations: The Western Thrace Minority." In *Turkish Foreign Policy: Recent Developments,* ed. Kemal Karpat. Madison, Wis.: n.p, 1996. 119–38.

———. *Atatürk Milliyetçiliği, resmî ideoloji dışı bir inceleme.* 5th ed. Ankara: Bilgi, 1999.

———. "Bir İnsan Hakları ve Çokkültürcülük Belgesi Olarak 1923 Lausanne Barış Antlaşması." In *Kopenhag Kriterleri,* ed. İbrahim Kaboğlu. Istanbul: Istanbul Bar Association Human Rights Center Publications, 2001. 210–19.

———. *Türkiye'de Azınlıklar; kavramlar—teori—Loza— iç mevzuat—içtihat—uygulama.* Istanbul: İleşitim, 2004.

Osler, Audrey and Hugh Starkey. "Fundamental Issues in Teacher Education for Human Rights: A European Perspective." *Journal of Moral Education* 23, no. 3 (1994): 349–60.

Özbudun, Ergun. "Constitutional Law." In *Introduction to Turkish Law,* ed. Tuğrul Ansay and Don Wallace. Boston: Kluwer, 1996.

References 321

———. *Contemporary Turkish Politics: Challenges to Democratic Consolidation.* Boulder, Colo.: Lynne Reinner, 2000.
Özbudun, Ergun and Serap Yazıcı. *Democratization Reforms in Turkey (1993–2004).* Turkish Economic and Social Studies Foundation (TESEV). http://www.tesev.org.tr/projeler/demokratiklesme_kitap.pdf (accessed 12 February 2005).
Özdek, E. Yasemin. "The Turkish Constitutional Court and the International Human Rights Instruments." *İnsan Hakları Yıllığı* 11 (1992): 25–37.
"Özel Okul Fiyatları Oxford Gibi." *Milliyet,* 13 October 2003.
Özerdem, Alpaslan. "Disaster as Manifestation of Unresolved Development Challenges: The Marmara Earthquake, Turkey." In *Natural Disasters and Development in a Globalizing World,* ed. Mark Pelling. London: Routledge, 2003. 199–213.
Özerdem, Alpaslan and Sultan Barakat. "After the Marmara Earthquake: Lessons for Avoiding Short Cuts to Disasters." *Third World Quarterly* 21, no. 3 (2000): 425–39.
Özerdem, Alpaslan and Tim Jacoby. *Disaster Management in Japan, Turkey and India: Earthquake Relief and Civil Society.* London: I.B. Tauris, 2005.
Özgen, Murat. *Türkiye'de Basının Gelişimi ve Sorunları.* Istanbul: Doğan Ofset, 2000.
Özkaleli, Murat and Umut Konuloğlu Özkaleli. "Myths and Realities About the Turkish Model." Paper presented at the annual meeting of the American Political Science Association, Philadelphia, 27–31 August 2003.
Özsever, Atilla. *Tekelci Medyada Örgütsüz Gazeteci.* Ankara: İmge Kitabevi, 2004.
Paker, Saliha, and Zehra Toska. "Yazan, Yazılan, Silinen ve Tekrar Yazılan Özne: Suat Derviş'in Kimlikleri." *Tarih ve Toplum* 39 (March 1997): 11–22.
Pan-Imvrian Committee of Athens. "Imvros and Tenedos—Violations of the Lausanne Treaty." Hellenic Resources Network. 1996. http://www.hri.org/docs/inter/93–10–06.doc.html (accessed 26 February 2003).
Payaslıoğlu, Arif and Ahmet İçduygu. "Awareness of and Support for Human Rights among Turkish University Students." *Human Rights Quarterly* 21, no. 2 (May 1999): 512–33.
Pervizat, Leylâ. "In the Name of Honor." *Human Rights Dialogue: An International Forum for Debating Human Rights* 2:, no. 10 (Fall 2003). www.carnegiecouncil.org/viewMedia.php/prmID/1061 (accessed 14 November 2003).
Petrol-İş. *Yearbook for 1995–96.* Istanbul: Petrol-İş, 1996.
———. "Labor Report 1995–99." Istanbul: Petrol-İş, 1999.
Pettersson, Bjorn. "Development-Induced Displacement: Internal Affair or International Human Rights Issue?" *Forced Migration Review* 12 (2001): 16–19.
Pevsner, Lucille W. *Turkey's Political Crisis: Background, Perspectives, and Prospects.* New York: Praeger, 1984.
Pişkinsüt, Sema. *Filistin Askısından Fezlekeye: İşkencenin Kitabı.* Ankara: Bilgi Yayınevi, 2001.
Plagemann, Gottfried. "Türkiye'de İnsan Hakları Örgütleri: Farklı Kültürel Çerçeveler, Farklı Örgütler." In *Türkiye'de Sivil Toplum ve Milliyetçilik,* ed. Stefanos Yerasimos. Istanbul: İletişim Yayınları, 2001.
Plender, Richard, and Nuala Mole. "Beyond the Geneva Convention: Constructing a De Facto Right of Asylum from International Human Rights Instruments." In *Refugee Rights and Realities: Evolving International Concepts and Regimes,* ed. Frances Nicholson and Patrick Twomey. Cambridge: Cambridge University Press, 1999. 81–105.
"Police Detain 29 People Demanding Kurdish Lessons." *Turkish Daily News.* http://www.turkishdailynews.com/FrTDN/latest/dom.htm (accessed 29 January 2002).
Pope, Nicole and Hugh Pope. *Turkey Unveiled.* London: John Murray, 1997.

————. *Turkey Unveiled: A History of Modern Turkey*. Woodstock, N.Y.: Overlook Press, 1999.

Population and Development Indicators. State Institute of Statistics. http://nkg. die.gov.tr/ (accessed 9 March 2003).

Preece, Jennifer Jackson. "Ethnic Cleansing as an Instrument of Nation-State Creation: Changing State Practices and Evolving Legal Norms." *Human Rights Quarterly* 20, no. 4 (November 1998): 817–42.

Prison Conditions in Turkey. Helsinki Watch Report. U.S. Helsinki Watch Committee. New York: Human Rights Watch, August 1989.

Project Underground (Supporting the Human Rights of Communities Resisting Mining and Oil Exploitation). *The Gold Album: Action Pack—Cyanide*. Section entitled "Two Communities Fight Back." http://www.moles.org/ ProjectUnderground/reports/goldpack/goldpack_i.html (accessed 6 November 2003).

Psomiades, Harry J. *The Eastern Question: The Last Phase*. Thessaloniki: Institute for Balkan Studies, 1968.

Rahman, Fazlur. *Islam*. Chicago: University of Chicago Press, 1979.

Randall, Vicky. "The Media and Democratisation in the Third World." *Third World Quarterly* 14, no. 3 (1993): 625–46.

Rajagopal, Balakrishnan. "Rule of Law in Conflict Management." In *Security, Development, and Human Rights in the 21st Century*, ed. Agnes Hurwitz. Boulder, Colo.: Lynne Rienner, 2006.

Rawls, John. *Political Liberalism*. New York: Columbia University Press, 1993.

Regular Report on Turkey's Progress Toward Accession. Council of Europe, Brussels, 9 October 2002, COM (2002) 700 final.

2004 Regular Report on Turkey's Progress Towards Accession. European Commission. http://europa.eu.int/comm/enlargement/report_2004/pdf/rr_tr_2004_en. pdf (accessed 12 January 2005).

"Relations with the European Union in the Field of Environment." Ministry of Foreign Affairs. (accessed 6 June 2005).

Reliefweb. *Guiding Principles on Internal Displacement*. http://www.reliefweb.int/ rw/lib.nsf/doc207?OpenForm&query=3&cat=Internally%20Displaced%20 Persons (accessed 18 March 2003).

Replies of the Turkish Delegation to the Question of the Pre-Session Working Group of the Committee on the Elimination of Discrimination against Women, United Nations, New York, 17 January 1997. http://www.die.gov.tr/CIN/ women/cedawpr.htm#REPLIES (accessed 4 August 2006).

Representation of the European Commission to Turkey. http://www.deltur.cec. eu.int/english/eu-turkey.html (accessed 5 May 2005)

Republic of Turkey Ministry of Foreign Affairs. "Turkey: 2003 Accession Partnership." http://www.mfa.gov.tr/MFA/ForeignPolicy/MainIssues/TurkeyAndEU/ TurkeyandtheEUmain.htm (accessed 5 August2006).

Resolution on the Human Rights Situation in Turkey, Document No. A2–117/ 85, the European Parliament, 23 October 1985. *Official Journal of the European Communities* C 343/60 (31 December 1985).

Reyna, Yuda and Yusuf Şen. *Cemaat Vakıfları ve Sorunları*. Istanbul: Gözlem, 1994.

Reyna, Yuda and Ester Moreno Zonana. *Son Yasal Düzenlemelere Göre Cemaat Vakıfları*. Istanbul: Gözlem Yayınları, 2003.

Risse, Thomas, Steven C. Ropp, and Kathryn Sikkink, eds. *The Power of Human Rights: International Norms and Domestic Change*. Cambridge: Cambridge University Press, 1999.

Robertson, Geoffrey, and Andrew G. L. Nicol. *Media Law: The Rights of Journalists, Broadcasters and Publishers*. London: Sage, 1984.

Robinson, Mary. Statement on Aarhus Convention. United Nations Economic Commission of Europe. http://www.unece.org/env/pp/statements.05.11.htm (accessed 6 August 2006).

Ross, Loretta J. and Meghna Gupta. "Bringing Human Rights Home: Human Rights Education for the 21st Century." *Social Education* 62 (1998): 377–80.

Rozakis, Christos. "The International Protection of Minorities in Greece." In *Greece in a Changing Europe*, ed. Kevin Featherstone and Kostas Ifantis. Manchester: Manchester University Press, 1996. 95–116.

Rumpf, Christian. "The Protection of Human Rights in Turkey and the Significance of International Human Rights Instruments." *Human Rights Law Journal* 14, no, 11–12 (1993): 394–408.

Rumford, Chris. "Human Rights and Democratization in Turkey in the Context of EU Candidature." *Journal of European Area Studies* 9, no. 1 (2001): 93–105.

Şahin, Haluk. "Broadcasting Autonomy in Turkey: Its Rise and Fall, 1961–1971." *Journalism Quarterly* (Autumn 1981): 395–400. Available from Makaleler Akademi. http://www.medyakronik.com/akademi/makaleler/makaleler08.htm (accessed 13 May 2005).

Samim, Ahmet. "The Tragedy of the Turkish Left." *New Left Review* 126 (1981): 60–85.

Sandole, Dennis. *Capturing the Complexity of Conflict: Dealing with Violent Ethnic Conflicts of the Post-Cold War Era*. London: Pinter, 1999.

Sarıbay, Ali Y. *Postmodernizm, Sivil Toplum ve İslam*. İstanbul: İletişim Yayınları, 1995.

Sarioglou, Irini. *Turkish Policy Towards Greek Education in Istanbul, 1923–1974: Secondary Education and Cultural Identity*. Athens: Hellenic Literary and Historical Archive (ELIA), 2004.

Secretariat-General for the EU Affairs. *Turkey: National Programme for the Adoption of the Acquis*. Section on "4.25.2 Asylum." Ankara, 2001.

Senturk, Recep. "Minority Rights in Islam: From Dhimmi to Citizen." In *Islam and Human Rights: Advancing a U.S.-Muslim Dialogue*, ed. Shireen T. Hunt. Washington, D.C.: CSIS Press, 2005. 67–99.

Shadow NGO Report on Turkey's Fourth and Fifth Combined Periodic Report to the Committee on the Elimination of Discrimination of Women. For submission to the CEDAW presession. July 2004. http://www.wwhr.org (accessed February 2002).

Shuibhne, Niamh Nic. "The European Union and Minority Language Rights: Respect for the Cultural and Linguistic Diversity." *International Journal on Multicultural Societies* (2001). UNESCO. http://www.unesco.org/most/vl3n2shui.htm (accessed 21 July 2001).

Sikkink, Kathryn. "The Emergence, Evolution, and Effectiveness of the Latin American Human Rights Network." In *Constructing Democracy: Human Rights, Citizenship, and Society in Latin America*, ed. Elizabeth Jelin and Eric Hershberg. Boulder, Colo.: Westview Press, 1996. 59–84.

Silicon Valley Toxic Coalition Web Site Media Advisory. "European Public Access to Environmental Information Enacted." http://www.svtc.org/icrt/rtk/aarhus_pr.htm (accessed 10 November 2003).

Sirman, Nüket. "Feminism in Turkey: A Short History." *New Perspectives in Turkey* 3, no. 1 (Fall 1989):1–34.

Skutnabb-Kangas, Tove. *Linguistic Genocide in Education or Worldwide Diversity and Human Rights*. Mahwah, N.J.: Lawrence Erlbaum, 2000.

324   References

Smith, Michael Llewellyn. *Ionian Vision: Greece in Asia Minor, 1919–1922.* London: Hurst, 1998.

Smith, Rhona K. "Moving Towards Articulating Linguistic Rights—New Developments in Europe." *Michigan State University-DCL Journal of International Law* 8, no. 2 (Summer 1999): 437–51.

Soltarides, Symeon. *Kemalikos Ethnikismos* [Kemalist Nationalism]. Athens: Nea Synora-Livani, 2000.

Southeastern European Women's Legal Initiative. "Turkish Report on National Machineries." http://www.seeline-project.net/NM/TurkeyNM.htm (accessed 20 September 2002).

Soysal, Mümtaz. *Anayasanın Anlamı.* Istanbul: Gerçek Yayınları, 1986.

Sönmez, Mustafa. "Türk Medya Sektöründe Yoğunlaşma ve Sonuçları." *Birikim* (December 1996): 76–86.

———. *100 Göstergede Kriz ve Yoksullaşma.* Istanbul: İletişim Yayınları, 2002.

———. *Filler ve Çimenler.* Istanbul: İletişim Yayınları, 2003a.

———. *İşte Eseriniz: 100 Göstergede Kuruluştan Çöküşe Türkiye Ekonomisi.* Istanbul: İletişim Yayıncılık, 2003b.

Söylemez, Alev. *Medya Ekonomisi ve Türkiye Örneği.* Ankara: Haberal Eğitim Vakfı, 1998.

Stammers, Neil. "Social Movements and the Social Construction of Human Rights." *Human Rights Quarterly* 21, no. 4 (1999): 980–1008.

Starkey, Hugh, ed. *The Challenge of Human Rights Education.* London: Council of Europe, 1991.

State Institute of Statistics (Devlet İstatistik Enstitüsü). Women Information Network in Turkey. http:// www.die.gov.tr/tkba/English_TKBA/kadin_haklari.htm (accessed 16 June 2003).

———. http://www.die.gov.tr/TURKISH/STATIS/Esg2/f.htm (accessed 15 March 2004).

———. http://www.die.gov.tr/konularr/isgucu04.htm. October 2002 (accessed February 2005).

State of the World's Refugees: Fifty Years of Humanitarian Action. New York: Oxford University Press for United Nations High Commissioner for Refugees, 2000.

NEAP, National Environment Action Plan of Turkey. Ankara, 1999. http://www.unescap.org/stat/envstat/neap-turkey.pdf (accessed 6 August 2006).

Statement by Prof. Yakın Ertürk, Head of the Delegation of Turkey to the Forty-Sixth Session of the Commission on the Status of Women. Permanent Mission of Turkey to the United Nations, New York, 5 March 2002.

Stathi, Penelope. "Ta tourkika scholika eghiridia sti Thraki" [Turkish Textbooks in Thrace]. *Sychrona Themata* [Current Issues] 63 (1997): 65–67.

Statute of the Mazlum-Der. Kayseri: Mazlum-Der, 1990.

Steiner, Henry J. and Philip Alston. *International Human Rights in Context.* Oxford: Oxford University Press, 2000.

"Students Signing Petitions for Kurdish Lessons File a Compensation Case." *Turkish Daily News.* http://www.turkishdailynews.com/FrTDN/latest/dom.htm (accessed 10 October 2002).

Talay, Birsen. "1979 Seçimleri ve Bakiye Beria Önger." *Tarih ve Toplum* 31 (March 1999): 183–88.

———. "'Temsili bir Karakter' ya da bir Karakterin Temsili: Bakiye Beria Önger." *Tarih ve Toplum* 37 (April 2002): 212–18.

Tan, Mine G. *Kadın-Erkek Eşitliğine Doğru Yürüyüş: Eğitim, Çalışma Yaşamı ve Siyaset.* Istanbul: TÜSİAD, 2000.

Tan, Mine G., Yıldız Ecevit, and Serpil Üşür. *Towards Gender Equality: Education, Working Life and Politics*. Istanbul: TÜSİAD Executive Summary, 2001.

Tan, Namık. *Toplu İş Sözleşmesi*. Ankara: Türk-İş, 1999.

Tanör, Bülent. *Türkiye'nin İnsan Hakları Sorunu*. Ankara: BDS Yayınları, 1994.

———. *Osmanlı-Türk Anayasal Gelişmeleri*. Istanbul: Yapı Kredi Yayınları, 1998.

Tarhanlı, Turgut. "Sığınmacı, Mülteci ve Göç Konularına İlişkin Türkiye'deki Yargı Kararları Konusunda Hukuki bir Değerlendirme." In *Sığınmacı, Mülteci ve Göç Konularına İlişkin Türkiye'deki Yargı Kararları*. Ankara: UNHCR, 2000. 1–34.

Taşkıran, Tezer. *Cumhuriyetin 50: Yılında Türk Kadın Hakları*. Başbakanlık Kültür Müsteşarlığı, Cumhuriyetin 50. Ankara: Yıldönümü Yayınları, 1973.

Tekeli, Şirin. "Emergence of the New Feminist Movement in Turkey." In *The New Women's Movement*, ed. D. Dahlerup. Beverly Hills, Calif.: Sage, 1986. 179–99.

———. "Women in the Changing Political Associations of the 1980s." In *Turkish State, Turkish Society*, ed. A. Finkel and N. Sirman. London: Routledge, 1990. 259–87.

———. "Birinci ve İkinci Dalga Feminist Hareketlerin Karşılaştırmalı İncelemesi Üzerine bir Deneme." In *75 Yılda Kadınlar ve Erkekler*, ed. Ayşe Berktay Hacımirzaoğlu. Istanbul: Tarih Vakfı Yayınları, 1998. 337–46.

"TESEV Anketi: AB'den yana olanların oranı yüzde 64/ Terör magdurlarının yüzde 43'ü idama karşı TESEV'in AB Anketi sunumu." TESEV. http://www.tesev.org.tr/basin/ab2002.php (accessed 15 May 2005). 2002.

TGC. *Türkiye Gazeteciler Cemiyeti'nin Basın Kanunu Tasarısının Maddelerine İlişkin Görüşleri*. http://www.tgc.org.tr/yasataslagi.htm (accessed March 2005).

Thornberry, Patrick. *International Law and the Rights of Minorities*. Oxford: Clarendon Press, 1994.

Tibbitts, Felisa. "Planning for the Future: Human Rights in Schools" Human Rights Education Associates. http://www.hrea.org/pubs/IHF.html (accessed 21 December 2004). n.d.

———. "Human Rights Education in Schools in the Post-Communist Context." *European Journal of Education* 29, no. 4 (1994): 363–76.

Tirman, John. *Spoils of War: The Human Cost of America's Arms Trade*. New York: Free Press, 1997.

Tomasevski, Katarina. *United Nations Commission Report by the Special Rapporteur on the Right to Education*. UN Doc. E/CN.4/2002/60/Add. 2–3 April 2002. Official Documents System of the United Nations. http://daccessdds.un.org/doc/UNDOC/GEN/G02/100/12/PDF/G0210012.pdf?OpenElement (accessed 6 June 2005).

Toprak, Zafer. "Cumhuriyet Halk Fırkasından Önce Kurulan Parti: Kadınlar Halk Fırkası." *Tarih ve Toplum* 9 (March 1988): 30–31.

Topuz, Hıfzı. *100 Soruda Türk Basın Tarihi*. Istanbul: Gerçek Yayınevi, 1996.

Toynbee, Arnold J. and Kenneth P. Kirkwood. *Turkey*. Reprint Westport, Conn.: Greenwood Press, 1976.

"Treaty of Peace with Turkey Signed at Lausanne, 24 July 1923." Brigham Young University, Harold B. Lee Library. http://www.lib.byu.edu/~rdh/wwi/1918p/lausanne.html (accessed 23 July 2002).

Troumbeta, Sevasti. *Kataskeuazontas tautotites gia tous Mousoulmanous tis Thrakis* [Constructing Identities for the Muslims of Thrace]. Athens: Kritiki, 2001.

Tseng, Chien-Yuan. "On People's Human Rights." Pt. 1. 8 January 2003. Association for Asian Research. http://www.asianresearch.org/articles/1150.html (accessed 6 November 2003).

Tunç, Aslı. "Faustian Acts in Turkish Style: Structural Change in National News-papers as an Obstacle to Quality Journalism in 1990–2003." In *Quality Press in Southeast Europe*, ed. Orlin Spassov. Sofia: Southeast European Media Centre, 2004. 306–22.

Turan, İlter. "Religion and Political Culture in Turkey." In *Islam in Modern Turkey*. London: I.B. Tauris, 1991.

Turgut, Nükhet. "The Right to Environment: Does It Reflect Environmental Ethics?" *Eubios Journal of Asian and International Bioethics 8* (November 1998): 169–71. http://www2.unescobkk.org/eubios/EJ86/ej86d.htm (accessed 27 March 2004).

Turkey: Call for Immediate Steps Against Isolation in "F-type". London: Amnesty International Publications, 2002.

Turkey: End Sexual Violence Against Women in Custody! London: Amnesty International Publications, 2003.

Turkey: Torture and Medical Neglect of Prisoners. London: Amnesty International Publications, 1988.

Turkey: Torture and Mistreatment in Pre-Trial Detention by Anti-Terror Police. New York: Human Rights Watch, 1997.

"Turkey Accepted the Compulsory Jurisdiction of the European Court of Human Rights: Declaration of 26 December 1989." *Human Rights Law Journal* 11 (1990): 458–59.

"Turkey's Public Realm." *Journal of International Affairs* 54, no. 1 (Fall 2000).

"Turkish Constitutional Court President Says Political Bans to Harm Ties with EU." BBC Worldwide Monitoring (26 September 2002). Last accessed via Lexis-Nexis on 6 August 2006.

Turkish Environmental Law and Some Other Related Legal Provisions. Environmental Problems Foundation of Turkey. Ankara: Önder Matbaa, 1988.

Turkish Foundation for Reforestation, Erosion Combat and Protection of Natural Habitats (TEMA). "Litigation." http://www.tema.org.tr/english/legal_campaigns/litigation.html (accessed 10 November 2003).

"Turkish Radio-TV Board Approves Private Kurdish Broadcasting" *Journal of Turkish Weekly*. http://www.turkishweekly.net/news.php?id=24261 (accessed 12 March 2006).

Türkiye Cumhuriyeti İlk Anayasa Taslağı [First Draft Constitution of Turkey]. Istanbul: Boyut Yayın Grubu, 1998.

Türkiye İnsan Hakları Kurumu Kuruluş Bildirgesi: Etkinlikler ve Belgeler. Ankara: TİHAK Yayınları, 2000.

United Nations. *Universal Declaration on Human Rights*. Fiftieth Anniversary of the Universal Declaration on Human Rights, 1948–1998. http://www.un.org/Overview/rights.html (accessed 2 November 2003).

——. "Rio Declaration on Environment and Development." *General Assembly Report of the United Nations Conference on Environment and Development*. http://www.un.org/documents/ga/conf151/aconf15126–1annex1.htm (accessed 3 November 2003).

United Nations Committee on Human Rights. General Comment 18 (37), "Non-Discrimination," adopted 9 November 1989. http://www.ohchr.org/english/bodies/hrc/comments.htm (accessed 7 July 2002).

——. Rights of Minorities. General Comment 23, p. 5.1, adopted 4 August 1994. http://www.unhcr.ch/tbs/doc.nsf/(s . . . /CCPR+general+comment+23.En?OpenDocumen (accessed 15 July 2001).

United Nations Country Team. "Common Country Assessment (CCA)." Ankara, December 2000.

UNDP (United Nations Development Program). Bureau for Crisis Prevention and Recovery. Disaster Risk Analysis for Turkey (Item # 3). http://gridca.grid.unep.ch/undp/cntry_profile.php?selectedCountry=232 (accessed 5 August 2006).

UNDP. *Human Development Report 2000.* New York: Oxford University Press, 2000.

———. *Human Development Report 2001.* New York: Oxford University Press, 2001.

———. *Human Development Report, Turkey.* Ankara, 1998.

———. *National Human Development Report for Turkey.* Geneva: UNDP, 2001.

——. *National Human Development Report for Turkey.* Geneva: UNDP, 2003.

UNEP (United Nations Environmental Programme). UNEP National Committees (NATCOM) http://www.unep.ch/natcom/assets/national_committees/natcom_turkey.html (accessed 27 March 2004).

UNHCR (United Nations High Commissioner for Refugees. *Collection of International Instruments Concerning Refugees.* Geneva: Office of the United Nations High Commissioner for Refugees (UNHCR), 1988.

———. *Sığınmacı, Mülteci ve Göç Konularına İlişkin Türkiye'deki Yargı Kararları.* Ankara: UNHCR, 2000a.

———. *The Collection of Turkish Jurisprudence on Asylum, Refugees and Migration.* Ankara: UNHCR, 2000b.

____. "Secretary-General's Representative on Internally Displaced Persons Concludes Visit to Turkey." http://www.unhchr.ch/huricane/huricane.nsf/view01/9230EA356745E6A1C1256BCF0042A86D?opendocument (accessed 30 July 2002).

Uras, Güngör. "Kentlerde Eğitimli Gençlerin Yüzde 29.1'i İşsiz." *Milliyet,* 7 October 2002. http://www.milliyet.com.tr/2002/10/07/yazar/uras.html (accessed February 2005).

U.S. Committee for Refugees. *The Wall of Denial: Internal Displacement in Turkey.* Washington D.C.: USCR, 1997.

U.S. Congress. Commission on Security and Cooperation in Europe. *The Continued Use of Torture in Turkey.* Washington, D.C.: Government Printing Office, 1997.

U.S. Department of State. Bureau of Democracy, Human Rights, and Labor. *Country Reports on Human Rights Practices: Turkey.* Washington, D.C.: Government Printing Office, 2001. Electronic version at http://www.state.gov/g/drl/hr (accessed 5 August 2003). N.d.

———. "2001 Annual Report on International Religious Freedom: Turkey." 2001. http://www.state.gov/ (accessed 17 December 2002).

———. "Turkey. Country Reports on Human Rights Practices-2001." 2002. http://www.state.gov/ (accessed 26 February 2003).

U.S. Department of State: *Turkey Country Report on Human Rights for 1996,* released on January 1997, http://www.state.gov (accessed 28 December 2000).

Üzüm, İlyas. "İslam'da Devlet Yönetiminin Yeri." *Köprü* 58 (1997): 54–60.

Varennes, Ferdinand de. *Language, Minorities and Human Rights.* The Hague: Nijhoff, 1996.

———. "Language Rights as an Integral Part of Human Rights." *International Journal on Multicultural Societies* 3, no.1 (2001): 15–25.

Verheugen, Günther. "Strategy Paper: Accession Partnership with Turkey and Progress Reports." SPEECH/00/419, European Parliament, Brussels, 8 November 2000.

Vieytez, Eduardo Javier Ruiz. "The Protection of Linguistic Minorities: A Historical Approach." *International Journal on Multicultural Societies* 3, no. 1 (2001): 5–14.

Vincent, Mark, and Refslund Sorensen. *Caught Between Borders: Response Strategies of the Internally Displaced.* London: Pluto Press, 2001.

Vlachos, Angelos. *Deka chronia Kypriakou* [Ten Years of the Cyprus Problem]. Athens: Hestia, 1980.

Volkan, Vamık D. and Norman Itzkowitz. *Turks and Greeks: Neighbours in Conflict.* Cambridgeshire: Eothen Press, 1994.

Weiker, Walter F. *The Turkish Revolution, 1960–1961: Aspects of Military Politics.* Washington D.C.: Brookings Institution, 1963.

Weisband, Edward. *Turkish Foreign Policy, 1943–1945.* Princeton, N.J.: Princeton University Press, 1973.

White, Jenny. *Islamist Mobilization in Turkey: A Study in Vernacular Politics.* Seattle: University of Washington Press, 2002.

White, Paul. "Economic Marginalisation of Turkey's Kurds: The Failed Promise of Modernisation and Reform." *Journal of Muslim Minority Affairs* 18 (1998): 139–58.

———. *Primitive Rebels or Revolutionary Modernizers? The Kurdish National Movement in Turkey.* London: Zed Books, 2000.

Wilson, Richard E., ed. *Human Rights, Culture and Context: Anthropological Perspectives.* London: Pluto Press, 1997.

Women in Turkey. Report by the United Nations Development Program and Directorate General for the Status and Problems of Women. Ankara, 1999.

Woodiwiss, Anthony. "Human Rights and the Challenge of Cosmopolitanism." *Theory, Culture, and Society* 19 (April 2002): 139–55.

World Bank. *Turkey: Marmara Earthquake Assessment.* Turkey Country Office. Ankara: World Bank, 1999.

World Organization Against Torture (OMCT). Press release. "OMCT observes the International Day for the Elimination of Violence Against Women." 25 November 2003. http://www.omct.org/base.cfm?page=article&num=3823&consol=close&kwrd=EQL (accessed 10 February 2004).

WWF-Turkey (World Wild Life Protection Foundation). "About WWF-Turkey." http://www.wwf.org.tr/tr/wwfhakkinda.asp (accessed 12 November 2003).

Yamanlar, Emine. *Demokrasi ve İnsan Hakları.* Istanbul: Ders Kitapları A.Ş., 2001.

———. *Lise İnsan İlişkileri.* Istanbul: Ders Kitapları A.Ş., 2002.

Yaraman, Ayşegül. *Türkiye'de Kadınların Siyasal Temsili.* Istanbul: Bağlam Yayıncılık, 1999.

Yavuz, Hakan M. "Towards an Islamic Liberalism? The Nurcu Movement and Fethullah Gülen in Turkey." *Middle East Journal* 53, no. 4 (Autumn 1999): 584–605.

Yeban, Felice I. "Introduction." In *HRE Pack: Human Rights Education Pack.* Published by Asia-Pacific Regional Resource Center for Human Rights Education (ARRC). May 1995. http://www.arrc-hre.com/publications_frameset.html (accessed 15 April 2003).

Yedinci Beş Yıllık Kalkınma Planı. Ankara: Devlet Planlama Teşkilatı, 1996.

Yeğen, Mesut. "The Turkish State Discourse and the Exclusion of Kurdish Identity." In *Turkey: Identity, Democracy, Politics,* ed. Sylvia Kedourie. London: Frank Cass, 1996. 216–29.

Yıldız, Ahmet. *"Ne Mutlu Türk'üm Diyebilene": Türk Ulusal Kimliğinin Etno-Seküler Sınırları, 1919–1938.* 2nd ed. Istanbul: İletişim, 2004.

Yücekök, Ahmet N., İlter Turan, and Mehmet Ö. Alkan. *Civil Society Organizations in Istanbul.* Istanbul: Tarih Vakfı Yayınları, 1998.

Yurdatapan, Şanar. "Throwing the Book at the State." *Index on Censorship* 27, no. 3 (May–June 1998): 125.

Zakaria, Fareed. "The Rise of Illiberal Democracy." *Foreign Affairs* 76 (November–December 1997): 23–43.

Zorn, Christopher and Steven R. Van Winkle. "Government Responses to the European Court of Human Rights." Paper presented at the International Conference on the Effects of and Responses to Globalization, Istanbul, 31 May–1 June 2002.

Zürcher, Erik J. *Turkey: A Modern History.* London: I.B. Tauris, 1993; rev ed. 1998.

Contributors

ZEHRA F. KABASAKAL ARAT is Juanita and Joseph Leff Distinguished Professor at Purchase College, State University of New York, where she teaches for the Political Science and Women's Studies programs. She is also Founding President of the Human Rights Section of the American Political Science Association. Her studies address theoretical and empirical questions of human rights, including their relation to democracy, gender construction, and development. Her publications include *Democracy and Human Rights in Developing Countries*; *Deconstructing Images of "the Turkish Woman"*; and *Human Rights Worldwide*.

BAŞAK ÇALI is Lecturer in Human Rights in the Department of Political Science, University College London. Her research focuses on the theory and sociology of international law and human rights. Currently, she is working on different taxonomies of human rights activism. She is coeditor of *The Legalization of Human Rights: Multidisciplinary Perspectives on Human Rights and Human Rights Law*.

DİLRUBA ÇATALBAŞ is Associate Professor of Journalism at the University of Galatasaray. She teaches and researches in areas concerning economic, political, international, and regulatory dimensions of public communication and journalism. She has published articles on media analysis of the coverage of the war in Iraq, Turkish-American corporate media relations, and civic journalism.

KENAN ÇAYIR is Assistant Professor in the Department of Sociology, İstanbul Bilgi University. is His publications and research interests involve questions that focus on human rights education and Islamic movements.

ÖZLEM DENLİ is a doctoral candidate in the Applied Ethics Program, Department of Philosophy, Norwegian University of Technology and

Natural Sciences. Her work focuses on the freedom of religion and belief, cultural and religious legitimacy of human rights, and Islamic human rights thought in contemporary Turkey.

YILDIZ ECEVİT is Professor of Sociology at the Middle East Technical University, where she also teaches in the Gender and Women's Studies Graduate Program. Her scholarship focuses on women's work and employment, as well as on women's movements and organizations. She has been also involved in the recent women's movement in Turkey as an active member of various women's organizations.

RICHARD FALK is Visiting Distinguished Professor at the Global Studies Program, University of California, Santa Barbara. Previously, he was Albert G. Milbank Professor of International Law at Princeton University. He is author of numerous books, including *Predatory Globalization: A Critique*; *Human Rights Horizons*; *The Great Terror War*; and *The Declining World Order*. He also served as a member of the Independent International Commission on Kosovo and the Human Rights Inquiry Commission for Palestine of the UN Human Rights Commission and is Chair of the Board of the Nuclear Age Peace Foundation.

FATMA GÖK is Professor of Education at Boğaziçi University. Her research focuses on educational policy and politics, gender and education, social foundations of education, and comparative education. She served as the chair of the work group "Right to Education" on the Democratic Education Congress organized by Eğitim-Sen (Teachers' Union) in December 2004, as well as on the editorial collective of *Pazartesi*, a bi-monthly feminist journal, between 1994 and 2001. Her books include: *Towards a Human Rights Conscious Educational Environment* (with Alper Şahin); *Education in 75 years at the Turkish Republic*; *Survey of Teacher Profile* (with Rıfat Okçabol); *Analysis of Citizenship and Human Rights Education Textbooks in Turkey*; and *Reflections on Education in "Multicultural" Societies: Turkish and Swedish Perspectives* (coedited with Marie Carlson and Annika Rabo).

DENİZ ILGAZ received her doctorate in political science and international relations from Boğaziçi University, where she is Assistant Professor in the School of Foreign Languages, Advanced English Unit. She has published articles on citizenship and EU membership, the Euro-Mediterranean partnership, the draft Constitutional Treaty of the EU, and intellectual property rights.

TIM JACOBY received his doctorate in political science from the University of York, where he continues to teach. In addition to numerous articles and book chapters on ethnicity and nationalism, Turkish nationalism, modernism, and nationalism, he is the author of *Social Power and the Turkish State*.

KEMAL KİRİŞÇİ is Professor of International Relations at Boğaziçi University. He is also Jean Monnet Chair in European Integration. He was a member of the External Research Advisory Committee of the UN High Commissioner for Refugees between 1996 and 2000. His books include *Turkey in World Politics*; *The Political Economy of Regional Cooperation in the Middle East*; *Turkey and the Kurds*; and *The PLO and World Politics*.

YASEMİN ÇELİK LEVIN teaches Political Science at the Fashion Institute of Technology, State University of New York. Her research interests focus on international law, international relations, and women's rights. She is the author of *Contemporary Turkish Foreign Policy*.

MARY LOU O'NEIL is Assistant Professor of American Culture and Literature at Kadir Has University in Istanbul. She is also the director of graduate programs in the same department. She has a Ph.D. in American Studies from the University of Kansas. Her publications include articles on the creation of public spheres for young people in the United States, juvenile justice in the United States, images of women's sexuality in women's magazines, discourses on the HIV/AIDS, and feminist legal theory.

BASKIN ORAN is Professor of International Relations at Ankara University. He is author of more than a dozen of books, including *The Western Thrace Question in Turco-Greek Relations*; *Kemalist Nationalism*; *The Unwritten Memoirs of General Kenan Evren*; *The Diary of a Political Prisoner*; *The State Against Itself*; *Globalization and Minorities*; and *Turkish Foreign Policy, Facts-Documents-Comments, 1919–2001*. Currently he is working on the history of Kurdish nationalism in Turkey.

SERA ÖNER holds an M.A. in political science from Virginia Tech. She is a doctoral student in the history program at Bilkent University in Ankara, where she works on Turkey-United States relations and labor rights in Turkey.

ALPASLAN ÖZERDEM is Lecturer in Post-War Recovery Studies at the Post-War Reconstruction and Development Unit (PRDU) at the Department of Politics of the University of York. In addition to numerous articles and book chapters on the reintegration of former combatants, post-conflict reconstruction of human settlements, and civil society-state relationships in the aftermath of disasters, he coauthored *Disaster Management and Civil Society: Earthquake Relief in Japan, Turkey and India* (with Tim Jacoby) and authored a forthcoming book on the disarmament, demobilization and reintegration of former combatants.

N. BURCU TAŞATAR PARLAK is an independent researcher and consultant who works on environmental issues, in general, and on the agricultural land and soil quality, in particular. She holds a Ph.D. in Agricultural Engineering from Ankara University. She has worked for the Ministry of Environment and participated in the drafting of the recent bill on environment.

THOMAS W. SMITH is Associate Professor of Government and International Affairs at the University of South Florida, St. Petersburg. He is author of *History and International Relations* (1999) and numerous journal articles in the areas of human rights and international law. He taught at Koç University in İstanbul from 1997–2000. He is currently writing a book about human rights and war.

FÜSUN TÜRKMEN is Assistant Professor of International Relations at Galatasaray University, where she also runs the exchange program with the European Union. Her teaching and research concentrate on U.S. foreign policy, human rights, and women's rights. Her publications include *The New Dimension of Human Rights: Humanitarian Intervention.*

EDWARD WEISBAND is Diggs Endowed Chair Professor in the Social Sciences, Department of Political Science, Virginia Tech. His books include *Turkish Foreign Policy*; *Resignation in Protest*; *Poverty amid Plenty*; and *Teaching World Politics*. He has served as senior consultant to a number of government and intergovernmental agencies, including the U.S. Agency for International Development and the Sectoral Committee and Technical Program of the International Labor Organization. He has received numerous awards for teaching excellence.

PRODROMOS YANNAS is Professor of International and European Relations and Chair of the Department of Public Relations and Communication at Technological Educational Institution (TEI) of Western Macedonia. He is also a senior editor of *Journal of Political Marketing*. His research and publications focus on foreign policy process, politics and culture in the Balkan and Eastern Mediterranean regions, and political communication. His most recent contribution is "Net Diplomacy," an entry in the three-volume *Encyclopedia of Digital Government*, edited by Ari-Veikko Anttiroiko and Matti Malkia.

Index

11 September attacks, xiv, xvi, 2, 287, 301

Aarhus Convention, 144
Accession Partnership, 147, 181, 257, 258,
    260, 295n, 300n
acquis (EU Acquis for accession), 122, 136,
    147–48, 180, 237, 243, 258, 260, 269
active geological fault line, 153
Adana, 164, 207
Additional Protocol for a System of Collec-
    tive Complaints, 258
Adıyaman, 295
advocacy, 3, 12, 168, 170, 180, 200–201,
    218, 227, 232, 276, 279, 282–83, 286
Aegean Continental Shelf, 42
Afet İnan, 190
Afghanistan, 112, 168, 289
Africa, 144, 146, 174
African Charter on Human and Peoples'
    Rights, 123
Agenda 21, 144
Agos, 290n
Air Quality Regulation, 141
Akdeniz and Others v. Turkey, 298
Akkuyu, 153
AKP (Adalet ve Kalkınma Partisi/Justice
    and Development Party), xiii, xv, xvi, 8,
    31, 32, 55, 87, 99, 277, 286
Aktaş Electric, 110
Alevi, 73, 88, 96–98, 135, 273, 274
Ali Kararname, 21
American Convention on Human
    Rights/Protocol of San Salvador, 123
Amnesty International (AI), 3, 183, 220,
    221, 227, 268, 276, 297

Amsterdam Treaty, 252
ANAP (Anavatan Partisi/Motherland
    Party), 7, 28–29, 255
Anatolia, 12, 59, 60, 72, 74, 75, 125, 132,
    161, 165, 228, 275, 295
Anatolian News Agency (AA), 22–24
Ankara, xiii, xiv, 2, 22–23, 35, 37, 59, 63,
    71, 126, 136, 161–62, 164, 166, 177,
    181, 192, 198–200, 207, 253, 255–57,
    261–62, 266, 269, 270–71, 273–74,
    293–94, 296n, 301n
Ankara Regional Administrative Court, 177
Annan Plan, 70
Antidesertification Convention, 146
Antiterrorism Law, 29–31, 45, 54, 77, 162,
    256, 266, 276, 282
AP (Adalet Partisi/Justice Party), 6, 26, 93
Arabic, 43, 90–92
Aras, Tevfik Rüştü, 59
Armenian, 9, 37–38, 50–52, 60–61, 69, 75,
    162, 272, 280, 284, 290n
armistice, 21
ASALA, 52
assimilation, 45, 76, 86, 280–81
Association Agreement, between Turkey
    and EU, 254–55
Association for Empowering Women, 192
Association for Human Rights and Funda-
    mental Rights and Freedoms (İnsan
    Hakları ve Temel Hak ve Özgürlükler
    Derneği), 219
Association for Investigating Women's
    Social Life, 192
Association for Rights and Freedoms
    (Haklar ve Özgürlükler Derneği), 297

Association for Protecting Women, 192
Association for the Protection of Human
    Rights (İnsan Haklarını Koruma
    Cemiyeti), 219
Association of Contemporary Lawyers
    (Çağdaş Hukukçular Derneği), 221, 228
Association of Democratic Women, 193
Association of Progressive Women, 192, 193
Association of Revolutionary Women, 193
Association of Soroptimists, 192
Association of Turkish Jurist Women, 192
Association of Turkish Mothers, 192
Association of Women Pharmacists, 192
Association of Women University Gradu-
    ates, 192
asylum, 12, 159–60, 170–83, 222, 224, 229,
    296
Asylum Regulation, 174–77, 179
asylum seeker, 12, 170–83, 222, 229
Aşkale, 61
Atatürk, Mustafa Kemal, xiii, xiv, xv, xvi, 2,
    4, 5, 21–22, 27, 30, 39, 50–51, 57, 63,
    75, 94, 106, 131, 134, 161, 189, 190,
    203, 236, 237, 294
Austria, 36
Aybar, Mehmet Ali, 220

Badr Khan, 161
Balıklı Rum Hastanesi Vakfı (Balıklı Greek
    Orthodox Hospital Endowment), 39–40
Balkans, 58, 173
bar associations, 179, 198, 225
Basic Law on National Education, 240
Batman, 163, 295, 299
Beijing, 197, 201, 207, 210, 297; Platform
    for Action, 207, 209, 297; Women's
    Conference, 209
Bergama, 153
besleme basın (foster-child press), 25
Bil, Hikmet, 63
Bilgin, Dinç, 33
Bilgin v. Turkey, 298
Biosafety Law, 148
Black Sea, 75, 146
Black Sea Environmental Program, 146
Bosnians, 172–73
Bozcaada, 58–59, 65
Britain, 62, 75
British Empire, 35
budget, 11, 40, 125, 126, 132, 136, 149,
    206, 244

buffer zone, 181
Building Law, 153
Bulgaria, 36, 112
Bumin, Mustafa, 265
Bursa, 173
Bush, George W., xii, 291
Büyükada, 68

Canada, 175
carbon emission, 147
Catholic Church, 89
Caucasus, 173
cemevi, 96
Central Asia, 146, 203, 289, 298
Central European Instrument for the
    Protection of Minority Rights, 83
Charter for a New Europe, 256
Charter of Fundamental Rights, 252
child labor, 11, 110, 121, 131, 280
children, 1, 11, 47, 54, 65, 76–77, 79, 82,
    119, 126–27, 131–32, 134–35, 189, 192,
    202, 204–6, 208, 210, 222, 276, 280
China, 160
CHP (Cumhuriyet Halk Partisi/Republican
    People's Party), 4, 5, 22, 24–25, 27,
    92–93, 106, 189, 191, 219, 294n
Christian, 37, 38, 59, 64, 69, 273, 291, 299,
    302
church, 10, 66–67, 95
Circassians, 167
Civil Code/Civil Law, 28, 90, 106, 193,
    196, 198–99, 201, 205, 208–9, 212
civil liberties, 161–62, 266. See also civil
    rights
civil rights, xvii, 10, 40, 58, 188, 220–22,
    224–25, 227, 259, 266–67, 277, 279,
    295n, 297n. See also civil liberties
civil servant, 109, 204, 222, 226, 234–35,
    237, 243
Clarendon, earl of, 249
Clinton, Bill, 291
Code of Criminal Procedure (CCP), 53–54
Cold War, xi, 25, 107, 170, 173, 249,
    251–52, 255, 289
collective bargaining, 107–8, 110, 113–15,
    117, 119, 121
Collective Bargaining, Strikes, and Lock-
    out Act, 107
collective offenses, 269
Commission of European Communities,
    68, 78–79, 260, 301

Commission on the Status of Women, 209

Committee for Policies for Women, 207

Committee for the Prevention of Torture, 270

Committee of Independent Experts of the Council of Europe, 119

Committee of Union and Progress, 21

Committee on the Elimination of Discrimination against Women, 211

Communist, 25, 48, 193, 301

communist block, 173

Conference on Environment, UN, 143–44

conflict, 3, 7, 20, 30, 39, 46, 57, 62, 72, 88, 93, 94, 99, 107, 113, 126, 159–60, 162–63, 165, 208, 223–24, 240–41, 243–44, 264–65, 267, 292n, 297n

Conflict Induced Displacement (CID), 159–60

Congress of the International Federation of Journalists, 27

consciousness, xvi, 98, 106, 137, 194–95, 236

Constitution, Turkish, xiii, 35, 45, 54, 82, 84, 90, 113, 116, 240–41, 253, 264, 266; of 1876, 21; of 1908, 106; of 1921, 22, 51, 137; of 1924, 22, 75, 96, 124, 137; of 1961, 5–6, 26–28, 47–48, 76, 92, 94, 107; of 1982, 6, 27, 29, 30, 37, 45–49, 51, 54, 75–79, 82, 84–85, 94, 96–97, 106–8, 113, 115–16, 124–25, 134, 153, 176, 190, 200, 207–8, 220, 222, 240, 241, 253, 257, 259, 264–65, 265, 272, 276, 292n, 302n

constitional amendments/reforms, 30–31, 54, 87, 97, 200, 207, 256–57, 259, 263, 272

Constitutional Court (Türk Anayasa Mahkemesi), 29, 37, 46–47, 49, 67, 77, 94, 133, 135, 153, 208, 264–65, 271–73, 286, 290n, 301n; party closings, and, 46–49, 77, 97, 135, 271, 286

Constitutional Monarchy, 21

constitutional right, 153, 204, 283

constructivist approach, 261

Consultative Council on Human Rights, 257

Convention against Discrimination in Education, 83

Convention against Torture and Other Cruel, Inhuman or Humiliating Treatment and Punishment (CAT), 177, 253–54

Convention concerning the Exchange of Greek and Turkish Populations, 291

Convention on the Elimination of All Forms of Discrimination against Women (CEDAW), 13–14, 195–97, 199–203, 205–8, 210–13, 253–54, 296n

Convention on the Elimination of All Forms of Racial Discrimination (CERD), 253

Convention on the Rights of the Child (CRC), 82, 85, 123, 127, 143, 237, 253–54, 300n

Coordinating High Commission of Human Rights (İnsan Hakları Koordinatör Üst Kurulu), 7

Coordination Council for Collective Bargaining in the State Economic Enterprises, 108

Copenhagen criteria, 20, 68, 87, 97, 182, 200, 252, 257–58, 261, 278, 300n

corporal punishment, 131

Council of Association, 256–57

Council of Europe, 50, 72, 79, 97, 112, 120–21, 123, 237, 239, 244, 251–54, 256, 267

Council of Europe Framework Convention for the Protection of National Minorities, 123

Council of Ministers, 23, 53, 64, 258

Councils for Preservation of Natural and Cultural Entities, 140

coup d'état, 5–7, 25–27, 44–45, 62, 77, 92–93, 107, 132, 193–94, 219, 221, 223–24, 229, 232, 254, 260, 297

Court of Appeals, 56, 265, 290n7

Criminal Procedure Code, 256

cross-ownership, 33

Cruz Varas v. Sweden, 172

cultural rights, xvii, 10, 224, 230, 253, 295, 298

culture, 13–14, 20, 28, 46–48, 50, 52, 55, 72, 76, 81–82, 93, 98, 135, 140, 182, 202–3, 213, 217, 227, 229, 232, 234, 239–41, 243, 245, 263, 283, 287, 295n, 299n, 302n

curricula/curriculum, 90, 92, 94, 134, 154, 234–36, 238–40, 244–45, 299

Customs Union, 256

cyanide, 152

Cypriot, 57, 62–63, 71, 273–74, 291n
Cyprus, xiii, 9, 27, 39, 57, 61–65, 68,
    70–71, 256, 258, 263, 272–74, 285,
    291n, 301n
Cyprus v. Turkey, 274
Czechoslovakia, 36

Çakıcı v. Turkey, 298
Çakmak, Fevzi (Marshall), 219
ÇEAŞ (Çukurova Elektrik Anonim Şirketi),
    110
Çelikel, Aysel, 265
Çiçek, Cemil, 265
Çiraklar v. Turkey, 301
ÇİTOSAN, 110

Danıştay (Council of State), 116, 153, 176,
    178, 264, 296
Dayton Peace Plan, 173
death penalty, 255, 257–59, 276
Declaration of Minimum Humanitarian
    Standards, 123
Declaration, of 1936, 38
Declaration on the Elimination of All
    Forms of Intolerance and Discrimina-
    tion Based on Religion or Belief, 292
deforestation, 152
DEHAP (Demokratik Halk Partisi/
    Democratic People's Party), 271
Demirel, Süleyman, 6, 162
democracy, xi–xv, xvii, 3–4, 45, 61, 71, 87,
    97, 99, 166, 194, 231, 236–37, 240, 242,
    258–59, 272, 282–83, 285–87, 289n,
    292n, 300n
democratization, xv, 2, 194, 220, 231,
    256–57
demonstration, 8, 45, 105, 114, 117, 194,
    272, 283, 291n
Deng, Francis, 160
Denktaş, Rauf, 274
Denmark v. Turkey, 269, 301n
DEP (Demokrasi Partisi/Democracy
    Party), 48–49, 270–71, 300n
deportation, 64, 175–79
Dersim, 76, 162
Derviş, Suat, 193
detention, 15, 117, 164, 220–21, 223, 226–
    27, 257, 262, 266–67, 269, 274, 281
Development Induced Displacement
    (DID), 159
devlet baba, 166

dialogue, 121–22, 196, 227, 229, 260
Directorate General on the Status and
    Problems of Women (DGSPW), 206–7,
    211, 296n
Directorate of Pious Foundations (Evkaf),
    90
dirigisme, 106
discrimination/antidiscrimination, xiii, 1,
    9, 11, 13, 39, 41, 50, 68, 72, 80–83, 95,
    111–13, 116, 121, 124, 126, 128, 144,
    197, 200, 202, 211–13, 224–26, 233,
    243, 267–68, 276, 279, 280–81, 287,
    292n, 302n
DİSK (Devrimci İşçi Sendikaları Konfed-
    erasyonu/Confederation of Revolution-
    ary Workers' Trade Unions of Turkey),
    107, 118, 293–94
disparity, 100, 211. *See also* inequality
displacement, 10, 12, 159, 160–63, 165,
    168–69, 280, 295
diversity, xvi–xvii, 4, 13, 29, 44, 49, 94, 99,
    101, 242, 258, 276, 279, 281–82
Diyânet İşleri Başkanlığı (Directorate of
    Religious Affairs), 10, 90–91, 98–99, 273
Diyarbakır, 163, 207, 223–24, 276, 295n,
    299n, 302n
Document of the Copenhagen Meeting of
    the Conference on the Human Dimen-
    sion of the Conference on Security and
    Cooperation in Europe, 82–83, 123
Doğan, Aydın, 28, 33
Doğan group, 33
domestic human rights NGOs, 13
domestic violence, 195, 210
DP (Demokrat Parti/Democrat Party), 5,
    6, 24–26, 92, 107, 219
Draft Declaration of Principles on Human
    Rights and the Environment, 143
Dulaş v. Turkey, 298

earthquake, 10, 123, 153, 166
eco-basin, 139
ecological equilibrium, 139
economic crisis/crises, 5, 34
economic rights, xvii, 10–11, 15, 105, 120,
    125, 172, 220, 227, 277–78, 298n
Ecumenical Patriarchate, 57–58, 63, 66,
    291n
Ecumenical Throne, 66
Eden, Anthony, 62
Edirne, 60

Education Protocol, 69, 291n
education, xvii, 5, 11, 14, 40, 46–47, 65,
    67–69, 72, 75, 79, 82–83, 85, 86, 90,
    92–94, 96, 98, 111, 114, 122–28, 131–36,
    139, 142–43, 148, 153, 154, 160, 163,
    188, 192, 202–5, 209, 210–13, 220, 227,
    233–36, 238, 240–41, 244–45, 273, 276–
    77, 279–80, 292n, 294n, 295n, 299n,
    300n, 302n; adult, 124–25, 128; environ-
    mental, 152, 154; human rights, 12, 14,
    155, 233, 238, 244. *See also* schooling
educational rights/right to education,
    10–11, 82–83, 86, 123–26, 134–36, 241,
    275, 279, 300n
Eğitim-Sen, 118, 135, 276, 294n, 302
Eight-Year Compulsory Basic Education
    Law, 210
emergency rule, 77, 270
Emergency Rule Law, 28
employer, xvii, 32, 106–9, 113, 115–17,
    120–21
employment, xvii, 32, 49, 59, 98, 109–12,
    120, 168, 202, 205, 280
energy consumption, 147
England, 35
Enosis, 62, 63
Environment Council (ENC), 139
Environment Organization, 139
Environmental Impact Assessment Regula-
    tion, 141
environmental impact assessment (EIA),
    140–42
Environmental Inspection Regulation, 141
Environmental Law, 140–42
environmental monitoring system, 148
environmental pollution, 137–38, 140, 142
Environmental Pollution Prevention Fund
    Regulation, 141
environmental rights, 11, 137–38, 142–46,
    152–54, 277
environmentalism, 153, 279
EOKA (National Organization of Cypriot
    Fighters), 62
EP (Emek Partisi/Labor Party), 47–48,
    220, 254–56, 270, 300n
Equality Framework Law, 201
Equality-Watch Committee, 213
Erbakan, Necmettin, 8, 93, 286
Erdoğan, Recep Tayyip, 66–67, 239, 261
Et Balık Kurumu (EBK/Meat and Fish
    Products Organizations), 110

étatism, 4
ethno-religious, 51
Eurogold, 153
Europe, xvii, 15, 41, 51, 66, 82–83, 85, 91,
    120–21, 146, 170, 173–74, 181, 222,
    234, 249, 250, 252, 254, 256, 260, 267,
    278, 285–86
European Commission against Racism and
    Intolerance (ECRI), 50
European Commission on Human Rights,
    50, 97, 145, 147, 149, 169, 180, 251,
    254, 300n
European Convention for the Protection
    of Human Rights and Fundamental
    Freedoms, 3, 14, 19, 53, 56, 80–81, 123,
    144–46, 172, 176, 237, 238, 249, 251,
    258–59, 262, 264
European Court of Human Rights
    (ECHR), 7, 14–15, 19, 30, 53–54, 56,
    97–98, 135, 145, 170, 172, 175–76, 178,
    182, 222, 224, 237, 238–39, 243, 251,
    254–56, 259–74, 286, 295n, 298n, 301n
European Environmental Agency, 149
European human rights regime, 15, 145,
    264, 274
European Single Act, 256
European Social Charter, 119, 120, 144,
    258, 278
European Training Foundation, 136
European Union (EU), xi, xiii–xiv, 3, 7–8,
    12, 15, 20, 30–31, 53, 55, 64, 68–72, 78,
    83–85, 87, 97, 99, 113, 116, 120–22,
    125, 136, 139, 147–49, 166–70, 174,
    180–83, 199–200, 208, 229–32, 237,
    239, 243, 250, 252–60, 263, 264–66,
    270–71, 277–79, 284–87, 295n, 298n,
    301n; draft constitution, 252
European Women's Lobby, 200
Europeanization, 249
Evren, Kenan (General), 6, 122, 132

Faculty of Divinity, 92
fair trial, 225, 262, 266–67, 269–70; right
    to, 268, 270–71, 283
Fatin Rüştü, 62
feminist, 190–91, 194–96, 198, 199, 201,
    211, 213; groups, 195, 198; pro-feminist,
    201
Fener Patriarchate (Fener Rum
    Patrikhanesi), 57, 66
First Legal Department, 39

Five-Year Development Plans (Turkey), 138–39, 147, 206
Fourth Financial Protocol, 254–55
FP (Fazilet Partisi/Virtue Party), 8
Framework Convention for the Protection of National Minorities, 82–83, 147
Framework Convention on Climate Change (UNFCC), 147
France, 35–36, 75, 175, 301
freedom, xiv, 2, 6, 9, 15, 19–21, 24–32, 34, 40, 47, 53–54, 58, 67, 69, 72, 80–84, 86–88, 94–98, 101, 105, 107–8, 111, 113–17, 120–23, 125, 135, 142, 171, 182, 191, 202, 204–5, 219–20, 222–24, 226–27, 231, 236, 239, 241, 255, 257, 259–60, 262, 265, 267, 269, 272–73, 276–77, 279–80, 283, 292, 299n, 301n; academic, 134; of assembly, 15, 262, 268; of association, 15, 97, 105, 107–8, 111, 113–17, 120–22, 220, 227, 257, 259, 262, 268; of communication, 259; of conscience, 88, 97, 268; from discrimination, 72, 80–81, 83, 224; of expression, 15, 19, 30–31, 53–54, 72, 80–84, 86, 97, 135, 219, 223, 227, 239, 257, 259, 262, 267, 269, 272–73, 280, 300n; from government interference, 72; individual, 6, 54, 87, 264, 276; of movement, 40, 259; of opinion, 117; political, 106; of press, 9, 19–21, 25–26, 28, 29, 32, 34, 279; of religion, 9–10, 58, 66, 67, 69, 87–88, 94–98, 101, 225–26, 263, 268, 273, 277, 282, 292n; of residence, 259; of speech, 277; of thought, 54, 88, 239, 255–59, 277, 301; from torture, 182
Freedom and Democracy Party (ÖZDEP) v. Turkey, 271
Freedom and Democracy Party (Özgürlük ve Demokrasi Partisi, ÖZDEP), 48, 135, 271
friendly settlement, 268–69

Gandhi, Mohandas (Mahatma), 302
GAP (Güneydoğu Anadolu Projesi/ Southeastern Anatolian Project), 162–63, 295n
Gaziantep, 164, 207, 295
GDP (Gross Domestic Product), 110–11, 164
gendarmerie, 179, 182, 235, 238

Gendarmerie General Command, 238, 243
gender, 11–12, 109, 111, 112, 121, 124, 127–28, 131, 134, 192, 195–97, 199–201, 205, 207–11, 213, 229, 259, 278, 280, 294n, 299n; discrimination, 11, 109, 111, 124, 128, 131, 134, 209, 229; equality, 12, 196–97, 199, 208, 210, 213, 259, 278, 299n; inequality/gap, 128, 201, 205, 294
Gender Empowerment Index, 205
Gender Equality Monitoring Commission, 201
Gender Equality Ombud, 201
General Assembly (UN), 1, 154, 171, 202–3, 233, 253, 299n
General Board of Legislation of the court, 39
General Directorate of Environment, 139
General Directorate of Foundations (Vakıflar Genel Müdürlüğü), 39, 53, 68
General Education Regulation of 1869 (Maarif-i Umumiye Nizamnamesi), 124
General Staff, Turkish Armed Forces, 285, 302n
Geneva Convention Relating to the Status of Refugees, 12, 170–71
geographical limitation, 12, 170, 173, 180–81, 183
Germany, 73, 170, 173, 254, 300
GINI coefficient, 7
Global Learning and Observations to Benefit the Environment (GLOBE) Protocol, 153
Gökçeada, 58–59, 65
gold mining, 152, 153
Grand National Assembly (of Turkey), 22, 60, 69, 75, 90, 93, 146, 188, 190, 204, 208–29, 230, 258–59, 294n
Greece, 9, 35–36, 39, 42, 58–59, 62–64, 69, 70, 255, 291n
Greeks, 2, 9, 25, 37–40, 42, 50–52, 57–65, 69–71, 75, 106, 273–74, 280–81, 291n. *See also* Rum Orthodox
Greek-Turkish Convention, 59, 64
Greek-Turkish Cultural Commission, 69
greenhouse gas emission, 147
Greenpeace, 151, 153
Gurani (Kurdish dialect), 74

hacı, 90
hafız, 90

HAK-İŞ, 118
Halide Edib, 188
Hanafi Medhab, 91
harmonization package, 20, 30–31, 55, 68, 97, 99, 166, 259
HAVAŞ (Airport Ground Transportation Services), 110
head scarve, xv, 8, 135, 201, 226, 273
health, 10–11, 19, 28, 111, 114, 116, 120–21, 137, 139–40, 143, 153–54, 160, 164, 189, 193, 202, 205, 209, 213, 295n; health care, 10–11, 121, 164
healthy environment, 12, 137, 153
Helsinki Summit, 97, 257
Heybeliada, 67–68, 71
Higher Council for the Environment (HCE), 139, 142
High Council of Judges and Prosecutors, 300
Higher Education Council (YÖK), 78, 94, 133, 240
Higher Islamic Institutes (Yüksek İslam Enstitüsü), 93
high-sulfur lignite, 147
Hizbullah Kurdish Revolutionary Party, 8
Hoda Jabari, 175
honor killings, 13, 201, 212–13, 278
honor, See also namus, 13, 201, 210, 212–13, 274, 278
human dignity, 1
human rights, xi–xviii, 1–5, 7–15, 19, 30, 36, 41–42, 44, 49, 50, 52, 57, 66, 68, 70, 72–73, 76, 78–79, 82, 86–88, 96–99, 101, 122–23, 137, 142–44, 152–55, 159–60, 161, 165–67, 169–72, 174–75, 180–83, 198, 201–3, 208, 210–11, 217–39, 241–45, 249–58, 260–65, 270, 274–86, 292n, 294n, 297n, 300n
human rights advocacy, advocates, 174, 224, 229, 231, 229, 282–83, 287
Human Rights Committee, 69, 251, 299
human rights council, 230
human rights groups, 170, 218, 283
Human Rights Investigation Commission, 229–30, 282
Human Rights Watch, 3, 20, 69, 164–65, 267–68, 291
humanitarian assistance/aid, 168–69
Hungary, 36
Hürriyet, 33, 290n9

ibadet, 91
idari mahkeme (administrative court), 177
identity, xvii, 3, 8, 10, 12, 30, 50–52, 66, 74, 77, 82–85, 127, 168, 187, 191, 219, 227, 240, 256, 264, 279, 280–81, 285, 291n, 293n; national, 5, 10, 50, 58, 75, 84–85, 91, 241, 279; sub-, 50; supra-, 7, 50–52
İHD (İnsan Hakları Derneği/Human Rights Association), 217, 221–26, 229, 231, 297n, 299n
İlisu Dam, 163
illegal immigrants, 179
ILO (International Labour Organisation), 113–14, 116–17, 120; Convention, 113–14; Equal Remuneration Convention, 203
imam-hatip schools, 93, 96
immigration, 170, 172, 183, 295
implementation, xvi, 13, 32, 55, 94, 119, 127, 136, 147–48, 164, 166–68, 175–76, 178, 182, 195–96, 201, 203, 206–7, 211, 213, 230, 234–35, 237–38, 251, 256, 258, 260, 275, 282–83, 292n, 300n
İncal v. Turkey, 270
independence, xi, 22, 46, 62, 271, 299, 300
Independence Tribunal, 22
industrial relations, 106–10, 113–14
industrialization, 6–7, 26, 106, 137–38
Inequality, 1, 5, 132, 205. See also disparity
informal economy/sector, 109–12, 121, 204–5
inhuman punishment, 176
İnönü, İsmet, 4–5, 64, 92, 190
in-service education/training, 131, 238–39, 245
inspection, 22, 148
Institute of French Priests and Others v. Turkey, 301
internally displaced people (IDP), 12, 78, 159–60, 162–65, 167, 169
International Bill of Rights, 279
International Court of Justice, 42
International Covenant on Civil and Political Rights (ICCPR), xviii, 19, 81–82, 85, 123, 172, 182, 251, 253, 292
International Covenant on Economic, Social and Cultural Rights (ICESCR), xviii, 10–11, 123, 143, 253, 300
International Criminal Court (ICC), 13, 251

International Human Rights Conference, 280
international human rights norms, 260–61, 284, 286
international human rights regimes, 2, 3, 15, 98, 144, 218, 222, 250, 252, 260, 284, 286
International Labor Organisation Equal Remuneration Convention, 203
international mining consortium, 153
International Press Institute, 25
international protection, 49, 159–60, 169, 171
international treaty, 1, 35, 54, 57, 72, 80–81, 113, 146, 208
inviolability of the domicile, 259
Iran, xii, 176, 180
Iraq, xi–xii, xv, 47, 52; Iraq War, xi, xv
İrtemçelik, Mehmet Ali, 257
Islam, xiii, xv, 10, 20, 37, 73, 87, 89–92, 94, 96, 99–101, 135, 225, 249, 289n, 292n, 302n
Islam Nation (Ümmet), 37
Islamist, 3, 7–8, 10, 29, 67, 92–94, 98–99, 101, 201, 227, 271, 277, 283, 286, 289n, 290n
İstanbul, 2, 21, 22, 24–25, 27, 52, 57–60, 62–67, 75, 106, 146, 162, 164, 173, 181, 188, 189, 190, 192, 194, 198–201, 207, 226, 250, 273, 290n, 294n, 297n; Martial Law administration, 194
Italy, 35, 36, 75, 125
itikad, 91
İzmir, 57, 59, 75, 106, 153, 164, 192, 198, 200
İzmir Economic Congress, 106
İzmit, 153

Jabari v. Turkey, 175–76, 178, 296n
Jandarma, 238, 243, 270. See also gendarmerie
Jews, 9, 37–38, 50–51, 60–61, 173, 280, 302n; Orthodox, 302n
Josephides v. Turkey, 301
Judaism, 73, 302
judicial protection and review, 172, 183

KA-DER (Association for the Support and Training of Women Candidates), 134, 197, 199, 212–13, 228, 296n
Kahramanmaraş, 164, 194

Kalaç v. Turkey, 273, 301
KAMU-SEN (Kamu Sendikaları Konfederasyonu/Confederation of Public Labor Unions), 114, 118
Kanadoğlu, Sabih, 271
Karabay, Köksal (General), 302
Kayseri Electric, 110
Kazakhstan, 298
Kemalism, 23, 262, 264
Kemalist, 3, 5, 12, 23, 25, 53, 55, 58, 90, 92, 94, 98, 132, 188, 191–92, 196, 240, 253, 263–64, 271; jurisprudence, 264; regime, 3, 12, 188
KESK (Kamu Emekçileri Sendikaları Konfederasyonu/Confederation of Public Laborers' Unions), 114, 118
Kıbrıs Türktür (Cyprus Is Turkish) Association, 63
Kılıç, Tuncer, 192–93, 285
KİGEM (Kamu İşletmeciliğini Geliştirme Merkezi Vakfı/Center for Improvement of State Owned Enterprises), 293, 294
Kilis, 295
King, Martin Luther, 302
Kingdom of Serbs, Croats, and Slovenes, 35
Kirmanshahi (Kurdish dialect), 74
Kıvrıkoğlu, Hüseyin, 166, 285
Kosovars, 173
Kuçuradi, İonna, 235
Kural, Adnan, 253
Kurdish, xii–xiv, xvi, 3, 5, 7–10, 12, 20, 22, 29–31, 38, 43–44, 47, 50–52, 55, 72–86, 106, 135, 161–63, 166, 174, 189, 223–24, 226–27, 256, 263, 265–68, 270–72, 276, 279–81, 283, 285–86, 292n, 295n, 300n; aspirations, xvi; citizens, 43, 80, 83–84, 86, 224, 279, 280; identity, 30, 77, 84, 256, 279, 280, 285; language, 9, 72–86, 162, 272; leaders, 22, 76, 286; movement, xiii, 84; nationalism, 3, 7, 55, 283; population, 72, 73, 224, 281; question/issue, xvi, 72, 76, 80, 226, 256, 265, 272, 280; separatists, 223, 226, 265, 266; uprising/rebellion/insurgency, 5, 29, 38, 51, 106
Kurdistan People's Congress (Kongra-Gel), 276
Kurds, xiii, 9–10, 43–44, 48, 52, 72–77, 80–86, 167, 265–68, 271, 274, 279n81, 286, 292, 300n; Iraqi, 74

Kurmanji (Kurdish dialect), 74
Kurt v. Turkey, 298
Kyoto Protocol, 147
Kyrgyzstan, 289n2

labor, 4, 6, 10–11, 25, 60–61, 105–22, 164,
    204–5, 209–13, 272, 274, 276–79, 294n;
    rights, 11, 25, 111, 121, 277–78; union,
    6, 11, 28, 105–9, 112, 114–19, 121, 150,
    211, 220, 222, 272, 276–77, 293n. *See
    also* trade union
Labor Unions Act, 107
laicism, 4, 10, 90, 94. *See also* secularism
language, 9, 10, 13, 15, 24, 30, 36, 38–41,
    43–48, 53–54, 58, 60, 65–66, 69, 72–89,
    91, 98, 101, 124, 135, 222, 240, 256–58,
    267, 279, 281
language rights, 9–10, 43, 72–73, 79–86,
    135, 279. *See also* linguistic rights
Latife Bekir, 190
Lausanne Peace Conference, 2
Lausanne, Treaty of, 9, 35–42, 44–45,
    47–49, 52, 57–58, 60, 65–66, 68–70, 75,
    80, 82–83, 96, 135, 167, 279, 280, 290
Law of Capital Levy (Varlık Vergisi), 60
Law on Associations, 46, 106, 259
Law on Collective Agreement, Strike, and
    Lockout (Toplu İş Sözleşmesi, Grev ve
    Lokavt Yasası), 108, 115, 117
Law on Foreign Language Education and
    Teaching, 79
Law on Foundations, 39, 53
Law on the Census, 79
Law on the Duties and Competencies of
    the Police, 269
Law on the Establishment and Broadcasts
    of Radio and Television Channels
    (LEBRTC), 53
Law on the Maintenance of the Order
    (Takrir-i Sükun), 22, 106
Law on the Protection of the Family, 198,
    210
Law on the Unification of Education, 124
League of Nations, 35, 37, 42, 58, 76
leftist, 26, 27, 162, 193, 219, 220, 221, 225,
    283, 297; organization, 162, 220;
    women, 193. *See also* left-wing
left-wing, 6, 8, 24, 26–27, 47, 93, 193–94,
    220–22, 225–66, 277, 282, 297n. *See also*
    leftist
legal norms, 15

legal reform, xiii, xv–xvi, 9, 32, 36, 87, 98,
    142, 196, 230–32, 265, 284–85. *See also*
    legislative reform
legislative reform, 30, 53, 55, 213, 257,
    259, 275. *See also* legal reform
Leki (Kurdish dialect), 74
Leonardo da Vinci, 136
liberal, xvii, 5–6, 14, 19, 24, 26–28, 76, 99,
    101, 125, 196, 225, 255, 263–64, 278,
    283–84, 292n
liberalism, 29, 271, 293
liberalization, xiii, 7, 29, 108, 110, 253,
    255, 259, 271–72, 277–78, 285
linguistic human rights, 10, 73. *See also*
    language rights
linguistic rights, 73, 79, 82, 292n. *See also*
    language rights
literacy, 127–28, 210–11
litigation, 12, 152, 283–84
lobbying, 196, 200–201, 283
Local Environment Committees (LECs),
    139, 294
local government, 114, 138
Loizidou v. Turkey, 302
London, 61–63, 220, 291
Lord Curzon, 42
Luxembourg, 257, 300

Maastricht Treaty, 252
marches, 195, 283
Mardin, 295
Marmara islands, 62
martial law, 6, 20, 22, 24–25, 27, 107, 270;
    martial law courts, 270
Marxist Revolutionary Eastern Hearth
    Organization, 76
May Day, 106, 117
Mazlum-Der (Association for Human
    Rights and the Oppressed), 217, 225,
    226, 228–29, 298n
MBK (Milli Birlik Komitesi/Committee of
    National Unity), 25–26, 92
McCarthyism, 36
Medi group, 33
Mediterranean, 58, 75, 132, 146, 150,
    153–54; Mediterranean Action Plan,
    146; Mediterranean Environmental
    Technical Assistance Program
    (METAP), 146
Megali Idea, 59
MEMUR-SEN (Memur Sendikaları

Konfederasyonu/Confederation of Civil Servants' Unions), 114, 118
Mehmet Efendi, 302
Menderes, Adnan, 5, 25, 62–63, 291
MGK (Milli Güvenlik Kurulu/National Security Council), 5, 7, 28, 30–31, 68, 258, 285
MHP (Milliyetçi Hareket Partisi/ Nationalist Action Party), 6
Middle East, xi, xv, 2, 73, 154, 174, 181, 207. 298
Middle East Technical University Development Foundation College, 154
military, xi–xv, 2–3, 5–7, 20, 24–27, 29–30, 39, 44–45, 47, 51, 59, 62–63, 65, 68, 77, 85, 92–94, 107, 114, 132, 161–63, 166, 176, 181, 193–94, 218–21, 223, 232, 239–40, 243, 249, 252, 254, 260, 264, 266–67, 270, 273–74, 276, 281–86, 289n, 300n, 302n
millet system, xvi, 37, 44, 51, 291, 302
Milli Görüş (National Vision), 8, 99
Milliyet, 19, 33. 302
Ministry of Environment (ME), 139–40, 148
Ministry of Environment and Forestry (MEF), 140, 148, 152
Ministry of Forestry, 140
Ministry of Interior (MOI), 51, 165, 173, 176–81, 269, 296n
Ministry of Justice, 198, 208, 237, 265
Ministry of Labor, 109, 110, 114, 119, 207
Ministry of Labor and Social Security, 109, 136, 206, 302
Ministry of National Education, 90, 124–26, 128, 133, 136, 154, 235–36, 240, 244–45, 294n, 299n
minorities, xv, 9, 35–38, 40–42, 44–46, 48–52, 57–58, 60–61, 66, 68, 70, 75, 80–83, 86, 94, 96–97, 124, 135, 166–67, 169, 218, 252, 280, 300n; ethnic, xvi, 218, 253; linguistic, 81; religious, 36–37, 58, 259, 272; rights of, xiii, 2, 35–36, 38, 41–42, 45, 49–50, 53–55, 57, 79–80, 167–68, 264, 276, 295n, 300n
MNP (Milli Nizam Partisi/National Order Party), 93
modernization, 3, 10–12, 55, 58, 70, 90–91, 124, 138, 191, 203, 240, 287, 299
molla, 90
Montagna, Jules Cesar, 42

mother tongue, 40, 43, 76–77, 79, 83, 85, 135, 258, 276, 279, 300n, 302n
MSP (Milli Selamet Partisi/National Salvation Party), 93
Municipal Law, 190
Muslim, xv, xvii, 2, 9, 36–44, 51–53, 58, 59–61, 68–70, 89, 92, 94, 96–97, 99–101, 172, 204, 225–26, 281, 291, 293n, 298n, 300n, 302n
Myanmar, 160

Nakşibendi, 91
namus, 204. See also honor
National Action Plan. See National Plan of Action
National Agenda 21, 147
National Biosafety Board, 148
National Climate Coordination Group (NCCG), 147
National Committee on the Decade for Human Rights Education, 234, 237, 244, 299n
National Environmental Action Plan (NEAP), 139–42, 147–49, 152, 154
national interest, 27, 30, 241, 250, 272
National Plan of Action: on human rights education, 14; of KA-DER, 197; on women's rights, 197, 209, 297n
National Program: for the Enhancement of Women's Integration in Development, 207; on human hights education, 134, 230, 233–39, 299n
National Programme for the Adoption of the acquis communautaire (NPAA), 148, 180, 237, 258–59, 269
National Security Political Document (Milli Güvenlik Siyaset Belgesi), 68
nationalism, xvii, 4, 30, 60–61, 190, 240, 264; Kurdish, 3, 7, 30, 55, 283; Turkish, 47, 55, 63, 70
Nationalist Front (Milliyetçi Cephe, MC), 93
nationalists, 2, 55, 75; Kurdish, 8, 29, 30, 44, 286; Turkish, 2, 35, 59, 75
NATO, 161, 285
natural disaster, 10, 138
natural gas, 147
natural resources, 140, 148
neo-Fordism, 108
Nezihe Muhiddin, 188–89, 190
Noise Control Regulation, 141

nongovernmental organization (NGO), 152, 208, 210–11, 213, 229, 259
non-Muslim, xv–xvi, 2, 9, 35–42, 44, 48, 51–54, 57–58, 60–62, 68–70, 75, 80, 82–83, 86, 94, 96–97, 100, 167, 229, 259, 280, 300n
non-refoulement, 171, 174–75, 178, 182–83
nuclear power, 153
Nurcu movement, 92

Optional Protocol to CEDAW, 200, 202–3
Organization for Security and Cooperation in Europe (OSCE), 50, 79, 83, 256, 295
Ottawa Convention, 13
Ottoman: Empire, xvi, 2, 21, 35–38, 50, 52, 55–58, 62, 72, 74–75, 88–89, 96, 291n; bureaucrats, 89; elite, 59; era, 2, 22, 105, 124; government/state, 74–75, 88–89, 124; heritage, xvi, 88; ideas, xvii; jurisprudence, 273; land/territory, 52, 89; policies, 302; rule, xvi, 39, 89; subjects/citizens, 59, 240, 292n; sultans, 292n; system, 249; tradition, 90, 96
Öcalan v. Turkey, 301
Öcalan, Abdullah, xiii, 7, 52, 72, 77–78, 166, 265, 266, 301n
Öndül, Hüsnü, 222
Önger, Beria, 192, 193
Özal,Turgut, xvi, 7, 28, 64, 77, 108, 253, 255–56
ÖZDEP (Özgürlük ve Demokrasi Partisi/ Freedom and Democracy Party), 48, 135, 271, 301
Özgür Gündem, 301

Paris, 50, 256
Paris Principles on National Human Rights Institutions, 299
Parliamentary Human Rights Commission, 299
Party of Rights and Freedoms (Hak ve Özgürlükler Partisi), 271
Pastures Regulation, 141
Patriarch Demetrios, 67, 291
Patriarch Vartholomeos, 67
Peace Association (Barış Derneği), 41–42, 221
Penal Code, 27, 30–32, 53–54, 92, 97, 142, 182, 196, 198, 200, 208, 210–11, 213, 256, 264, 269, 272, 276, 292, 298

Permanent Board of Consultants for Environmental Problems, 139
persecution, 20–21, 171–72, 176, 283
Pişkinsüt, Sema, 282
PKK (Partia Karkaren Kürdistan/Kurdistan Workers' Party), 7–8, 29–30, 52, 55, 72, 77–78, 162–63, 166, 174, 223–24, 265–67, 269, 272, 276
Platform of Solidarity for the Revolutionary Prisoners (Devrimci Tutsaklarla Dayanışma Platformu), 297
Poland, 36, 43
Police Academy, 269
Polish Minorities Treaty, 36–37
political criteria, 166, 200, 257, 258–59
political participation, 188, 256
political pluralism, 256
political power, xiii, 140, 193, 196
political rights, xvii, 10, 40, 58, 107, 188–89, 192, 220–22, 224–25, 227, 257, 259, 267, 277, 279, 295n, 298n
polluter pays principle, 140
pollution prevention, 138
Pomaks, 172
population, xvii, 2, 7–11, 15, 38, 43, 51, 57, 64, 72–74, 77, 91, 94, 109, 120–21, 127, 133, 136, 140, 159, 161, 163–65, 194, 224, 238, 280, 283, 291n
post-Fordism, 108
poverty, xvii, 1, 11, 113, 127, 163, 227, 277, 297n
power generation, 153
pre-accession, 170
pre-parliamentary, 296n
prejudice, 243, 280
Press Advertising Corporation (Basın İlan Kurumu), 26
Press and Broadcasting Directorate, 24
Press and Intelligence Directorate, 22
Press Association Law, 24
Press Congress, 23
Press Honor Council (Basın Şeref Divanı), 26
Press Law, 21, 23–25, 30–32, 53
Prime Ministry, Turkish, 7, 122, 152, 230, 234–35, 301n
private schools, 65, 125, 132–33, 153
privatization, 105, 108–12, 120–21, 132, 277, 278
Program Coordination Unit, 146
progress report, 149

Progressive Republican Party (Terakkiperver Cumhuriyet Fırkası), 22
protest, 6, 12, 25–26, 77, 78, 94, 107,
152–53, 195–96, 198, 201, 218, 225–26,
283; public, 32, 155, 211, 277, 296n,
302n
public agencies, 138
public interest, 239
public school system, 128
Purple Roof Women's Shelter Foundation,
213

Qur'an, 91–93, 96, 273, 293n

Radiation Safety Regulation, 141
Radio and Television Supreme Board
(Radyo ve Televizyon Üst Kurulu,
RTÜK), 29, 78, 79, 154
raison d'état, 89
rape, 195, 198, 200, 210
readmission agreements, 180
realpolitik, 15, 250, 260–61, 286
reception centers, 180
Red Cross, International Committee of
the, 165
refugee, 50, 120, 159–61, 170–83
Regional Agenda 21, 146
Regional Environmental Center, 146
regional waste, 139
Regulations, environmental, 136, 141–42
Representative for Displaced People
(RSG), 160, 165, 167, 169
repression, 5, 6, 9, 11, 13, 15, 74, 76, 105,
135, 162, 187, 200–201, 222, 224, 229,
242, 254, 257, 259, 275–77, 279, 280, 283
reproductive rights, 13, 194, 202, 212–13
Republic of Northern Cyprus (TRNC),
274
Republic of Turkey, 4, 11, 21–22, 35, 40,
44, 46, 50, 52, 72, 79–80, 82–84, 88, 96,
106, 137, 187–88, 280, 292, 297, 301
reservation, 82–83, 85, 119, 135, 200, 202,
205–7, 210, 253–54, 258, 285, 291n
resettlement, 74, 119, 159, 163–65, 175,
177, 180–81
resolution, 52, 71, 243–44, 256, 300n
Return to the Village Project, 164–65, 168
Revolutionary People's Liberation
Party/Front (DHKP/C), 8
rights, fundamental, 30, 54, 97, 239, 241,
260, 265 to adequate standard of living,

143; to assembly, 117; to association,
28; to asylum, 17; to be informed,
271–72; to collective bargaining, 113,
119, 121; to demonstration, 117; to
development, 144; to education, 11,
82–83, 123–26, 134, 136, 241, 275, 279,
300n; to fair remuneration, 119; to
health care/medicine, 11, 120; to
health/healthy environment, 137–38,
144; to healthy conditions of work, 119;
to language (see language rights); to
life, 171–72, 175, 182, 259, 262, 269,
274; to livable wages, 11; to organize,
113, 119; to privacy, 287; to property,
209, 212, 259; to run for office, 188; to
self-determination, 2; to social security,
11; to strike, 107, 114–15, 117, 121;
third generation, 142; to vote, 190, 204;
to work, 209. See also human rights;
freedom
Rio Declaration on Environment and
Development, 144
Rıza Nur, 37
Romania, 35–36, 112
Rome Statute, 13
RP (Refah Partisi/Welfare Party), 87, 94,
271, 273, 286
rule of law, 97, 166, 228, 252, 281–83,
300n
Rum Orthodox, 57–59, 61–71, 291n
Rumbold, Horace, 41

Saadet Rafet, 190
San Francisco conference, 252
Sakharov Peace Prize, 300
Sayyid Nursi, 292
schooling, 11, 126, 128, 131, 136
Sebatay Sevi (Sabbatai Sevi), 302
Second Legislative Branch of the court, 39
secularism, xv, 4, 8, 10, 29, 87–88, 92, 96,
135, 190, 225, 292n. See also laicism
secularization, 8, 11, 12, 58, 60, 88–90,
101, 132
security, xii–xiii, xv, 1, 14, 23, 27, 30, 49,
53–54, 68, 86, 111–12, 114, 116,
120–21, 161, 163, 164, 171–72, 175,
181–82, 219, 223–24, 236, 238–39, 242,
259, 262, 265, 268–70, 275, 278, 282,
285, 290n, 300n; human, 159, 275;
national, xi, 4, 19, 28, 31, 46, 51, 116,
174, 183, 236, 240, 242, 267, 287, 290n

security threat, 8, 29, 39, 110, 115, 236, 267, 282, 302n

Selçuk, Sami, 265

Serbest Cumhuriyet Fırkası (Free Republican Party), 23

Serbian-Croatian-Slovenian State, 36

service sector, 110–112

Settlement Law, 76

Sèvres Paranoia/Syndrome, 36, 50, 52, 55, 85, 276, 302

Sèvres, Treaty of, 35, 52, 75

sexual harassment, 200–211

Sezer, Ahmet Necdet (President Sezer), 29, 31, 166

Sheik al-Islam, 292

Sheik Said, 10, 22, 91, 161; revolt, 91

Shia, xii, 73, 89, 96

Siirt, 295

social and economic rights, 10, 11, 15, 105, 120, 125, 172, 277, 278. See also economic rights; social rights

social rights, xvii, 10–11, 15, 105, 120, 125, 144, 172, 220, 227, 277, 278, 298

social security, 11, 111, 120–21, 194, 212

Socrates, 136

soil erosion, 138, 152

Soil Pollution Control Regulation, 141

Solid Waste Regulation, 141

Solidarity Association of the Families of the Detained and Imprisoned (Tutuklu ve Hükümlü Aileleri Dayanışma Derneği, TAYAD), 297

South Eastern Mediterranean Environment Project (SEMEP), 154

Southeast Asia, 174

sovereignty, 2, 75, 98, 161, 165, 169, 252, 293

Soviet Union, xiv, 173

SP (Sosyalist Parti/Socialist Party), 48

Special Felony Courts, 276

special temporary measures, 201

Spyridon Polychroniades, 59

Sri Lanka, 168

state agency, 13, 22, 53, 153–54, 196, 199, 244

State Ministry, 230, 256

state of emergency, 7, 78, 223–24, 258, 266

State Security Courts (Devlet Güvenlik Mahkemeleri, SSCs), 257, 266–67, 270–71, 276

Stockholm Declaration on the Human Environment, 143

STP (Sosyalist Türkiye Partisi/Socialist Turkey Party), 48

strike, 106–7, 109, 114–17, 121, 268, 282

subsidy, 33, 133

sufi orders (tarikat), 91

Sultan Mahmud, 161

Sunni, xii, 37, 51, 73, 87, 89, 91, 94, 96–99, 135, 225–26, 273

super high schools, 133

Supreme Board of Coordination for Human Rights, 257

Supreme Court, 39, 68, 290

Supreme Court of Appeals (Yargıtay), 39

Surani (Kurdish dialect), 74

Surp Haç Armenian Lycée Foundation, 51

sustainable development, 139, 142, 144

Syria, 73, 112, 162

Şahin v. Turkey, 302

Şanlıurfa, 163, 295

Şeriat, 90

Şırnak, 131, 295

Takrir-i Sükun, 22, 106

Tan, 24, 28, 110–11, 114, 117, 134

Tanzimat, Decree of, 21, 124

taşeron, 110

Tatars, 172

Tatil-i Eşgal Kanunu, 106

tawhid, 293

TBKP (Türkiye Birleşik Komünist Partisi/ Turkish United Communist Party), 48

Teheran, 280

Tenth Year Speech, 50

TEP (Türkiye Emekçi Partisi/ Labor Party of Turkey), 47–48

terrorism, 6, 45, 55, 267, 272, 283

terrorist, 7, 8, 29, 45, 52, 54, 162, 218, 223, 242–43, 267, 276

teşmil system, 119

textbooks, 14, 65, 69, 134, 234, 236, 238–45, 299n

Theological Seminary, Chalki (Heybeliada), 64, 67

Thessaloniki, 63

Thrace, 58, 60, 69–70, 75, 291

TİHAK (Türkiye İnsan Hakları Kurumu/Human Rights Institution of Turkey), 217, 226–27, 297n

TİHV (Türkiye İnsan Hakları Vakfı Human Rights Foundation of Turkey), 217, 224–26, 231, 297n, 299n
Timurtaş v. Turkey, 298n
TİP (Türkiye İşçi Partisi/Turkish Workers' Party), 26, 47, 77
tolerance, xvi, 79, 98, 233, 244–45, 265, 276, 280–81, 287, 299n
Tomasevski, Katarina, 125–26, 294
torture, xiii, 1, 54, 77, 172, 175, 182, 220–21, 223, 224–27, 238, 255, 258–59, 262, 266–70, 274, 276–77, 281–82, 300n
Trade Union Act, 107
trade union, 105–9, 113–14, 116–17, 119–21, 194, 207, 222, 225. *See also* labor union
transnational advocacy, 218
treason, 22, 78, 266
Tripartite Advisory Board, 121
Tripartite London Conference, 63
TRT Law, 31
Truman doctrine, 25
Turkey Report for United Nations Environment Programme (UNEP), 139, 151
TÜRK-İŞ (Türkiye İşçi Sendikaları Konfederasyonu/Confederation of Turkish Labor Unions), 107, 118, 211, 293n
Turkish Armed Forces, 302. *See also* military
Turkish Association of Journalists, 32
Turkish Coastal Law, 141–42
Turkish Economic and Social Council (ESC), 122
Turkish Economic and Social Studies Foundation (TESEV), 285
Turkish Foundation for Reforestation, Erosion Combat, and Protection of Natural Assets (TEMA), 150, 152
Turkish Industrialists' and Businessmen's Association (TÜSİAD), 286
Turkish Job Security Act (İş Güvencesi Yasası), 112
Turkish Parliament, 201, 257, 270. *See also* Grand National Assembly
Turkish Press Council, 19
Turkish Radio and Television Broadcasting Corporation (TRT), 26–29, 31
Turkish Wireless and Telephone Company (TTTAŞ), 22, 23
Turkish Women's Party, 188

Turkish Workers and Peasants Liberation Army (TİKKO), 8
Turkish-Greek rift, 256
Türkiye Halkı, 51
Türkiyeli, 51
Turks, 48, 50–51, 60–61, 65, 72, 74, 85, 96, 106, 173, 203, 240, 266

Ubaidullah, 161
ulema, 89, 292
ummah, 93, 100
Umut Foundation, 245
unemployment, 11, 110–12, 120, 122, 277, 285, 294
UNESCO, 123, 125, 154, 294; Convention against Discrimination in Education, 123
Union of Journalists, 32
Union of Laboring Women, 193
Union of Revolutionary Women, 193–94
United Communist Party of Turkey and Others v. Turkey, 271
United Nations (UN), 1, 3, 12–15, 42, 49–50, 70, 72, 79–80, 82–83, 97, 125–26, 128, 139, 143–44, 147, 151, 154, 159–62, 165, 167, 170–71, 177, 196, 201–3, 207, 209, 219, 233–34, 249–55, 284, 292n, 295n, 298n, 300n; Charter, 1, 161, 219, 251, 295; Commission on Human Rights, 7, 143, 219, 299, 301; Decade for Human Rights Education, 14, 154, 233; Development Programme, 147; Economic Commission for Europe, 144; General Assembly, 1, 154, 171, 202–3, 233, 253, 299n
High Commissioner for Refugees (UNHCR), 12, 159–60, 165, 167–68, 170–80, 182; Undersecretariat of Environment, 139, 296n
United States (U.S.), xi–xiv, xvi–xvii, 2, 25, 36, 43, 153, 163–65, 287, 292n
Universal Declaration of Human Rights, xviii, 1, 3, 19, 50, 80, 88, 123, 142, 171–72, 182, 233, 237, 241, 251, 253
university, xv, 8, 25, 26, 67, 78, 93–94, 96, 98, 125, 131, 133–34, 154, 201, 204, 207, 226, 235, 257, 273, 275, 296; entrance examination, 134
USEK (Ulusal Sağlık Emekçileri Konfederasyonu/Confederation of National Health Workers), 114, 118

Ülkü Ocakları ([Nationalist] Ideal
  Hearths), 6

Vakıflar, 60, 68, 228
Vakıfname, 39
Video, Music, and Works of Arts Supervisory Board, 31
Vienna Convention on the Law of
  Treaties, 42
Vienna Programme of Action, 298n, 299n
Village Centers Project, 164
village guards, 7, 163–64
village institutes, 125
violation, xiii, 9–12, 38–40, 46–48, 50, 60,
  65, 70, 73, 96, 98, 112, 116–17, 135,
  153, 159, 171, 175–77, 180, 198, 201,
  210, 212, 218, 220–22, 224–26, 230,
  233, 240, 251–52, 255, 259, 263,
  267–71, 274–80, 282–83, 285, 287,
  291n, 302n
virginity test, 198
Vivarajah v. United Kingdom, 172, 295n
vocational training/education, 119, 128;
  vocational/technical school, 126, 239
voluntary return, 165, 167, 171

wages, 11, 108–12, 114–15, 277, 280
War of Independence, 2, 22, 35–36, 44, 51,
  57, 59, 70, 75, 106, 219

Water Pollution Control Regulation, 141
watershed water quality, 139
welfare state, 132
weltanschauung, 255
westernization, 8, 12, 190, 249
Wolfowitz, Paul, xi
women, xiii, xv, xvii, 12–14, 90, 111, 119,
  121, 124–25, 127, 131, 134, 187–213,
  226, 229, 253, 264, 276, 278–79, 286,
  294n, 296n
workers, 105–22, 173, 194, 205, 212, 221,
  225, 235, 295n. *See also* laborers
World Bank, 10, 211
World Conference on Human Rights in
  Vienna, 233, 280
World Food Programme (WFP), 160
World War I, xvi, 2, 21, 35–37, 41–42, 52,
  57, 60, 74–75, 106, 162, 219, 252
World War II, 24, 42, 57, 60, 106, 171,
  173, 219, 252–53

Yassıada, 62
Young Turks, 106
Youth Community Action Programme, 136
Yugoslavia, 168, 173

Zana, Leyla, 270–71, 300n
Zaza (Kurdish dialect), 74
Ziya Gökalp, 203, 240